From Colonial Cuba to Madrid

From Colonial Cuba to Madrid examines the largest and most complex freedom suit litigated in the highest court of the Spanish empire at the end of the eighteenth century. Filed by hundreds of re-enslaved Afro descendant people who had lived in quasi-freedom in eastern Cuba for more than a century, this action drew on local customary practices and broader cultural, political, and legal discourses rooted in the Spanish Atlantic world to put forward novel claims to collective freedom and native-based rights at a time when questions of slavery, freedom, and citizenship were igniting in many parts of the Atlantic world. Intersecting law, society studies, and the history of slavery, María Elena Díaz offers a carefully researched study of one of the few communities of Afro descendants that managed to secure freedom and political and legal recognition from the Spanish Crown during the colonial period.

María Elena Díaz is Associate Professor of Latin American History at the University of California, Santa Cruz. She is the author of *The Virgin, the King, and the Royal Slaves of El Cobre, 1670–1780*, which was selected as an ACLS Humanities ebook.

Afro-Latin America

Series editors

George Reid Andrews, *University of Pittsburgh*
Alejandro de la Fuente, *Harvard University*

This series reflects the coming of age of the new, multidisciplinary field of Afro-Latin American Studies, which centers on the histories, cultures, and experiences of people of African descent in Latin America. The series aims to showcase scholarship produced by different disciplines, including history, political science, sociology, ethnomusicology, anthropology, religious studies, art, law, and cultural studies. It covers the full temporal span of the African Diaspora in Latin America, from the early colonial period to the present and includes continental Latin America, the Caribbean, and other key areas in the region where Africans and their descendants have made a significant impact.

A full list of titles published in the series can be found at:
www.cambridge.org/afro-latin-america

From Colonial Cuba to Madrid

Litigating Collective Freedom and Native Rights in the Spanish Empire, 1780–1814

MARÍA ELENA DÍAZ
University of California, Santa Cruz

CAMBRIDGE
UNIVERSITY PRESS

CAMBRIDGE
UNIVERSITY PRESS

Shaftesbury Road, Cambridge CB2 8EA, United Kingdom

One Liberty Plaza, 20th Floor, New York, NY 10006, USA

477 Williamstown Road, Port Melbourne, VIC 3207, Australia

314–321, 3rd Floor, Plot 3, Splendor Forum, Jasola District Centre, New Delhi – 110025, India

103 Penang Road, #05-06/07, Visioncrest Commercial, Singapore 238467

Cambridge University Press is part of Cambridge University Press & Assessment, a department of the University of Cambridge.

We share the University's mission to contribute to society through the pursuit of education, learning and research at the highest international levels of excellence.

www.cambridge.org
Information on this title: www.cambridge.org/9781009494199

DOI: 10.1017/9781009494212

When citing this work, please include a reference to the DOI 10.1017/9781009494212

First published 2025

A catalogue record for this publication is available from the British Library.

A Cataloging-in-Publication data record for this book is available from the Library of Congress

ISBN 978-1-009-49419-9 Hardback
ISBN 978-1-009-49422-9 Paperback

Contents

Figures and Tables

FIGURES

TABLE

Acknowledgments

Another book hereby enters a rapidly changing world where AI may soon displace human authors or dispense with the enormous human labor it takes to research and write that beautiful but increasingly quaint artifact called a book. As a human-produced work, *From Colonial Cuba to Madrid* had a slow process of gestation that I will not go into here. Suffice it to say, it had many iterations in my head and that, like the mythical Greek Penelope, I've woven and unwoven that cloak many times. Its final iteration, the version leading to the present book, emerged during the Covid pandemic lockdown. The pandemic was a singular global event that shook the world. Along with the havoc, however, also came opportunities to rethink our lives and projects. Covid made the world slow down and turn local; it pushed some people to shift priorities, take up new projects, learn instruments, write books long waiting to be written, take walks, long to connect in new ways. It provided time for deep reading and thinking even if we were not sure if we would survive the onslaught. We did, but now it seems we're facing even more inauspicious times. The book comes out in an age of deep internal turmoil and expanding forever wars.

Family–related memories and acknowledgments come first. Perhaps the person I have most to thank for this book is my sister Marissa Díaz Walker. During the Covid hiatus she made her own career change and earned a graduate degree in technical communication. Her drive inspired me to set my own project goals and to work steadily with deadlines in mind. Marissa read many of the initial chapters, made suggestions as a nonspecialist reader, copyedited previous versions of the manuscript, and cleaned up and formatted the final one. Our mother, Lilita Balsera, would have loved to see us collaborate in this manner. My other sister, Viviana Díaz-Balsera, herself an academic, read and critiqued a former introduction and provided much moral support while busy with her own book project. My niece Alexandra Walker took on the responsibility of double-checking and formatting the footnotes and bibliography with great accuracy.

Others contributed to the making of this book in less immediate ways. I want to thank my department and the University of California, Santa Cruz (UCSC) for the quarter-long sabbatical policy that allows faculty, young and old, to take time off periodically to focus on research and travel to archives. Despite shrinking resources for research, especially in the Humanities, that policy still stands. I also thank my colleague and department chair Alice Yang Murray for offering me a teaching course relief to manage the last stages of the book. At UCSC, I also want to thank our IT Systems Administrator Alejandra Sicairos who has helped me navigate all kinds of computer breakdowns and technological challenges at many points in the writing and production process and has always done so with a friendly disposition.

In a less official capacity, my colleague and friend, Cynthia Polecritti, herself a very good writer, read and approved an early version of Chapter 6 that, alas, has become unrecognizable after several re-writings. My US history colleague Catherine Jones and I formed a twosome reading group one recent summer to discuss relevant comparative bibliography on race and the law. Catherine also pointedly critiqued one of the earlier versions of the book's Introduction. Through the years, I have informally discussed multiple ideas that eventually made their way into the book with many other colleagues and friends (some of them by now departed). Wittingly or unwittingly they have collectively contributed to the making of this book.

On archival matters, I want to especially thank Antonio Sánchez de Mora and the staff at the Archive of the Indies in Seville who through email communication during Covid times helped me locate documents and order high-resolution images for the book, all with surprising rapidity given the Covid moment. More recently, in the University of Miami's Cuban Heritage Collection, Juan Antonio Villanueva was extremely efficient in helping me find some mining images that I needed for the book and fast tracking their high-resolution reproduction.

On the manuscript's publication process, I thank Alejandro de la Fuente and George Reid Andrews as editors of this important series for taking an interest in my manuscript and considerng it for review. I want to especially thank Karen Graubart and another anonymous reviewer for putting in the considerable labor that reading such a long manuscript entailed (it is now shorter) and for doing it with such care. The manuscript is all the better for their feedback. I bear responsibility for the final product, however. Another special thanks goes to Cecelia Cancellaro at Cambridge University Press for shepherding the manuscript through the review and publication processes as well as through the "marketing" requisites of university presses these days. Cecelia has also been very accommodating with my work rhythms and with my requests for the book's illustrations. Her assistant, Victoria Phillips, has endured questions galore on the technicalities of submitting maps, images with the correct resolutions, copyright permissions, and all that. I thank her for her patience too.

This book is my swan song before retirement (hopefully not yet before the encounter with "la Pelona"). As a meditation on many themes, it has entailed a lot of thought, reading, and work as swan songs often do. I hope the book will open new questions for discussion and for future research. Meanwhile, I will be pursuing smaller academic and nonacademic projects.

Introduction

> I have given myself to this great defense that is this pretended freedom that was so confused and dark and deep that it has been necessary to found it with much efficacy and saintly zeal.
>
> —Gregorio Cosme Osorio, Madrid, 1795

> I was sold like a cargo slave [*esclava de armazón*] even though I was born, raised and educated in a Pueblo of our Catholic monarch's domains [El Cobre].
>
> —Margarita González, Sancti Spíritus, Cuba, 1792

> Nativeness is one of the greatest obligations people can have with one another ... [it] converts them into a single unit through the long practice of loyal love.
>
> —Siete Partidas, 13th c.

The words in the first two epigraphs were written more than 230 years ago, at a time when freedom was taking a central role in political and philosophical discourse in the Atlantic world, but its meanings were elusive. A time when slavery, freedom's main antithetical condition then, was expanding and morphing into a "second slavery" in many regions of the American hemisphere, including Cuba.[1] This book is about the shocking enslavement of more than 1,000 women, men, and children who had lived as a pueblo in colonial Cuba for more than 100 years and about the unprecedented freedom lawsuit they took to the highest imperial court in Madrid in the last two decades of the eighteenth century.

[1] Dale Tomich has aptly termed this new wave of slavery expansion in the Atlantic world a "second slavery" in *Through the Prism of Slavery*. For Cuba, see Ferrer, *Freedom's Mirror*, 12. For the new Spanish imperial thinking and policies undergirding the aptly named "slaving fever," see Schneider, *The Occupation of Havana*, 270–84.

The first epigraph comes from the letter of a freedman who had once been a royal slave in that pueblo but was then residing in the imperial court in Madrid.[2] For more than a decade, Gregorio Cosme Osorio had been in exile acting as the legal representative (*apoderado*) of the enslaved plaintiffs who were seeking freedom and return to a pueblo they considered their local homeland. Finding all legal channels of redress in the colony exhausted, Cosme and another companion, a pardo (Brown) artisan named Carlos Ramos, traveled covertly to Madrid under the sponsorship of a middling Spanish merchant residing in Havana named Don José Espinoza de los Monteros. Transatlantic journeys of this kind were uncommon for Afro descendant subjects and more generally for non-Spaniards in the empire too.

Once in Madrid, the three men filed jointly a petition in the Council of the Indies in 1784. In that document, they presented themselves as "natives" (*naturales*) of different localities in the empire: one from villa Manrique in the Spanish "kingdom of Seville" and the other two from the aggrieved community, a pueblo named Santiago del Prado (aka El Cobre) on the island of Cuba. The petitioners also referred to the enslaved plaintiffs whom they were representing as "natives of that pueblo in Cuba": they sought justice, their petition said, "on behalf of the rest of the natives of the said pueblo of more than 6,000 souls who have been dispossessed of their freedom and handed out as slaves."[3] Although the 6,000 souls cited as the *naturales* of Santiago del Prado constituted an inflated population count (the number was closer to 1,400), their invocation of that seemingly descriptive category was significant. Or rather, they *made it* significant in the freedom action they presented to the court. A few years later, Margarita González, one of the plaintiffs covered by the collective action in Madrid, also filed a freedom petition in the colony's lower courts. The basis for her freedom, as the second epigraph suggests, was essentially that she was a native of a pueblo, and therefore not a slave, and that her local homeland was part of Spain's Catholic empire.[4] Those were unusual grounds to claim freedom in the Spanish empire, or even in the Atlantic world, at least in traditional legal terms.

[2] Gregorio Cosme Osorio, Madrid, October 6, 1795, No. 75, Archivo General de Indias (hereafter AGI), Santo Domingo (hereafter SD) 1629.

[3] Memorial of Don José Espinoza de los Monteros, Gregorio Cosme Osorio, and Carlos Ramos, Madrid, April 4, 1784 (hereafter Memorial Madrid, 1784), AGI-SD 1629.

[4] Petition of Margarita González, Sancti Spíritus, September 5, 1792, in Autos Teresa Ramos alias Coba, No. 34, AGI-SD 1628.

But again, this legal (and political) action was unusual in many ways, and so was the community behind it. The lapidary words in the third epigraph went farther back into medieval times, to the thirteenth century Castilian foundational legal code of the *Siete Partidas*. Yet they were still part of a cultural, social, and political understanding of belonging for many subjects throughout the Iberian world, and they undergirded Margarita González's freedom claim in the colony too.

Hundreds of men and women from the pueblo of El Cobre fought tooth and nail during the 1780s and '90s in Madrid and Cuba against the transformations taking place as part of the Bourbon Crown's imperial reforms in this region in eastern Cuba: policies that were also creating other kinds of unrest elsewhere in the empire.[5] The lawsuit at the center of this book became the largest and most complex freedom action in the annals of Spain's colonial archive at least up to the early nineteenth century, perhaps beyond too. Set mainly within the framework of Spanish Atlantic legal and political discourse, this controversial freedom suit put forward novel claims associated to nativeness (*naturaleza*) and native rights that expanded notions of freedom and belonging among Afro descendants in this region at a time when questions of slavery and freedom were igniting many parts of the Atlantic world. What can the claims of this remarkable legal action and the events and litigants that sustained it reveal to historians of Cuba, the Spanish empire, and the wider Atlantic world?

Located in eastern Cuba, barely twelve miles from Santiago de Cuba, the regional capital, El Cobre is one of the oldest pueblos in Cuba. By the eighteenth century, however, this community had become an unconventional pueblo in the Spanish Atlantic world due to its irregular social profile. In the 1780 regional census of Santiago de Cuba's jurisdiction, for instance, 99 percent of this pueblo's 1,406 inhabitants were recorded as Black or Mulatto.[6] And whereas 33.5 percent of villagers in this census

[5] Perhaps the greatest unrest came in the Andean region with the Tupac Amaro rebellion in 1780–83, the revolt of the Comuneros in New Granada in 1780, and other more localized reactions. See Walker, *The Tupac Amaru Rebellion*; Phelan, *The People and the King*.

[6] Census of Santiago de Cuba and Jurisdiction, Santiago, February 24, 1780 (hereafter Census of Santiago, 1780), AGI-Cuba 1272. Censuses for this period are only approximations. Additions are often incorrect and there is considerable variability between different censuses. For instance, although the 1780 regional census gives a population of 1,370, the corrected figure that I will be using throughout the book is of 1,406 souls. Only two years before, the Census for the Island of Cuba from 1778 (hereafter General Census, 1778) provides a higher population count of 1,482 (again corrected from the reported 1,492) souls for El Cobre. In the 1778 general census, 1.3 percent of El Cobre's inhabitants were

were categorized as free people of color, an overwhelming 65.5 percent were inscribed as slaves. A village of African descendants did not fit properly into Spain's plural legal grid where only Spanish and Indian pueblos (or republics, as they were formally known) were sanctioned by written law per the *Recopilación de las Leyes de Indias* (1680).[7] Blacks and racially mixed colonial subjects were supposed to reside in Spanish republics in a subordinate capacity. Moreover, a village with such a high percentage of enslaved persons, in this case also considered members of the pueblo, constituted an even more unorthodox formation. How did such a mismatch situation between law and reality come about? And how would the legal action at the center of this book attempt to legitimize that mismatch?

El Cobre had sprung up at the end of the seventeenth century in the midst of a derelict mining settlement near the city of Santiago de Cuba. After the Crown confiscated the allegedly exhausted mines of Santiago del Prado from their private contractor in the 1670s, the former mining slaves became the "king's slaves" (*esclavos del Rey*). Profound reconfigurations of the status of these enslaved subjects and of their labor and defense obligations to the state developed in the course of the next century. I have written elsewhere an ethnographic and social history of the changes involved in the gradual makeover of these former mining slaves into a hybrid pueblo of slaves of the king and free people of color.[8] Suffice it to say that the growing pueblo's location in a military inter-imperial frontier in the Caribbean region (see Figure 0.1) provided a favorable context for these former mining slaves to informally negotiate flexible arrangements resonant of quasi freedom in different areas of life. A small Marian Christian sanctuary with an allegedly miraculous image of the Virgin of Charity also gave this unusual pueblo religious legitimacy and some regional fame. With time, these royal slaves and their free relatives came

inscribed as Whites; 35 percent as free of color; and 98.7 percent are slaves. General Census of the Island of Cuba, Havana, December 31, 1778, AGI-Indiferente 1527.

[7] *Recopilación de Leyes de Indias* 1680, the basic source of colonial law, only recognized Spanish and Indian republics or pueblos. There was no allusion anywhere in it to Black republics and pueblos, although it did not explicitly ban them either. There tend to be various uses of the term "republic" by scholars and contemporaries. In its singular form – the Republic of Spaniards and the Republic of Indians – it refers to separate general jurisdictions and legal regimes for Spaniards and Indians. In the plural form, "republics" of Spaniards and of Indians, the term refers to actual municipal entities related to those regimes: cities, towns, and pueblos. I use the term in this book in its second inflection. For other iterations of the term see Graubart, *Republics of Difference*.

[8] Díaz, *The Virgin, the King*.

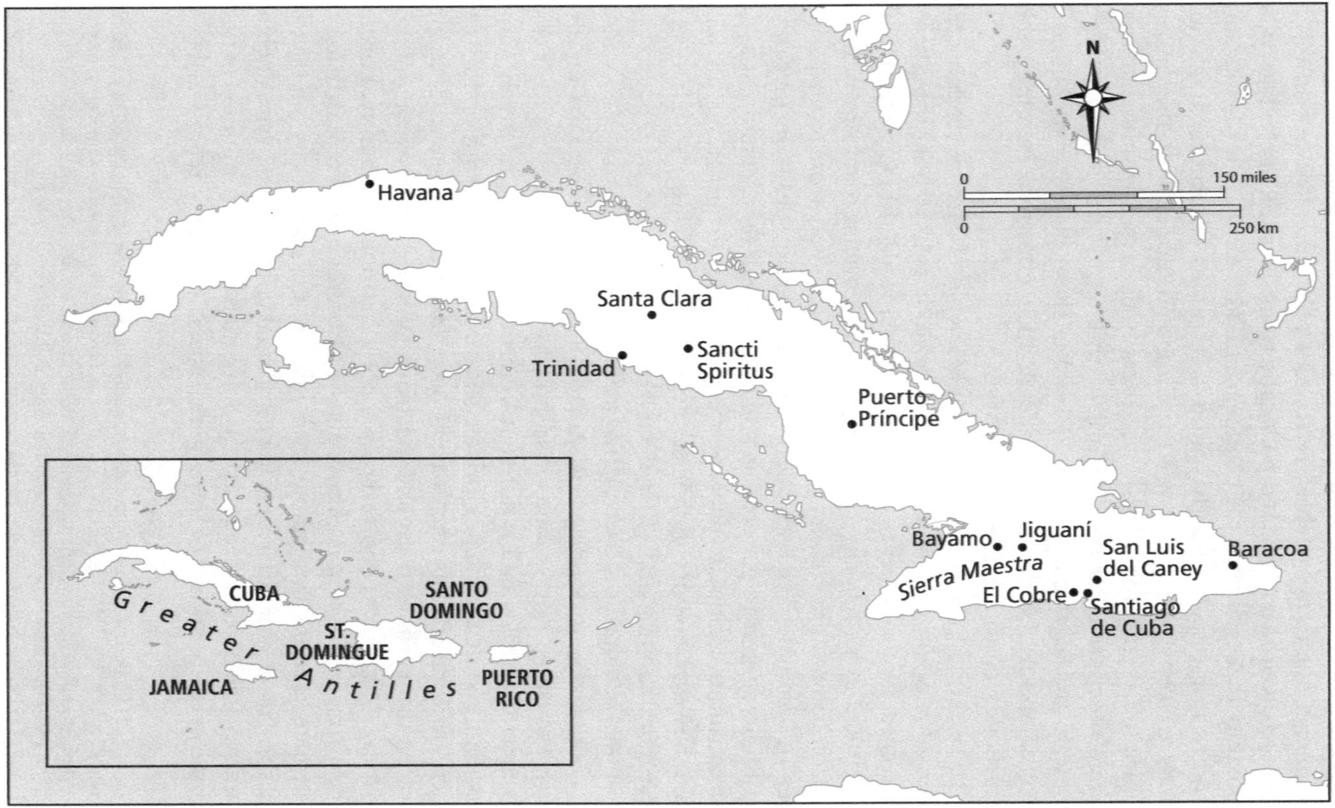

FIGURE 0.1 Map of Cuba and the Caribbean. Map by David McCutcheon FBCart.S. www.dvdmaps.co.uk

to identify themselves as cobreros or natives of the pueblo of El Cobre. In Spanish, the term "pueblo" refers to a physical entity in a locality (a village) as well as socially and politically to its constituents (villagers), an ambiguity that facilitated the confluence of both terms. The identification as natives of a pueblo was based on old notions of local birthright and bonds of conviviality that were widespread throughout the Spanish empire (third epigraph). Although generally dismissed by historians as a merely descriptive category of origin, this term carried deep cultural, political, and legal meanings that I argue these plaintiffs mobilized in their composite freedom action and in their efforts to legitimize their unorthodox customary social formation.

To be sure, El Cobre was not the only pueblo of Afro descendants that emerged in Spain's Atlantic empire. A few others have been identified in the record. None, however, had the unusual profile of El Cobre, a pueblo constituted in its majority by enslaved people, even if royal slaves. Illegal maroon communities (communities of fugitive slaves) arose in the peripheries of colonial slave societies where they could subsist in precarious conditions subject to persecution and capture. But these communities did not constitute legitimate pueblos: they were illegal formations. In some cases, however, colonial authorities negotiated an amnesty with leaders of these communities and gave them recognition in an ad hoc way as colonial pueblos of free Afro descendants. Nuestra Señora de Guadalupe de los Morenos de Amapa in Mexico is perhaps the best known example of this kind of ad hoc recognized pueblo.[9] Other Afro descendant pueblos had a different kind of origin. The relatively short-lived San José de Gracia in Florida emerged in the eighteenth century as a sanctuary for runaway slaves from other imperial powers and became part of the peripheral colony's defense system with its own military functions.[10] El Cobre, however, was not a maroon community, nor had it been one in its origin. Although the cobreros made repeated use of marronage actions throughout their history, the community's trajectory and formation was different. Other informal communities, even pueblos, of mostly free Afro descendants may have materialized for limited periods of time in the periphery of the empire, especially in the circum-Caribbean

[9] Taylor, "The Foundation of Nuestra Señora de Guadalupe de los Morenos," 439–46. See as well San Basilio de Palenque in Colombia in Borrego Plá, *Palenques de negro*; Carroll, "Mandinga," 488–505. For one under negotiations for its legitimation, see Yingling, "The Maroons of Santo Domingo in the Age of Revolution," 25–51.

[10] Landers, "Gracia Real de Santa Teresa de Mose," 9–30. For Costa Rica, Cáceres Gómez, "La Puebla de los Pardos en el siglo XVII," 83–113.

region, but perhaps because the footprint they left in the archive is too weak or fractured we know little about them.[11] El Cobre, however, holds special interest to the historian not only for its profile but for the voluminous documentation it generated. Because this was a valuable royal mining jurisdiction and most villagers after the 1670s were considered slaves of the king, official local recordkeeping was requisite. Moreover, the legal action at the center of this book itself led to the collection of otherwise dispersed local and imperial records in a gargantuan dossier in the Archive of the Indies that enables the modern scholar to document the relation between local, colonial, and imperial levels in a wider Atlantic world.

The conflict and collective litigation examined in *From Colonial Cuba to Madrid* unfolded at a time when the Spanish Bourbon Crown deployed a broad series of "enlightened" policies to renovate – and modernize – its overseas colonies by making them more productive and, effectively, more "colonial."[12] The Bourbon monarchs' so-called enlightened economic and pro-slavery policies took hold more rapidly and effectively in some American localities than in others. In the Caribbean, and especially in Cuba, imperial reforms were geared toward upgrading commercially unproductive military colonies and transforming them into slave-based agribusinesses for the production and export of cash crops, mainly sugar. Havana led the transition into a full-fledged sugar plantation regime based on the massive importation of African slave labor.[13] The effects of Havana's "sugar revolution" were enduring and profound as sugar became "King" in the island for the next two centuries. Other regions, less dynamic, but not less affected by the imperial reforming impulse, are less well known. Eastern Cuba, and its jurisdictional capital in Santiago de Cuba, lacking capital, trade outlets, and resources at the time, lagged behind in the "modern" upgrading of the region and complained of lesser royal attention than Havana.[14] Yet lagging behind fast-track Havana did

[11] Marcela Echeverri, for instance, makes reference to "towns of free Blacks" in Popayán in New Granada, some created "illegally" by escaped slaves and others "legally" by free Blacks, but there is little discussion about them, especially about the latter. Her study focuses instead on the mobilization of "communities" living mostly as mining slave gangs. See her *Indian and Slave Royalists*, 120–21.

[12] Gabriel Paquette, *Enlightenment, Governance and Reform*; Brading, *Miners and Merchants in Bourbon Mexico*.

[13] Moreno Fraginals, *El ingenio*; Knight, *Slave Society in Cuba*, and more recently, Ferrer, *Freedom's Mirror*; Schneider, *Occupation of Havana* and "African Slavery and Spanish Empire," 3–29.

[14] Belmonte, *Ser esclavo en Santiago de Cuba*. See as well, Chira, *Patchwork Freedoms*.

not mean, especially in this new period, remaining isolated from or untouched by imperial policies and wider global trends in some isolated periphery as it is sometimes assumed. For it was here, in this so-called backwater of the empire, where the Crown tried to jump start another kind of industry and where that policy had immediate visible and controversial results as this book shows. In this case, however, the enlightened reform policy was directed at the revival of an extractive metal industry based on El Cobre's once rich copper mines. Crucial for the production of artillery, copper was at the time a valuable strategic resource for the Spanish Crown.[15]

The global imperial conflict of the Seven Years' War and the British occupation of Havana at the end of that war called for the urgent overhaul of the empire's military defense system and its arms industry. In 1779, as part of its military and mining revival policy in the empire, the Bourbon Crown privatized this old copper mining jurisdiction, with devastating consequences for El Cobre villagers whose long-established customary rights were suddenly upended. The newly privatized site – with its "mines, land and slaves" – was handed over to three distant heirs of a seventeenth-century mining contractor, Don Juan de Eguiluz, with the expectation that they would reactivate the dead mines and the large-scale extraction of copper. Instead, the beneficiaries of the privatized mining estate, reacting to the new colonial juncture of high demand for slaves in the island, divided up among themselves their newly acquired enslaved villagers and, asserting full property rights over them, removed them from El Cobre and sold many in the island's expanding slave markets. Margarita González, the enslaved litigant mentioned in the second epigraph who asserted that she was born, raised, and educated in a pueblo in

[15] The history of silver and gold mining in the Iberian overseas empires has received extensive scholarly attention. Copper mining studies, however, are limited. For early modern Spain, see Goodman's short overview in *Power and Penury*, 109–17. For copper production in Spain's Río Tinto mines, see Avery, *Not on Queen Victoria's Birthday*. The fundamental study of copper mining in the Spanish overseas empire is Barrett, *The Mexican Colonial Copper Industry*. For the copper mining industry in Cuba there is even less. The most important years in the early period were from 1599 to 1640. Thereafter, large-scale mining came to a stop and production became artisanal, see Díaz, *The Virgin, the King*. The most important production period s of El Cobre's mines during the colonial period was in the nineteenth century (1830s–60s) under British exploitation (see Chapter 9). There is an important article on this nineteenth-century mining industry by González Loscertales and Roldán de Montaud, "La minería del cobre en Cuba," 255–99. A full study of the copper mining industry at the imperial level and at the colonial and national levels is still needed.

the Spanish empire, was among those captives: she was sold in the town of Sancti Spíritus, a region in central Cuba. Although the literate Gregorio Cosme was later able to purchase his freedom and become the community's apoderado in Madrid, he, too, was enslaved and removed from El Cobre along with his wife and children. Multiple cases of re-enslaved people in the archive and in the memory of the African diaspora are reminders of the precarity of African descendants' lives in slave societies (Blacks living in post-slave modern societies continue to experience precarity in various ways as the Black Lives Matter Movement reminds us).[16] Yet an enslavement – or re-enslavement, the distinction became significant to some – of this magnitude, involving more than 1,000 people and sanctioned by royal edict, raised disturbing questions even at a time when state-backed pro-slavery policies were in ascendancy. The modern reader can begin to sense the legal, moral, political, and social conflicts latent in this privatization scenario, not to mention its shattering human impact.

One response to the resulting massive enslavement turned out to be remarkable: an unprecedented composite emancipation action that also protested the privatization of land and pueblo. What possibilities of fighting back slavery and protecting other customary entitlements did the law provide in a case like this? Or were the more conventional routes of individual purchase of freedom papers (*coartación*) or illegal marronage (fugitivity) the only – or best – options available to these villagers to resist enslavement, removal from birthplace, and the loss of resources such as land? I closed my earlier book *The Virgin, the King and the Royal Slaves of El Cobre, 1670–1780* precisely before the new period of Bourbon reforms hit the region and this tragic event took place. Beyond that moment lay disruption of the local community arrangements that had been negotiated for more than one hundred years, an idiosyncratic yet forgotten world that I had carefully culled out from the archival record and reconstructed in that book.

Although I knew that the cobreros had launched a legal action in the Council of the Indies and that in 1800 they had obtained freedom and recognition as a pueblo by royal edict, questions lingered about how that emancipation had been attained, especially in the new climate of strong

[16] Cases of re-enslavement can be found in the judicial archive of colonial Latin America and Cuba. For some examples, see Scott and Venegas Fornias, "María Coleta and the Capuchin Friar," 727–62; Chaves, *María Chiquinquirá Díaz*. The problem of kidnapping and re-enslavement was common elsewhere too. For the United States, see McDaniel, *Sweet Taste of Liberty*. For Brazil, Grinberg, "Re-enslavement, Rights and Justice."

pro-slavery forces that had thrown that local world off kilter in the first place. José Luciano Franco's pioneering *Las Minas de Santiago del Prado y la rebelión de los cobreros, 1530–1800* (1975), one of the first books in socialist Cuba on Black history, had produced a resistance narrative claiming that a long tradition of marronage and insurgency among the cobreros had finally forced their freedom through the Edict of April 7, 1800.[17] That resistance narrative was inserted in a larger revolutionary metanarrative of guerrilla action and liberation preceding and leading to the Cuban Revolution. In a Cuba by then playing down racial conflict or displacing it into the past and into other spots in the contemporary world, this was an acceptable, even compelling narrative (one that could even displace the general religious and cultural associations of El Cobre with the sanctuary to the Virgin of Charity there).[18] The narrative also resonated with a nascent 1970s and 1980s historiography of marronage and slave rebellions in the African diaspora especially in relation to the Haitian Revolution.[19] Although by no means inaccurate, Franco's account of marronage and insurgency was a simple narrative that contained and concealed other stories of mobilization, other venues for emancipation, and other notions of freedom tapped by the cobreros at the time. The cobreros' judicial mobilization, not to mention their involvement in a litigation of this magnitude, went for the most part unremarked in Franco's narrative.[20] The right historiographical context for the study of legal mobilizations had not arrived.

17 Franco, *Las minas*.

18 Díaz, *The Virgin, the King*, 2–5; Portuondo Zúñiga, *La Virgen de la Caridad*.

19 Richard Price's classic anthology *Maroon Societies* (1st ed., 1973) was among the first works to open research on marronage. Eugene Genovese studied slave revolts in various locations in the Americas and argued that there was a revolutionary shift in their ideological orientation toward freedom and equality after the Haitian Revolution. See his *From Rebellion to Revolution* (1979). Since those decades, the literature on slave rebellions and conspiracies also saw a boom: marronage and rebellion now became the exemplary forms of slave resistance. For Cuba, see Childs, *The 1812 Aponte Rebellion* (2006); Barcia, *The Great African Slave Revolt of 1825*; Finch, *Rethinking Slave Rebellion in Cuba*. For the Caribbean, see Geggus, "Slavery, War, and Revolution" and more generally, Gaspar and Geggus, eds., *A Turbulent Time*. For a recent overview of these forms of resistance in the Americas, see Helg, *Slave No More*, 43–63, 90–109, 221–29, 245–73. For a more controversial and complex approach to slave rebellion, see Tomlins, *In the Matter of Nat Turner* ; see also Aptheker, *Nat Turner's Slave Rebellion*.

20 Following Luciano Franco, more recent works on Santiago that make reference to the cobreros' mobilization in this period refer almost exclusively to marronage. See Belmonte, *Ser esclavo en Santiago de Cuba, 1780–1803*; Chira, *Patchwork Freedoms*. Though Chira's work focuses on legal actions in Santiago, she did not have access to the cobreros' lawsuit covered in this book.

A new turn in the scholarship of colonial Latin America to subordinate subjects' dynamic use of the law and a new body of work on law, slavery, and race in the African diaspora, spurred a new interest in me in the cobreros' freedom suit and in these villagers' deep engagement with the judicial system, which I, too, had sidestepped, at least in relation to this critical legal action. My previous book had focused on a different period and set of issues. And although in it I had called attention to the king's slaves' use of the courts in previous decades, I had not delved deeply into judicially related questions nor for that matter into a collective freedom lawsuit that had not come up before in the community's local history. The new historiography beckoned. Rather than focusing on abstract colonial legal regimes as many earlier studies such as those based on the famous Tannenbaum thesis had done, new studies turned to a more dynamic "law in action" approach focusing on litigants' *use* of the law.[21] Mirroring the more general shift in historical and postcolonial studies that placed subordinate subjects at the center of narratives as active makers of history, new studies located in the ample field of law, politics, and society focused on subordinate litigants' active use of the courts to make claims and contest rights.

Indigenous subjects, women, free people of color, and, particularly, enslaved people took center stage in this new line of work. Bianca Premo demonstrated the surge in civil legal actions filed by subordinate groups, including enslaved people, in different localities of colonial Latin America during the mid- to late eighteenth century as they increasingly turned to royal courts with their claims and protests.[22] This trend had its counterpart among enslaved subjects in North America after the American

[21] For a discussion on the problems of the Tannenbaum thesis, see the debate by de la Fuente, "Slave Law and Claims-Making in Cuba"; Diaz, "Beyond Tannenbaum"; and Schmidt-Nowara, "Still Continents," 339–76. For more dynamic applications of Tannenbaum, see McKinley, *Fractional Freedoms* and more recently, de la Fuente and Gross, *Becoming Free, Becoming Black*.

[22] Premo, *The Enlightenment on Trial*. Premo attributed the surge in legal actions in royal courts in Mexico and Peru to what she termed a "popular Enlightenment" manifested in colonial Spanish America (though not in the peninsula). I do not wish to enter the polemic on locations (or criteria) of the Enlightenment because, in my view, it tends to rest on linear notions of history, and ultimately, on a Eurocentric benchmark that other localities in the world supposedly meet, surpass, or lag behind on. For a critique of those arrow-based notions of history (to which scholars unwittingly return to) see Tomba, *Insurgent Universality*. However, the phenomenon of the surge is interesting and may be due to a multiplicity of reasons, including reactions to the disruptions created by the Bourbon reforms throughout the overseas empire. These disruptions may in turn have led to reformulations of claims in bolder terms or couched in more eclectic discourses as

Revolution, only to close down in subsequent decades in the Southern slave states.[23]

Enslaved litigants, as quintessentially oppressed subordinate subjects with few, if any, juridical protections garnered special attention in this new historiography as they came to emblematize the fundamental battle for emancipation (or at other times more modestly, for specific minimal human protections). A good part of this scholarly work called attention to the role of enslaved people in emancipating themselves, that is, to their strategies as "agents of their own freedom," especially through the legal venue of self-purchase or coartación.[24] Although at times there has been tension in the literature between legal actions conceptualized as accommodating, individual, or ineffective, and other forms of resistance such as marronage or rebellion seen as revolutionary, these actions should not be compartmentalized or opposed to each other in either-or terms.[25] As I claim in this book, judicial and extrajudicial actions such as marronage were entangled with each other in this case and ultimately emancipation and recognition as a pueblo would not have come about without their use as combined forms of political action. But I'm getting ahead of myself. In any case, regardless of the question of efficacy, judicial cases enable the historian to explore other kinds of questions regarding discourses, sources, and forms of mobilization.[26] The conflicts presented in these cases, and the terms in which they were presented, allow scholars to probe understandings of categories and rights that often remain implicit in social and political life.

happened in El Cobre's case. The reasons for the surge need further research as well as the discursive terms in which legal actions were cast.

[23] De la Fuente and Gross, *Becoming Free, Becoming Black*; William, *A Question of Freedom*.

[24] Hunefeldt, *Paying the Price of Freedom*; Aguirre, *Agentes de su propia libertad*; Chira, *Patchwork Freedoms*; Chaves, *Honor y Libertad*; and even earlier Scott, *Slave Emancipation in Cuba*.

[25] In colonial Latin American history, this polemic was once played out in the early 1980s with regard to Indian litigation by Stern in *Peru's Indian People* and Borah's *Justice by Insurance*. It runs even more strongly through the literature on slave resistance with the emphasis on rebellion. See Thomas, *A Question of Freedom*, 7–8. In some ways, the question of litigation constitutes a question of strategy in many movements to this day. It was discussed among abolitionists in the United States and today for many groups. It is an issue among Palestinians and their use of Israeli courts or international legal fora. For the latter, see Erakat, *Justice for Some*.

[26] Even if unsuccessful, the enormous tenacity, agency, and exertion that many subordinate litigants displayed in pursuing legal battles merit scholarly and popular interest in themselves. After all, rebellions were usually unsuccessful, and yet they do not lack scholarly attention.

Recent works on law, politics, and society in colonial Latin America have taken different directions. Some move beyond the tenet that subordinate subjects were active participants in legal conflicts by focusing on how they made law through their actions and the kind of cases they pressed on the court.[27] Others focus on the significance of briefs coauthored by plaintiffs and *letrados* (legal professionals) and the arguments deployed in them. New work like Karen Graubart's on the early modern Andean region begins to examine the interrelated intellectual production that such legal activity generated.[28] Comparative work by Ariela Gross and Alejandro de la Fuente explores questions of the relation between understandings of race and freedom across space and time, while Rebecca Scott goes a step further examining the challenges of legal mobilization across transnational legal regimes.[29] Microhistories, in their capacity to represent actors at a human scale (Braudel's short durée) and situationally in relation to an array of factors inside and outside the courts, have been rightfully acquiring much popularity as a genre.[30] A handful of new studies by Bianca Premo, Michelle McKinley, and Brian Owensby also examine the judicial apparatus of ecclesiastical and secular tribunals in the Spanish empire and the logistics of Spanish law to better convey what operating in the colonial judicial arena entailed.[31] If, as some scholars claim, a surge in subordinate subjects' legal suits, including freedom actions, took place in the late eighteenth century, another kind of surge has recently taken place in scholarship about them. *From Colonial Cuba to Madrid* draws from this growing body of work and then moves in other directions.

As I turned back to the archive to research the cobreros' late eighteenth-century collective freedom action, I found that the available

[27] Premo, *The Enlightenment on Trial*; de la Fuente, "Slaves and the Creation of Legal Rights"; Chira, *Patchwork Freedoms*; Yannakakis, *Since Time Immemorial*. In the United States, for free Blacks, see Jones, *Birthright Citizens*.

[28] Graubart, "Pesa más la libertad," 427–58.

[29] De la Fuente and Gross, *Becoming Free, Becoming Black*; Scott, "Slavery and the Law in Atlantic Perspective"; and Scott and Hébrard, *Freedom Papers*.

[30] Scott has been engaging in the genre in a recent series of works. See especially Scott and Hébrard, *Freedom Papers*; Scott and Venegas Fornias, "María Coleta and the Capuchin Friar." In the United States, see particularly McDaniel, *Sweet Taste of Liberty* and more amply, Thomas, *A Question of Freedom*.

[31] McKinley, *Fractional Freedoms*, on Lima's sixteenth-century ecclesiastic courts; Premo's *The Enlightenment on Trial*, on late eighteenth-century royal courts; Owensby, *Empire of Law*, on the Indian Tribunal of New Spain and on freedom suits in seventeenth-century tribunals, "How Juan and Leonor Won Their Freedom." See also Cutter, *The Legal Culture of Northern New Spain*.

documentation was richer than I thought. Tentatively, I began to make my way through the labyrinths of Spanish colonial plural law and jurisprudence. Slowly, I began to delve into the historiography of freedom suits and legal oriented studies on Latin America and the United States.[32] Against that backdrop, I gradually realized that the cobreros' freedom lawsuit was not a run of the mill freedom case. We know now that freedom suits, though by no means common or successful, took place in all the slave societies of the Americas regardless of their slave regimes or imperial background.[33] Although each freedom suit was unique in its own way, the cobreros' action was distinctive in more than one way. No other freedom suit on record involved so many plaintiffs in a single legal action; and whereas freedom suits everywhere tended to be individual or familiar, this emancipation claim was collective – more importantly, it was communal and corporate. Moreover, the plaintiffs of El Cobre took their judicial fight against enslavement beyond the lower colonial courts and Audiencia (high regional appeal court) where most freedom actions throughout the empire took place and filed it directly in the highest tribunal of empire in Madrid where it blended with issues of state. This multiple level of litigation triangulated the conflict and its judicial manifestations in important ways that transcend the usual binary

[32] Slaves made use of the courts for a range of claims. Only a portion of slave litigation were freedom suits per se. Major studies of slave litigation, especially freedom suits, aside from those referenced in the notes above include the following: Scott, "Social Facts, Legal Fictions, and the Attributions of Slave Status"; Schweninger, *Appealing for Liberty*; Schafer, *Becoming Free, Remaining Free*. For Peru: Arrelucea Barrantes, "Slavery, Writing and Female Resistance." For Mexico, Bennett, *Africans in Colonial Mexico*; Owensby, "Legal Personality and the Processes of Slave Liberty." For Brazil, Grinberg, *Liberata*, as well as *A Black Jurist in a Slave Society*; and "Freedom Suits and Civil Law in Brazil and the United States"; Townsend, "Half My Body Free"; Chaves, "Slave Women's Strategies for Freedom"; as well as *María Chinquinquirá Díaz*. In Cuba, Scott, *Slave Emancipation in Cuba*, began these studies. Castañeda Fuertes, "Demandas judiciales de las esclavas en el siglo XIX cubano." Document anthologies show multiple abridged cases. For Cuba, see García Rodríguez, *Voices of the Enslaved in Nineteenth Century Cuba*. See also Peabody and Grinberg, *Free Soil in the Atlantic World*.

[33] Consider the total number of enslaved people's actions in court – not only freedom cases – in different localities across time. Freedom litigants in Santiago de Cuba amounted to 104 individual suits in fifty years (1820s–1860s) in Chira, *Patchwork Freedoms*, 145. Cases of slaves acting as litigants (not just freedom suits) from 1750–99 amounted to 28 cases in Mexico City, 192 in Lima, and 48 in Trujillo, Peru, in Premo, *The Enlightenment on Trial*, 196. In the US South there were 2,023 freedom suits (1,360 at the county level and 663 appeals between the beginning of the American Revolution and the Civil War) most of them in the Upper South, in Schweninger, *Appealing for Liberty*, 3–4, for breakdowns in tables, see the appendix, 291–307.

framework of colonizers and colonized. Finally, even more significant in this remarkable legal action were the substantive issues that the case presented to the court regarding the meaning and reach of freedom rights for Afro descendants as natives of a pueblo.

In *From Colonial Cuba to Madrid*, I examine this transatlantic collective lawsuit and its derivative legal actions in the colony from various angles. The book explores three major themes: the more obvious one is concerned with the question of freedom, albeit in this case with the more controversial proposal of collective freedom. Related to the claim to collective freedom is the meaning of the category of natives of a pueblo and its alleged rights, an especially significant question in the case of Afro descendant subjects. The third theme deals with the politics of litigation and subordinate subjects' use of the courts in the context of Spanish colonialism and absolutism in the late eighteenth century. The focus on a single collective case (and its individual offshoots), rather than on an aggregate collection of legal actions as in most legal studies, not only provides the proverbial depth rather than breadth to the study, but it also allows me to better link the judicial sphere to its political and social context, including the often- overlooked Bourbon reforms in this region and the later geopolitical conflagrations of the 1790s in more specific ways. Finally, in interweaving these themes, this book not only attempts to bridge the usually compartmentalized historiographies of slavery, African descendants, Indigenous people, and colonial plural law in the field of colonial Latin America, but it also tries to broaden the scope of the study by relating the local to wider trends in the Spanish Atlantic world rather than remaining enclosed in separate national histories and historiographies.

THE CASE FOR COLLECTIVE FREEDOM AND RIGHTS: A DISTINCTIVE ARGUMENT

Legal mobilization for collective freedom in an increasingly pro-slavery climate like that at the end of the eighteenth century constituted an important form of political mobilization and activism by subordinate colonial and enslaved subjects.[34] In absolute monarchies with little if

[34] Even though new work holds that the law is pliable, that it offered openings for contestation, and that its customary aspects made it subject to community norms, it is important not to lose sight of its hegemonical character. If before legal action was often dismissed by many scholars as ineffective and almost irrelevant, now the pendulum risks

any space for political organization, expression, and mobilization in civil society, the courts constituted a main arena where debates over rights and justice formally took place, even if in restricted or summary ways. Several scholars of colonial Latin America have suggested that courts constituted a venue of political engagement for subordinate colonial litigants at the time, a point superbly exemplified in the case depicted in this book.[35] In his study of empires, Frederick Cooper also calls attention to different forms of challenging power from below. He warns us that if we are to study power in empires from below, we need to understand the importance of "making claims for resources, rights or access on an empire on the basis of belonging to empire."[36] Cooper adds that courts became an instrument through which Indigenous subjects in empires could become "legal actors" and manipulate the plural legal systems of empire. That is what the cobreros were up to when they filed their composite legal action in royal courts claiming freedom, land, and corporate rights as imperial subjects and as natives of a pueblo in the Spanish empire.

The two main themes that I cover in *From Colonial Cuba to Madrid* are the question of collective freedom and the significance of local nativeness and native rights in late eighteenth-century colonial Cuba and the Spanish empire. Both constitute related substantive issues in the legal action at the center of this book. I treat them through a discursive approach to the memorials, petitions, and depositions generated for the court, and, when possible, in their manifestation outside the courts too. As the first epigraph shows, Cosme wrote that the cobreros' freedom was so obscure and confused and so lost in the past that it had to be refounded. That effort would require revising the past and reappraising their present and future. This judicial action offered an opportunity for *letrados* (men of letters or of the law) and jurists to reflect on the legal and

swinging too much to the other extreme and regarding it as too flexible and conducive to self-emancipation. Going to court was very difficult. Furthermore, the very legal character of slavery itself and the asymmetrical power relations involved especially in that system was a fact – a point perhaps that made these freedom suits all the more admirable when they actually took place. That said, litigation-oriented studies can also illuminate the intense work and resources required to challenge the law as well as the social and political factors that enable such a contest. Even if ultimately doors to freedom through the tribunals remained closed, the failed and sometimes futile legal mobilization effort in itself is worthy of study.

35 Owensby, *Empire of Law*, 5; Premo, *Enlightenment on Trial*; Taylor, "Between Global Processes and Local Knowledge"; Yannakakis, *The Art of Being In-Between* and *Since Time Immemorial*.

36 Cooper, *Colonialism in Question*, 32.

political challenges that the cobreros' unusual story, experience, and claims presented. Although the arguments and assessments of the case that emerged in the plaintiffs' briefs and memorials were, of course, not necessarily accepted by the court, their interest resides in the novel approaches and interpretations they could produce and in their implications. The memorials also point to incipient antislavery critiques and alternative proposals to the expansive slave plantation regime surfacing at that time.

Regular freedom cases for the most part turned around a set of issues regarding genealogy of maternal ancestry (sometimes explicitly linked with race, especially in the United States): unkept promises of masters in life and postmortem, terms of manumission and coartación (self-purchase), conditional or quasi possession of freedom, wrongful enslavement (including re-enslavement), and touching free soil. Obviously, the significance of these legal emancipation actions varies, for instance, regarding the master's own disposition and will to manumit in any given case. More profound principles undergirding a case were usually left implicit as suits focused on more narrow legalistic issues.

In the Iberian Atlantic, the closest a case tended to come to a conflict over foundational principles was in the invocation of the jurisprudential question regarding the extent to which the juridical and moral injunction that magistrates should "always favor freedom" (versus dominium or property rights) apply in any given case, if at all.[37] This was a first principle of justice enshrined in Spanish medieval legal sources that courts often struggled with in freedom suits; but as with other principles, it was malleable and subject to various interpretations and applications as the case of El Cobre will show. Did the confusing and indeterminate status of cobreros, or the fact that they had lived and acted in various ways as free for a long period of time, favor their freedom according to this juridical and philosophical rule? Or could having once lived as free or quasi free as in the cobreros' case be thereafter reversed into the inferior state of slavery? Questions could also be raised in this case regarding the force of customary norms versus ambiguous principles in written law: whether, for instance, royal slavery was the same as private slavery since it did not

[37] *Las Siete Partidas*, Book 7, Title 33, Law 13 briefly mentions a general "rule" (not a positive law) grounded on natural law: "It is proper rule [*regla derecha*] that all judges should favor freedom [*ayudar la libertad*] because it is a friend of nature and loved not only by men but also by all animals." This principle also enshrined in the Portuguese Ordenações Filipinas (1603) and earlier medieval codes was also invoked in myriad ways by lawyers in nineteenth century Brazil. See Grinberg, *A Black Jurist*, 55–57.

entail private dominion (which is how many cobreros read their standing). Of particular interest in El Cobre's case, however, was a novel dilemma based on what rights should have preeminence: private property rights over people and land, Crown prerogatives based on public utility and reasons of state, or the (natural) rights undergirding the bonds of nativeness to land and pueblo community that were brought to bear in this case. The cobreros' briefs and memorials were multilayered and included legal, moral, and policy-oriented arguments, making them rich sources to understand priorities in the thinking of the time.

Freedom is an abstract term that has myriad specific historical meanings and manifestations across time and place. Freedom suits, particularly those of wrongful enslavement such as this one, constitute ideal vehicles for probing understandings and criteria of freedom in various historical contexts.[38] Even better, they allow us to examine the range of acts that were reclaimed as rights of freedom in different localities.[39] The cobreros pressed on the court a series of local customary practices and arrangements that had been established through the decades, but re-configured them now as criteria of freedom and as freedom rights that could not be revoked. The implicit and explicit "rights" – or claims to rights – asserted thereby were not necessarily articulated in the modern terms of Enlightenment discourse, however.

Above all, the criterion of freedom that distinguished this case from other more standard freedom legal actions was the claim – turned into argument – that belonging to a pueblo constituted a way of enacting and producing (or prescribing) freedom, and of doing so collectively. Here the

[38] Rebecca Scott's article, "Social Facts," beautifully addresses these issues that have jurisprudential relevance in disputes of modern slavery. For performances of freedom and race, see Gross, *What Blood Won't Tell* as well as "Beyond Black and White." Tamar Herzog makes the point of performance in relation to the categories of nativeness (*naturaleza*), vecino, and vassalage, which were not explicitly parsed in legal codes. *Defining Nations*.

[39] For the US South, Laura Edwards has argued that after the American Revolution, the language of rights was avoided at the local level in favor of that of "the Peace" and that the legal rights language that appeared at the state and federal level related to constitutional and natural rights discourse excluded women, Blacks, and minors. Edwards, *The People and Their Peace*. I argue that in colonial Cuba (and the Spanish empire) a language of rights undergirded freedom claims of African descendants, as per some of the memorials on behalf of the plaintiffs. At other times, the freedom claims were more customary or made in terms of the "king's" orders and law. For a more Enlightened-oriented rights language in late eighteenth-century colonial Latin America, see Premo, *The Enlightenment on Trial*. Tamar Herzog also uses the language of rights in discussing the meaning of nativeness and *vecindad* (local citizenship) in *Defining Nations*.

case entered new terrain. At stake was an innovative claim based on notions of corporate belonging in the Spanish Atlantic world especially related to municipal bodies like a pueblo. Helen Nader in *Liberty in Absolutist Spain* claims that municipal autonomy represented "one of the highest aspirations of Castilian political life" and remained the main way through which Castilians, especially in small towns, thought about and exercised freedom from the sixteenth to the nineteenth century.[40] One of the briefs on behalf of the natives of El Cobre presented to the court further parsed an important distinction between civil and local political freedom that drew out explicitly the implications of living as a municipal corporation, the space in which limited sovereignty and political rights could be enacted locally in an absolute monarchy. In this iteration, the cobreros had not only enjoyed individual civil freedom in the past, but as natives of a pueblo they had collectively enjoyed political freedom rights too. I draw out the bold implications of this claim for Afro descendants at large who at most could only enjoy civil freedom and rights in the empire.

NATIVE BONDS AND RIGHTS

The cobreros' freedom arguments were linked to the notion of naturaleza (nativeness) widespread in the Spanish Atlantic world and more specifically to local nativeness in a pueblo. Here the cobreros' freedom suit suggests novel questions that lead my study in yet other directions. Nativeness in the Spanish Atlantic was a category of belonging primarily (but not exclusively) defined by birth, descent, and co-residence in a political community and territory. Its general ideological meaning goes back at least to the medieval *Siete Partidas* (epigraph 3). According to this conception, being native of a place created "natural" affective bonds of solidarity (or "love") among those sharing a territory and the municipality constituted the basic political unit of place on which local nativeness was literally grounded. The identity of "cobreros" was the vernacular analogue of the formal term "natives of the pueblo of El Cobre" and thus a local identification pressed on the court from below. Although in this book I examine some of the vernacular manifestations of the cobrero identity on the ground, I probe especially the use of the term "native" of a pueblo in the legal briefs and the claims made through the category.

[40] Nader, *Liberty in Absolutist Spain*, 8.

The term "native" was a common identifier in colonial records that scholars have taken for granted as a mere descriptor of place of birth and little else. But on closer inspection, nativeness was a capacious and flexible discursive category that could do different things and could be mobilized in different ways. In her book *Defining Nations*, legal historian Tamara Herzog has shown that the social terms *natural* (native) and the related one *vecino* (resident or citizen) were basically legal constructs that carried rights and duties that could vary across time and place in the Spanish Atlantic world.[41] According to Herzog, the categories' implicit meanings surfaced especially in court disputes over rights and duties. It is through these sources that she reconstructs the variable meaning of these categories in Castile and the Spanish overseas empire during the seventeenth and eighteenth centuries mainly in relation to the construction of Spanish nativeness. Herzog argues that although originally linked to a local municipal polity (pueblo, town, city), the term "naturaleza" became more elastic and evolved into supralocal forms of belongings (province, kingdom, empire) that converged in the identity of "Spanishness" across the Atlantic and across kingdoms in the peninsula.[42] However, in focusing on the supralocal Spanish native identity that emerged in the overseas colonies during the sixteenth century and that was enacted in the Spanish republics in America, Herzog stopped short of examining the uses people of color made of the category locally in the overseas colonies. Although Herzog rightly points out that Indians, Blacks, and racially mixed subjects were excluded from the category of Spanish nativeness, we know that these excluded racialized subjects were also regularly identified, and they self-identified, as natives and vecinos of (Spanish) republics (municipalities) such as Santiago, Havana, Sancti Spíritus in Cuba, or in Lima, Cartagena, or Mexico elsewhere in the empire; that is, they identified as natives of the locality in which they were born, raised, and resided. What, if anything, did local belonging as natives in Spanish republics in the

41 Herzog, *Defining Nations*.

42 The scope of the term nativeness could be elastic. Although the main referent in this study is the local pueblo or city, nativeness could apply concurrently to broader entities such as kingdom (as Castile or Aragon or later America); province, country, nation, as in the Spanish nation; and even empire. At times it referred to even broader regions such as Africa or, in the case of Indians, to natives of the Indies. Nancy Van Deusen, in *Global Indios*, has shown several broad usages of *naturaleza* in sixteenth-century Castile to determine provenance of enslaved Indian subjects and possible criteria for emancipation. In some recent work Herzog revisits the category of Indian nativeness structurally in terms of static (Spanish) legal doctrine, rather than in local terms or in dynamic disputation. Herzog, "Colonial Expansion" and "The Appropriation of Native Status."

Americas mean in the cases of racialized and otherwise excluded non-Spanish subjects? Did they invoke nativeness in their legal and vernacular actions? If so, for what purposes and to make what kind of claims? These are the kinds of questions that Herzog's study triggered for me but that her focus on other issues of interest did not address.

Although, in covering Spanish America, Herzog mostly focuses on the Spanish community, with some summary coverage of Indian republics, I use her approach in *Defining Nations* as a starting point but take my inquiry in other directions. Like Herzog, I argue that this category was also used to assert rights and make claims. But in my book, I focus on the dynamic uses of the term "native" of a pueblo in the case of the inhabitants of El Cobre who were not part of a Spanish republic. The cobreros' case shows the social, legal, and political importance of this category and how it could be mobilized in different ways by non-Spanish racial subjects to make claims. Yet, as mentioned before, nativeness was a capacious identity that especially by the seventeenth and eighteenth century could take on supra local meanings too. Yet, supra local meanings of nativeness did not displace local ones; they coexisted and were used in different contexts. Although I also explore the deployment of some of these broader meanings of belonging to make solidarity claims with subjects beyond the local polity, this study is focused for the most part on the local invocations of nativeness by the cobrero plaintiffs and the social, political, and legal meaning attributed to that identity in their judicial briefs.

And yet, the cobreros' case becomes more complicated – and fascinating – due to ambiguities in the meaning of native or *natural* in the overseas empire where it also referred to Indianness or Indigeneity, another meaning that was also wielded ambiguously in the court briefs of the natives of El Cobre.[43] In this formulation, the natives of El Cobre had Indian ancestry, or had coexisted with Indians as natives of El Cobre

[43] Indigeneity is an encompassing modern term that refers to a late twenty and twenty-first century resurgence (and reinvention) of Indigenous identities and movements in a globalized neoliberal world. The movements are political and cultural; they also seek legal grounding and expansion of rights in international human rights law and new constitutions. Recent scholars have been historicizing the category and examining its legal deployments and underpinnings in different historical contexts. I will be using the terms Indianness, Indigeneity, Indigenous and (Indian) Natives more or less indistinctly here. It is understood, however, that all of these terms constituted historical constructions based on Spanish law though subject to variation and disputation on the ground. For the exploration of global manifestations of these resurgent movements, see Clifford, *Returns*, especially 13–32. For the national period, see Earle, *The Return of the Native*. For the colonial period, see especially Yannakakis, *Since Time Immemorial*; Premo, *The*

in the past, or by legal analogy had a similar standing to Indians by virtue of their customary living arrangements. Although Indigenous nativeness entailed a subordinate colonial status, conflating natives of a pueblo with Indigeneity provided a legal opening to assert free status, land rights, and a protected corporate pueblo status for African descendants and racially mixed cobreros in this case.

The invocation of nativeness as Indianness in Cuba is particularly interesting given the fading presence of Indigenous people resulting from the demographic collapse and "great dying" brought about by the Spanish conquest during the early sixteenth century. Yet, there were at least two pueblos with official Indian native pueblo protected status in eastern Cuba – San Luis del Caney in the environs of El Cobre and San Pablo de Jiguaní near Bayamo – that could have served as models for allusions to nativeness through Indian ancestry in El Cobre's case (see Figure 0.1). There were also vernacular stories circulating in the village and region regarding the relation of Indians and former Black slaves as natives of El Cobre. I argue that in invoking nativeness, the cobreros' case bridged plural regimes of colonial slave and Indigenous law and race norms in heretofore unexamined ways.

With some exceptions, the intersectionality between Afro descendant and Indigenous legal and social regimes has barely begun to be probed by historians of colonial Latin America.[44] In the United States, a number of recent studies examine how slave litigants used Indigenous maternal ancestry as a way to claim freedom in the courts of the new American republic.[45] More recently, a subfield of Black Indian studies has emerged in US historiography that focuses on Black slave, freedmen, and Indian relations, rights, and conflicts of belonging in Indian reservations in the past, in some cases with ongoing conflictive implications to this day.[46] But there is still little along those lines in the Latin American scholarly literature. For colonial Spanish America, Karen Graubart has keenly

Enlightenment on Trial, 159–90; Penry, *The People Are King*. See also Herzog, "The Appropriation of Native Status."

44 The displacement of Blackness into the "Indio" category among Dominicans has been noted for the modern period in the Dominican Republic but not sufficiently probed in the past. See Torres-Saillant, "The Tribulations of Blackness," 126–46.

45 Gross, *What Blood Won't Tell*; de la Fuente and Gross, *Becoming Free, Becoming Black*, 95–98; Sachs, "'Freedom by a Judgement'"; Wallenstein, "Indian Foremothers"; Ablavsky, "Making Indians 'White'"; Vandervelde, *Redemption Songs*, 39–56.

46 See among others, Miles, *The House on Diamond Hill* and *Ties That Bind*; Littlefield, *The Cherokee Freedmen*; Saunt, *Black, White, and Indian*; Chang, *The Color of the Land*.

explored attempts by an African descendant petitioner to claim the rights of Indian status in early colonial Peru (with negative results).[47] Matthew Restall has documented the presence of both groups in Yucatan, though ultimately he treated them separately.[48] More recently, Marcela Echevarri has brought these groups together by comparing their royalist alignments during the Independence wars in Popayán and their sharing of a colonial discourse based on the king's protection and justice that went back to earlier colonial times.[49] This kind of alignment applies to the cobreros' case to an even greater degree given their century-long trajectory as the king's slaves and their interpretation of that standing. But the imbrication with Indigeneity in El Cobre's case comes up in even more complex ways through overlapping corporate identifications and analogies in the logistics of judicial argumentation and mobilization. Although plural regimes existed that separated the experiences of Spanish, Afro descendants (free and enslaved), Indian, and racially mixed subjects (*castas*), their legal boundaries were sometimes bridged, or implicit claims were made for their social and legal expansion or reconfiguration as the cobreros' case shows. Emerging liberal tendencies in the Spanish Atlantic during the nineteenth century, however, would erode plural regimes and the protections and rights that Indigenous corporate municipal entities could invoke (or reinterpret) through plural law. In this sense, El Cobre and the two Indian pueblos of eastern Cuba would face similar challenges in the emerging era of liberal trends under Spanish colonialism in the nineteenth century (Chapter 9).

Overall, in *From Colonial Cuba to Madrid*, I argue that the plaintiffs' use of the term "natives of El Cobre" straddled both Spanish/Castilian and Indigenous socio-legal regimes and that there was an unresolved tension and ambiguity between these two notions of nativeness that could be mobilized to claim rights in the case of this unconventional community of African descendants. I push the end point of this study to the period of the Cádiz Constitution of 1812 to examine to what extent the civil and (local) political freedoms aspired to by the cobreros as natives of a corporate pueblo – eventually obtained in the Freedom Edict of 1800 – fit into the new liberal scheme of belonging to the greater Spanish nation

[47] Graubart, "Pesa más la libertad," 427–58. See also O'Toole, *Bound Lives*.

[48] Restall, *The Black Middle*; Landers in *Black Society in Spanish Florida* has documented Spanish use of communities of both groups for defense purposes and work exists on the friendly and hostile relations between these groups as part of a wider US historiography.

[49] Echeverri, *Indian and Slave Royalists in the Age of Revolution.*

and its (short lived) project of democratization through the expansion of local political citizenship rights. I end the study by examining the issues that the natives of corporate communities such as El Cobre and the two other Indian pueblos in eastern Cuba faced as new and old Atlantic and colonial forces converged in this region in the nineteenth century.

THE POLITICS OF LITIGATION

The third theme examined in *From Colonial Cuba to Madrid* focuses on the politics of legal action as they played out in this case. As mentioned before, legal actions constituted a form of political action through which imperial subordinate subjects could use the law to make claims on royal courts. Scholars have casted coartación and other individual freedom legal processes as forms of self-emancipation within the framework of slavery. But the cobreros' action was even more consequential due to the magnitude of the collective mobilization involved in this case, the corporatist discourse and freedom rights that plaintiffs invoked, and the implicit and explicit critiques of slavery that appeared in their briefs. Politics, as this case shows, imbued the litigation conflict at different levels, both inside and outside the courts – and it could not have been otherwise given the increasing centrality of issues about slavery and freedom at the time.

The cobreros' social bonds and (informal) organization as a pueblo enabled their strong collective action in the legal arena. In that sense, their situation placed them closer to the experience of Indigenous subjects who litigated in common as corporate entities than to African descendants who usually did not live in that kind of formation. The cobreros empowered Gregorio Cosme Osorio (first epigraph), a freedman and native of the pueblo, to be their apoderado in the royal court in Madrid, a rare liaison position for a colonial man of African or Indigenous descent in the imperial capital and another extraordinary aspect of the case. Yanna Yannakakis's research on Indigenous intermediaries has shown the agency of Indian colonial subjects in legal actions and the predicaments they faced in colonial courts. José Carlos de la Puente Luna and Alcira Dueñas have shown that some Indigenous and Mestizo litigants made it to Madrid, but not enough is known about their actions in the royal court.[50] Cosme, in particular, but also his local counterparts in El Cobre, took the role of legal representation to a new level, especially

[50] Yannakakis, *The Art of Being In-Between*; de la Puente Luna, *Indigenous Cosmopolitans*; Dueñas, *Indians and Mestizos in the "Lettered" City.*

for African descendant litigants. The close examination of their activities in this book throws further light on subordinate litigants' possibilities of mobilization in transoceanic and transregional royal court networks. Cosme's extant correspondence with the community constitutes an extraordinary source that allowed me to document his political and legal agency in Madrid and to probe his views on the law and the community's case.

In Cuba, individual enslaved and runaway cobreros in different towns also accessed the courts for hearings when lower instance courts offered openings. In this sense, the conflict went beyond its epicenter in Santiago and became a widespread legal action across various cities on the island and involved a broad series of actors: cobreros, slaveholders, magistrates, notaries, attorneys, witnesses, and, overall, lay people who heard and saw edicts posted calling for the hearings. The cobreros' legal mobilization, therefore, took place at different levels in colonial and imperial tribunals resulting in an extensive trans-local and transatlantic action that required wide ranging networks of communication.

Although in this book I focus mainly on different aspects of the cobreros' legal action, I show that political action on their part also took place through extrajudicial actions such as civil disobedience, marronage, and even armed ambushes to recover captured cobreros. Even though these actions are usually treated separately in the historiography of emancipation and resistance to slavery, I show that they were entangled with judicial actions and impacted each other. Rather than a mere flight from slavery into an elusive freedom, these combined actions were part of a broader political action that affirmed specific agendas of freedom.[51]

In *From Colonial Cuba to Madrid*, I also examine the political considerations that informed shifts in court decisions at the imperial level between the 1780s and the 1790s. Geopolitical factors such as the Revolution in Saint Domingue and imperial war with the British added a new and broader political context to the case in the 1790s. The larger question of Saint Domingue that haunts the historiography of the Age of Revolution in the Caribbean also comes up in this case. Did Saint Domingue have an impact on the cobreros' mobilization for freedom?

[51] The initial and classic empirical studies are presented in Richard Price, ed. *Maroon Societies*, but the literature is extensive. For Cuba, see La Rosa Corzo, *Runaway Slave Settlements*. For more theoretical reflections of marronage, see Edouard Glissant's cultural classic, *Caribbean Discourse* and more recently, from a political theory perspective, Roberts, *Freedom as Marronage*. For a discussion of this issue, see Chapter 7.

Launched in the early 1780s as a response to the Crown's privatization of El Cobre, this lawsuit represented a reaction against the effects of that Bourbon policy and the new order of unbridled slavery expansion rapidly becoming dominant. The radical revolutions in France and next door in Saint Domingue that abolished slavery and extended the rights of man in a universalizing way did not materialize until the 1790s, a full decade after the cobreros' freedom suit began to run its course in Cuba and Madrid.[52] The cobreros' response represented a legal and political mobilization within the Spanish Atlantic that challenged with its own discursive and legal tools the approaching tsunami of slavery expansion early on in the game – and as I argue in the book, it even presented an alternative to the plantation regime on the rise. The revolution in Saint Domingue cast its influence over the cobreros' case indirectly and influenced the outcome of the case in 1799 due to imperial security concerns. But the significance of some of the cobreros' freedom rights arguments and proposals were distinctive, even radical, in their own terms, as I hope to show in this book. Some of them have reemerged in the late twentieth century in other localities of Latin America under upgraded democratic constitutions as I point out in the Conclusion.

SOURCES AND ORGANIZATION OF THE BOOK

The small pueblo of El Cobre has a disproportionally large presence in the imperial state's archive. Most of the available local documentation regarding the case – including local censuses (*padrones*) and even baptism records – was forwarded to Madrid for the adjudication of the case. The lawsuit itself generated its own harvest of legal records – petitions, briefs, memorials, depositions, rulings – that document the legal process and the issues under contestation. Other documentation in the dossier was generated at different levels of empire and by different groups and stakeholders in the conflict: policy deliberations in the Council of the Indies; representations by the heirs, colonial correspondence between governors and captain generals, the bishops and clergy's reports, *autos* of court hearings and trials in the colony and in Madrid. The record even includes

[52] For the radical significance of the claims for universal freedom and citizenship posed by the revolution of Saint Domingue and the other French colonies, see Dubois, *A Colony of Citizens* and *Avengers of the New World*. For the paradoxical relation of Cuba and the Haitian Revolution, see Ferrer's *Freedom's Mirror*. For a discussion on the indirect influence of the Haitian revolution in the cobreros' legal case, see Chapter 8.

correspondence between the cobreros in El Cobre and Madrid. Such a compilation would have been virtually impossible to assemble by a single historian (at least until the archive is fully cataloged and digitalized). In short, this dossier, located in the imperial General Archive of the Indies in Seville, constitutes a true mine (so to speak) of documentation on a local community of racialized colonial subjects' engagement with the imperial judicial system. Additionally, I have made use of documentation scattered through other sections of that archive and, especially for the nineteenth century, to documents in the National Historical Archive in Madrid.

The chapters in this book examine from different angles and points in time the relation of law, politics, and society undergirding the conflict at the center of this book. On "genre," rather than casting the work in a single genre, say a narrative approach, the book alternates microhistory, narrative, and discursive analysis to explore various aspects of this action. Topics covered in the first two chapters relate mostly to the political and social contexts that gave rise to the legal action filed in Madrid in 1784. Focusing on the relation between imperial, colonial, and local levels, Chapter 1 opens by tracing the imperial logic informing the Bourbon Crown's decision to privatize the mining jurisdiction of El Cobre, that is, with the process of making law and policy according to the imperial state's reform imperatives of the time. A growing demand for slaves in the colony and a stronger interpretation of slave law and property rights led instead to an island-wide traffic of enslaved cobreros.

Chapter 2 turns to the local level of the pueblo of El Cobre and its response to the privatization order. It examines the unorthodox character of this community that exposed it to the enslavement actions of 1780 and the villagers' vernacular collective self-identification as "cobreros" – natives of El Cobre – with which they countered their captivity. The chapter then turns trans-local as it traces the cobreros' apoderados travails to reach the imperial court from colonial Cuba and the networks created to do so.

The next three chapters turn to various aspects of the judicial battle itself. Chapters 3 and 4 are central to the book. Based on discursive analysis, they focus on the memorials produced in Madrid and the colony to mount the plaintiffs' case. Whereas Chapter 3 examines the battery of legal tools deployed in the plaintiffs' memorials to buttress their case for collective freedom, Chapter 4 focuses on the meaning and deployment of the novel category of "natives" of a pueblo to bolster their claims. It also compares the unconventional standing of El Cobre with that of the Indian pueblos of El Caney and Jiguaní in the island's eastern region to explore the cobreros' equivocal claims to Indian ancestry.

Chapter 5 turns to the law in action and the politics of litigation involving adjudication and conflictive interpretations of the law. The chapter opens with an examination of the Council of the Indies' confusing response to the freedom memorial filed in Madrid in 1784. The ruling gave way to a cascade of legal actions in lower-level colonial courts contesting its actual scope and application. Ordinary enslaved and fugitive cobreros dispersed throughout the island, and not just in El Cobre, became direct participants in the judicial arena at this point as they directly engaged in the politics of litigation.

The following chapters move forward in time from the 1780s to the 1790s, a period when a shift began to take place regarding the case at the imperial level. Cosme's extant letters from Madrid from 1795 are the focus of Chapter 6. They provide a close view of a cobrero leader's legal and political views on the case, the effect his letters had on the community, and his crucial role as liaison between the court and his home pueblo. Chapter 7 moves back to the colony. Here the story of legal action merges with one of extrajudicial actions such as fugitivity and more violent action and shows how judicial and extrajudicial actions were intertwined. Factoring into the escalating threat of violence and political conflict on the ground was the broader Atlantic context of revolution in Saint Domingue and war with the British during the 1790s. Chapter 8 goes back to the imperial state level to examine the legal and political logic informing the final adjudication of the case in 1799 in favor of the cobreros' freedom, yet with several caveats. The chapter ventures into the immediate aftermath of the Edict of 1800 to examine the immediate challenges that emerged in the actualization of the decreed emancipation.

Focusing on the afterlife of the Freedom Edict of 1800, Chapter 9 moves the story into the nineteenth century: into a period of imperial crisis, the emergence of liberal trends in the empire reflected in the Cádiz Constitution of 1812, as well as of new stakeholders in the region's historical context such as French refugees from Saint Domingue and British miners. The chapter focuses on the problems the emancipated cobreros faced in actualizing a corporate community model along the lines of colonial Indian law in the new liberal-oriented historical context. Questions about native rights, race, and citizenship, about civil and political rights and about corporate and individual land rights emerged in this new political context. The book concludes with a reflection on the significance of the category of local nativeness for racial colonial subjects and the political uses and rights claimed for this category in changing historical contexts in the past and its reemergence in various Latin American nations in the late twentieth and early twenty-first century.

1

Imperial Reform, Privatization, and Enslavement

> It can be stated as an absolute principle that the prosperity of this island depends mainly on the importation of slaves.
>
> —Marshall Alejandro O'Reilly, 1767

> The Council thinks that the public utility of the mines should be the principal object in whatever decision is taken on the matter.
>
> —Council of the Indies, 1778

In 1784, the Council of the Indies issued a ministerial order to facilitate the importation of African slaves in Spain's overseas empire. The preamble to that order reflects the Bourbon state's voice and the tenor of its broader colonial renovation policy.

> The paternal love of the King our Lord ever zealous in providing his beloved vassals of America with all those means which will contribute to their greatest prosperity and wealth, recognizes that one of the most useful and necessary means to this end, is that of facilitating the introduction of negro slaves into those dominions as the only laborers [*brazos*] for agriculture and mining in the greater part of those dominions which are the bases upon which depend the commerce and happiness of these [in the Peninsula] and those kingdoms [overseas].[1]

The new imperial slave expansion policy – with all the violence that it entailed – was sheathed in a benign royal ideological mantle of paternal love, utility, and necessity wedded to the promise of happiness and prosperity to imperial subjects. Some of the terms used – such as utility and agriculture – were linked to the creation of happiness and wealth.

[1] Ministerial Order of José de Gálvez, San Lorenzo, November 4, 1784. In Andrew and Cleven, "Ministerial Order," 274.

The use of these terms was fairly new in the Spanish imperial state's mission rhetoric.[2] Whereas the preamble indirectly recognized the political pressure exerted by colonial vassals in support of slave labor, it presented it as a favor bestowed by His Sovereign Majesty on his beloved subjects. Havana's export plantation agriculture advocates were especially aggressive in pushing pro-slavery policies that would eventually culminate in the deregulation of the slave trade market in 1789 – paradoxically, a policy of international "free" trade in unfree human property. The "second slavery" period was opening up.[3] Although Havana was at the center of that story in the Caribbean region, other so-called peripheral locales were also impacted by the Bourbon reforming impulse.

Even more pertinent to the story of this book was yet another kind of imperial policy directed specifically at mining, which was also in need of slave labor as the edict's preamble notes. The mining jurisdiction of Santiago del Prado (aka El Cobre) in the island's eastern region held the promise of happiness for the imperial state and considerable wealth for imperial subjects in that region's lagging economy: rich copper deposits and slaves. The importance of those copper mines in the history of this region has been generally overlooked by scholars and so has the impact of Bourbon reforms whose study has focused on Havana.

In this chapter, I unpack what has been termed the modern utility logic undergirding the Bourbon policy of privatization of the mining estate of El Cobre in the late 1770s and place it within the broader context of imperial copper mining policy in the Spanish Atlantic.[4] I then turn to the policy's implementation in the colony where it intersected, on the one hand, with the slave expansion policy mentioned above and the high demand for slaves on the island and, on the other, with the uprooting of an unconventional but long-established pueblo in the jurisdiction. Imperial arms production and resource extraction policy, colonial private sector interests related to slave (and land) property, and small community-based interests clashed in the new reform juncture in this corner of empire. The consequent enslavement of hundreds of quasi-free villagers and the disruption, nay, the axing, of traditional customary

[2] G. Paquette, *Enlightenment, Governance, and Reform.*

[3] Tomich, *Through the Prism*; Schneider, *Occupation of Havana.*

[4] On the "modernity" of the Bourbon state's reforming impulse, see G. Paquette, *Enlightenment, Governance, and Reform.* For Mexican Bourbon mining reforms: Howe, *The Mining Guild of New Spain*; Brading, *Miners and Merchants.* For Peru: Fisher, *Silver Mines and Silver Miners in Colonial Peru*; Kuethe, "Mining and the Bourbon Reforms." For copper mining policy in New Spain, see Barret, *Mexican Colonial Copper Industry.*

arrangements shook up various aspects of the colonial order in this transitional historical moment. The privatization and enslavement raised questions about the meaning and limits of slavery and freedom, of property versus community rights, and of royal law versus customary rights at a time of considerable change. The disputes that emerged extended all the way from colonial Cuba to Madrid. This chapter represents the voices and interests that converged and clashed around this momentous event. Chapter 2 focuses on the perspective of the affected villagers.

SANTIAGO DE CUBA AND THE EASTERN REGION

Despite its standing as the capital of Cuba's eastern region, Santiago de Cuba was, in the late 1770s, a mid-size, lusterless provincial port city subject to the jurisdiction of the booming capital city of Havana. Atlantic port cities in the Americas at the end of the eighteenth century ranged between 4,500 and 45,000 inhabitants.[5] Santiago, the island's second most important city, had an urban population of about 10,280 souls in 1778, roughly one-fourth of Havana's population of almost 40,000 (Table 1.1).[6] To be sure, Havana may have been one of the largest port cities in the hemisphere then (the other was Philadelphia), but the population scale of these cities was not large by modern standards: no larger than US university campuses in our early twenty-first century, to take a familiar point of reference.[7] Whereas Havana was the seat of the highest Bourbon colonial officials, the intendant and the captain general, Santiago de Cuba sat a governor and a smaller provincial colonial administrative and military bureaucracy (Figure 0.1).

[5] J. Price, "Summation ... Atlantic Port Cities," 263.

[6] General Census of Cuba, 1778, AGI-Indiferente 1527. I have made corrections in Table 1.1 based on some recalculation of the numbers in the 1778 census. For instance, although the General Census of 1778 gives an urban population for the city of Santiago of 10,070 souls, I calculated 10,280 including clergy and nuns. When the rural population (*partido*) is included, Santiago's population increases to 12,476 souls. For Havana, the 1778 census gives an urban population of 40,737, which I recalculated to 39,741 inhabitants. I have not included here Havana's rural population because the city had multiple rural districts.

[7] J. Price, "Summation ... Atlantic Port Cities," 262–76. Philadelphia was the largest with 42,444 souls in 1790. The Brazilian cities of Salvador, Bahia, and Rio de Janeiro in 1780 had almost the same population as Havana (around 39,000) and New York had 33,131. Santiago de Cuba's population in 1778 was in the range of that of the important port of Cartagena de Indias (11,500 in 1772) and was larger than Saint Domingue's Port au Prince, which had only 6,000 inhabitants in 1789.

TABLE 1.1 *Population in various localities – by race and status, 1778*

	Race		Status of population of color		
Localities	White	Of color	Free	Slave	Total population
Santiago					
urban	4,268	6,012	3,795	2,217	10,280
% of total population	41.5	58.5	36.9	21.6	
Santiago					
urban & rural	4,487	7,989	4,009	3,980	12,476
% of total population	36.0	64.0	32.1	31.9	
Baracoa					
urban & rural	776	1,142	1,012	130	1,918
% of total population	40.5	59.5	52.8	6.8	
El Cobre					
urban & rural	19	1,463	519	944	1,482
% of total population	1.3	98.7	35.0	63.7	
El Caney					
urban & rural	662	297	164	133	959
% of total population	69.0	31.0	17.1	13.9	
Jiguani					
urban & rural	1,054	278	263	15	1,332
% of total population	79.1	20.9	19.7	1.1	
Bayamo					
urban	4,062	5,350	3,606	1,744	9,412
% of total population	43.2	56.8	38.3	18.5	
Havana					
urban	21,211	18,530	7,111	11,419	39,741
% of total population	53.4	46.6	17.9	28.7	

General Census of Cuba, December 31, 1778. AGI-Indiferente 1527

And while Havana had its own bishopric, Santiago was the seat of the regional archbishopric with its own ecclesiastical staff. Like other Spanish "republics" or cities in the empire, cities like Santiago and Havana also had their own municipal government or *cabildo* that represented local self-government. Although in principle the cabildo represented the interests of the city and allegedly of all its free *vecinos* (residents and citizens), it was constituted by distinguished local citizens – all of them of Spanish

FIGURE 1.1 General view of Santiago de Cuba and Bay, ca. 1890.
The engraving from a scientific publication of the late 19th century aptly captures the eastern capital's character as a seaport surrounded by mountains and its provincial urban feel through the depiction of a narrow street lined with modest, tile roof colonial houses. From E. Reclus' famous *Universal Geography*, vol. 17, VII Cuba, 372, 1890. The Print Collector/Alamy/ Heritage Images/From Universal Geography, Maps and Illustrations, Vol. XXXIV [*sic*], Virtue and Co. Limited (London ca. 1890)

descent and alleged racial purity. As the capital of the island's eastern region, Santiago had other districts and villages under its jurisdiction. Aside from the unusual village of El Cobre (population 1,482 in 1778), two villages considered Indian pueblos or republics were also under its direct jurisdiction: San Luis del Caney (El Caney), near Santiago, and San Pablo de Jiguaní (Jiguaní), near the town of Bayamo (Figure 0.1).[8]

[8] Census of Santiago, 1780, AGI-SD 1272. Although the 1780 census lists under Santiago's jurisdiction the cities of Baracoa and its district and Holguín and its district, the General Census of Cuba of 1778 (AGI-Indiferente 1527) included only El Cobre, El Caney, and Jiguaní under Santiago's jurisdiction. The Census of Santiago of 1780 gives a population count for El Cobre and its district of 1,370 souls; however, my recalculation of the numbers in the census comes to 1,406 inhabitants, which is the figure I will be using hereafter for 1780. The census of 1778 gives a higher population count of 1,492 inhabitants for El Cobre.

In 1778, Santiago was a majority Afro descendant city where people of color, free and slave, constituted more than half of the city's population (58.4 percent) and an even higher percent if the rural population is included (64 percent) in a still sparsely populated region (see Table 1.1 for urban and combined rural and urban populations). At the top of the city's social and racial hierarchy stood those considered Whites at 41.5 percent of the city's inhabitants. About a third of the urban population (36.9 percent) were free people of color and more than a fifth (21.6 percent) was enslaved. A combined urban and rural population alters the proportions somewhat with roughly a third for each group. Yet Santiago was not unique in terms of its racial composition.

Other so-called Spanish republics (cities and towns) in the island's eastern region also had majorities of African descendants and did so in even more striking combinations. In Baracoa, a huge 52.7 percent of the urban and rural population of the district were free people of color (a much higher proportion than in Santiago) and only 7 percent were enslaved persons. In the town of Bayamo, a considerable 38.3 percent of the urban population was made up by free people of color and 18.5 percent were urban slaves – but the racial and class dynamics in these towns still await scholarly attention. On the western side of the island, in fast growing Havana, White people predominated making up 53.3 percent of the city's population, while at almost 18 percent, free people of color constituted a much lower proportion, and enslaved persons made up a high 28.7 percent of the city's inhabitants.[9]

The pueblo of El Cobre, however, had the most unusual racial and status profile on the whole island: a huge 64 percent (almost two-thirds) of its population were considered slaves, specifically slaves of the king, and only 1.3 percent were Whites. Finally, whatever Indigenous people, or racially mixed people with Indigenous blood, may have remained in eastern Cuba's two Indian pueblos by 1778, they were rendered invisible in the island-wide censuses that began to be produced by Bourbon administrators in the late 1770s. Contrary to mainland censuses, those generated in the colony of Cuba utilized an exclusive racial classificatory framework of White, Black, and Mulatto so that racial nuances outside this scheme were lost. In 1778, Whites overwhelmingly predominated in these two small pueblos (69 percent in El Caney and 79.1 percent in Jiguaní) mainly

[9] General Census of Cuba, 1778. AGI-Indiferente 1527.

because people with Indian ancestry were re-classified as Whites. I will come back to this issue in Chapter 4.

Although the capital of the island's eastern region, Santiago de Cuba was a provincial port city whose economic growth lagged behind that of Havana. Its (White) elite vecinos were aware of their diminished status in comparison to Havana's political power and mushrooming prosperity. A 1780 entry in Santiago's municipal records lamented the city's lethargic economy and its decadence in an almost comic way. Striking a nostalgic tone for the loss of a chimerical imperial glory, it said: "The sad state of this city, which is without a regular slaughterhouse, without a dock, with impassable streets and a Capitular House [Sala Capitular] in a state of total lack of decency; a city like this ... which has the honor of once having had Hernán Cortés as *alcalde ordinario* (bailiff) and which is the second capital which was founded in America, after Santo Domingo."[10] Recent warfare, earthquakes, climatic catastrophes, lack of trade and capital, and a stagnated economy had exacerbated the city's deterioration, reflected in its allegedly subpar infrastructure. Compared to fast growing Havana, the economic situation of Santiago looked sluggish but not dead. Large slabs of the overseas empire may have resembled Santiago's provincial condition (Figure 1.1).

Santiago's economy in 1780 was based on the production of sugar, tobacco, and cattle. Coffee would not become a major export crop until the late 1790s with the arrival of French exiles from neighboring Saint Domingue's revolution; and copper mining would not really take off until the 1830s, when production became spectacular under British exploitation. If sugar was at the time the great indicator of agricultural growth, "prosperity," and commerce in the Atlantic colonial world, Santiago's production infrastructure was far behind Havana's. The eastern city had less and smaller sugar *ingenios* (sugar mills or plantations) than Havana: of Santiago's 50 ingenios in 1786, the largest 5 (10 percent) held between 40 and 43 slaves. Havana, on the other hand, had three times as many ingenious (150) and more than half were larger than Santiago's 5 largest ingenios, but they were also dispersed in a much larger region.[11] Of the

[10] Bacardí, *Crónicas Santiago*, July 17, 1780, 206.

[11] Amores, *Cuba*, Appendix 2, 497–501. Years before, the Census of 1778 recorded a total of 138 ingenios in all the 33 districts of Havana's jurisdiction (but they were found in a few districts, with the highest concentration in the pueblo and district of Managua with 31 ingenios). The smaller district of Santiago de Cuba, however, had 48 ingenios (43 of them in the city's surrounding district). There is no breakdown in the census of the number of slaves that were employed in these sugar concerns, only general numbers for rural districts.

96 sugar estates in Havana for which the number of slaves was recorded, 54 had over 40 slaves; and the largest 14 had between 100 and 183 slaves by the mid-1780s.[12]

Tobacco production in the colony was under Crown monopoly. It was a small farmer's cash crop that inserted White and free people of color into a commercial circuit, even though the royal monopoly limited their incomes.[13] Many other free people of color and poor Whites lived in a food-producing economy based on small farms. Cattle ranching took up enormous expanses of land but did not need a large labor force.[14]

Santiago de Cuba's strategic frontier location in a multi-imperial Caribbean region enhanced the city's military value for the Crown, particularly at a time of increasing warfare between Spain, France, and Britain, Spain's main imperial rival at the time (see Figure 0.1). A magnificent garrison protecting the entrance to Santiago Bay made visible its strategic status as a military colony in Spain's Caribbean imperial system (Figure 1.2). Especially important in oiling the city's modest economy was the silver coming in from Mexico, the so-called royal military *situado* (subsidy) shared with Havana for defense purposes. This silver represented a valuable input of liquid currency into the economy that long supported contraband trade.

Santiago complained that few legal ships visited its port, preferring other ports of trade, although it had traditionally conducted considerable inter imperial contraband trade with neighboring Jamaica and other islands, a trade that the Bourbon reformers were especially intent on containing. The struggling eastern capital city, however, wanted to move beyond its military colony status and become an agricultural and commercial emporium like its rival Havana and wanted more commercial freedom to trade with foreign merchants, particularly in the neighboring British colony of Jamaica.

12 Amores, *Cuba*, Appendix 2, 497–501.

13 Ortiz, *Contrapunteo cubano*; Levi Marrero, *Cuba*, vol. 11, 1–46; Costner, *The Golden Leaf*; Chira, *Patchwork Freedoms*, 46–50, 198–202. The 1778 General census did not count *vegas* or tobacco farms, just generic family small farms or *estancias*. For an anthology of the role of tobacco and the royal monopoly in the Spanish empire, including Cuba, see González Enciso and Torres Sánchez, eds., *Tabaco y economía en el siglo XVIII*.

14 Santiago's rural district also had in 1778 the considerable number of 87 hatos, large open landed estates for pasturing and raising cattle. General Census of Cuba, 1778, AGI-Indiferente 1527.

FIGURE 1.2 San Pedro de la Roca Castle, Santiago de Cuba.
The imposing fortress defended the entrance to the Bay of Santiago in a multi-imperial Caribbean region and gave the city a military character. Generations of cobreros worked as royal slaves in the construction and maintenance of this fortification until 1780. Arterra/Universal Images Group/Getty Images

Barely twelve miles away from Santiago was the royal mining jurisdiction of Santiago del Prado (aka El Cobre), an abandoned copper mining settlement that by 1778 had grown into an unconventional rural village of about 1,482 inhabitants, most of them small farmers and peasants, descendants of former mining slaves (see Figure 0.1). About two-thirds of this informal village's inhabitants were considered slaves of the king and the other third were free people of color. Chapter 2 provides an in-depth profile of this community. Suffice it to say that the royal slaves in this Caribbean frontier region of empire were incorporated into the Crown's defense system. They worked in the construction and maintenance of nearby fortification projects and guarded the coastal port of Guaycabón from the approach of enemies. The pueblo had four militia companies that included the free and royal slave inhabitants of the pueblo who fought against British invasions in the 1740s and of Havana in 1762. However, El Cobre lost its own militias as a result of the Bourbon reform of the military in the mid-1760s. Thereafter, these royal slave villagers' role in the imperial defense system was downgraded to that of only laborers in the maintenance of the fortification projects (Figure 1.2).

Although royal slaves were also employed in the fortification projects in Havana, Havana's royal slaves never enjoyed the unusual customary arrangements that the royal slaves of El Cobre were able to negotiate through the years. Like slaves elsewhere, Havana's royal slaves worked full time and were housed in barracks; and after the mayor fortification reconstructions following the British occupation of Havana were completed in the 1780s, hundreds, if not thousands of them, were sold off to private slaveholders given the high demand for slaves in the island.[15] Even though the royal slaves living in El Cobre had been able to negotiate very different labor arrangements through the years, in the late 1770s the Bourbon state further changed its policy regarding the use of its royal slaves in El Cobre envisioning more productive roles for them in a privatized mining industry.

A quick turn to El Cobre's complex history as a mining settlement before it became a village of Afro descendants incorporated into the colony's defense system will provide context for the shift in imperial policy that led to the privatization of the mining estate and its inhabitants through the Executory Order of 1779.

BOURBON IMPERIAL COPPER MINING POLICY: PUBLIC UTILITY AND PRIVATIZATION

The importance of this mining jurisdiction goes back to the turn of the seventeenth century when an important royal mining-agricultural-cattle ranching complex developed around some rich copper mines discovered in the late 1520s. At one point in the 1610s, the complex included more than 300 slaves making it the largest venture in the island and in the Caribbean at the time.[16] The story of the privatization and de-privatization of the mining complex that went back to this period created an obfuscating tangle of possession rights in this jurisdiction that affected the privatization of 1779. Briefly, in 1599, the Crown, claiming eminent domain, de-privatized, enclosed, and created a Real de Minas, a royal mining jurisdiction around these mines. The Crown directly exploited the rich copper mines for two decades, creating an extractive industry of a strategic metal with other satellite agricultural and cattle ranching ventures in the jurisdiction's land. Between 1614 and 1620, a shift in policy in

[15] Jennings, "Paths to Freedom," 121–42; Schneider, *Occupation of Havana*, 285.

[16] Inventory of the Mines, February 1620, AGI-SD 1631; see also Díaz, *The Virgin, the King*, 29–35.

the Council of the Indies led to the decision to "privatize" the mining concern and, in modern parlance, outsource copper production for its arms industry. Don Juan de Eguiluz won a public bid for the mining contract and took over the mines in 1620. Because copper was a strategic resource, the privatization came with a contract to provide the Crown an annual quota of 2,000 quintals of copper at a fixed price. It was then that most of the confusion began. Just what kind of possession rights did Eguiluz negotiate over the estate? Was it an *asiento* (a leasing contract), a property transfer and sale of the full estate, or something in between? We need not enter into those details here. Suffice it to say that by the 1660s, large scale mining production in the privatized concern had ceased for a series of reasons and the mines lay for all purposes abandoned. In 1670, the Crown impounded the mining concern from the Eguiluz family for breach of contract. Because the contractor Eguiluz's heirs were unable to pay the outstanding debt for undelivered annual copper quotas, the mining estate – mines, slaves, land, and tools – reverted to the Crown. After roughly half a century of erratic production under private hands, the mining estate was again de-privatized. Although the Crown periodically sought miners to reactivate mining production, no further offers came through. A lack of expertise, technological know-how, and capital, together with the low value of the metal (unlike gold or silver) and exhaustion of the deposits closer to the surface did not attract further investment and thereafter the mines lay idle and in ruins under Crown control. The imperial state then incorporated the repossessed slaves into its defense system, allowing them to live in the abandoned mining settlement. It was in this vacuum that the former mining slaves in the settlement became a community of royal slaves that, with the passing of time, acquired the attributes of an informal pueblo.

While the Bourbon silver mining reforms in the mainland were effective in creating an upsurge in silver production in Mexico and Peru in the mid- to late eighteenth century, the case of copper mining in the empire was different. The Spanish Crown had long been forced to depend on foreign providers to import part of the copper for its foundries in Seville and Barcelona. Contrary to silver mining, technological knowhow regarding the refining of copper was lacking in the Spanish empire, which constituted an obstacle for large-scale production.[17] At times, the Crown

[17] Suppliers had included Habsburg Hungary, Flanders, and Sweden. Copper was also produced in Rio Tinto mines in Spain, in Mexico, Peru, and Chile. Barret, *Mexican Colonial Copper*, 46–50. See also Goodman, *Power and Penury*, 110–17.

attempted, with erratic results, to produce and import copper from the colonies, particularly Mexico, but its needs were never sufficiently met. After the abandonment of large-scale extraction in El Cobre and the Crown's confiscation of the mines in the 1670s, the villagers turned to a small scale artisanal production that provided limited amounts of copper for domestic markets but not enough for regular export.[18] Although copper production in Mexico was also limited, its extractive industry produced sufficient copper for the Crown's own foundry in Mexico City, for commercial domestic needs, and still some for export to the metropolis.[19]

The Bourbon Crown's overhaul of its imperial defense system after the mid-1760s also required renewed attention to the armament industry in the empire. Although Mexico had sent remittances of 3,000 annual quintals to the metropolis since the late 1740s, recurring warfare, specifically during the American Revolutionary War, shot up the Crown's demand for colonial copper by 1780 to an unprecedented 15,000 annual quintals, a situation that gave way to what Elinore Barrett has called a "copper crisis" in the empire.[20] The public utility imperative associated with the reactivation of copper production in El Cobre was linked to this copper supply crisis. In addition, copper had other forms of commercial applications too. The metal's heat conduction properties made it an ideal material for the cauldrons used in the sugar processing and refining processes. Demand for copper in the sugar commercial sector both in Mexico and especially in Cuba also increased and had to be met, especially given the Crown's interest in the development of this agricultural industry. By the mid-1790s, Cuban planters' requests reached a base line of 700 annual quintals of copper to meet the needs of the rapidly expanding sugar industry.[21]

In the mid-1770s, almost a hundred years on the dot after the mining estate of El Cobre reverted to the Crown, the distant heirs of the seventeenth-century private mining contractor Don Juan de Eguiluz and of his son-in-law Captain Francisco de Salazar approached the Council of the Indies to reclaim what they argued were their legitimate property rights over the family's confiscated mining estate (Figure 1.3: Nos. 1 and 3). In 1776, Don Manuel Garzón, a vecino of Santiago de Cuba and a distant descendant of the contractor Eguiluz, traveled to Madrid to

[18] Diaz, *The Virgin, the King*, 214–16; "Mining Women, Royal Slaves."

[19] Barrett, *Mexican Colonial Copper*, 2–10, 104–7. [20] Ibid., 25–42.

[21] Ibid., 43–53, 106–9.

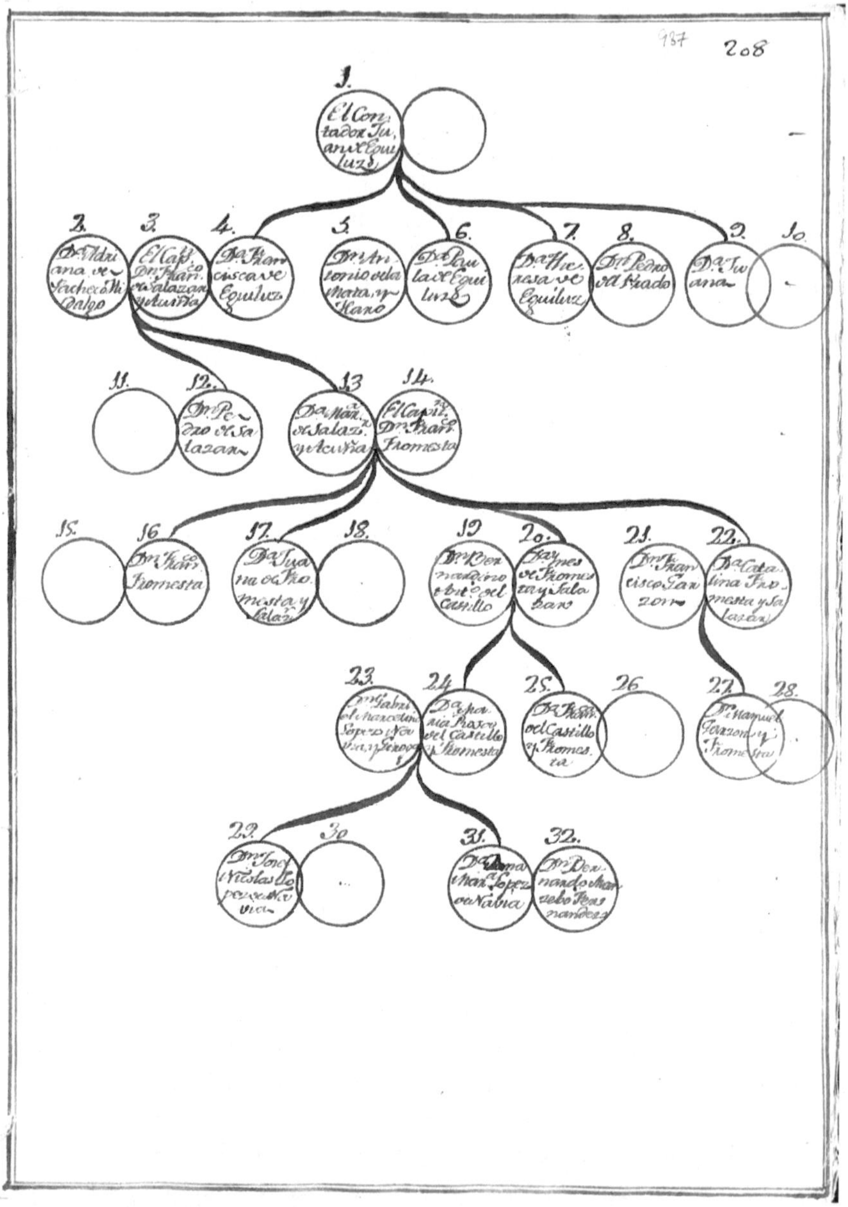

FIGURE 1.3 Genealogical tree of Don Juan de Eguiluz and heirs (ca. 1620–1780). The tree covers the descendants of the original mining contractor Eguiluz (ca. 1620) down to the generation that claimed ownership of the mines as his heirs in the late 1770s. Ministerio de Cultura y Deportes. Archivo General de Indias. Árbol genealógico del contador Juan de Eguiluz, AGI, Santo Domingo, 1627. fol. 208r.

claim the family's property rights to the mining estate of El Cobre (Figure 1.3: No. 27).[22]

Garzon's contrived rationale for the claim was that that the sums entered in the Royal Treasury from the *coartaciones* (self-purchases) of a number of slaves throughout the century and from the rents of some lands belonging to the jurisdiction had liquidated the outstanding family debt his ancestors had incurred with the Crown.[23] The negotiations between the Council and the heirs were speedy and expedient. In three years, Garzón obtained an executory order issued on August 21, 1779 (hereafter the Executory Order of 1779) to privatize (or re-privatize) the mining estate.[24] Thus, a hundred years after the confiscation of the mines in the 1670s, the Council offered the heirs of Eguiluz restitution of their alleged possession rights to the mining estate but did so on the condition that they activate mining production in a prescribed period of time. The Council did not challenge the alleged heirs' claims and rationale; it basically refinanced the old debt thereby lifting the Crown's hold on the estate.[25] Eguiluz's heirs were given four years, later extended to ten, to activate mining and pay back their re-calculated debt.

Although an initial attempt was made to resolve the question of possession rights in judicial terms, the legal issues were too tangled up and the fog of the past obscured the legal basis of the heirs' rights. The fiscal of the Council's Sala de Gracia y Justicia (Justice section)recognized the confusion noting that "This *causa* [case] in its actual state cannot be decided in terms of rigorous justice given the confusion of facts it offers and the difficulty of rushing it [*apurarlos*] after the many changes [*alteraciones*] it has undergone [through the years]," an accurate portrayal of the confused state of the story of rights to those copper mines.[26] The Council admitted the policy-minded criteria informing its decision to restore possession rights to the heirs: "The Council thinks that the *public utility* of the mines should be the principal object in whatever decision is

[22] Junta's report on the case of El Cobre, Madrid, October 31, 1799, AGI-SD 1146.

[23] Ibid.

[24] Council's Sentence, Madrid, March 20 and November 12, 1778, AGI-SD 1138.

[25] The Council accepted the heirs' deduction claim but recalculated the heirs' debt to the Royal Treasury by taking into consideration the copper they failed to provide during the century after the embargo and adding a percent interest rate to the refinanced debt. Debt deductions included 10,075 total pesos from coartaciones of 188 slaves through almost a century and 25,700 pesos for the rent of the pasture lands (*hato*) of Barajagua for 100 years. Council's Sentence, Madrid, March 20 and November 12, 1778, AGI-SD 1138.

[26] Council of Indies, Sala de Justicia, Población de El Cobre Madrid, November 23, 1778, AGI-SD 1138.

taken on this matter. And having the successors of Don Francisco de Salazar, an in-law of Eguiluz [Figure 1.3: No. 3], offered to execute it, they have the right to be reinstated in their possession, especially after the experience of so many years in which the efforts to find a contractor or work the mines on His Majesty's account has been fruitless" (my italics).[27] "Public utility" was a wild card, so to speak, whose invocation gave the absolutist state an enormous discretionary power. There was no autonomous sphere of the law in the legalistic obsessed Spanish administration, but nor were there completely arbitrary rulings either. Criteria associated with each sphere were often weighted in high court rulings. In this case, governance policy and public utility had explicit primacy over other possible considerations – a good exemplification of Bourbon enlightened absolutism.

There was absolutely no mention in the negotiations of how many slaves were included in the old mining estate: slaves were mentioned only in passing, as part of "the lands, mines, tools and slaves" of the estate. The Council apparently had no idea of their numbers or the fortune they represented, or it did not care. Nor was there any mention of a pueblo in the midst of the mining jurisdiction: the erasure of this community from the negotiations was, wittingly or unwittingly, almost complete. The question of land, however, got more attention from the state. The heirs wanted to recover all the land that the mining jurisdiction had lost through the years to encroaching private landowners and had the land surveyed. The Council ordered neighboring hacienda owners to present their land titles to ensure they were in rightful possession of the land and if not, that it be returned to the mining estate. This issue, of course, had the potential to become a point of contention between the beneficiaries of the mines and other landowners in the city who could then find themselves opposing the privatization.

Bourbon technocratic policy thinking in this case seemed haphazard, uninformed, and hasty. Although the reactivation of the mines was considered a policy matter of "public utility," there was no probing into the economic viability of exploiting seemingly exhausted copper mines or the problem of technical knowhow.[28] The only discussion about possible

[27] Ibid.

[28] Around 1777, when the heirs of Eguiluz were negotiating the recovery of the mines in Madrid, the crown commissioned a viability study of the costs of exploiting the mines of El Cobre. Lieutenant Isidro Limonta made a superficial exploratory investigation and reported that there was abundant copper in them but that the costs of its extraction were too high and thus their exploitation probably not feasible. Isidro Limonta's report, Cuba, November 6, 1778. Minas del Cobre, f. 1111–13, AGI-Cuba 1231. For technological issues in large-scale production and reform efforts in Mexico, see Barrett, *Mexican*

mining challenges took place in a petition from the heirs to extend the payment of their debt to ten years instead of four. Garzón justified the request due to the ruined state of the mines, the lack of any mining expertise in the island (and for that matter in the empire), the need to find some mining expert from New Spain or Peru willing to direct the revival, and the considerable capital needed to invest in production. Indeed, those were the very reasons why the mines had lain idle for decades. The Council readily accepted the need for a longer period to ensure that those issues be resolved and large-scale copper production be set on a strong foothold, but it did not question the feasibility of such a project or the heirs' capacity to manage it. Nor did it set benchmarks or requisitions for the copper produced as in the case of New Spain. An urgent demand for copper in the empire, and even in Cuba, may have guided the Council's hasty decision.

Although the Bourbon Crown imposed a monopoly over copper distribution in Mexico to meet its increasing needs, this "public utility" mandate was not successful in stimulating an expansion of copper production in New Spain until at least 1799 when the price of copper was deregulated.[29] In Cuba, it was worse. The recipients of the privatized mining estate of El Cobre, the heirs of Eguiluz, did not even jump-start the mining operation. The new owners had their eyes on another more lucrative business. A profitable commerce based on the pool of available slaves in the mining estate trumped by far the investment risk that the development of a large-scale copper industry could entail. To any savvy onlooker, the heirs' mining agreement served as a front for far more lucrative slave-trading operations, especially in the juncture of the 1780s.

AN INITIAL COLLECTIVE SELF-PURCHASE OFFER AND A CHANGING BOURBON POLICY ON *COARTACIÓN*

In 1780, the heirs of Eguiluz presented to interim Governor Vicente de Zéspedes (1779–80) the Executory Order of 1779 they had obtained from the Council to privatize the mining estate.[30] Zéspedes would be the only governor of Santiago in a long series of five in the next twenty years who provided some support to the cobreros in resisting their private

Colonial Copper, 64–89 and for economic ones, 54–56. While there were labor problems in Mexico too, in El Cobre these were to be met through El Cobre's slaves.

[29] Barret, *Mexican Colonial Copper*, 61–62.

[30] Autos Minas El Cobre, August 5, 1796, No. 2, f. 29v–31v, AGI-SD 1627.

enslavement. Claiming lack of clarity in the Executory Order regarding a surety deposit and raising military defense concerns during the American Revolutionary War, Governor Zéspedes placed a stay on the Executory Order and sent up his concerns to the Intendant of Havana, the royal official charged with the implementation of the privatization writ. That stay opened a brief window for the cobreros to organize, seek alliances, and figure out how to deal with the privatization order. The cobreros first tried to counteract the enslavement threat through the long-established practice of *coartación* (self-purchase) to which they added some novel spins. Given the scholarly attention that the practice of coartación in Havana has garnered, it is worth delving into its significance in the cobreros' history and how their experience reflected Bourbon policy changes in the late 1770s in relation to this practice too.[31]

Coartación was a manumission practice that allowed enslaved persons to purchase their own freedom upon an initial down payment on an agreed price followed by installments. Although not as extensive as in the Spanish empire where it became the most common and expedient way to freedom, manumission through self-purchase was also practiced in some slave states in the United States and in Brazil.[32] Sometimes considered a humanitarian act that helped break the perpetuity of slavery, this form of emancipation placed the burden of compensating the master on the enslaved victim: yet some scholars have come to see it as an important form of self-emancipation involving the agency of the enslaved person and a network of support.[33] The practice, like any sale of slaves, developed its own protocols over time: a notarized transaction, an assessment of value and price, a down payment, installments, and freedom papers at the completion of the process. Basically, in these market transactions, the enslaved person would take on the dual role of commodity and buyer. Many issues related to this practice, including value set in the slave appraisals, unacknowledged payments, split ownership and labor

[31] De la Fuente, "Slaves and the Creation of Legal Rights"; and de la Fuente and Gross, *Becoming Free, Becoming Black*. Focusing on Havana, de la Fuente stressed the continuity of the practice of coartación rather than the smaller shifts. Other references focus mostly on the nineteenth century. See also Varella and Barcia, *Wage Earning Slaves*.

[32] For an overview of manumission in colonial Spanish America and Brazil, including self-purchase, see Johnson, "Manumission in Colonial Buenos Aires." For cases in the US South: Schaffer, *Becoming Free*; Schweninger, *Appealing for Liberty*; Thomas, *A Question of Freedom*.

[33] See Scott, *Slave Emancipation*; Hunefeldt, *Paying the Price*; Aguirre, *Agentes*; Chira, *Patchwork Freedoms*. A less positive view of coartacion is put forth by Varella and Barcia in *Wage-Earning Slaves*.

time between master and slave in incomplete purchases, status of children in the womb and children of women in the process of buying their freedom, and rights to change masters were disputed in court through the years.[34] Perhaps the major contested issue was the extent to which the practice of coartación constituted a legal "right" to which slaves were entitled upon initiating the payment or if property rights gave the master any discretionary power to refuse to sell the slave's liberty to the slave. Although Alejandro de la Fuente has argued that in Cuba coartación had become a legal right recognized in written law by the 1840s, scholars are unsure about other localities.[35] The cobreros' case brought up other kind of issues.

Although there are references to the practice of self-purchase in Havana that went back to the sixteenth century,[36] the oldest recorded official legitimation of self-purchase in eastern Cuba is found in a royal Edict of May 30, 1673, that the Crown issued dictating policy regarding the mining slaves in the confiscated mines of El Cobre.[37] Using the medieval formal term of *rescate* (ransom), the Edict of 1673 ordered that the king's newly acquired slaves be offered the possibility of self-purchase at easy prices or otherwise be sold to private slaveholders or sent to work in the royal works of Havana (see Chapter 3). The first document of an actual coartación of a royal slave living in El Cobre was from 1689. Other coartaciones from El Cobre followed through the years (188 in 84 years).[38] Thus, royally sanctioned coartación practices had an established precedent in El Cobre.

On August 16, 1780, the cobreros presented a petition to Governor Zéspedes requesting the *rescate de nuestro pueblo* (literally, the ransom or liberation of our pueblo) by offering an initial down payment of 5,000 pesos.[39] In this case, the request was more unusual since it involved a

34 For a sample of these disputes in Havana, see García, ed., *Voices of the Enslaved.*

35 De la Fuente, "Slaves and the Creation of Legal Rights." The tribunals in Brazil explicitly disputed the issue in a 1853–54 case that went up from first instance into higher appeal levels. Ultimately, the court decided that the masters had the right as property owners to deny to sell them. Burton, ed., *Children's of God's Fire*, 6–8, 267–73.

36 De la Fuente, "Slaves and the Creation of Legal Rights."

37 Memorial Madrid, April 4, 1784, AGI-SD 1629.

38 List of *cortes y libertades* by virtue of Edict of 1673, f. 98–101, AGI-SD 451; List of coartados, No. 28/37, AGI-SD 1628; and List of manumissions 1743–75, AGI-SD 1627.

39 Petition of natives and vecinos of El Cobre, Santiago de Cuba, August 16, 1780, No. 37/29, 1780, AGI-SD 1628. A court reporter's (*relator*) account with some scratched lines stated(perhaps confusedly or with access to another lost document) that after the initial 5,000 pesos payment, subsequent annual payments of 3,000 pesos would be made until the total amount at which they had been assessed was covered. The annual payments would be deposited at the Contaduría (Treasury) from whence "the owners" would be paid. Autos, August 5, 1796, No. 2, f. 33v, AGI-SD 1627.

collective self-purchase. In fact, it was unprecedented in that it involved a pueblo ("our pueblo") and not just any group of slaves. Although an offer of coartación meant acceptance of slave status (since they were purchasing their freedom), this petition also effectively constituted a request for recognition of their standing as a pueblo. At the document's closing it added another surprising request: "If you admit the *rescate* of *our pueblo*, that it be *with lands and everything* so that we can find where to work these quantities [of money] because we find ourselves too cramped in these hills and we can't find where to extend ourselves to" (my italics).[40] This was a "package" of land and people (and an ambiguous "everything") that ensured the continuity of the community and land as a pueblo. But it was to be bankrolled by the cobreros themselves through a financial transaction that effectively allowed them to repossess their bodies, their labor, and their land. The petition recalled elements of what Helen Nader has identified as the early modern Hapsburg practice of purchasing town liberty in Habsburg Castile.[41] These actions entailed the purchase of municipal autonomy and "liberation" from seigneurial dependence or dependence on another city or town. In the case of El Cobre, though, the liberty package referred to the villagers' actual freedom from enslavement, although presumably it also referred to liberty of the pueblo from the private dominion or sovereignty of the heirs. Some of these town liberty purchases took place again in Castile during the late eighteenth century when the Crown was in desperate need for funds to finance its wars.[42] The cobreros' advocate may have used that Castilian precedent in this unusual petition for collective coartación as a pueblo with land, but again, the idea may have come up as a juridical solution to the royal slaves' own practices in the derelict mines and to their aspirations for the future.

Regardless of precedents and language, the petition still constituted basically a request for coartación from slavery. The petitioners admitted that 5,000 pesos in cash may be a low down payment, but it was all they could come up with in such a short span of time. They would submit to individual appraisals and after the total sum was determined, the governor could specify the terms for subsequent installments. The individual appraisals of the royal slaves amounted to a total of 193,480 pesos, a

[40] Petition of natives and vecinos of El Cobre, Santiago de Cuba, August 16, 1780, No. 37/29, 1780, AGI-SD 1628.

[41] Nader, *Liberty in Absolutist Spain.* [42] Ibid., 204–5.

mindboggling amount for a poor community.[43] Although purchase prices of the coartaciones of royal slaves of El Cobre had traditionally been relatively low, the assessments of 1780 increased their price dramatically. For instance, during the fifteen years between 1760 and 1775, as many as eighty-two cobreros obtained their freedom papers, with seventeen doing so just between 1770 and 1775, the last period recorded before the privatization took effect in 1781. The range of prices in that last five-year period fluctuated between 50 and 150 pesos (with two male outliers at 175 and 180 pesos) reflecting the low appraisals that by the Edict of 1673 and by custom had prevailed for almost a century.[44] The cobreros may have expected similar low prices for their liberty now. But the new appraisals in 1780 amounted to almost twice the value at which they had been appraised in previous years.[45]

The new assessed values reflected a recent policy shift regarding coartaciones that had taken place in 1778. At that time, the Crown had made some concessions to Havana's slaveholders who had challenged previous norms on coartación on the grounds that they were detrimental to their interests and property rights.[46] Jurists in Havana challenged a capping price rule arguing that the slave's value should be contingent on improvements and actual value (market value, though the term was not in use). In 1778, the Council accepted to adjust the rules to support the interests of property holders. The new rule called for an appraisal of the slave's "actual value" (rather than original purchase price with no profit margin on the sale).

Alternatively, master and slave could "agree" on a price, reflecting a "market" negotiation between seller and purchaser over the commodity of freedom.[47] The cobreros' higher appraisal in 1780 reflected this shift to a rule based on market value rather than the fixed lower customary values of former times. An increase of more than 100 percent in the assessment price made coartación more difficult for the cobreros. And in subsequent market sales enslaved cobreros' prices would even fetch higher market prices.

The cobreros' hybrid petition for collective freedom was sent up to the Intendant of Havana, the official directly overseeing financial and military

[43] Petition of natives and vecinos del Cobre, Santiago de Cuba, August 16, 1780, No. 37/29, 1780, AGI- SD 1628.

[44] Assessments 1765–75 in List of manumissions 1743–75, AGI-SD 1627.

[45] Some thirty-seven cobreros were able to purchase their freedom between 1780 and 1805 and a few others did so in other cities. Belmonte, *Ser esclavo en Santiago*, 233.

[46] Council of the Indies, Opinion over rules on slave sales, alcabala payments, coartación and other matters of slaves, Madrid, February 17, 1778, AGI-SD 1138.

[47] Ibid.

matters for the Crown, who denied the request on July 28, 1781. The intendant considered the offer an "inadmissible recourse to freedom on credit [*al fiado*] at negligible prices [*ínfimos precios*]" and mandated that the Provision of 1779 be immediately enacted.[48] The intendant's denial of the cobreros' initial offer reflected a break with customary practice and a shift in coartación policy. Yet, despite the harsher new terms, some individual cobreros did enter the coartación process, albeit on an individual basis, not collectively. For instance, fourteen-year-old María Manuela Borrero was sold *coartada* for 350 pesos – a very high sum for the time – to Don Antonio Rollo in Havana "so that she cannot be [subsequently] sold at a higher price."[49] Her parents or relatives probably put down the initial down payment that would fix her price before she was shipped to Havana, but it is not known if they were eventually able to purchase her freedom papers.

After the arrival to Santiago of the new Governor Nicolás de Arredondo (1781–88), interim Governor Zéspedes moved on to his new post in Florida. The Council's reiteration of the Executory Order of 1779 set into motion once again the interrupted privatization of the mining estate. Governor Arredondo oversaw the privatization of the estate and allowed the division and sale of the re-enslaved villagers as private property. The military repossession of the village described by some as a surprise raid took place on August 1, 1781.[50] Although some cobreros managed to escape to the *monte* (forest/mountains) or had long ago emigrated from the village, some 800 cobreros were distributed among the heirs at this time. Forced removals of cobreros followed in subsequent months. A list of cobreros from 1784 contained notes such as "Lorenzo de Rosas and Juana Cruzata and all of their children are enslaved and all of their grandchildren." "Martina Josefa Norate and four children of hers have been sold."[51] The heading of another undated list compiled by someone in the community recorded the last group of captive cobreros sold: "Note on the sons of this pueblo who the Señores heirs have sold now, the last of the remaining ones [*los últimos que habian quedado*]."[52] Sons (and daughters) of the pueblo had been turned into full human commodities in the privatization process. The calamities of privatization touched every family in El Cobre.

48 Autos Minas El Cobre, August 5, 1796, No. 2, f. 32v, AGI-SD 1627.
49 Autos, María Manuela Borrero, Havana, 1786, No. 37/45/2, AGI-SD 1628.
50 Memorial Havana, December 10, 1783, AGI-SD 1627.
51 List of cobreros enslaved and sold, ca. 1784, No. 39, AGI 1627. 52 Ibid.

Many of the newly enslaved cobreros were sold off in the island's markets, others were commodified in other ways. Some were retained as domestic workers in the houses of the newly rich heirs, who were now also making their way into the city's power circles with positions in the municipal government (cabildo). Many others were rented out, their commodified labor constituting a source of steady income for their masters. Some cobreros, especially in the 1790s, negotiated the payment of *jornales* (wages) to their masters to be allowed to return to El Cobre; in this sense, their masters rented them to themselves or their families who were willing to pay the wages to get their relatives back. Enslavement rights, wages, and land rents all became sources of conflict in subsequent years.

The heirs of the privatized mining estate among whom the 800 enslaved cobreros (and some 265 deserters) were divided constituted a small group of at least three persons and their spouses that later grew to perhaps up to seven relatives (Figure 1.3: Nos. 24, 27, 31).[53] Each of the three heirs would have received more than 250 enslaved cobreros (out of the pool of 800), which would place them way above the top slave owners in Santiago's district. The top slave owner in Santiago in 1786–1787, an outlier, had 70 slaves between his two sugar plantations and the second, another outlier, had 53 in his two properties. As a group, however, the leading planters in the district had 40 to 43 slaves in each sugar mill, the largest slave-based concerns at the time, and most had only 20 to 25.[54] To own 250 slaves, made each of the three heirs truly powerful slave owners by the standards of Santiago and even Havana.

TRAFFICKING ENSLAVED COBREROS: GLIMPSES OF A DOMESTIC SLAVE TRADE NETWORK

Although the Crown had supposedly made the re-possession of the mining estate and its royal slaves conditional to the revival of mining, the Council of the Indies was silent on the question of whether the slaves of El Cobre could be sold off, that is, whether the transfer of the mining estate to the heirs entailed full property rights over the slaves. Royal

[53] The number of heirs is uncertain, especially since some were spouses and others appear to be subdivided into other branches of the family. The Council left open the possibility of other heirs appearing in the future. Council of the Indies, Madrid, May 20, 1778. AGI-SD 1138. Not all the heirs who received enslaved cobreros appeared in the genealogical chart in Figure 1.3. In a memorial of 1783, as many as seven heirs were mentioned. are. Memorial Havana, December 10, 1783, AGI-SD 1627.

[54] Amores, *Cuba*, Appendix 2, 499–501.

policy in general had recognized the need for slave hands in the transformation of the colony's economy, so in this sense, opening up the slave "pool" in the mining jurisdiction of El Cobre to the market was arguably in alignment with this imperial economic policy. Moreover, the supply bottlenecks that Santiago faced in relation to the importation of African bonded labor during the 1770s and '80s and the increasing importance of this human commodity in the island's markets turned slave trading into a lucrative business venture.

Slave supply and distribution problems in the island were exacerbated in the case of Santiago and the eastern region due to Havana's gobbling up the still limited foreign human imports supplied by a regulated international slave trade business. During the fourteen-year period immediately preceding the privatization of El Cobre (1765–1779), the Spanish Compañía Gaditana de Negros had an exclusive contract to import slaves to the island. During this period, only 1,700 slaves, mostly from Barbados and Jamaica, were legally introduced by the company into Santiago – an annual average of 121 slaves – while Havana received 22,000 or about 1,500 a year, still a limited volume given the voracious demand for slaves in the expanding economy of the western region.[55] An unknown number of other enslaved laborers were brought to the island through contraband trade. With Spain's entrance to the American Revolutionary War in 1779, Jamaica, the source of three-fourths of imported slaves to the island, was effectively closed down and the Compañia Gaditana's contract was not renewed. Given Britain's enemy status, the official slave trade was carried out during the war through a policy of open trade with the allied French colonies. North Americans also carried on a brisk trade with Havana if not with Santiago.

After the war, and until 1789, when the slave trade with foreigners was deregulated, the Spanish Crown initiated a series of trial measures to supply slaves to the island. These included lowering the taxes of imported slaves and the issuance of licenses to Spanish individuals to travel to foreign colonies to buy slaves, (the licenses also became the object of speculation and proxies for British traders). During 1786–88, the Crown went as far as making an asiento with the major Liverpool-based company Baker and Dowson to supply slaves to the island.[56] And yet, supply problems persisted. For instance, while the British firm delivered

55 Ibid., 127.

56 For an excellent summary of the state's new thinking and policies on what Schneider calls the "slave fever" during this period, see *The Occupation of Havana*, 270–84.

2,000 annual slaves to Havana, only 200 arrived in Santiago during that period.[57] The deregulation of the foreign slave trade decreed in the (in) famous Edict of February 28, 1789, provisionally lifted the bottlenecks that allegedly put a break on the island's economic development and opened the door to the mass importation of African slaves.

Despite the postwar measures to procure slaves in the 1780s, Santiago continued dealing with the unsatisfactory delivery of slaves, competition over the few African arrivals, speculation over import licenses, and resale of imports through Santiago into more distant slave markets in the island. Purchasers of imported slaves were also accused of reselling the enslaved laborers rather than directly employing them, suggesting entrenched speculation in internal slave trading activities.[58] Governor Arredondo wrote in 1787 that there had been 406 potential buyers requesting a total of 1,992 slaves for a shipment in 1786 and that he could only serve 144 purchasers with 190 slaves.[59] Many of these must have been the petitions of the friends he was accused of favoring, suggesting a politics over the distribution of a valuable commodity in the city involving royal officials. Given the intermittent shipments of slave captives to Santiago during this decade and the difficulties of legally importing African slaves to this region, El Cobre's pool of 800 to 1,065 enslaved cobreros constituted a considerable domestic source of human captives during the early 1780s.

In the assessment of 1780, the 1,065 enslaved cobreros were valued at 193,480 pesos, a formidable fortune at the time. Although only about 800 captives were available (at least 57 were marked as *desertores* or deserters and valued at a minimum of 50 pesos), sales of enslaved cobreros commanded high prices and showed considerable profit margins that exemplified a robust capitalist dynamic.[60] For instance, enslaved cobrero children three to five years of age who were assessed at between 80 and 110 pesos in the already dramatically increased assessments of 1780 discussed before were sold for as much as 150 pesos in the "free" market of the 1780s.

Adolescent girls who were assessed at 300 pesos in 1780 (and may have been valued at 150 pesos in previous decades) sold in the market for 350 pesos. A twenty-two-year-old woman, Marcelina de los Reyes,

[57] Amores, *Cuba*, 156–58. [58] Amores, *Cuba*, 156.

[59] Amores, *Cuba*, 156. In 1787, the cabildo of Santiago announced the arrival of 200 African slaves to be distributed to hacendados in most need. Bacardí, *Crónicas de Santiago*, 227.

[60] Assessment of slaves of Mines of Santiago del Prado, 1780, No. 37/29, f. 14v and 24v, AGI-SD 1628.

assessed at 325 pesos, and her six-year-old son Pedro, valued at 180 pesos, were sold for 590 pesos, 85 pesos over their assessed price of 505 pesos. Some working-age male adults went for 485 pesos, although the highest value males were assessed for was 350 pesos.[61] Enslaved creole cobreros commanded high prices in the island's markets.

Domestic slave trade networks sent many of the captives from El Cobre to dynamic regions in the island where slave labor was in demand. Of the 137 sold cobreros listed in the last batch on record, 41 were sold in nearby Santiago de Cuba, 9 in Holguín, 14 went to Bayamo, and the largest contingent, 73 cobrero captives, were sold in Puerto Príncipe, a central province with a fast-growing economy whose capital had become the island's third most important city and the second in population (see Table 1.1).[62] Although Havana had its own external sources of African slaves more reliable than those available to buyers in the eastern and central jurisdictions, at least thirty enslaved cobreros ended up as far as Havana. What developed out of the sudden availability of this pool of captive cobreros was a considerable intra island domestic slave trade.

Colonial officials, for the most part, cooperated with these transactions and with the trafficking in cobrero slaves. Royal administrators were involved in providing certifications, treasury officials certified that the 6 percent sales tax was paid, private notaries certified titles of ownership, and licences were issued to embark or transport slaves. Whether in good or bad faith, the administration seems to have operated as an intermediary in private market exchanges or in officializing the sales of cobreros. The pardo enslaved cobrero Pedro Antonio Moreno, sold in Sancti Spíritus, reported that he was "among those whom the Administrator of Royal Finances [Rentas Reales] sold with the authorization [*poder*] of those who appropriated the [cobreros]."[63] Governor Arredondo who had approved the sale and trafficking in privatized cobreros when he oversaw the transfer of royal slaves from the Royal Treasury to the private hands of the heirs in 1781, received, probably as a gift, two young cobrera

[61] For the 1780 assessed values, Assessment of slaves of the Mines of Santiago. 1780, No. 37/29, AGI-SD 1628. Subsequent sale prices were obtained from various hearings carried out between 1786–90. Autos, Simona and Manuel José, No. 38/46/3; Autos, Isabel Cruzata and María Francisca Moreno, No. 43/51/8; Autos, Marcelina Antonia de los Reyes, No. 35/43; Autos, Antonio Vicente Norate, No. 55/63/20. All these hearings are located in AGI-SD 1628.

[62] List of cobreros enslaved and sold, 1784, No. 39, AGI-SD 1627. On Puerto Príncipe, see Amores, *Cuba*, 73.

[63] Autos, Pedro Antonio Moreno, Sancti Spíritus, No. 42/34, AGI-SD 1628.

sisters. He sold one in the town of Baracoa for 350 pesos and his wife took the other one to Madrid to serve her there around 1787.[64]

The business networks of merchants, brokers, and traders are not readily visible on the record. Although they may have followed networks already in place to channel African slaves entering the island's markets through Santiago, the transaction networks I was able to uncover were modest in scale, and personalized, as perhaps was the case for creole slaves in general. Although at times transfer of enslaved cobrero took place through family and kin, more often transactions took place through commissioned purchases or through merchants, and perhaps specialized traffickers, who bought and sold enslaved cobreros. Historians have examined the transactions of the inter-imperial Atlantic trade, particularly by the large firms, but there is little on the smaller capillary circuits through which the internal trade took place throughout the island.[65] The heirs had their own network of apoderados in different cities – in Santiago, Sancti Spíritus, Havana, San Felipe, and Santa Clara – through whom sales and purchases, including a few individual coartaciones, took place. Sometimes these apoderados were relatives of the heirs, personalizing further the networks through which the traffic unfolded: for instance, the parish priest of the town of Santa María del Rosario, Don Nicolás Ambrosio Mancebo, was the brother-in-law and apoderado of the heir Bernardo Garzón in Havana.

The traffic could also take place through third parties who acted as mediators between sellers and buyers in various cities. In some cases, the procurement was made through military networks, an especially gruesome linkage since to many the cobreros' former military service would have exempted them from enslavement. For instance, as early as 1782 the captain of militias of Bayamo bought the eighteen-year-old Isabel Cruzata (coartada for 350 pesos) and, more disgracefully, the sub-inspector of the Pardo Militias in Santiago, Don Francisco Sánchez Griñán, in whose battalion many free cobreros may have served, bought the twelve-year-old María Francisca Moreno (for 300 pesos), both on behalf of Doña

64 Damiana Ortiz and Barbara Rodríguez in Cosme vs. Francisco Creagh, Madrid, 1787, No. 7, AGI- SD 1627.

65 For the Atlantic slave trade, see Curtin, *The Atlantic Slave Trade*; Murray, *Odious Commerce*. For the domestic slave trade in the United States, see Johnson, *Soul by Soul*. For the British intra colonial slave trade, see O'Malley *Final Passages*. O'Malley stresses that the distribution of captives in this trade was carried out in small batches alongside other commodities that made them difficult to notice and be counted.

Bárbara Hernández, a resident of Havana.[66] Militia officials were apparently privately charged with capturing and transporting some enslaved cobreros perhaps using their military capacity to do so. In another instance, the captain of the regiment of Havana, serving in Santiago, was sent by one of the heirs to grab the cobrero Simón de la Paz in El Cobre and take him to sell in Havana, but the cobrero escaped.[67] Lieutenant Colonel Hilario Estenoz served as apoderado of Don Bernardo Mancebo and two other heirs in Havana through whom sales were transacted.[68]

At other times, buyers, perhaps even slave traders, came to Santiago to buy slaves. The merchant Don José Girbert, perhaps a domestic slave trader, embarked on his *bergantín* (vessel) two cobrero children aged three and five whom he bought in Santiago directly from one of the heirs, Doña Graciana Meneses.[69] A Don Manuel Sorribás bought the fourteen-year-old cobrera María Manuela Borrero from the heir Bernardo Mancebo in Santiago, took her to Havana and sold her to Doña Nicolasa Menocal, who in turn sold her to Don Antonio Rollo.[70]

Transfers also took place through donation or inheritance: Don José Antonio Barzaga inherited Isabel Cruzata from his mother and sold her to a militia officer in Bayamo who in turn sold her in Havana.[71] Slaveholders of enslaved cobreros in Havana included prominent citizens such as Don Sebastián Peñalver y Calvo, a member of one of the wealthiest sugar planter clan on the island. Peñalver did not hold a legal title for the eighteen-year-old enslaved cobrera Josefa Sánchez, which he attributed to having received her from his father-in-law in Santiago.[72] The transfer may have been a case of an illegally trafficked cobrera or a maneuver by one of the wealthiest citizens to avoid paying the sales tax to the Crown.

REACTIONS IN SANTIAGO

The enslavement and trafficking of cobreros sanctioned by colonial authorities produced considerable fissures in Santiago de Cuba. Don

[66] Autos, Isabel Cruzata and María Francisca, 1786, No. 43/51/8, AGI-SD 1628.
[67] Autos, Simón de la Paz, 1788, No. 65/57/22, AGI-SD 1628.
[68] Autos, Pedro Cárdenas, No. 46/54/11, AGI-SD 1628.
[69] Autos, Simona and Manuel José, No 38/46/3, AGI-SD 1628.
[70] Autos, María Manuela Borrero, No. 37/45/2, AGI-SD 1628.
[71] Autos, Isabel Cruzata and María Francisca Moreno, no. 43/51/8, AGI-SD 1628.
[72] Autos María Josefa Sánchez, No. 53/61/18, AGI-SD 1628.

Francisco Mancebo, one of the heirs, himself a letrado who redacted most of the family's legal representations and petitions, lamented that: "vecinos [local citizens] in this locality [*vecindario*] have viewed *our rights* [*nuestros derechos*], benefit and wealth with hatred and diabolic envy so that *almost all the vecinos* have been influential against us and corruptors of *our slaves*"(my italics).[73] Mancebo invoked the language of property rights and implicitly of slave law to validate the possession of cobreros and the immense wealth they had generated for the family. He also deployed the moral rhetoric of sinful passions to invalidate the basis of critics' attacks on their legal rights.

Mancebo's own virulent rhetoric mirrored the intensity of the conflict that began to make its way from the ground into the tribunals. "The vecinos [of Santiago] in general have been hostile to us," wrote Mancebo, "but, speaking more concretely, the Regidor Don Esteban de Palacios and the Sublieutenant of Militias Don Manuel Poveda have lived against us as rabid dogs in continuous barking, movements, conversations, to the point of writing representations to His Majesty and papers on behalf of the free cobreros so that they would fulminate processes against us."[74] Although the councilman (*regidor*) Esteban Palacios was a prominent citizen who owned a middling sugar hacienda with twenty slaves, and thus was a slaveholder himself, he actively opposed the cobreros' enslavement and counseled them to challenge it in court.[75] Poveda was a White militia officer who had once overseen the village's militias of color. Although some military men were involved in the trafficking of enslaved cobreros, Poveda represented a sector in the military that recognized the utility of the population of color in the island's defense system. He was, however, accused by some of having a personal interest in supporting the cobreros because he had a farm in El Cobre. Other citizens of Santiago even recognized the distinction many cobreros had accrued in their military service in the past. Poveda may have shared those views.[76]

Insulted at the criticism that some members of the heirs' own class and even family were expressing, Mancebo threatened that he would "go to the tribunals against them despite the third and fourth degree of kinship and friendship that links us ... just as they have not respected those very ties of piety to stop destroying us, [and] our honor, it will not be

[73] Francisco Mancebo, Santiago, August 14, 1792, No. 9, AGI-SD 1627.
[74] Francisco Mancebo, Santiago, October 16, 1792, No. 9, AGI-SD 1627.
[75] Amores, *Cuba*, Appendix 2, 500.
[76] Schneider, "African Slavery" and *The Occupation of Havana*.

inappropriate given their spirit of hate and vengeance that I petition the tribunals to contain them."[77] Complaints like these provide rare glimpses into the passions that the cobreros' enslavement triggered in the city even among elites. What vernacular understandings and what interests may their enslavement have violated to produce this kind of pushback from even White vecinos in Santiago, some of whom would constitute covert allies of the cobreros?

Military service and merit in Spanish imperial defense became a criterion in the public's eye precluding the cobreros' enslavement. To those who still remembered the cobreros' militia service in the past, that service was incompatible with the degradation of slavery. Francisco Mancebo protested that one of the city's councilmen, who was not even among the citizens who had most "doggedly" opposed the heirs rights over enslaved cobreros, "had nonetheless said in my own house angrily and bluntly [*con zafamiento*] that the cobrero Norberto Martínez could be and merited being Captain General of the Royal Armies."[78] What military feats had Martínez accomplished that had won him such words of respect from the anonymous councilman? "Captain General of the Royal Armies" was the highest military title and honor that could be granted in the Spanish imperial polity. In raising Norberto Martínez's reputation to such an exalted level, even if only as a rhetorical expression, the councilman suggested that earned military distinction made Martínez a respectable veteran and imperial citizen whose status should not be degraded – or betrayed – with enslavement. Mancebo's emphasis on the manner in which the councilman had uttered his view – "angrily and bluntly" – suggests deeply felt opinions on the issue even within the heirs' own social circles. Military performance and distinction informed local support for the cobreros among some important sectors of colonial society making their enslavement morally and politically offensive as well as pragmatically imprudent.

Reported rumor can shed some light on the standing of the cobreros among vecinos in Santiago and what motivated opposition to the heirs' claims among them. Mancebo himself provided a sampling of the critical gossip circulating in the city.

> [Some vecinos say] the poor cobreros. Others, this cannot be. Others, they *have always been free*, how are they going to adapt [*se van a acomodar*] now to being slaves? Others why don't the *owners* ask the King for African slaves [*bozales*]? Others, why didn't they ask the King some reward [*premio*] for all of them? Why

[77] Francisco Mancebo, Santiago, October 16, 1792, No. 9, AGI-SD 1627. [78] Ibid.

didn't they ask the King for *something else in compensation* for this fortune? Others: the cobreros are *very brave*, they are the Devil, very bad, nobody can do anything against them. Others so that the *owners of El Cobre* become very rich, the rest of the vecinos have become impoverished. Or, it is better that the owners of El Cobre leave this. It would be better to leave them in El Cobre, or from whence do these people [*esta gente*] get the idea that they *are the cobreros' masters* [*amos de los cobreros*?] Others have laughed at us. Others have encouraged them to return to El Cobre (my italics).[79]

Alleged responses ranged from pity and commiseration with the vulnerable victims, as in "the poor cobreros," to respect, even admiration, and solidarity with actively resisting subjects, as in "the cobreros are very brave ... nobody can do anything against them."[80] Some of these informal reactions had their counterparts in juridical rhetorical discourse that ranged from the passive victim trope symbolizing pure innocence (the *miserables*) to the active resisting agent that could easily be bent into a predatory trope of aggression, insubordination and criminality (i.e., the fugitive, the insurgent, the bandit) that was often deployed by the heirs and their allies against the cobreros. Perplexity and indignation at perceived injustice also inspired – then as now – solidarity with the injured party. Yet self-interest and competition over resources seemed to motivate alignments in colder calculating ways too. The somewhat cryptic reference to the zero-point game whereby the privatization of El Cobre meant the impoverishment of some vecinos in Santiago could have alluded to some sectors' previous licit and illicit access to the cobreros' labor or to conflict over disputed land boundaries that the privatization affected.

The repeated use of the term "cobreros" in the passage was a place-based identity that seemed already entrenched in local people's vernacular speech. Many vecinos questioned the legitimacy of the cobreros' removal from El Cobre and urged them to challenge the heirs' illegitimate rights of dominion and return to their pueblo despite the civil disobedience that such a return entailed. The strongest and most explicit statement of the villagers' status and rights was the comment that affirmed the cobreros' freedom by custom since time immemorial: "They have always been free." In this formulation, having lived openly as free far back in memory made the cobreros' freedom a fait accompli, or at least it made the return to slavery untenable and unbearable ("this cannot be," "how are they going to adapt now to being slaves?"). These manifestations of public opinion rested on assumptions that living or acting as free people had

[79] Ibid. [80] Ibid.

greater legitimacy than any formal claims to property by the heirs or even perhaps than royal orders: that de facto freedom carried greater weight than de jure slavery or that the long-standing exercise of de facto freedom was irreversible.

But there were also more restrictive views regarding the cobreros' status in this chorus of critical voices. References to the "owners of El Cobre" (*los dueños del Cobre*) seemed to acknowledge possession rights at least over the estate, if not fully over its inhabitants. Others subtly questioned royal orders and judgment by suggesting alternatives like indemnification for the "fortune" the cobreros represented. A "reward" or "something else" referred here to acceptable material forms of indemnification that could exempt the cobreros from crass commodification. Although indemnification by the state was out of the question given the usual indebted state of the Crown, especially after another war, the allusion here may have referred to some possible compensation scheme such as profitable licenses to import African slaves that could be sold as discussed before or perhaps to compensate the alleged owners of El Cobre with other kinds of lucrative import trade licenses.[81] Many years later, one of the heirs, the widow Doña María López de Navia (Figure 1.3: No. 31), faced with the loss of her portion of enslaved cobreros, suggested one such deal. She petitioned the Crown to grant her the "mercy of bringing in from the French, British, Dutch, and Danish foreign colonies 10,000 barrels of flour and another 10,000 of lard [*manteca*] or meat to sell in Cuba," as compensation for the loss of freed cobreros.[82] Even those who recognized the heirs' property rights over the estate, and perhaps the slaves, felt troubled by the commodification and removal of the cobreros preferring other solutions.

Religious faith and popular devotions may have also played a role in creating empathy and support for the cobreros among Santiago's vecinos. As I argued in my previous book, the long veneration of the regionally famous Marian image located in the village's sanctuary may have accounted for the sympathies of many devotees in the region.[83] Although the bishopric in Santiago had traditionally protected the village's parish as part of its duties and was particularly keen to protect the

[81] As discussed before, there were mechanisms employed in the 1780s to supply demand in the island and santiagueros competed with habaneros for concessions from the Crown and for supply of slaves from the larger monopoly asientos.

[82] Petition of Doña Ana Maria López de Navia, Santiago, November 22, 1802, No. 131, AGI-SD 330.

[83] Díaz, *The Virgin, The King*.

Marian sanctuary with the regional cult it sustained, a shift or a split in the bishopric seems to have taken place in this crisis. Then Bishop Santiago Echevarría y Elguezúa (1770–88), the scion of one of the wealthiest patrician families in the city, effectively used his ecclesiastical power to support the heirs' rights to human property. He dictated excommunication decrees against the cobreros who had fled to the mountains in 1781, forcing those who wanted to be part of the church and save their souls to return to the service of their new masters.[84] Although, according to Mancebo, the old parish priest Don Antonio Alvarez Viceo was involved in the initial writing of representations against the heirs, Alvarez passed in 1783.[85] During the next decade, the pueblo's parish fell into neglect and a sickly and often-absent priest filled the vacancy left by the former priest.[86] The Marian cult also went into decline.

Things dramatically changed years later when Bishop Joaquín Osés y Alzúa (1793–1823) took over the bishopric of Santiago in 1793. Contrary to his two predecessors, Bishop Osés became perhaps the cobreros' most powerful ally in the city, for which he incurred the wrath of colonial officials and the heirs' supporters (Chapter 7). The bishop's educational formation was broad, and he represented Enlightened religious reformers of the Church. He had seminary and university educational training in philosophy and theology, degrees in secular and canon law obtained as recently as 1783, had practiced jurisprudence in several positions (*oficios*), and was approved and licensed as an attorney (*abogado*) by the Royal Council.[87] With his educational credentials as a lawyer, the bishop, who also held antislavery views (Chapter 3), was in an exceptional position to aid the cobreros in the judicial field too. He backed the cobreros' legal struggle in Madrid by writing amicus briefs and by facilitating access to mail channels that had ecclesiastic immunity protections to avoid the government's interception of the community's correspondence with Madrid. Thus, by the 1790s, allies in the city came to include powerful church figures like Bishop Osés (and the bishopric)

[84] Havana Memorial, December 10, 1783, AGI-SD 1627. On the Bishop, see Amores, *Cuba*, 73.

[85] Francisco Mancebo, Santiago, October 16, 1792, AGI-SD 1627.

[86] José Luciano Franco mentioned that the Presbítero Bernardo Antonio del Pico y Redín, from the Archbishopric of Santiago, gave the cobreros a contact letter for Madrid, which may have indicated church support from earlier on, but the dates are unclear. *Las Minas de Santiago del Prado*, 59.

[87] Aguirre, "El informe del obispo Joaquín." The bishop was elected deputy to the Cortes for Santiago in 1821, but he did not accept, AGI-SD 2229.

who acted as a de facto protector of the natives of El Cobre. Similarly, the young Canarian priest, Father Alejandro Paz y Ascanio, took on an active role in support of his parishioners after his appointment to the village in 1793.

Although interim Governor Vicente de Zéspedes (1779–80) made efforts to support the cobreros' stay in their village and block their enslavement, successive governors of Santiago were more hostile. As mentioned before, Governor Nicolás Arredondo (1782–88) authorized the privatization and sale of cobreros. Governor Juan Bautista Vaillant (1788–96), Governor José Nepomuceno de Quintana (1796–98), and Governor Sebastián Kindelán (1799–1814) followed similar policies in defense of slave property in line with the frenzy toward slavery expansion. Although eventually commissioned to oversee the investigation over the case, the island's captain generals also backed the heirs' property rights to the enslaved cobreros during two long decades. Many of the cobreros' supporters were drawn from private citizens who for various reasons opposed the enslavement or the heirs. Some loyal royal officials who may have suspected fraud against the Crown by the sale of the Crown's former slaves seem to have also covertly provided support to the cobreros' efforts to denounce the privatization of the mining estate as suggested in other chapters.[88]

[88] In addition, there may have been other intrigues, and even conflicts, between vecinos favoring the opening of the slave trade to the British and those favoring peninsular merchants, but I have been unable to unravel this larger context. See Amores, *Cuba*, 153–58.

2

An Unorthodox Pueblo and Its *Apoderados*

> [Cosme wants] to take for himself all the honors and rewards of having freed his compatriots from the slavery and tyranny that they suffered.
>
> —Don José Espinoza, Madrid, 1784

Madrid, December 1784. In a petition to Minister Don José Gálvez, head of the Council of the Indies, the freedman Gregorio Cosme Osorio decried the "ruination" of his pueblo in Cuba. On a more personal and human level, he entreated the powerful minister to "pity me [*se duela de mí*] for my wife and four children have been sold and I do not yet know where they are."[1] He signed his petition "Gregorio Cosme Osorio Covrero" (Figure 2.1). By appending the moniker "covrero" or cobrero (the vernacular term for a native of El Cobre) to his individual and family name, Cosme deliberately entwined his personal identity with a collective one that invoked local birthplace and belonging. His signature compresses information about his historical background, affiliations, gender, literacy, indirectly his race, and perhaps even his aspirations. (To a graphologist, Cosme's handwriting, and curlicue may also reveal other personal traits.) Affixing "covrero" to his autograph asserted his claim in court to speak as a native of El Cobre and to invoke a common voice with other cobreros.

This gesture was all the more significant given the events that threatened to upend the meaning and bonds on which his cobrero identity had long been based. Cosme was in Spain to represent his village, which through privatization was now facing an existential threat. Most

[1] Gregorio Cosme Osorio to Minister José Gálvez, Madrid, ca. December 13, 1784, f. 35, AGI-SD 1628.

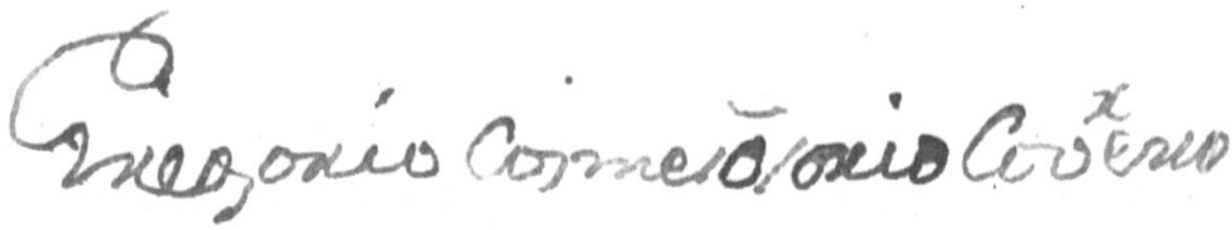

FIGURE 2.1 Signature of Gregorio Cosme Osorio, 1784.
The signature in a petition to Minister José Gálvez in Madrid on behalf of the natives of El Cobre constitutes a graphic image of this literate cobrero apoderado. See the autograph in its larger context in Figure 2.7. Ministerio de Cultura y Deportes. Archivo General de Indias. Petición de Gregorio Cosme Osorio, AGI, Santo Domingo, 1627. No. 49, fol. 35r.

cobreros, including his own family, had been enslaved and removed from the village. Although the status of the pueblo had long stood on shaky ground, the village had been able to grow and gain some degree of legitimacy – until recently. Underlying his complaints was a conflict over the social, political, legal, and even moral meaning of place. Whereas the Spanish Crown viewed El Cobre as a mining jurisdiction whose main value and utility resided in the extraction of a valuable imperial resource (copper), and the heirs saw it as a private estate with a bountiful source of human property to use, rent, or sell in the island's slave markets and of private land to lease out, the cobreros' competing notion of place was instead more human-centered. It was based on linked notions of pueblo community and local homeland that were widespread throughout the Spanish empire. (We may add to this assortment of conceptions of place the church's view of this site primarily as a parish of Christian souls and as hallowed ground in which a Marian sanctuary of regional fame stood, notions of religious community that most cobreros also shared.) But although pueblos and *villas* (towns) in the empire took various forms, El Cobre's makeup was unorthodox, making its political and legal sustainability harder to uphold in the face of new challenges. As a community of mostly people of African descent, El Cobre was an outlier in the empire's social landscape. Yet the cobreros asserted their common bond based on a local social and political entity that they aspired to be officially legitimized. In fact, this very unconventional situation, especially in the case of Afro descendant subjects, incubated alternative proposals in the empire's social landscape, some of which are being revived and reconfigured in various regions in Latin America today (see Conclusion).

In this chapter, I re-center the book's narrative in local space and push it as far down as records allow to the level of ethnography and microhistory. The account moves in time between the cobreros' past and the aftermath of the privatization of El Cobre. The first part of the chapter traces the long-standing customary norms and arrangements in the pueblo and explores what it meant to be a cobrero, the identity that Cosme embraced. It also asks what made El Cobre an unorthodox pueblo community in the empire's social landscape. I am using the term "community" here specifically as a social and political entity (a pueblo and later a villa or town) and not vaguely as a social (and racial) one. I probe the singularities, ambiguities, and divisions that undergirded the pueblo's precarious situation leading to the enslavement of most of its members in 1781. But I also appraise the social bonds and customary practices that for generations had constituted them as members of a pueblo and that they channeled into judicial actions. That is, despite official distinctions in the statuses of individual villagers, they collectively asserted their communal identity as cobreros and natives of a pueblo to make claims.

This chapter also introduces two local legal and political activists who became the main public face of the pueblo, especially in the judicial sphere: Gregorio Cosme Osorio at the imperial level in Madrid and Justo Cruzata at the colonial local and regional level in El Cobre and Santiago de Cuba. Although other prominent cobreros acted as local *apoderados* (legal representatives) of the community too, these two freedmen became the most prominent apoderados throughout the two decades of the conflict and in the case of Cruzata thereafter. Yet, however significant the roles of these two local leaders may have been, without the collective support of the grassroot community and of other prominent well-off villagers and proxy granters who backed the litigation socially, politically, and economically, the legal action would have foundered early on. I argue that this collective legal effort in itself constituted an important (albeit contested) judicial assertion of cobrero identity and an enactment of communal pueblo bonds. I also consider the human and the material resources that enabled these beleaguered villagers to pull off this high-profile protracted legal action. I suggest that it was precisely this customary collective affiliation as a pueblo, however informal or irregular, that facilitated the far-reaching legal and political mobilization of these subjects. The (controversial) unconventionality of this community's bonds undergirded, paradoxically, both its vulnerability and its strength.

The second part of this chapter is trans-local. It moves beyond the local village and the neighboring city of Santiago in eastern Cuba all the way to Havana and Madrid in an exploration of the resources and networks required by colonial subordinate subjects to engage in a legal mobilization of this order. Seeking royal justice in the imperial court in Madrid was not for the faint of heart. African descendants, Indigenous commoners, and Mestizo colonials from troubled regions in the Spanish Atlantic faced even greater challenges than other royal vassals from the colonies. Whereas powerful individuals, corporations, and cities had agents in the court to lobby for their interests and at times traveled themselves to Madrid, it was harder – though not impossible – for imperial vassals farther down the social hierarchy to do so. Some of the impediments were economic, but others were political and administrative, and still others were racial. Few, if any cases, are on record or have yet to receive scholarly attention.[2] This made Cosme's journey to Madrid even more remarkable. Rather than a passive wretched colonial subject sponsored by a proper Spanish protector, Cosme pushed boundaries when the time came by pressing for his official recognition as apoderado of the community. He also set in place a communication circuit through a network connecting El Cobre, Santiago, Havana, and Madrid. In doing so, the natives of El Cobre projected themselves way beyond the horizon of their pueblo.

THE PUEBLO OF EL COBRE

El Cobre in 1780 was a colonial village of some 1,406 inhabitants.[3] Its formal name was Real de Minas de Santiago del Prado, a name that reflected the locality's official standing as a mining jurisdiction. Some records squeezed into the official title the term "pueblo" as in the convoluted "pueblo and Real de Minas de Santiago del Prado" that reflected the dual character of place. But informally, and even formally in most official local records, including censuses, the place was known as the pueblo of El Cobre. The moniker "El Cobre" referred eponymously to the copper (*cobre*) mineral once extracted in large scale from the mines (and later, informally and at a very small scale, by women in the locality). Scattered across the landscape were the still-visible scars of abandoned mines and

[2] Dueñas has traced a handful of these Indigenous and Mestizo apoderados from colonial Peru who traveled to Madrid from the sixteenth to the eighteenth century, sometimes legally with permission from viceroys or archbishops and sometimes clandestinely. This handful of educated apoderados authored memorials on behalf of their constituents. Contrary to Cosme, most of them were noble caciques or Mestizos. See *Indians and Mestizos* and especially 61–62 and 84n8. De la Puente Luna has uncovered a wider array of Andean Indigenous travelers in various capacity in his *Andean Cosmopolitans*.

[3] Census of Santiago, 1780, AGI-Cuba 1272.

covered shafts of former times. El Cobre's designation as a "pueblo" in most local records indicated the transformation over the years from a derelict royal mining settlement into a parish and an informal village housing mainly the descendants of former mining slaves, now royal slaves, and other free people. The moniker "cobreros" may have evolved from a vague occupational association with the producers of copper and its descendants to a collective vernacular identity of belonging attached to birthplace and pueblo – despite the ambiguous status of its inhabitants. Cosme's signature was not just a manifestation of a subjective identification: it was a political assertion of it too.

Notwithstanding the exaggerated portrayals of local prosperity before 1781 that were intentionally displayed in memorials on behalf of the cobreros, El Cobre, by 1780, was a modest subsistence-based agricultural community, with some cash crop producers. The small-scale production of copper was a complementary source of income of what had become largely an agricultural community. The pueblo's core consisted of seven unpaved streets laid out in uncertain order named after Catholic saints. Although the census of Santiago of 1780 reported 513 houses in the pueblo, internal household censuses from 1773 and 1775 recorded 104 thatched-roof houses of various sizes, often grouped as multifamily households dotting these streets.[4] Only six tiled-roof houses, a sign of relative wealth or distinction of their owners, stood out in the landscape of more ephemeral thatched-roof dwellings.[5] Signaling the village's informal character, there was no school, no municipal house for the on-and-off *cabildo* (local government) to meet, and when it did so to elect officials and discuss other business, they did so in the parish priest's house. Jail was provisional detention in the house of whoever held the *alcalde* (bailiff) position in any given year. The only public buildings in El Cobre were religious ones: a modest parish church in the midst of the pueblo and a larger sanctuary housing a miraculous image of the Virgin of Charity that sat on top of a hill near the mines. A long stairway leading up the hill to the sanctuary's perron would have added pizzazz to the pueblo's otherwise lackluster small urban hub. Next to the Marian shrine was a small guesthouse, called a hospital, funded by the church for regional pilgrims seeking cures in the sanctuary. This famed Marian

[4] Ibid. The 1780 census reported 177 houses in the rural partido that may have referred to *estancias* (small family farms).

[5] Household censuses of El Cobre, 1773 and 1775, AGI-SD 1628. Census of Santiago 1780, AGI-Cuba 1272.

image, its sanctuary, and the festivities associated with it magnified the visibility of this modest pueblo. Considered the pueblo's patroness, this imperial symbol of Catholic Christianity became a collective symbol of local community and of cobrero identity; these associations had considerable weight in legitimizing the outlier status of this community through the years.[6]

More distant from the center were small family subsistence farms (*estancias*) and tobacco farms (*vegas*), pastures for animals, and the like. There were between 98 and 167 estancias in El Cobre between 1778 and 1780.[7] Further out lay the *monte*, the forest or uncultivated land, in the neighboring hills, which provided an open space for hunting, foraging, gathering botanical resources, conducting illegal encounters, and perhaps practicing banned spiritual practices. When conflict with authorities ran high, the monte had often provided refuge for villagers who ran away. After 1781, the space of the monte became even more integrated into village life as multiple trails became rehearsed routes of escape into the rugged terrain of the hills in case of raids in the village. Two main roads, one leading to Santiago and the other to the town of Bayamo, had long connected the pueblo to Spanish city hubs but also to an Indian pueblo in the region, El Caney. Other small trails connected the village to encroaching large haciendas and neighboring estates belonging to *vecinos* of Santiago de Cuba. El Cobre was by no means an isolated inaccessible village in the mountains. It was part of a wider colonial, imperial, and in some cases trans-imperial web.

Land, the most valuable resource for the inhabitants of this rural village, had long been in short supply, perhaps due to El Cobre's closeness to the city of Santiago. Population growth and encroachment from neighboring estates had reduced the productive land available to the community for its subsistence. The majority of cobrero families were food producers: they had a small family farm (estancia) where they grew manioc and the staples of a subsistence economy and helped provide the city of Santiago. Some held pigs, cows for their milk, chicken, and turkeys in these farms. Most cobreros held usufruct rights to house plots and farms, although some may have owned land in the surrounding area as well. However, after the privatization of the mining estate, villagers lost

[6] For the famed Virgin of Charity image and shrine that emerged in El Cobre and its local political deployments see Díaz, *The Virgin, the King*, chapters 4 and 5.

[7] General Census of Cuba, 1778. AGI-Indiferente 1527. The Census of Santiago of 1780 (AGI-Cuba 1272) reported 167 estancias, however.

their customary possession rights to the land that they had worked and improved for generations, and the heirs began to demand rent from those who were not removed from El Cobre. Land rights became another major local transformation that created additional conflict between cobreros and heirs after 1781.

Women worked on the family farms and also sold the small quantities of copper they scavenged from the riverbanks to local brokers or to a handful of smelters in the village.[8] The privatization undoubtedly undermined this small-scale copper industry too since most women were enslaved and removed from the pueblo. The village had a handful of other skilled artisans: a painter, a tailor, a blacksmith, and several carpenters who perhaps served locals or patrons in nearby Santiago de Cuba. They either also farmed or had relatives who did.[9]

Not all agriculturalists were peasants engaging in subsistence farming, however. There were some cobrero families that engaged in a modest cash economy and had acquired the economic and social status of a rural petite bourgeoisie. The most prominent clan in El Cobre were the Cosmes who owned at least one cattle hacienda. Like 10 percent of the farmers in this community, they also cultivated tobacco, one of the island's most important export products at the time, over which the Crown held a monopoly. The González clan family grew tobacco as well as owned a small *ingenio* (sugar mill), the only one in the village, possibly to supply molasses and alcohol to local residents.[10] Some of them even owned a few personal slaves. The assets of the petite bourgeoisie in this village were limited, but they were critical to underwrite communal legal actions in Santiago and Madrid.

El Cobre may not have been too different from other small rural pueblos throughout the overseas empire, including Cuba. Looking closer, however, the unorthodox contours of this pueblo – and what made it so vulnerable to existential threats – comes into greater focus. As mentioned before, this was solidly a pueblo of Afro descendants: the census of 1780 registered 99 percent of El Cobre's population as *pardos* and *morenos*.[11] Or rather, it was mainly a pueblo of racially mixed people since most of its inhabitants (87.2 percent) were inscribed as pardos (Brown or Mulattoes). Either way, the racial profile of El Cobre turned it into an unorthodox municipal formation in the imperial landscape.

[8] Díaz, "Mining Women, Royal Slaves."

[9] Household censuses of El Cobre, 1773 and 1775, AGI-SD 1628.

[10] Ibid. 1773.

[11] Census of Santiago, 1780, AGI-Cuba 1272.

Although the *Recopilación de Leyes de Indias* of 1680 called for free Blacks and Mulattoes to reside in Spanish households in Spanish cities, by now free Afro descendants lived all throughout the empire and in Cuba in their own households and many had their own farms – but with some exceptions, they could not and did not live in their own pueblos, even though they could have their own parishes and militia regiments and lay brotherhoods.[12] By law, neither African descendants nor racially mixed people could constitute pueblos of their own in the Spanish empire. Only Spanish and Indian republics or municipal jurisdictions existed under separate laws.[13] Thus, despite large populations of free people of color on the island, and especially in eastern Cuba, they could not constitute republics or municipal entities of their own. Instead, they resided in the Spanish cities and towns such as Havana, Santiago, and Bayamo as subordinate colonial subjects with no local political rights, however

[12] *Recopilación Leyes de Indias*, Book 7, Title 5. Law 3. In the seventeenth century, the regulation that they had to live with Spanish employers or masters because they were "people *sin asiento* (without settlement) and a certain place [of residence]" was linked to the collection of tribute that the employers were required to pay from their wages. But it was also recognized in Law 1, which was also related to tribute regulations, that many had their own *granjerías* (produce) and possessions. Also, the militia service of these free morenos in some regions was recognized as a basis for some abstract entitlements (*preeminencias*) that should be respected (Laws 10 and 11), and which usually meant exemption from tribute and the recognition of other *fueros* (privileges), but these did not include constituting a pueblo. However, the laws of the Indies in the *Recopilación* did not explicitly ban Afro descendant pueblos either. For the presence of free Afro descendants in rural and urban villages throughout New Spain where they sometimes constituted a majority over Spaniards, see Vinson III, *Bearing Arms for His Majesty*. Vinson notes a case where the pardo soldiers of several pueblos in the province of Zacatula in the Pacific coast of Mexico (with some 1,000 Afro descendant households) petitioned for Crown land collectively offering to constitute a *república* (or pueblo) of pardo soldiers, but the litigation collapsed, 100–102. A more successful effort was what Vinson calls the "atypical" racially based pueblo of San Fernando Aké in Yucatan that was founded in 1795 by a corps of Black auxiliaries who had fought for Spain in the Haitian Revolution. The community was internally divided by military hierarchies and language. However, by 1806 there were only 230 individuals in the community although a few Indians and Whites had settled in it. Vinson does not elaborate on the formal organization and running of the settlement (see 216–19). Marcela Echeverri mentions the existence of Black communities in New Granada in passing but does not discuss them. See *Indian and Slave Royalists*, 120–21. However, Black pueblos in the northern Cauca region of Colombia did emerge after abolition of slavery in 1851 through the collective purchase of land by former slaves, but again little is still known about them. See Carabalí, "Los afronortearaucanos," 390–94. In general, the standing of Afro descendant and racially diverse pueblos throughout the Spanish empire needs further research. The study of El Cobre is a starting point.

[13] *Recopilación Leyes de Indias*, Book 4, Titles 7–13 for Spanish settlements and Book 6, Titles 3–6 for Indian Pueblos.

constrained these local rights may have been for everyone under an absolute monarchy. For instance, Afro descendant and other racially mixed subjects (*castas*) had no rights of representation in local municipal governments (cabildos), which were controlled by Spanish descendant elites in the Spanish republics or by Indians in the Indian republics. In Cuba, mostly in the eastern region, the long-declining Indigenous population still had two pueblos of Indians by the late eighteenth century and into the nineteenth: El Caney and Jiguaní. However, Whites, free Afro descendants, and slaves also resided at the time in these mixed and changing Indian pueblos.

El Cobre, on the other hand, had emerged as a separate racialized community that was neither a Spanish republic nor an Indian republic: it was an informal, semi-autonomous entity in between a Spanish and an Indian pueblo. To be sure, there were some pueblos of Afro descendants or racially mixed colonial subjects scattered throughout the Spanish overseas empire, but they had emerged in an ad hoc way under divergent circumstances (see Introduction). El Cobre, as discussed before, had emerged in the site of derelict mines, close to a colonial center in Santiago; its members, descendants of former mining slaves, were virtual squatters who were allowed to live and work the land in the abandoned royal jurisdiction while subject to a series of labor and military obligations to the imperial state. Thus, the community's status as a village or a semi-autonomous república was officially anomalous. El Cobre was a work in progress, so to speak, an experiment interrupted by the privatization of 1781. This irregular status was what the cobreros' judicial mobilization, in part, sought to regularize and legitimize in the face of the privatization of 1781.

Even more unconventional, and ultimately problematic, than El Cobre's racial contour, however, was the strange profile of its inhabitants' status. The census of 1780 registered almost two-thirds (65.5 percent or 921) of El Cobre's total population (1,404) as slaves and one-third (33.5 percent or 471) as free. By all measures, this constituted an unusually high proportion of slaves to free. However, the census did not register that these slaves were "*esclavos del Rey*" (slaves of the king) rather than regular private slaves, as if, officially, the royal qualification did not matter – but, did it matter in local practice? Nor did the census capture the distinction – or relation – between the royal slaves and the free in the community, all of whom self-identified, and were identified by outsiders, as cobreros or natives of the pueblo. Just how could slaves, or even royal slaves, be considered part of a pueblo? Or were they? Therein lay an important source of the controversy that erupted after 1781 and the basis of the community's precarity – but also of its strength.

Regardless of some internal class-based differentiation in El Cobre, the most critical internal distinction, at least from the official point of view, was one between villagers who were classified as *esclavos del Rey* and those marked as *libres* or free. This fundamental distinction had been regularly inscribed in all kinds of state and church records since the turn of the century. Local censuses, draft lists, even ecclesiastical documents such as baptism and death records systematically registered these villagers under one of these two officially significant categories. Military authorities in Santiago conducted annual *revistas* (inspections) to keep track of His Majesty's slaves in the village. The distinction became crucial in 1780 since it marked the subjects officially targeted for private enslavement by the heirs.

The most important pragmatic distinction between royal slaves and the locally free before the privatization of the mining estate was that royal slaves were subject to forced rotational labor drafts on the fortifications of Santiago, an arrangement not unlike the Indian *repartimiento* or *mita* systems on the mainland. Single women labeled royal slaves had to work their stints in Santiago's royal hospital or do personal labor for royal officials in the city; married women with children tended to be excused from these forced labor services.[14] Although some royal slaves had become *ausentes* (absent) through the years and had moved elsewhere on the island, the king's slaves were for the most part subject to restricted movement and residence in the village. Despite this forced labor service, the category of royal slaves did not signify regular slavery to the cobreros and to many others in Santiago. Because there was no private master, because they were subject to militia service, and because both royal slaves and free lived quasi autonomously in the pueblo, royal slaves were not considered by many to be living as slaves; if anything, their servitude was considered closer to royal vassalage. Those distinctions and boundaries would be contested after 1781.

A third of the inhabitants of the pueblo were registered as free in 1780. These free cobreros were, for the most part, the inhabitants who stayed

[14] Díaz, *The Virgin, the King*. Another distinction is that free men and women were free to leave the pueblo and settle elsewhere. Those marked as royal slaves had no such freedom of mobility since their labor was important to the state and to royal officials in Santiago. They were labeled *ausentes* and *deserters* (absent and deserters) in the royal lists of annual inspections.

behind in what remained of the village after those deemed royal slaves were privatized and forcibly removed from the pueblo after 1781. They were the ones who would mobilize to litigate on behalf of their enslaved co-villagers. Who were the free in El Cobre and how had they become free? In this community, as elsewhere on the island and in other Spanish colonies, free status was most often obtained through individual self-purchase (*coartación*), a long-established practice in this community. Other free people in the pueblo were outsiders who had married into the community and formed families there.

As mentioned in Chapter 1, although most descendants of the mining slaves never purchased their freedom, some 188 cobreros (over a period of eighty-four years) became sufficiently prosperous – or "industrious" as one memorial would claim – to buy their manumission from the state and formally move into the local ranks of the free. Although there had been no difference in the gender rate of coartación among cobreros until the 1730s, 76 percent (112 of 147) of the recorded coartaciones in the village from 1743 to 1773 went to men.[15] This gender shift seems to have coincided with military operations against General Vernon's short-lived British occupation of Guantánamo in 1747, in which El Cobre's militias took part, and later in the British invasion of Havana in 1762, where cobrero militias also fought. This shows the gendered emancipatory possibilities that military service and veteran status could provide to enslaved men at the time; but these were reduced after the militias of El Cobre were dissolved as part of the Bourbon military reforms in the late 1760s.

It is difficult to ascertain how official distinctions between royal slaves and freed people may have played out among the cobreros themselves. Kinship, marriage, godparenthood, friendship, and other factors would have downplayed these official distinctions in local social life, especially as they also shared birthplace and residential identity and local rights as cobreros. Although all members of the nuclear unit were either free or royal slaves in many cases, many other families were mixed, with some members of the family designated as royal slaves and others as free.[16] For example, in some families a free cobrero or an outsider was married to a royal slave woman, and their children, following the maternal status rule of slave societies, were inscribed as royal slaves. Even when the entire

[15] List of *cortes y libertades* by virtue of Edict of 1673, f. 98–101, AGI-SD 451; List of *coartados*, No. 28/37, AGI-SD 1628; List of manumissions 1743–75, AGI-SD 1627.

[16] Díaz, "Of Life and Freedom."

nuclear family was free, most extended families included a mix of free and royal slave members. It is possible that mixed-status households may have recognized the differences in status between free and enslaved members of the family, just as mixed-status households of documented and undocumented migrants in the United States today can experience intrafamily strains.[17] Nonetheless, bonds crisscrossing through families and households would have reinforced solidarity among these villagers as all would have been affected to some degree or another by the consequences of the privatization of 1781. Moreover, the identity of cobreros – grounded on pueblo-based bonds – also reflected and reinforced collective bonds over and above individual and family distinctions between slave and free.

In fact, other than the labor obligations to the state, distinctions between free and royal slaves seemed to have little practical significance in the internal affairs of the community. For instance, all cobreros held family estancias with usufruct rights and house plots in the pueblo, regardless of status. In even more important ways, notwithstanding their official status, cobreros labeled royal slaves lived and acted as free cobreros by holding positions of power in the pueblo. For example, militia officer positions were held by free and royal slaves. In 1739, two cobreros were inscribed with the title of "Captain," one was listed as royal slave and Mulatto, the other as free and Black (*negro*). And about sixteen years before the dissolution of the pueblo's militias, the local household census of 1750 listed at least three cobreros with the title of "Captain," two were marked "slaves of the king" and one, José Cosme, was labeled "free"; two other cobreros who had the title of "Lieutenant" were also labeled royal slaves.[18]

Similarly, for years, official status had seemed irrelevant to who became part of the pueblo's local cabildo. As early as 1708, for example, Félix Cosme (Gregorio Cosme's grandfather) had sufficient standing to be elected alcalde of the pueblo despite his designation as a royal slave.[19] A list of the last "sons of this pueblo" who had been sold after

[17] Ten percent of documented residents and US citizens live with an undocumented family member in Fresno and in the United States in general; that is, they live in "mixed-status" families, creating distinctions in access to services, work, and, today, fear of deportation inside the family. Flin, "Growing Up Undocumented."

[18] Household census of El Cobre, 1739, AGI-SD 385. Household census of El Cobre, 1750, AGI-SD 1630.

[19] Household census of El Cobre, 1709, AGI-Escribanía 93A. Official titles and status of cobreros serving in the cabildo were not inscribed in all of the local censuses; only in a few.

1781 included many who had held local governance positions despite their official royal slave status. The annotations in a list of enslaved cobreros suggested the enormity of the breach involved in enslaving people who had once had local political standing:

> Salvador Quiala, main bailiff (*alcalde de primer voto*) and enslaved, and Juan Bautista Sanches, second *alcalde*, sold [as] slaves. Francisco Sánchez, main commissioner (*comisionado mayor*), is sold, and all of the councilmen (*regidores*) from the generation of Juan Crisóstomo González, all are enslaved [*todos están esclavos*]; Juan Bautista Sanches, regidor, is sold; Cristóbal Francisco de Salas, main commissioner of the coast, has been sold and those who are not here are with their owners.[20]

Their positions pointed to the existence of local municipal government and some limited self-rule before the privatization of 1781. Thus, rights analogous to those enacted regularly by Spanish descendants in Spanish republics or Indigenous subjects in Indian republics had also been enacted by villagers in El Cobre despite their African ancestry and the royal slave formal status of most of the villagers. However, these men's political and social standing evaporated after 1781 when the heirs' property rights eradicated customary practices in the pueblo and turned respectable cobrero men into common slaves. The injury and humiliation involved in the reversal of status indicated in this list of sold sons of the pueblo were profound.

Whereas royal slave and free status constituted the main (official) fault line within the community threatening the cobreros' future as a pueblo after 1781, the cobreros' racial status in colonial society presented other challenges. Race was a fundamental axis of distinction and organization in Iberian colonial society (and colonial societies in general). As mentioned before, this was a solid 99 percent African descendant pueblo with 86.3 percent of the population classified as racially mixed *pardos* and 12.7 percent as Blacks.[21] It is unclear how important racial identity or coloration was in the internal dynamics of this community, but racial thinking was unavoidable in the broader colonial setting. Authorities relentlessly divided and classified subjects in colonial society into racial and color terms. Church records of baptism, marriage, and death were usually kept in separate books for Whites and people of color. Identification of people in depositions called for racial identification

[20] List of cobreros enslaved and sold, 1784, No. 39, f. 1453–54, AGI-SD 1627.

[21] Census of Santiago, 1780, AGI-Cuba 1272. The census reported 14 Whites, 1,214 Pardos, and 178 Blacks out of a total population of 1,406 souls.

(if not White) among other anchoring criteria such as age, status, birth, or residential place. The institution of colonial militias was segregated into White, Black (*moreno*), and Brown (*pardo*) companies. Even though in El Cobre militia companies had not been divided by racial status of pardo or moreno, but by free and royal slave companies, after the Bourbon military reform of 1767 dismantled them, free cobreros were recruited into the segregated pardo or moreno militias of Santiago.

Although for royal authorities the recurring and inexorable markers of the village's inhabitants was free or royal slave status; racial distinctions were often but not always recorded. The first extant local household census of 1709 registered only free villagers' racial status as pardo or moreno (there was also a "*mozo blanco*" (young White man) who was married to a cobrera who resided in the village), but it did not explicitly tag royal slaves racially because they were all presumed to be of African ancestry. Subsequent local household records from 1731 and 1735 did not mark racial status for anyone, but that of 1739 systematically inscribed free and royal slaves' race and used the categories of White, Mulatto, and Black, instead of the polite terms moreno and pardo. Mostly everyone, except the clergymen and their families, was Black or Mulatto in 1739. There were at this time two White men who were married to cobrera women (one of them the parish priest's nephew). Overall, the two exceptions of White and non-White interracial marriages in the midst of hundreds of married Mulatto and Black couples in these *padrones* (local household censuses) suggests that the wider colonial White supremacist norm that shunned interracial marriages between Whites and non-Whites was well alive in El Cobre and in the region. Although outsiders of color married and settled in El Cobre across time, Whites, other than clergymen and sometimes their families, for the most part did not marry or even settle in this basically Afro descendant pueblo, although they may have had intimate relations with female (or male) villagers.[22]

Coloration was added to racial entries in the local household census of 1765. Entries ranged between "negro," "negro claro," "mulata," "mulata oscura," and "mulata clara." Who made and inscribed the distinctions and for what reason is not clear, but it must have been a royal official or more likely the parish priest. It is difficult to make out if other racial mixes, as, for example, with a fading Indigenous population, existed or were recognized

[22] That was not the case in colonial Mexico, especially during the eighteenth century, where militia men of color, and to a lesser extent civilians, also married Mestizas and *españolas*. See Vinson, *Bearing Arms*, 123–28.

since, contrary to censuses in the mainland that included Indians and Mestizos, the racial classificatory system that authorities used in Cuba was based on a three-tier Spanish/African axis of White, Mulatto, and Black. Within an expansive and ambiguous pardo or Mulatto category, there may have been mixtures with Indian ancestries as well.

Although race and coloration had political and cultural significance in colonial society, it is not clear how important they were internally among the cobreros themselves. Racial tags did not appear either in the extant internal correspondence among Gregorio Cosme, Justo Cruzata, and other cobreros. Cosme applied it only once, collectively, in a petition in his own hand to identify the cobreros when referring to General Bernardo Gálvez whom he asserted "was of great satisfaction to all of us [people] of color."[23] Generally, there was no reference to race in his petitions in Madrid nor in his letters to the pueblo. The cobrero Martín Salazar, however, did make explicit references to race and coloration in a letter to Cosme where he denounced the heirs' most recent raid on the pueblo seeking runaway cobreros and land rents. Salazar recounted that the heir Mancebo "went to the sugar mill of Francisco González, a *white and free mulatto* [man] ... slapped him, beat him, and kicked him and he endured it without a word .... From there [Mancebo] went to ... the house of Sale Cruzata, asking for his *captive* son and, not finding him, he ordered the father, who is *pardo of white color and free*, be tied-up and punished with one hundred lashes" (my italics).[24]

Salazar's descriptors had social and political significance: they highlighted that the rights of these cobreros had been egregiously violated despite their free condition *and* their light skin, as if coloration aggravated the transgression. The memorial would have been written down by a White letrado who may have added these qualifications. Although Salazar's use of these color-based labels reflected broader colonial expectations of racial rights, it is perfectly plausible that the labels may have also marked internal hierarchies among the cobreros' themselves. Salazar's account also shows the mix of free and captive cobreros within a nuclear family and the solidarity bonds that led kin to provide refuge to their runaway relatives in their houses and farms in the pueblo. Although he ended his letter with a status-based identification to make claims – "Friend, all these events have happened to *free people*, men and women

[23] Gregorio Cosme Osorio to Minister José Gálvez, Madrid, ca. December 1784, f. 35, AGI-SD 1628.

[24] Martín Salazar, El Cobre, August 21, 1792. No. 1, f. 209–10v., AGI-SD 1627.

of honor" – he closed with a collective pueblo-based identification: "May Our Lord praise and guard your life for many years, as your most humble *compatriots* wish you and *on behalf of all*, Martín Salazar" (my italics).[25]

Racial thinking was used, at least by letrados and allies, to politicize the cobreros' standing and protections. A memorial drawn up in the colony questioned the slavery "of those natives that the named Don Julián Garzón [one of the heirs] and his compatriots want to call their own . . . but from that [Black] color there is not even one in that pueblo, or its surroundings."[26] That same memorial used the local racial ideology of "whitening" and coloration to upgrade the cobreros' status and counteract racial representations that associated the cobreros with slavery.

One local story in a memorial filed in Havana in 1783 textualized the political and cultural deployment of these racial and color categories and entangled them with a gendered ideology. Although the incident was also a critique of political gifting mechanisms in Santiago de Cuba that had strong gender and sexual overtones, it lay bare racially ingrained assumptions that equated Blackness with slavery and abjection and Whiteness with freedom and honor. The story pointed out that when interim Governor Zéspedes took office in Santiago in 1780, the alleged beneficiaries of the mines

> presented him (as with others) six *mulatta* maidens *white and blonde* as a gift for his service; but since this gentleman was not an interested man, and in truth, he was struck by the strange gift. . .of some women *who seemed whiter* [*más blancas*] *by birth and* [*therefore*] *not subject to slavery*, the suspicion of the [heirs'] attempt to trample the natives of El Cobre, began to ring in his ears (my italics).[27]

Race, color, gender, and sexuality intersected in this account in ways that may have well reflected racial ideologies at work in the city. The broader principle undergirding this passage was that quasi White (racially mixed) persons in the colonies were close enough to White Spaniards as to exempt them from the stigma of slavery, "Blackness," and dishonor. The passage above explicitly used the color term "white" and "blonde," to make the White supremacist rule explicit, using it to erase traces of slavery from the cobreros' bodies.

If the correlation between "Whiteness" and freedom was one manifestation of colonial White supremacist ideology, a fundamental gendered corollary of this association was respecting female sexual honor. The gifting of these women among men suggested an immoral violation of

[25] Ibid. [26] Memorial Havana, December 10, 1783, AGI-SD 1627. [27] Ibid.

womanhood, more serious, the passage insinuated, because of these women's quasi Whiteness. The women embodied and symbolized the larger cobrero community and therefore signaled their presumed freedom – and honor. If the "ruin of the pueblo" that the cobreros generally denounced meant forced removal of population, as well as loss of local citizenship positions in the pueblo, separation of families, and loss of land, it was also sometimes represented, as in the gifted women passage above, in more explicit gendered terms as loss of control – or sovereignty – over cobrera female bodies and sexuality, along with the private and collective dishonor that entailed. Several apoderados of El Cobre protested in court in 1791 that during one of the heirs' raids "two young maiden cobreras [*cobreritas doncellas*] suffered the cruelty of a punishment and the embarrassment of being raped in front of their parents with the greatest scandal."[28]

It is difficult to know what kind of gender divisions and barriers existed within the pueblo and families. Cobreros in the pueblo shared the same patriarchal gender norms as the free people elsewhere on the island and throughout the empire. In fact, the ability to enact patriarchal norms defined them in many ways as free cobreros. As elsewhere, gender created internal exclusions in what may be called local active citizenship: women were excluded from the prestigious institution of the militias and the greater access to individual freedom veterans acquired. Again as elsewhere, women could not hold cabildo offices, they could not be legal representatives of the pueblo, they could not, or did not, sign documents giving proxy power to Cosme in Madrid, even if they were heads of households. Women did not appear as witnesses in the individual freedom hearings that took place later (see Chapter 5).

That is not to say that cobrera women had no informal political influence, as I have discussed elsewhere.[29] Whereas women could not represent the community in court as apoderadas, they could represent themselves and their children in court. Some of the most active individual litigants were female cobreras. The cobrera friends Rafaela Sánchez, Margarita González, Teresa Cobas, and María del Rosario Rodríguez went to court jointly in Sancti Spíritus as captive cobreras, sharing information, contacts, counsel, and witnesses (Chapter 5). And the cobrera Marcelina Antonia de los Reyes became the most persistent litigant

[28] Petition of the free natives of El Cobre, Santiago de Cuba, February 3, 1792, AGI-SD 1629.

[29] Díaz, "Mining Women, Royal Slaves."

dragging her slaveowner through courts in four cities. Her master railed against "the brazeness with which my slave attempted this [judicial] proceeding and the tenacity with which she pursues it."[30] Nor did gender-based disabilities mean that cobrera females had no economic power. Female cobreras controlled an informal surface mining industry in the pueblo that provided some limited income.[31] Although farming was considered the sphere of men, women also worked in family estancias, especially if they were widows or single. House plots in the pueblo's urban hub seemed to be the possession of and were passed down through female lines in families.[32] Women owned property, some even a few personal slaves. Like male cobreros, female cobreras had no personal master to serve. They lived in their own homes with their own families, if anything they were subject to their parents and their mothers (and perhaps to their husbands too).[33] José Basilio Maestre testified that he knew the cobrera Rafaela Sánchez "[when] she was enjoying her freedom with no subjection other than to her mother."[34] Women had been impacted as much as men by the privatization. Gender norms and relations in the pueblo had also been deeply affected by the removal of women, the breakup of families, and land rents.

El Cobre was not a "community" in the loose social or racial sense of the term that is often used in the literature of the African diaspora. Despite its irregular profile, El Cobre had developed into an informal hybrid pueblo over the course of a century. After the initial offer for a collective purchase of freedom and land was denied by the state in 1781 (Chapter 1), leaders of the pueblo turned to other forms of legal action – and to a reformulation of claims. Nativeness to El Cobre, from then on, would be associated with presumption of freedom. The cobrero Francisco Quiala informed a magistrate that "it is notorious in all the island that there have never been slaves among the natives of El Cobre."[35] This was the case they would dispute in the courts in subsequent years as discussed in the next chapters. But what resources were available to a decimated

[30] Autos Marcelina Antonia de los Reyes, No. 35/43, 1797, AGI-SD 1628.

[31] Díaz, "Mining Women, Royal Slaves." [32] Díaz, *The Virgin the King*, 175–77.

[33] For a closer examination of the life cycle of women and their family relations see Díaz, "Of Life and Freedom."

[34] José Basilio Maestre, Sancti Spíritus, 1792, in Autos Teresa Ramos alias Coba, No. 34, f. 358, AGI-SD 1628.

[35] Francisco Xavier Quiala, Santi Spíritus, 1792, in Autos Teresa Ramos alias Coba, No. 34, f. 362v., AGI-SD 1628.

community to access royal courts? And what kind of relations and identities was the state willing to protect?

TWO ACTIVISTS AND LEADERS: THE FACES OF THE PUEBLO

One of the most remarkable aspects of the cobreros' legal mobilization was to make their case in common. Cobrero identity, based on native pueblo-related bonds, led free cobreros to represent their enslaved compatriots in court in communal terms, not as individuals or families. Gregorio Cosme's signature in a Madrid petition, discussed at the opening of this chapter, displayed that communal cobrero identity, as did his work as apoderado of the natives of El Cobre in Madrid asserting judicial corporate personhood as natives of a pueblo. In Santiago de Cuba, other cobrero leaders filed petitions on behalf of the community, for instance: "Ventura Cosme, Justo Cruzata, and Gregorio González, free pardo *natives of the pueblo of El Cobre for themselves and on behalf of the rest* [*por sí y a nombre de los demás*]" (my italics).[36] Whereas other prominent men in the pueblo also took on the role of apoderados of the cobreros in Santiago, Gregorio Cosme Osorio and Justo Cruzata became the most important legal representatives of the community on both sides of the Atlantic. Others contributed in further capacities to the communal legal actions financially or as proxy granters.

Although opponents contested the cobreros' right to speak in one voice and questioned the standing of their apoderados to represent the enslaved cobreros in court, the leaders pressed their claim to this right by continuing to file collectively and thereby assert corporate judicial personhood as natives of El Cobre. Filing and acting collectively in court in this (ambiguous) case constituted a form of legal activism as discussed further in Chapters 3 and 4.

The capacity to receive proxy powers to represent and act on behalf of a constituency constituted a political right that only free males in the empire could perform, with attendant racial limitations, as the above petition opener suggests. Although White men could become apoderados of constituencies of any race (or gender), free men of color, and for that matter Indigenous and Mestizo men, could only legally represent those of their own race and not White or other racial constituencies. And whereas Indigenous pueblos and constituencies throughout the Spanish empire

[36] Petition Ventura Cosme et al. ca. March 15, 1791, AGI-SD 1629.

sent their own representatives to local or Audiencia courts, occasionally even to Madrid, that was more rarely the case with African descendants mainly because they did not tend to constitute pueblos in the empire. Although in principle Afro descendant men could represent other kinds of smaller corporate entities such as lay brotherhoods, African cabildos, or even pardo or moreno militia regiments, their role in this capacity needs further research. In the case of El Cobre, the litigation was facilitated by communal solidarities and by the existence of a petite bourgeois sector in the pueblo that was willing to guarantee loans for the common good. Their tight bonds and commitments as a pueblo facilitated this type of legal mobilization, which would have been out of reach to individuals or families willing to litigate. Yet, although the cobreros acted communally like Indigenous pueblos, or like Castilian pueblos in the Habsburg era, they did not do so officially through a cabildo-sponsored and -managed action.[37] Theirs was a looser ad hoc affair but still a communal one in which they acted communally as natives of a pueblo.

Financing communal litigation could be a costly affair. Larger Spanish towns and cities had *solicitadores* (solicitors) of their own and *propios* (communal assets) to fund legal actions and legal agents in the Audiencias or in Madrid. Indigenous pueblos paid for communal litigation with funds from their *caja de comunidad* (local communal treasury) or by issuing special ad hoc taxes called *derramas*.[38] In contrast, the cobreros did not have a caja de comunidad nor propios to finance these actions, a fact that points to the informal standing of El Cobre as a pueblo. The local leaders did not have the power to impose local special taxes either. Instead, they depended on funding by the better off members of the pueblo and on loans and voluntary contributions from poorer villagers. In 1788, as many as twenty-nine cobreros and two "criollos mulatos" from Santiago de Cuba who resided in El Cobre and were vecinos of the pueblo signed a power grant, pledging their finances as collateral for the litigation costs; and in 1792, another group of twenty-five cobreros gave Cosme notarized power to spend as much as 6,000–7,000 pesos or more on the community's business in court.[39] Gregorio Cosme singled out in his correspondence the principals who gave him power of attorney and to

[37] Owensby, *Empire of Law*, 155–62; Penry, *The People are King*, 101–23. For Castilian pueblos' litigation, see Nader, *Liberty in Absolutist Spain*, 164.

[38] Yannakakis, *The Art of Being In Between*, 120–22.

[39] *Poderdantes* (proxy granters) of the Mulato Gregorio Cosme Osorio, Santiago de Cuba, March 31, 1788. AGI-SD 1629; Francisco Mancebo, Santiago, July 1792, "Escritos presentados," No. 7, AGI-SD 1627.

whom he was obliged to keep personally informed: "I always live writing to all the vecinos and mostly the *poderistas o poderantes* [power grantors] of this villa of Santiago del Prado [El Cobre] about whatever matters are taking place or have taken place for the benefit of all in general."[40]

But participation was also broader. Justo Cruzata also "collected in the Pueblo the money to send to the apoderado and for other expenses."[41] Legal costs, indeed, could represent a considerable burden on the community, especially without the labor and resources of so many enslaved cobreros removed from their village. Legal actions in the colony, although not as expensive as in Madrid, entailed considerable burdens too. Costs for legal actions ranged from a moderate 27 and 28 pesos to the considerable sum of 175 pesos.[42] In 1792, Cruzata was penalized for the legal expenses of a land action on behalf of the cobreros and tobacco bundles were confiscated from his house to pay for it. Although there was a good possibility of claiming indigence (as "miserables") to obtain legal aid through reduced fees (in the range of 27 to 28 pesos) and special legal paper, even these actions could end up being costly. At other times, payment of legal expenses depended on who won the case.

Taking on the apoderado role, especially in El Cobre's case, could entail considerable political risks too. An official report in 1795 identified the "free cobrero" Justo Cruzata as "the protector and apoderado of the natives [of El Cobre] and the one who makes their defenses and legal actions [*recursos*] and whose conduct [Governor] Brigadier Don Juan Bautista Vaillant always heeded ... to the point of having him jailed for the influence he had in depraved maxims over the *vecinos*."[43] In Madrid, Cosme also faced surveillance and jail by even higher authorities in the Council of the Indies. In 1786, Minister José Gálvez tried to have Cosme "a mulatto" investigated and arrested for "writing papers against the Council of the Indies."[44]

Despite somewhat different social trajectories, both Cruzata and Cosme inherited the status of royal slaves from their cobrera mothers. But by the time Cruzata assumed his activist role, he had moved up into

[40] Gregorio Cosme, Madrid, n.d., ca. 1795, f. 102–7, AGI-SD 1631.

[41] Report of José Emigdio Maldonado, Santiago, July 11, 1796, No. 73, AGI-SD 1629.

[42] Assessment of costs (tasación) of the natives of El Cobre's legal action, Santiago de Cuba, ca. October 24, 1792, Autos Cuba, No. 6, f. 1022–23, AGI-SD 1629.

[43] Report of José Emigdio Maldonado, Santiago, July 11, 1796, No. 73, AGI-SD 1629.

[44] Report of Pedro Muñoz de la Torre, Madrid, October 8, 1786, in Expediente sobre crímenes atribuídos al mulato Gregorio Cosme (hereafter Expediente crímenes Cosme), AGI-SD 1529.

the ranks of the free petit bourgeois families in the pueblo. Whereas there is no extant coartación record for Gregorio Cosme, Cruzata purchased his own freedom in 1764.[45] Then, a decade or so after becoming a freedman, Cruzata married the freeborn daughter of a well-to-do free couple in the village and their children were born free. Although other members of his extended family, as well as neighbors and compatriots, were enslaved and removed from El Cobre, Cruzata and his immediate family were all free. This made his willingness to take risks on behalf of fellow enslaved cobreros especially commendable.

Cosme, on the other hand, was a directly injured party: his wife and children were enslaved as a result of the privatization.[46] Although there is no record of Cosme's coartación, a 1788 legal document granting him proxy powers to represent the community referred to him as "Gregorio Cosme Osorio *mulato cobrero liberto* [freedman] of Doña Josefa Andrea Mancebo y Betancourt, one of the heirs."[47] It is possible that he negotiated his coartación privately with the aid of well-off cobreros in order to travel or, subsequently, to serve as apoderado of the pueblo. Cosme's own petitions never mentioned his status. He quietly passed as free, without distinction between freed or freeborn, while identifying only as a cobrero in Havana and Madrid. Because of his more modest background, Cosme fashioned his public persona as apoderado by embellishing aspects of his personal biography. Cosme proudly represented himself as "the son of Commander José Cosme Osorio who governed that pueblo during thirty-one years in a military capacity and as alcalde, regidor, and other employments such as guarding the coasts."[48] His direct association with a prominent local patriarch turned Gregorio Cosme into a distinguished son of the pueblo and allowed him to draw social capital from his purported father's service and merits. In a 1784 petition to José Gálvez, president of the Council of the Indies, Gregorio Cosme sought the minister's patronage "for the many services provided to His Majesty by my father and me."[49] But the claim was implausible at best. Commander José Cosme was only eleven years older than Gregorio and could not have been his progenitor. Rather, the local patriarch may have been an uncle,

[45] List of manumission, 1743–75, AGI-SD 1627.

[46] Assessment of slaves of Mines of Santiago del Prado, 1780, No. 37/29, AGI-SD 1628.

[47] Gregorio Cosme was referred to as a *liberto* (freedman) in a report listing his thirty-one proxy granters, Santiago, March. 31, 1788, f. 181–82, AGI-SD 1629.

[48] Memorial Havana, December 10, 1783, AGI-SD 1627.

[49] Petition of Gregorio Cosme to Minister José Gálvez, Madrid, ca. December 1784, AGI-SD 1628.

more likely a cousin, or simply a distant maternal relative in the extended Cosme family. Uncles, aunts, and cousins may well have been considered close family, the line between extended and immediate family was often faintly drawn. Or the filiation was understood as a metaphor of the collectivity. Cosme also sought to capitalize on his and his father's war veteran status.

Veteran status also was a basis to claim merit and reward. Commander José Cosme served his Majesty for thirty-one years and was a veteran of two military conflicts: Admiral Vernon's occupation of Guantánamo in 1741 and the British occupation of Havana in 1762. Gregorio Cosme claimed to have accompanied him in these battles and to have himself served his Majesty for twenty-two years. In another petition, Cosme even claimed that his father had been wounded during the capitulation of Havana in 1762 and had later died of those wounds. He asserted that he, too, had been wounded and bore the scars of war in defense of the Spanish empire: "two bullets, one in his hand and the other in his right leg."[50] His body served as a living document of his loyal service. After the recovery of Havana from British hands in 1763, many free soldiers of color sought and received recognition and reward for their services; and many enslaved subjects filed claims for freedom based on their services and wounds in military action. The Crown had reviewed some cases – there were too many claims to consider them all – and purchased some of these men's freedom from their owners after the war.[51]

Although several men in the pueblo could at least sign their names, one important qualification that Gregorio Cosme and Justo Cruzata shared – and put at the service of the common good as apoderados – was their literacy, a highly regarded skill in the Spanish empire, more precious for its association with state and legal craft in the "lettered city." Although literacy was not a prerequisite to access the courts, or even to hold the position of apoderado, as the cases of many Indian representatives in the Indies show, it was crucial to autonomous long-distance communication across the ocean in this case. As the main liaison between court and community, Cosme wrote extensively to his constituency, especially to distinguished vecinos in the pueblo. The correspondence was always among men, and usually among some six leading community members with the political power and economic means to back the collective enterprise, especially as *poderdantes* (granters of power of attorney).

[50] Ibid. [51] Schneider, *The Occupation of Havana*, 238–49.

Cosme's style and tone tended to be polite and respectful, sometimes even formal, as if to reflect the honor of the correspondents.

Collective legal mobilization became a significant political assertion of communal bonds by the cobreros: a form of activism as a community. Whereas Cruzata and other prominent free male local figures acted as the community's apoderados in the courts of Santiago, Cosme's task would be to move beyond the pueblo's immediate jurisdiction in order to expand the beleaguered community's social and political networks to the colony's capital and, if possible, all the way across the ocean to the highest seat of power in Madrid. Whether Cosme ever entertained the possibility of traveling first to Santo Domingo, the seat of the regional Audiencia (high court) where freedom suits were supposed to be initially heard, or whether his sights had been set on Madrid all along, it is difficult to say.[52] It seems that the latter was the case given that this was not a garden-variety freedom case.

In any case, if a journey to Havana may not have been an uncommon undertaking for a subordinate colonial subject, even for one residing at the other extreme of the island, an Atlantic crossing was a more far-fetched endeavor for a lowly subject. What would it take for Cosme to go so far? Sometime in November 1782, Cosme arrived in Havana as the cobreros' envoy with some documents in hand.[53]

FROM HAVANA TO MADRID

Havana was the seat of imperial rule in the island and commercially a flourishing city. The capital's more than 40,000 souls in 1778 made it a formidable port city at the time (Figure 2.2).[54] Both the captain general, who oversaw internal colonial governance, and the intendant, who was charged with supervision of military and fiscal matters and who had denied the cobreros' petition for the collective coartación (Chapter 1), resided in the capital. The port city was also an Atlantic commercial hub of increasing importance. Havana's businessmen welcomed the trading opportunities with American merchants that Spain's engagement in the American Revolutionary War opened up, at least for some years.

[52] *Recopilación Leyes de Indias*, Book 7, Title 5, Law 8.

[53] Memorial of Carlos Ramos, Madrid, November 17, 1784, No. 44 f. 11–11v, AGI-SD 1627.

[54] General Census of Cuba, 1778, AGI-Indiferente 1527. For Havana's busting economy, commerce and militarization see Schneider, *The Occupation of Havana*, especially 66–89.

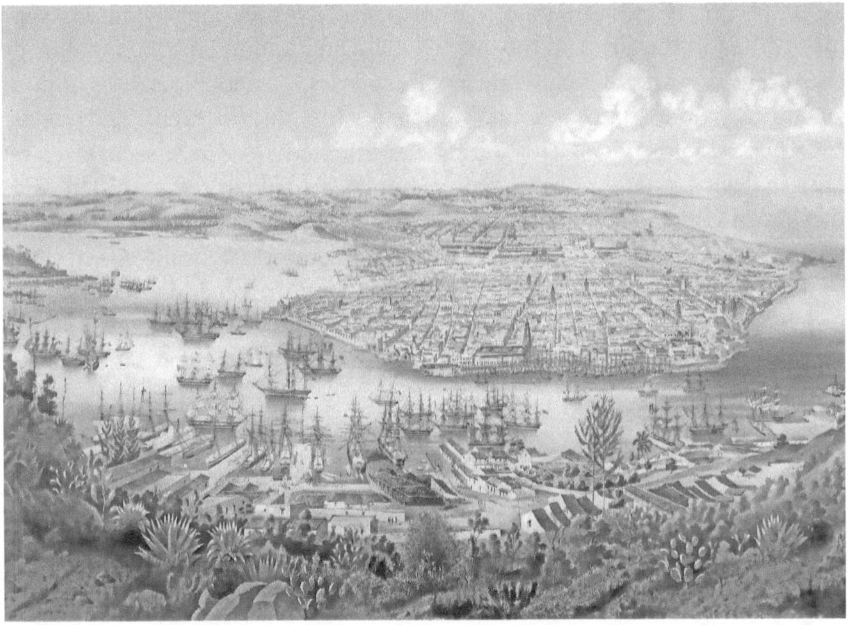

FIGURE 2.2 View of Havana and Bay, engraving by L. Marquier and E. Laplante, ca. 1860.
The engraving by these French and Cuban artists captures the dimensions of this booming port city and capital in the mid-nineteenth century; but by the 1780s, Havana was already a bustling seaport and the second largest Atlantic port city in the hemisphere. Photo by DeAgostini/Getty Images, ca. 2002

Robust political and commercial activity drove the expansion of the city's judicial apparatus and litigating culture. Seventy-two attorneys practiced in the city in 1786, a ratio of 1 attorney per 555 free and enslaved inhabitants. In contrast, Santiago only had ten, or roughly one per thousand.[55] The proportion of legal professionals to inhabitants in Havana was like that in the city of Lima, a viceregal capital.[56] Years later, Captain General Conde de Santa Clara described Havana as a city where "money circulates as nowhere else in America. Commerce is great and the incidences that result from it are vast, the rents of houses are over 100 pesos a month, and like that everything else, suits in the tribunals are many."[57] He did not attribute the litigation surge to the commercial

[55] Amores, *Cuba*, Appendix 1, 491–95.

[56] Lima in 1790 had 91 attorneys (*abogados*) for a population of roughly 50,000, or one lawyer per 549 inhabitants Premo, *The Enlightenment on Trial*, 104, 109.

[57] Conde de Santa Clara to the Council, Havana, February 18, 1797, AGI-SD 328.

boom. Santa Clara attributed it instead to "the many bad lawyers [*abogados*] in the city and the quarrelsome and bad intentioned ones that encourage disputes to create improper expenses ... since regardless of how small the action is in that country expenses are big for [even] the three or four papers with which any recourse is initiated."[58] There seemed to be faith in legal venues among a litigious public. Seeking to reduce or expedite the out-of-control volume and cost of litigation in that city, the captain general proposed to Madrid a reform to hold summary oral trials in cases under 500 pesos. The Council denied the captain general's request and ordered him "to continue with the customary practice up to now," so the surge in lawsuits, small and large, continued.[59] The Bourbon state seemed interested in expanding the use of royal courts in the colony. Freedom lawsuits and suits by other subordinate groups such as women may have been part of this litigation surge as they were, according to Bianca Premo, elsewhere in the empire.[60] Although the cobreros' legal action had problems taking off in the colony, the pueblo's apoderados filed legal actions in the governor of Santiago's court, and ordinary cobreros embraced local courts in various cities once their doors opened to them (see Chapter 5).

A few cobreros had migrated or run away to Havana over the years and worked in the city and its districts by the early 1780s. They were now in danger of re-enslavement, as the heirs were contracting slavers to find dispersed cobreros that could be reclaimed as their human property. Other cobreros were trafficked and sold in Havana after the privatization (see Chapter 1). They all became part of both the wider group of plaintiffs in Cosme's collective legal action and part of the network in Havana. Cobrero-based ties took on a new force that now stretched across the island. Aiding cobreros were also people who had once lived in El Cobre or had relatives and friends there. Carlos Ramos, an Afro descendant artisan, was one of them. Ramos was a successful silversmith in the city, the most prestigious craft among the manual arts, and owned his own shop.[61] His mother-in-law had apparently been affected by the enslavement.[62] He became one of the earliest and most important contacts Gregorio Cosme relied on when he arrived in Havana in 1782.

58 Ibid. 59 Response of the Council, Madrid, September 7, 1797, AGI-SD 328.

60 On the surge of legal actions by subordinate subjects in royal courts in Mexico and Peru during the last three decades of the eighteenth century, see Premo, *The Enlightenment on Trial*, 96–101; Appendix II, 241–50.

61 Memorial Carlos Ramos, Madrid, November 17, 1784. No. 44, f. 11, AGI-SD 1627. For eight months of lodging Ramos charged 160 pesos.

62 Petition of Gregorio Cosme, Madrid, January 14, 1785, AGI-SD 1627.

Carlos Ramos fits the profile of the upper ranks of the urban petite bourgeoisie of color in Havana, a group that was part of the 7,111 free people of color (17.9 percent) living in the capital in 1778 (see Table 1.1).[63] Although free people of color had a subordinate role in Spanish controlled cities, there were opportunities for limited prosperity among the artisan class, especially in Havana. These men also served in the militias of color and became officers in them.[64] Military experience and veteran credentials also linked Ramos and Cosme. Ramos had reportedly once been a sergeant in the volunteer militia companies of Santiago de Cuba. Like Cosme, Ramos stated that his father had died fighting during the British occupation of Havana and that he had also fought in that war.[65] These acts of sacrifice were especially worthy of reward in the monarchy's economy of rewards.

Ramos lodged Cosme in his house during the eleven months of preparations for the journey to Madrid; he loaned him money for the cause and eventually became part of the three-man delegation that traveled to the court in Madrid more than a year later. Ramos reportedly sold 269 pesos worth of property, including horses and pigs, a gold watch, and tools valued at 150 pesos to help finance preparations for the trip (Figure 2.3).[66]

Ramos' reasons for investing in and undertaking the risky journey to the court may have gone beyond familial obligations. A petition he filed in Madrid called attention to "the merit he has earned by coming with the other two to inform about the tyranny executed against the six thousand [*sic*] souls of the pueblo of El Prado Cobre" (my italics).[67] Tyranny, it is worth noting, was an old politically charged term but one that when applied to slavery was but a step away from the radical language of the Age of Revolutions and of nascent antislavery movements in the Atlantic world.[68]

63 General Census of Cuba, 1778, AGI-Indiferente 1527.

64 Deschamps Chapeaux, *Los batallones*; for economic opportunities and the military role of the free population of African descent in Havana, see Schneider, *The Occupation of Havana*, 295–97. According to Schneider their military role began to decline in the late eighteenth century with the shift to a plantation economy (294–303).

65 Petition of Carlos Ramos, Madrid, December 21, 1784, AGI-SD 1627.

66 Memorial Carlos Ramos. Madrid, November 17, 1784, No. 44, f. 11–11v., AGI-SD 1627.

67 Petition of Carlos Ramos, Madrid, December 21, 1784, AGI-SD 1627. The 6,000 souls of El Cobre was an exaggeration. I will address this issue in next chapter.

68 For seventeenth century deployments of the terms "tyranny" and "tyrannies" see Owensby, *Empire of Law*, 256–58. For the eighteenth century and its relation to Natural Law see Premo, 31, 146–47, 198, 305n134.

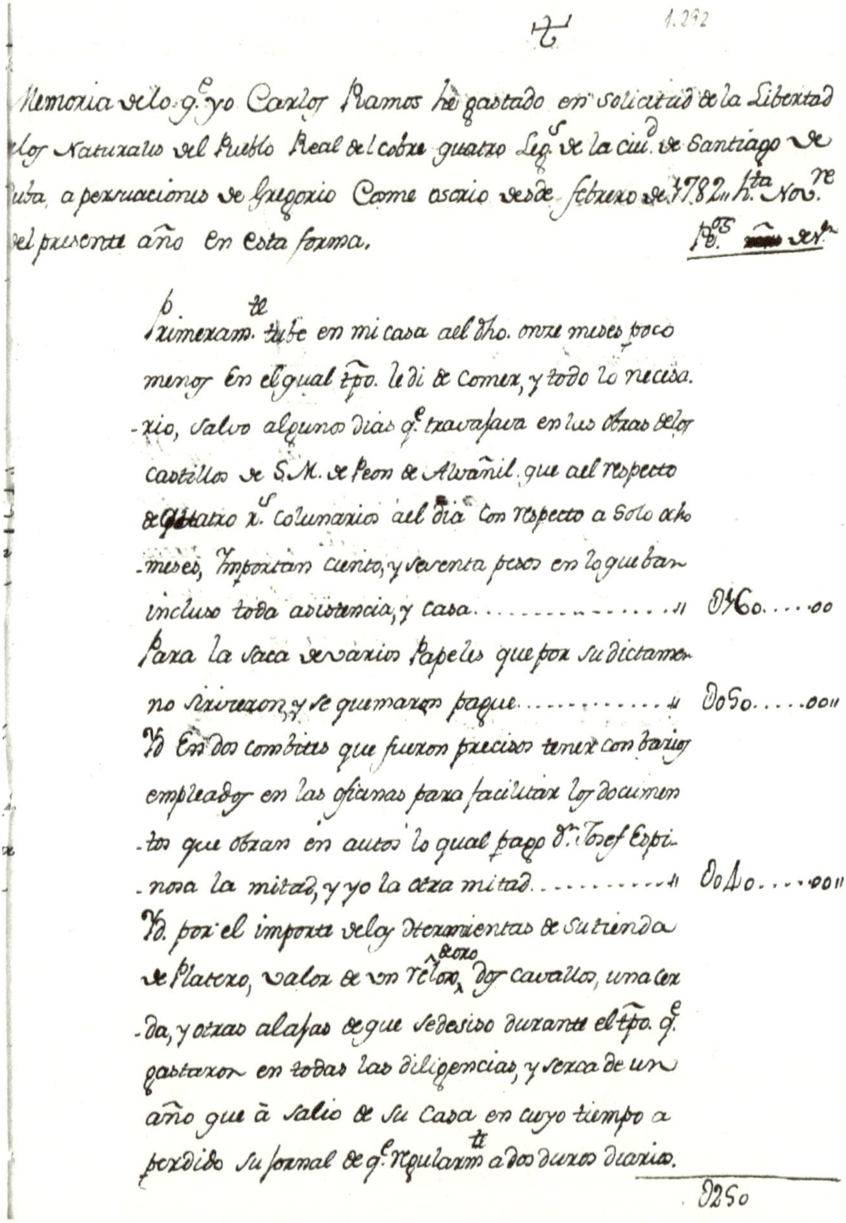

Memoria de lo q.e yo Carlos Ramos he gastado en solicitud de la Libertad de los Naturales del Pueblo Real del cobre quatro Leg.s de la ciud. de Santiago de Cuba, a persuaciones de Gregorio Come osorio desde febrero de 1782 h.ta Nov.re del presente año en esta forma. Ps. rs.

Primeram.te tube en mi casa al dho. onze meses poco menos en el qual tpo. le di de comer, y todo lo necesario, salvo algunos dias q.e travajava en las obras de los castillos de S.M. de Peon de Albañil, que al respecto de quatro r.s colunarios al dia con respecto a solo ocho meses, importan ciento, y seenta pesos en lo que van incluso toda asistencia, y casa ... 0160....00

Para la saca de varios Papeles que por su dictamen no sirvieron, y se quemaron pague ... 0050....00

Yd. En dos combites que fueron precisos tener con varios empleados en las oficinas para facilitar los documentos que obran en autos lo qual pago D.n Josef Espinosa la mitad, y yo la otra mitad ... 0040....00

Yd. por el importe de las herramientas de su tienda de Platero, valor de un relox de oro, dos cavallos, una cerda, y otras alajas de que se desiso durante el tpo. q.e gastaron en todas las diligencias, y cerca de un año que à salido de su casa en cuyo tiempo a perdido su jornal de q.e regularm.te a dos duros diarios. ... 0250

FIGURE 2.3 Preparations for the Madrid trip: Account of expenses, 1784. The document filed in Madrid lists the expenses that Carlos Ramos incurred in Havana in preparation for the trip to the royal court in Madrid for which he expected repayment. Ministerio de Cultura y Deportes. Archivo General de Indias. Memoria de los gastos de Carlos Ramos, AGI, Santo, Domingo, 1627, No. 44, fol. 11r

Although the artisan Carlos Ramos provided fundamental support during Cosme's eleven-month stay in Havana, his financial, political, and social possibilities as a man of color were limited. Somehow, Cosme made contact in Havana with a middle-class Spanish merchant named Don José Espinoza de los Monteros, who sponsored his travel plans in ways that were beyond the means of Ramos. Espinoza was a minor member of the city's peninsular merchant class. A native of Villa Manrique, near Seville, Espinoza had once been a shipbuilding carpenter (*carpintero de la rivera*) and may have worked in Havana's large shipyard. His clunky signature reveals his limited education and lower social origins (Figure 2.4).

While Cosme and Ramos had an alleged history as officers and veterans in the volunteer militias of color in former times, the Spanish merchant was a mere "distinguished soldier" in the urban (White) militias of Havana. This low rank spoke to his subordinate status among the city's elite White vecinos who held high military ranks. Espinoza was also hoping to obtain rewards and merit from the king by sponsoring the cobreros' cause. In addition, he was to profit directly from the cobreros through transactional exchanges for his mediation services. Espinoza loaned money for the journey, functioned as liaison with the colonial bureaucracy, and helped with the logistics of the trip, including obtaining fake embarkation papers. Once in Spain, he served as sponsor for the litigants in court. Cosme would eventually have a showdown with Espinoza in Madrid over who had the rights and credentials to act as apoderado and represent the natives of El Cobre in court in Madrid. Control over the position of apoderado of El Cobre became one of Cosme's personal and political battles in the royal court.

Cosme's network in Havana included yet another military connection. José Valentín Sánchez, sergeant in a volunteer (White) militia in that city, served as apoderado for Cosme and the cobreros after Cosme, Espinoza, and Ramos left for Madrid. Espinoza and Sánchez eventually became the main apoderados in Havana. One of Sánchez's letters to Gregorio Cosme illustrates his liaison role and provides a short glimpse of the (initially) friendly, even egalitarian, working relations developed among Sánchez, Espinoza, Ramos, and Cosme regardless of class or racial status. Addressing Cosme with the respectful "*usted*" [formal you] Sánchez also wrote in familiar terms: "Friend Gregorio ... on the 15 of September, three cobreros, an Ortiz, a Quiala and a González... came by to bring a piece of paper for the *Reverendo Señor* of which I'm sending you by mail on this occasion. I am well, thanks God, and my family too, that of my

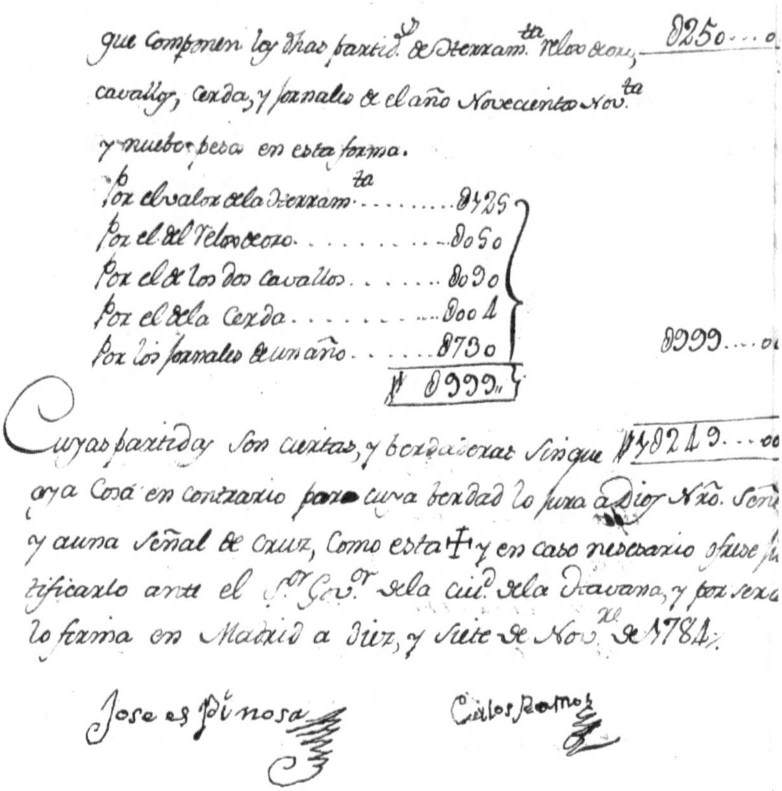

FIGURE 2.4 Signatures of Carlos Ramos and José Espinoza de los Monteros, 1784.
Note the wobbling autograph of the Spanish merchant Espinoza suggestive of his low literacy level. Espinoza also signed for Ramos who was illiterate. The signatures lay at the end of Ramos's bill of expenses for the journey and stay in Madrid. Ministerio de Cultura y Deportes. Archivo General de Indias. Memoria de los gastos desembolsados por Carlos Ramos, AGI, Santo Domingo, 1627, No. 44, fol. 11v

esteemed friend Espinoza is without any novelty, as is the wife of the friend Ramos, to whom you will all give a thousand affectionate expressions and to God."[69] The note points to the operating network that had also developed among cobreros from the village, including those in other towns, all the way to Havana. A prominent cobrero, Rafael Cosme, wrote from El Cobre to Sánchez: "With great joy I learn that Vuestra Merced is

[69] José Valentín Sánchez to Cosme, Havana, October. 14, 1784, f. 1475v., AGI-SD 1627.

the apoderado of Gregorio Cosme and ours who will send the letters of obligatory correspondence."[70] And later, he invoked the notion of tyranny in vernacular terms: "As our protector in that city we send you a very old paper for His Majesty ... and another one for the Señor Intendant so that he stops all the rigors of these tyrants" (my italics).[71] Rafael Cosme closed a letter to the apoderado Sánchez invoking his identity as native of El Cobre when he signed "I bear witness as cobreros [*doy fe como covreros*] [*sic*]."[72] Whereas the apoderados in Santiago were natives of El Cobre and free men of color, the apoderados of Havana, Espinoza and Sánchez, were White. Sánchez would now mediate communications to Madrid via Havana. Over time, Cosme built a transatlantic legal network of apoderados in El Cobre, Santiago, and Havana, although his most direct connections would be with the local leaders in El Cobre through their secret correspondence.

The Spanish merchant also helped circumvent other travel impediments of a political and racial nature. The memorial presented in Madrid vaguely attributed the plaintiffs' travel difficulties to obstruction of justice by the heirs and their cronies: "due to the influence of the persecutors of that pueblo, it seemed impossible that any of its inhabitants could cross to this peninsula to inform about the harassment [*las molestias*] they were suffering."[73] Gregorio Cosme claimed that Captain General Juan Manuel Cagigal had misplaced or lost (*refundido*) the official papers he had brought from Santiago "on purpose so that they could not come to this court to claim their freedom."[74]

But racial status also posed an obstacle for travel to the metropolis. Ramos declared that he and Cosme were "pardos and in this quality [*calidad*] lay the difficulty of the passage [to Spain]."[75] Travel bans to the court for colonials of color was a major issue for Indigenous subjects too.[76] High-level royal officials could deny travel licenses in politically controversial cases like that of the cobreros. Given the near impossibility

70 Rafael Cosme to José Valentín Sánchez, El Cobre, July 27, 1784, f. 1470, AGI-SD 1627.

71 Rafael Cosme to José Valentín Sánchez, El Cobre, August 19, 1784, f. 1474, AGI-SD 1627.

72 Rafael Cosme to José Valentín Sánchez, El Cobre, July 27, 1784, f.1471v., AGI-SD 1627.

73 Memorial Madrid, November 17, 1784, AGI-SD 1627.

74 Petition of Gregorio Cosme to Minister José Gálvez, Madrid, December 10, 1784, AGI-SD 1628.

75 Petition of Carlos Ramos, Madrid, December 21, 1784, AGI-SD 1627.

76 *Recopilación Leyes de Indias*, Book 6, Title 7, Law 17. De la Puente Luna cites earlier royal edicts from the 1560s that prohibited noble or common Indigenous subjects from seeking favor and redress in person in Madrid, yet his study discusses different ways

of getting legal visas, Espinoza bought illicit *criado* (servant) travel licenses and forged identity papers for Gregorio Cosme and Carlos Ramos. Cosme and Ramos traveled under assumed names as Juan de la Cruz and Domingo Ramos. Posing as the merchant's companions (*camaradas*), and perhaps also employees, who were returning to their local patria of Ayamonte in southern Spain, they paid for their own sea fare by tending poultry and cattle on board.[77]

The *Rosario de los Gremios* docked in Cádiz sometime early in the winter of 1784. Gregorio Cosme and Carlos Ramos made it through customs as Juan de la Cruz and Domingo Ramos. They were luckier than other African descendant travelers from the colonies who attempted to cross the imperial geographic and racial border at Cádiz. That year, three free Black militiamen from Rio de la Plata, also heading to the court, were refused entry into Cádiz and deported to Buenos Aires because they lacked the required papers.[78] Cádiz was the first stepping stone in the three colonial envoys' long winter journey into the heart of empire. After almost three weeks in the city, the travelers made their way to Madrid. The next year or so would be trying as the three men navigated new terrain in the court. Relations among them would also grow strained over various matters and eventually reach a breaking point. Madrid in the 1780s was, for the most part, an inauspicious place for a freedom case, however.

NAVIGATING THE ROYAL COURT IN MADRID

Madrid, as imperial capital and the seat of the royal court (Figure 2.5) may have been an overwhelming environment for men from Santiago, Havana, or even Cádiz. At mid-century, the city had an estimated

through which the prohibition was circumvented, especially through patronage. But the number of travelers who actually crossed the ocean voluntarily is unknowable. *Andean Cosmopolitans*, 7–9, 124. Dueñas documents a 1750 memorial to the king from a noble Inca from Cusco residing in the royal court in Madrid on behalf of other noble caciques and military Indians in that city demanding the rights of free passage of Indians to Spain. Ferdinard VI denied the general request in an edict but reiterated the law in the *Recopilación* that the viceroy could grant a license in individual cases if justification for the trip was deemed acceptable. *Indians and Mestizos*, 67 and 86–87n26.

77 In the Madrid Memorial, April 4, 1784, AGI-SD 1629. De la Puente Luna also discusses the Indigenous subjects that could travel to Madrid as *criados* or servants and employees in subordinate relations as Cosme and Ramos did. *Andean Cosmopolitans*, 96–102. In Cosme's case, a commercial transaction was behind the patron-client pretense.

78 Borucki, *From Shipmates to Soldiers*, 84.

FIGURE 2.5 Royal Palace in Madrid.
Constructed in the eighteenth century, the palace constituted the iconic site of the royal court. Photo by David Espejo/Getty Images

population of 156,672 souls, up to one-third were immigrants or colonials from throughout the empire seeking favors or doing business in court. By the end of the eighteenth century, the city's population spiked to almost 200,000 inhabitants.[79] As the seat of the imperial court, more than six thousand people were employed in the king's service – almost half the population of Santiago de Cuba.[80]

Madrid had a bloated administrative bureaucracy and many letrado professionals, including 595 attorneys, 257 scribes, and an indefinite number of agents and *procuradores* working for clients throughout the empire. There were by then 122 guilds of judicial professionals, attorneys, and solicitors.[81] Although Gregorio Cosme Osorio would soon learn to navigate the court labyrinth with surprising assurance, it was Espinoza who seemed initially to have dealt with the court bureaucracy and the professionals required to prepare a new dossier. Espinoza also covered the costs of these judicial operations.

Claiming he had run out of funds and did not have enough money to return to Havana, Espinoza, through proxy powers that Cosme had given him in Madrid, applied in the Royal Treasury for an 8,000 pesos loan to be paid by the cobreros in the colony.[82] The move reveals that credit mechanisms were in place in the court for long-distance money transactions. Once the loan was approved, however, Espinoza refused to continue funding Cosme, leaving him stranded in Madrid. Cosme claimed

[79] López García, *La esclavitud*, 46–47. [80] Ibid., 48–50.
[81] Kagan, *Lawsuits and Litigants*.
[82] Memorials of José Espinoza and Carlos Ramos, Madrid, November 17, 1784, No. 44, AGI-SD 1627.

FIGURE 2.6 South facade of Palace of the Councils, Madrid, 1847.
Since the early 1700s this Palace housed the councils of the different kingdoms of the empire, including the Council of the Indies. Engraving from *L'album giornale letterario e de belli arti,* August, 14, 1847. DEA/Biblioteca Ambrosiana/Getty Images

later that had he realized Espinoza's promised funds were insecure, he "would not have decided to come to Spain until I had found the means of doing so without the risk of facing the hardships in which I now find myself."[83]

Overall, Espinoza claimed that the costs of the journey and litigation had amounted to the extravagant sum of 3,425 pesos.[84] Cosme explained that he and Espinoza had made a written agreement (*un papel*) under which Espinoza committed to lend the two other men who depended on his finances up to 500 pesos in Madrid but had failed to do so.[85] The agreement basically established that Cosme committed to pay Espinoza a three thousand pesos "gratification" for a private loan of five hundred or one thousand pesos (the amount is unclear) on top of expenses or, effectively, for services of transacting the trip and sponsoring them at court.[86] The eight-thousand-peso loan from the Royal Treasury may have been devised to pay up immediately on the expenses and services. It is

83 Petition of Cosme, Madrid, January 14, 1785, AGI-SD 1627.

84 Memorial of José Espinosa, Madrid, November 17, 1784, No. 44, f. 10–10v, No. 44, f. 10–11v, AGI- SD 1627.

85 Petition of Cosme, Madrid, January 14, 1785, AGI-SD 1627.

86 Petition of Gregorio Cosme, Madrid, ca. December 1784, AGI-SD 1628.

plausible that Cosme and the cobreros could have viewed the predatory financial deal with Espinoza as analogous to an investment in a general coartación or collective purchase of freedom: the money originally intended for the denied coartación offer discussed in Chapter 1 may have been redirected toward litigation for collective freedom in Madrid. An even more onerous deal is suggested by another letter exchange between Sergeant Valentín Sánchez, the apoderado in Havana, and one of the principal leaders of the pueblo, Rafael Cosme, deceased Commander José Cosme's brother. The note suggests that the cobreros may have informally agreed to pay a considerable lump sum of up to 40,000 pesos if their freedom suit succeeded. Considering that the total cost of their freedom through coartación was assessed at 190,000 pesos, 40,000 pesos may have seemed a less expensive, alternative deal – if they obtained their freedom. However, since the cobreros were still in captivity, a guarded Rafael Cosme was unwilling to advance anything until the enslaved cobreros were freed and back in the pueblo.[87] The note also suggests that Cosme had agreed to take the eight-thousand-peso loan jointly with Espinoza, perhaps as part of a previous agreement between them to finance expenses or pay for Espinoza's sponsorship services. But how the loan went through without Rafael Cosme's approval is unclear.

Espinoza may have also wanted to be recognized by the Council as the main apoderado of the cobreros' cause. In a display of supreme confidence, Cosme effectively challenged Espinoza's sponsorship and tried to emancipate himself and the plaintiffs from his judicial and financial patronage. He penned a few petitions himself, used legal services to pen others, and sought his own web of patronage in court. In his effort to recover control of the case, Cosme tried to revoke the proxy power he had extended to Espinoza and Ramos to disqualify them from representing the community in any capacity arguing that they were not part of the aggrieved community. Claiming nativeness to El Cobre as the defining criteria for the apoderado role, Cosme asserted that he was the "sole legitimate and true representative of the natives [of El Cobre]."[88] Espinoza referred to Cosme's deft moves to undercut his power as "the sinister designs of Gregorio" and accused him of wanting to "take for himself all the honors and rewards of having freed *his compatriots* from

[87] Rafael Cosme to José Valentín Sánchez, El Cobre, August 22, 1784, f. 1478–79, AGI-SD 1627.

[88] Petition of Cosme, Madrid, January 14, 1785, AGI-SD 1627.

the *slavery and tyranny* that they suffered, perhaps also trying to collect payment for the expenses that he has not made" (my italics).[89] In the Spanish merchant's view, regardless of possible misleading financial claims, Cosme, as a cobrero, had political aspirations of emancipating his fellow villagers from slavery and tyranny, again conflating the enslavement with tyranny. Chapter 6 turns to Cosme's letters, where he indeed conveyed aspirations along those lines. The political emancipatory significance of the legal action was recognized by contemporary actors themselves. And Cosme would not share the role of liberator.

Recognizing the importance of the politics of patronage in a highly hierarchical court, Cosme sought patronage from the two most powerful figures in colonial affairs at the royal court at the time: General Bernardo Gálvez, Spanish hero in the American Revolutionary War who had been appointed Captain General of Cuba in 1784, and his uncle, Minister José Gálvez, the powerful president of the Council of the Indies, who had presumably approved the privatization provision when it first came up in 1779. Apparently, Cosme had previously obtained an audience with General Gálvez, where he personally recounted the cobreros' enslavement and sale with the complicity of the Governor of Santiago, Nicolás de Arredondo. He may have brought other information and complaints, especially related to contraband activities with the British in Jamaica by two prominent merchants of Irish descent and a network of officials in the city. The contraband activity had taken place during the American Revolutionary War; therefore, it had the potential of being considered a high crime during war.[90] Cosme connected the denunciations against (illicit) enslavement of the cobreros and the destruction of the pueblo to other criminal activities perpetrated by powerful people and officials in Santiago – what General Gálvez would call the "disorders in Santiago."

In a petition to Minister José Gálvez, written in his own hand, Cosme suggested that he was seeking his patronage at nephew General Bernardo Gálvez's instigation "who ordered me to come to Your Excellency among

[89] Memorial of José Espinoza, Madrid, November. 17, 1784, No. 44, f.10–10v., AGI-SD 1627.

[90] Anonymous representation from a vecino of Santiago to the Conde [Bernardo] de Gálvez, October 30, 1784, AGI-Cuba 1374. In this representation, a whistleblower accused the Governor of Santiago, Nicolás de Arredondo, the merchant's relatives, Juan Francisco and Antonio Creagh, and others in Santiago of contraband trade with Jamaica and the tyrannies that oppressed the poor in the city. These reported "tyrannies" resonated with the enslavement of the cobreros too.

other things to make it clear that I am the apoderado of the said cause."[91] He even referred to "Señor Don Bernardo Garves [*sic*], a godfather [*padrino*] to all of us [who are] of color" and was now turning to José Gálvez "as godfather of my merits."[92] Cosme boldly pulled patronage strings to claim official recognition of his status as sole apoderado of the natives of El Cobre in their freedom suit (see Figure 2.7)

Finding himself stranded and indigent in court, Cosme requested from the Council another loan of eight thousand pesos for himself, which he offered to guarantee with his own and the community's properties in El Cobre.[93] He devised a way to pay for the loan by making an offer to reactivate the mines with the cobreros, an interesting offer that the Council ignored.[94] He would have to wait at least two more years living in precarious conditions before he received in 1787 proxy powers from well-off cobreros to represent the community and to take loans in court. Meanwhile, Espinoza and Ramos returned to Havana after the Council's ruling came down in late September 1784.

After the two other travelers returned to the island, Cosme lived on credit in the basement of an inn in Madrid awaiting a new loan and overseeing the progress of the legal action. A surveillance report on Cosme said that he "maintains himself from the little food [*bocado*] that a washerwoman or the owner of the inn, to whom he owes 6,000 reales, give him."[95] According to the spy, Cosme reportedly led the life of a recluse, staying most of the time in his basement. When he ventured out, he went to a couple of houses that were not investigated, except to point out that one of them was a house of *extranjeros* (foreigners from Madrid) near his pension. The spy reported that Cosme had recently been "ill and bled" (*enfermo y sangrado*), adding physical debilitation to his economic troubles and reclusion. Still awaiting his loan, Cosme was actually living close to indigence.

Adding to Cosme's difficulties, the report also revealed that he had lost letters from the Indies and was now receiving his correspondence through the widow of a former royal official from Santiago de Cuba, revealing

91 Petition of Cosme to Minister José Gálvez, ca. December 1784, AGI-SD 1628.

92 Ibid. Black militia troops from Cuba had fought in the American Revolutionary War under General Bernardo Gálvez (although no cobreros did so), see Schneider, *The Occupation of Havana*, 297.

93 Petition of Cosme, Madrid, January 14, 1785, AGI-SD 1627.

94 Petition of Cosme to Minister José Gálvez, Madrid. December 13, 1784, AGI-SD 1628.

95 Report of Pedro Muñoz de la Torre, Madrid, October 8, 1786, in Expediente crímenes Cosme, AGI-SD 1529.

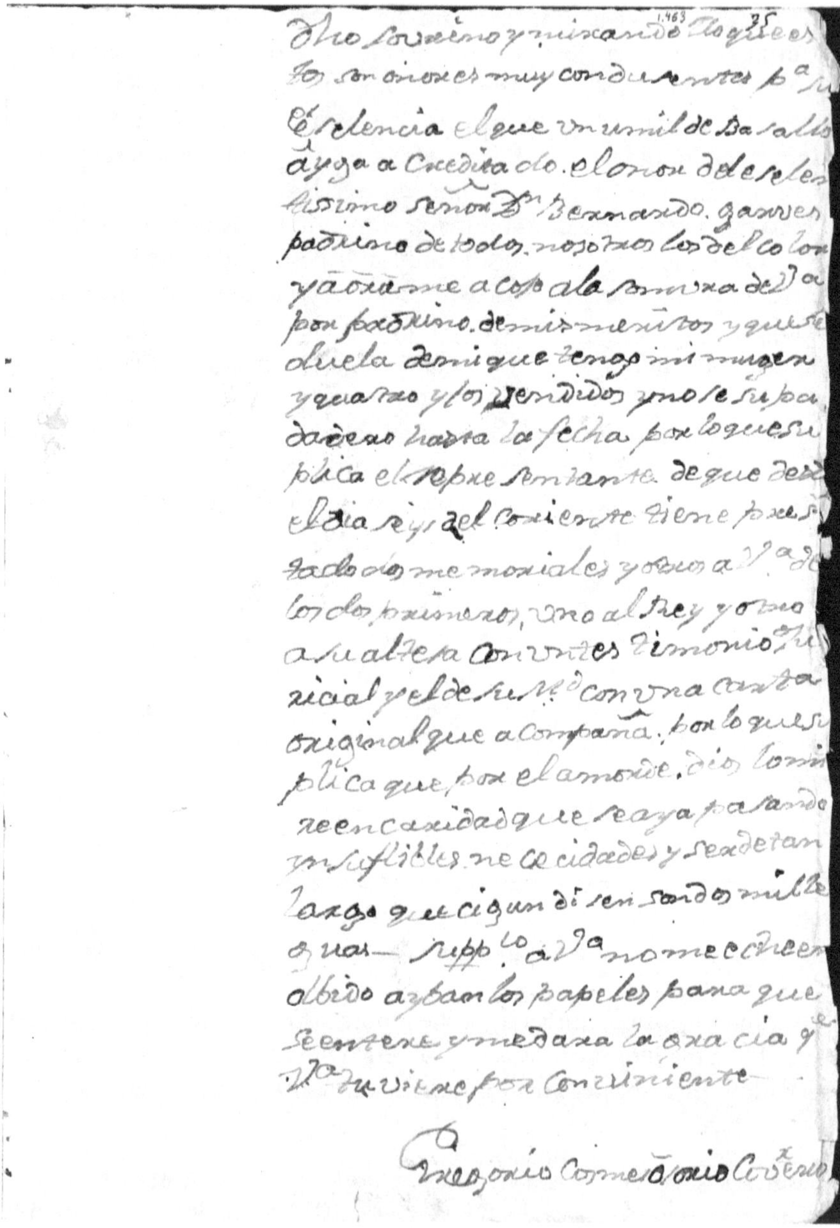

FIGURE 2.7 Handwritten petition by Gregorio Cosme Osorio to Minister Gálvez, 1784.
Last folio of a petition penned by the apoderado of El Cobre, Gregorio Cosme Osorio, to Minister José Gálvez, head of the Council of the Indies, seeking the powerful minister's patronage. Note Cosme's signature as a cobrero at the bottom. Ministerio de Cultura y Deportes. Archivo General de Indias. Petición de Gregorio Cosme Osorio, AGI, Santo Domingo, 1627. No. 49, fol. 35r.

friendly networks that Cosme had been able to establish in Madrid.[96] The problem of lost letters suggests that Cosme's correspondence was intercepted. We know that this correspondence was Cosme's lifeline to the community back home. It was vital to the legal business and perhaps to Cosme's emotional sustenance. For instance, in one of the only extant letters from the early period, from Salvador Quiala in El Cobre, Quiala gave Cosme personal news about his family ("your wife and family until now are well although with a lot of travails") and updated him on the grim local situation: "Brother, please hurry because the second masters already treat us like capital enemies."[97] Losing his regular communications obstructed Cosme's work and left him vulnerable and isolated even from his community back home.

The importance of the cobreros' case in the Council of the Indies and the risks Cosme faced on his own in court are reflected in that surveillance investigation that had been ordered in 1786 by no other than Minister José Gálvez. Having received a confidential note from a snitch in Cádiz informing him that "a mulatto" from Cuba was "writing papers against the Ministry," Gálvez tried to have Cosme arrested and his papers confiscated.[98] The high-level ministerial intervention into a low-level inquiry illustrates not only how surveillance networks operated in court but also how much Cosme must have troubled some high figures in the imperial hub. It also indicates that Cosme had high placed enemies in the royal court, not surprising given the magnitude of his denunciation. Cosme was saved by another minister charged with surveilling Cosme's activities who did not find cause for arrest.[99] By 1786, any protection that General Bernardo Gálvez may have once promised was gone. General Gálvez died that same year, soon after his promotion to Viceroy of New Spain. Minister José Gálvez, in turn, felt threatened by Cosme's denunciations and had tried to get the colonial "mulatto" out of the way. Incarceration would have meant disappearing in Madrid and a break in the communication networks between Madrid and El Cobre. The ordeal of mobilizing

[96] Ibid. There is no clear evidence that Cosme asked for financial aid or *ayuda de costa* from the Crown as many other stranded travelers did by invoking the standing of miserables. Cosme seems to have asked for a loan but he may have received aid especially when ill. For *ayudas*, see de la Puente Luna, *Andean Cosmopolitans*, 148–54.

[97] Salvador Quiala to Cosme, El Cobre, August 19, 1784, AGI-SD 1627.

[98] Expediente crímenes Cosme, Madrid, October 12, 1786, AGI-SD 1529.

[99] Report of Pedro Muñoz de la Torre, Madrid, October 8, 1786, in Expediente sobre crímenes atribuídos al mulato Gregorio Cosme (hereafter Expediente crímenes Cosme), AGI-SD 1529.

in Madrid turned out to be riskier and more taxing than initially expected. Chapter 6 provides a more searching view of Cosme's varied activities as apoderado in the mid-1790s. By then, more than a decade after his arrival, he was a more experienced legal agent and intermediary, and his secret line of communication with the local apoderados back home had become more critical precisely as the case began to take a new turn.

IDEOLOGICAL CLIMATE IN MADRID ON THE QUESTION OF SLAVERY

Although well-off colonials had agents in the court to look after their business and interests, those who had the means came for periods of time to carry out business personally and very powerful ones established a permanent residence in the court. Havana's elites, often with new noble titles, maintained personal business in court and represented the city's cabildo and the pro-slavery sectorial interests, especially those linked to the growing sugar industry. Perhaps the most famous apoderado in the island's history, Francisco Arango y Parreño, arrived at court in 1787, only three years after Cosme. He came on family business and stayed there until 1794, obtaining important slave-trading concessions for the city. The main one was the deregulation of the slave trade with foreigners in 1789: the first major rupture in the Crown's mercantilist policies.[100] Cosme, of course, would not have been accepted in those exclusive social cum political circles. Like them, he may have been a Christian, a monarchist, an avowed loyal royal vassal, and a free man (albeit a freedman), but his race and class confined him to a far lower circle in a highly hierarchical world. Not even a relation of patronage in this case would have brought them closer, for they backed divergent projects and futures. And although all were part of the Spanish empire, perhaps even natives of the same empire, to be a native and apoderado of Havana was different than being a native and apoderado of a place like El Cobre. Yet there they were: de facto activists representing different constituencies in the hub of empire and striving for different futurities.

The 1780s was a time when pro-slavery policy deliberations to propel production, wealth, and the "happiness" of (some) royal vassals were

[100] Pierson, "Francisco de Arango y Parreño"; Tomich, "The Wealth of Empire"; Moreno Fraginals, *El ingenio*. For new thinking in Madrid, see Schneider, *The Occupation of Havana*, 270–79.

rapidly advancing in the Council's "Mesa de Negros" (Chamber of Slave Commerce) with strong pressure from colonial lobbyists.[101] However, summary news about nascent antislavery debates and organizations in Britain, France, and the United States were also arriving in Madrid at the time. News arrived, for instance, in the incipient and timid free press of Madrid during the mid- to late 1780s.[102] Although this modest press was suppressed in 1791 due to the breakout of the French Revolution, at least briefly, emergent antislavery views circulating elsewhere were reported especially in *El Espíritu de los mejores diarios literarios que se publican en Europa*, a sort of a digest of news abstracts from other European papers. Brief news appeared about the first wave of antislavery movements, petitions submitted to the British Parliament, letters, excerpts, and even widespread discussions in Britain, where, a paper reported, the topic was so prevalent that it was even discussed in "ladies' salons."[103] In its issue of September 4, 1787, for instance, *El Espíritu* printed a negative review of an anonymous pro-slavery work, *An Apology for Negro Slavery*, that had been recently published in London. The reviewer wrote, "It is embarrassing and even horrible that in the century of Enlightenment [*siglo de las luces*] and philanthropy there can be defenders of Black slavery and that they can be found in a nation whose fanaticism for liberty is well known and that brags of respecting more than any other the rights of man and of nature. The work does not merit any consideration given its odious title."[104] It is difficult to know if Cosme or his attorneys were familiar with this kind of international news and with the philosophy there represented.

No abolitionist movement emerged in Spain at the time (not until the 1860s!) that could help Cosme navigate the royal court and publicize the cobreros' case.[105] The lack of a strong civil society in Spain, where ideas could be debated and associations mobilized, was an important reason for this absence. In this absolutist monarchy, no parliamentary power could be lobbied to influence the laws on slavery and the slave trade. There was

[101] Amores, *Cuba*, 129–37. [102] Jensen, *Children of Colonial Despotism*, 4–6.

[103] Morgado García, "Zinda," 187–219. Other papers included *Correo de Madrid* and *El correo de los ciegos*. For the "first wave" of antislavery movements and ideas in the north Atlantic, see Sinha, *The Slave's Cause*, Part I.

[104] Morgado García, "*Zinda*," 187–219.

[105] Abolition of slavery in peninsular Spain took place with the liberal Constitution of 1837, but it was not extensive to the colonies. For the (late) abolitionist movement in Spain, see Schmidt–Nowara, *Empire and Antislavery*.

no robust press either to provide a platform for public discussions and dissemination of views. At best, external antislavery movements were reported for a short time, but internal debates over the question of slavery in the colonies did not take place publicly. News did circulate orally but the courts remained the main path in the empire to consider and contest questions of freedom and slavery as well as other issues indirectly. The cobreros' case may have represented such an opportunity.

Legal advocates' arguments and memorials may be a good place to begin to examine whether strands of antislavery discourse and sentiments entered the fray in actual court battles or what other policy-related issues connected to freedom in the cobreros' case were brought to the table and how they could be argued. What questions did the native plaintiffs of the distant village of El Cobre bring to the imperial court?

3

Making the Case for Collective Freedom

This, Señor, is the miserable state [of enslavement] to which *the Pueblo* of Santiago del Prado [aka El Cobre] has been reduced, and this the painful destiny [*suerte lastimosa*] of the very loyal *vassals of Your Majesty* [who] *after their grandparents freed themselves of their primitive slavery have only recognized Your Majesty* [as their Lord] (my italics).

—Madrid Memorial, 1784

If Man individually is presumed to be free, with how much more reason should it not be presumed that a Villa [town], community, political body or municipality composed of many who governed themselves and form a state in civil society [is free].

—Memorial of Simón Echenique, Madrid, 1793

On April 4, 1784, Gregorio Cosme, Don José Espinoza de los Monteros, and Carlos Ramos filed a long memorial to the king in the Council of the Indies denouncing the wrongful enslavement of the natives of El Cobre.[1] The memorial referred to the cobreros' enslavement as a violation of the "sacred rights of humanity," the only ideological reference to rights in universal terms in this judicial brief. As basically a wrongful enslavement case, the argumentation depended on proving the plaintiffs' possession of freedom in the past to secure it for their future. The universal sacred rights of humanity that had been violated referred here to those of free subjects who had been enslaved, rather than to the sacred natural rights of all persons not to be enslaved. But again, the more radical universal claim would not have begun to pass muster in the Council of the Indies at a time of strong pro-slavery policies upheld by established slave law.

[1] Memorial Madrid, April 4, 1784, AGI-SD 1629.

The challenge had to be more limited and circumscribed within the parameters of the law.

Although the cobreros had gone to court before on the island and even in the Audiencia of Santo Domingo, this was the first time that they filed a legal action for collective freedom.[2] To be sure, about a third of the villagers were free by 1780, having emancipated themselves individually through the years by purchasing their freedom as discussed in Chapter 2 or, subsequently, by being born free. In a letter to the cobreros spotlighting his work as *apoderado* in the royal court, Cosme stressed the new – and distinctive – aspect of this collective action by differentiating between two kinds of emancipation: "Look at how many years have gone by since this *villa* [town] was founded and no one has [ever] asked for freedom, nor obtained it from Kings for you," he wrote, "I think no one, and if some had it [freedom], it was because of their money [self-purchase]."[3] *Coartación* represented for Cosme an individual and transactional form of emancipation, a commodified freedom that had a fundamentally different value than a royally declared general emancipation or a judicially obtained collective freedom based on belonging to a long existing villa. Such grounds for freedom constituted the most distinctive aspect – and one of the most controversial facets – of the cobreros' legal action. Although this chapter examines a series of arguments for freedom and implicit critiques of slavery deployed in the briefs on the cobreros' behalf, it will highlight the significance and implications of the connection Cosme sketched in that passage.

Regarding the turn to claim collective freedom for the first time, recall as well that as recently as four years before, in 1780, the cobreros had submitted in Santiago a collective petition for coartación that entailed acknowledgment of their status as (royal) slaves (Chapter 1). (That petition also reflected an awareness of the need to secure rights to the land they had worked for decades to provision themselves.) Having been denied the collective offer to purchase their freedom and land and facing a brutal policy of enslavement – or re-enslavement – in the almost frenzied pro-slavery climate of the time, the cobreros shifted gears and turned to the courts. They now made a claim to wrongful enslavement that called for a revisionist narrative of their past. Years later, Cosme wrote in one of his letters that he had given himself "to this great defense that is the pretended freedom [which] was so confused and dark and deep that it

[2] Díaz, *The Virgin, the King*, chapter 11.

[3] Gregorio Cosme, Madrid, October 6, 1795, No. 75, f. 195–207, AGI-SD 1629.

has been necessary to found it with much efficacy and saintly zeal."[4] His work had consisted in clarifying a freedom that had laid confused and almost forgotten in the past and putting it on solid ground for the future. The memorials filed in court aimed to do just that.

This was not, however, a regular freedom dossier like most of those scattered through the dockets of colonial and postcolonial courts.[5] This freedom case was further complicated by its collective character – encapsulated in the term "natives of a pueblo" – and by its composite dimension. It was a hard case that posed tough legal, political, and moral questions to the imperial court at a time of rapid transformations in the island and the empire. In fact, I argue that there were also important incipient political claims with broader future implications for free African descendants implicit in this legal action. Aside from legal-based arguments, moral- and policy-based ones were invoked too, some bordering on antislavery discourse. Could the plaintiffs persuade the imperial court to condemn the enslavement that its own mining and privatization policy had generated? This was a politically charged legal action that basically went against the grain of recent Bourbon colonial policy and the strong lobby favoring the expansion of slavery in the colony.[6] In calling for the protection of their collective freedom, the plaintiffs indirectly also questioned the priorities of the Bourbon state, exposed the darkest sides of slavery, and provided an alternative future to the increasingly dominant slave-based plantation model then rapidly advancing in the island.

Legal professionals in Madrid did not mount this complex case anew. They revised and edited a memorial that the three travelers brought with them from the colony and adapted it to the standards of the legal culture in the royal court, probably with some further oral feedback from Cosme, the only one of the three travelers with deep personal knowledge about local events in El Cobre. At least three versions of the same collective memorial, constituting a sort of palimpsest, can be found on the record: one produced in the colony in 1783 and two in Madrid (1784 and 1793). I focus in this chapter on the arguments made in the Madrid Memorial of 1784, which became the official memorial that the Council of the Indies

4 Ibid.

5 For a recent study of the type of freedom suits that were filed in nineteenth-century lower instance courts in Santiago, see Chira, *Patchwork Freedoms*. See also Scott and Hebrard, *Freedom Papers*; Townsend, "Half My Body." For Brazil, see Grinberg, "Freedom Suits." For the US South, see Schweninger, *Appealing for Liberty*.

6 Amores, *Cuba*, 125–58.

responded to in the initial ruling of September 1784, but I analyze iterations of the arguments in the other two briefs when pertinent.

Although redacted for the most part in plain language, these legal briefs reflected mostly the voice of the professionals who crafted the documents with the tools available in Spanish law and jurisprudence to mount a freedom case. Whereas plaintiffs pressed on the court claims from real life and their own vernacular understandings of them (not always easy to unravel), legal professionals adapted – or translated – those claims into judicial discourse, at times expanding, restraining, or reconfiguring the plaintiffs' original claims. The memorials and petitions they produced constitute forms of legal advocacy that adapt a messy, perhaps even contradictory, vernacular story into a legally feasible narrative. Legal professionals looked for loopholes and ambiguities in the law to press their clients' claims as far as possible. At times, they also used other political and moral discourses to complement the judicial ones. The problem with separating and distinguishing vernacular and professional voices in legal documents comes up repeatedly in the chapters of this book. I dedicate some reflection to that problem when that distinction becomes particularly significant. Although the cobreros' voice, especially that of Cosme and the local apoderados, could become entangled with that of the letrados' they worked with (Chapter 6), I treat them for the most part separately in this chapter (barring some of Cosme's comments in his letters).

All three extant petition briefs contained the same facts, relied basically on the same narrative, and used the same battery of legal instruments and arguments available in Spanish jurisprudence, but with subtle variations. They also argued for collective freedom from similar subject positions – free subjects, natives of a pueblo, royal vassals/imperial subjects, and in a more formulaic, but still relevant, way as *miserables* (wretched subjects) in need of special court protection. I will probe the significance of most of these categories, including the novelty of that of "native" in Chapter 4. Suffice it for now to note their centrality in the legal briefs.

All three memorials lodged their arguments in a narrative of past and present and indirectly of future too. The metanarratives in which the more specific story of this community became embedded was, first, a story about the "rise and fall" of a prosperous pueblo in the Spanish empire, which in turn became intertwined with another metanarrative about powerful subjects who unjustly oppressed wretched (miserable) ones – in this case through wrongful enslavement – and tried to block their access to justice. The latter was a staple in the juridical discourse of "miserables" probed more recently by Brian Owensby in relation to Indian subjects.[7] These metanarratives inexorably called for the intervention of the Crown to restore law, justice, and prosperity to one or another corner of empire.

The first extant version of the memorial was filed in Havana on December 10, 1783, right around the time the three travelers embarked for Spain. It is likely that the Havana Memorial closely followed one drafted in Santiago since it was full of local anecdotes and references that the subsequent Madrid versions deleted.[8] That memorial drafted in the colony was cast in what may be called old regime discourse, which made considerable use of religious language and moral references that the Madrid versions purged. It also included many local anecdotes that were also deleted from subsequent memorials in Madrid as if not fit for the more professional legal culture of the royal court. The Havana memorial of 1783 may have been redacted by a clergyman in the island familiar with the case with some oral input from Cosme.[9] Four months later, on April 4, 1784, the three travelers filed in Madrid a recycled version of the first, which became the second and official version of the memorial.[10] The advocacy rhetoric of this memorial was the most restrained of the three memorials laying out the cobreros' case. A third version of the memorial, filed on March 12, 1793, based on the official one of 1784, was signed by another apoderado in Madrid named Simón Echenique.[11] Although in line with previous memorials, the Echenique Memorial parsed furthest the legal, political, and philosophical significance of facts and notions that were often left implicit in the previous two briefs. This memorial grasped best the most distinctive aspect of the cobreros' freedom case and drew

[7] Owensby, *Empire of Law*, especially 53–60. See also Borah, *Justice by Insurance*.

[8] Havana Memorial, December 10, 1783, AGI-SD 1627. According to the heir Francisco Mancebo, the first "fulminations" were redacted in Santiago in 1780 among which the original (or master) version may have been produced. Other briefs filed in Santiago, particularly in 1791 and 1792 used some, not all, of the same arguments nor were they formatted as a historical narrative as the Havana and subsequent ones in Madrid were.

[9] Cosme may have decided what version of various memorials drafted in Havana suited him best and settled for the version of the Havana memorial of 1783. Carlos Ramos stated that he loaned Cosme fifty pesos "to obtain various papers that in his [Cosme's] opinion were not helpful and were burned [*Para la saca de varios papeles*] *que por su dictamen no sirvieron y se quemaron*]." Those papers may have referred to memorial drafts. Memorial of Carlos Ramos, Madrid, November 17, 1784. No. 44, f. 11–11v, AGI-SD 1627.

[10] Memorial Madrid, April 4, 1784, AGI-SD 1629.

[11] Memorial of Simón Echenique, Madrid, March 12, 1793, No. 11 (hereafter Echenique Memorial), AGI- SD 1627.

out, so to speak, a subtext that the more cautious and legalistic Madrid Memorial of 1784 was unable – or unwilling – to fully engage.

There were three salient lines of argumentation in the memorials. The first questioned the legitimacy of the heirs' property rights to the mining estate and therefore to the original mining slaves (and their descendants). The legal claim was that the heirs had been contractors or leasers of the mines – not owners – so they could not make property claims over the descendants of the original mining slaves. The argument is briefly summarized in the following passage: "They [the natives of El Cobre] find themselves now subject to a harsh captivity ... because of the unjust pretension of the heirs of a contractor who was never their proprietary owner and who, far from having done any service to Your Majesty, caused serious damage to the Royal Treasury and died indebted [to the Crown]."[12] There was even an insinuation that the heirs had committed fraud against the Spanish Crown in appropriating and selling the slaves in the mining estate. I will not discuss this argument further since it touched on the cobreros as presumed property of the estate. Effectively, it boiled down to a contest between the Crown and the heirs over contract terms and possession rights to the mining estate. I will return to this matter when discussing the final adjudication of the case in Chapter 8.

In this chapter, I focus on the more pertinent second and third lines of argumentation for collective freedom. The main claim in the second line of argumentation was that the plaintiffs had long been (free) vassals of the Crown and (free) natives of a pueblo who had been indistinctly and wrongfully enslaved in 1781. As the first epigraph suggests, the natives' freedom was located in an emancipation narrative of the past, so that the memorial's task was to trace the legal paths through which that emancipation had once taken place. The third line of argumentation was based on the claim of wanton violence against the plaintiffs, especially during – and after – the privatization and enslavement of 1781. The border between the substantive part of the wrongful enslavement argument and the transgressive violence of its execution was fuzzy, and they impinged on one another, but they were considered juridically distinct in the brief. This argument called for the immediate return to the status quo ante 1781 before any substantive legal disputation could even begin to take place. I also argue that, wittingly or unwittingly, the illicit violence argument and its rhetorical dramatization – particularly in the Havana

[12] Memorial Madrid, April 4, 1784, AGI-SD 1629.

Memorial – echoed critiques of slavery made in some earlier antislavery discourses in the Spanish Atlantic, and in nascent ones in the north Atlantic world.

But whereas the illicit violence argument resonated with some critiques of slavery made by two late seventeenth-century abolitionist Capuchin friars in Havana and even echoed Bartolomé de Las Casas' sixteenth-century rhetoric against Indian enslavement, the Echenique Memorial of 1793 critiqued slavery by using more current notions associated to Enlightenment discourse (second epigraph). Thus, the cobreros' case prompted incipient antislavery formulations in the briefs that may have reflected more broadly circulating critiques of slavery in the island and in the Atlantic at a time when notions of freedom were enkindling small and big battles in the Age of Revolution.

A word on the "facts" presented in the memorial (and the problem of "truth"). As often is the case in legal disputes and briefs, there were misrepresentations and exaggeration of the facts presented in the memorial (the heirs called them outright "falsities") that constituted rhetorical subterfuges. Most appeared initially in the Havana Memorial that was produced in Cuba for a distant audience and were reproduced, sometimes augmented, in the subsequent Madrid Memorials. For instance, there were enormous exaggerations in terms of the reported enslaved population (an alleged 6,000 inhabitants were reported when the actual number was around 1,065), the number of houses (an alleged 3,000 when a brief from the colony reported 300 – a subtle intended or unintended "typo" that could make a huge difference), the value of the landed property and the types of farms that the natives owned (which may have included the whole jurisdiction of Santiago and its precincts and not just the pueblo of El Cobre), and the amount in tithes they allegedly paid.[13] These altered "facts" did not fundamentally modify the basis of the case; they were meant to boost the policy-based argument of a flourishing pueblo, its utility to the empire, and the magnitude of its destruction as a result of the privatization policy. In a way, the memorials' enhanced picture of the pueblo of El Cobre constituted a fantasy – or an aspiration – of what the cobreros' pueblo could become in an ideal future rather than what

[13] For the reference to 300 houses, Petition of Justo Cruzata, Martín Salazar, et al., Santiago de Cuba, November 11, 1791, f. 289, AGI-SD 1629. For intentional and unintentional errors made by notaries, see Burns, *Into the Archive.* On misrepresentations of narratives in collective village petitions for township status in early modern Castile, see Nader, *Liberty in Absolutist Spain*, 6.

it had been in the past, before, to use Las Casas' famous term, its devastation in 1781.

LEGAL ARGUMENTS AND INSTRUMENTS UNDERGIRDING THE NARRATIVE OF EMANCIPATION

The plaintiffs' memorials constructed a speculative narrative of emancipation and pueblo formation around a few available written documents, memories, and hearsay accounts. Political and moral arguments were sometimes embedded in the narrative too. The general argument of wrongful enslavement – based on presumption of freedom – is summarized in the closing argument of the Madrid Memorial of 1784. Also sketched in this passage are the contours of the narrative about the emergence and fall of a pueblo of considerable value to the empire.

> This, Señor, is the miserable state [of enslavement] to which the Pueblo of Santiago del Prado [aka El Cobre] has been reduced, and this the painful fate [*suerte lastimosa*] of the very faithful vassals of Your Majesty [who] *after their grandparents freed themselves of their primitive slavery* have *only* recognized Your Majesty, [and have] enjoyed their freedom for more than a century, forming a considerable settlement [*población*] of laborious vassals *useful* to the state who paid their tithes to the Church and taxes [*derechos*] to the Royal Treasury. *After they were in possession of the said freedom,* they have exercised themselves in the defense of the patria and of the domains of Your Majesty under the military discipline obtaining ranks only conferred on free persons, and in *civil employments for the political governance of their Pueblo* never conferred to those who are not [free] (my italics).[14]

The argument juxtaposed several temporalities – a present, a far past, and a century sandwiched in between them – to frame the freedom narrative. The pivotal moment on which the argument rested was the story of the grandparents' emancipation in the far past. The memorial's task was to legally substantiate an emancipation that allegedly had once taken place. Note as well the practices highlighted as major badges of freedom in the near past before 1781. The last one particularly stands out. I flag it here but will return to the significance that the Echenique memorial read into it later.

The narrative of the plaintiffs' past opened with the general "beginnings" of the mining settlement of El Cobre and its population makeup – a moment already full of potential legal meaning in the story: El Cobre

[14] Memorial Madrid, April 4, 1784, AGI-SD 1629.

"was composed in its beginnings of Indian natives of the country [*Indios naturales del País*] and some Black slaves [*negros*] that were *brought in by account of His Majesty* to work in the mines of that place" (my italics).[15] That moment was followed by another legally significant moment when the concessionaire Don Juan de Eguiluz took over the operation of the copper mines in 1616. From the initial episode, the narrative sought to establish that the mining slaves were the property of the Crown, not of the private contractor Eguiluz. Undergirding this was also a legal argument based on confused genealogies that I will discuss in Chapter 4. Suffice it to say here that the memorial insinuated as part of its wrongful enslavement argument that the descendants of Indians in the village had been improperly enslaved along with the descendants of the mining slaves.

The memorial's narrative focus then turned to how most of the mining slaves had become emancipated. Royal edicts became the main and preferred legal instruments in the brief whereby the descendants of the early mining slaves had allegedly attained freedom in the past. The first cited in the Madrid Memorial was the Royal Edict of May 30, 1673, which ordered the disposal of the 275 existing mining slaves either through *rescate* (i.e., coartación) or through their sale to private persons.[16] However, a royal edict per se was not evidence of its enforcement. Although the edict could be considered evidence of the Crown's intention to facilitate the freedom of its mining slaves, the edict itself was not a grant of manumission. Manumission here depended on individual purchases of freedom. As discussed in Chapter 2, some cobreros across several generations had obtained freedom through this means, but most had not purchased it and were therefore considered *esclavos del Rey*. Turning to speculation, the brief argued that most of the 275 original (or "primitive") mining slaves in the 1670s must have taken advantage of this manumission opportunity and subsequently purchased their way out of slavery. Those who did not, the memorial argued, would presumably have been sold away as slaves to private individuals and removed from El Cobre by their purchasers. Those who purchased their freedom, on the other hand, would have remained in El Cobre as freed persons and their descendants would have been born free and become part of the natives of El Cobre who had been recently wrongfully enslaved. Although it was a

15 Ibid.

16 As I discussed in Chapter 1, this was the first formal edict on record, at least in eastern Cuba, whereby coartación was explicitly recognized as a legal venue to freedom.

narrow and problematic argument that could contravene the collective thrust of the case, the Madrid Memorial put particular attention on this dubious legal strategy.

As evidence of the edict's enforcement, the brief attached to the Edict of 1673 an extant *carta de libertad* (manumission certificate) from 1689 belonging to a female slave named Juliana. The memorial speculated "it is very regular that the same would have happened [*sucediese*] with many of the other 275 slaves" and spuriously claimed that "since then, no one ever saw again any among those who remained established in the pueblo, or their descendants, subject to slavery, rather all have been in possession of [freedom] as free vassals of Your Majesty exerting the acts proper of such and taking care of the cultivation of their farms and cattle."[17] Thus, according to the memorial, the legal foundational act of emancipation was located in the Edict of 1673 and in the individually purchased freedoms that it had enabled. In this formulation, freedom-related practices – highlighted in the memorial as badges of freedom – came after formal emancipation through coartación. This was, for all purposes, a conservative (if speculative and redundant) argument. There was nothing too novel about it.

The Madrid Memorial, however, made a long explicit digression into an interesting – but problematical – discussion of evidential procedural issues. The evidential issue hinged on written proof versus public reputation and enactment as evidence of freedom. The memorial acknowledged that a sign (*cartel*) had been posted in the parish church's door right after the enslavement of 1781 announcing that "those who manifested their legal titles of freedom within a deadline were exempted from slavery [enslavement]."[18] This sign acknowledged that there were distinctions among the freed and slave natives of El Cobre. But the memorial claimed, perhaps from Cosme's telling, that this evidential requirement was almost impossible to meet "because the titles of freedom that *undoubtedly* were issued in the previous century were not issued to the actual inhabitants, who were already born free, but to their grandparents who were the slaves" (my italics).[19] Two things had allegedly happened: the first, according to the memorial, was that the natives of that time, "incapable of foreseeing the persecution that would be unleashed against their descendants, did not take the care to request testimony of their freedom to protect their right, or they had lost it with the passing of time."[20] These

[17] Memorial Madrid, April 4, 1784, AGI-SD 1629. [18] Ibid. [19] Ibid. [20] Ibid.

emancipated ancestors had taken for granted a freedom that several generations later could be challenged, thereby demonstrating the vulnerability of free status for African descendants. The memorial implicitly asked: for how many generations did a free family of color have to hold on to the freedom papers from an ancestor to feel secure from re-enslavement?

The second related issue that the memorial raised was that even the presentation of a title of freedom could constitute insufficient evidence of free status because cobreros also had "to prove the identity and descent of the living persons from that [freed] trunk" and they were not given enough time to find this proof.[21] The memorial suggested that these difficulties – lack of titles and genealogical proofs – contributed to the mistaken enslavement of all the natives. These procedural reflections suggested questions such as: Was freedom so fragile and so riskily contingent on a title of manumission? Were generations of natives living in freedom, acting as free men and women, not sufficient evidence of freedom? Did public knowledge of status carry any weight before the law? Was presumption of slavery and freedom so based on race that Black and racially mixed people needed written proof of freedom?

The digression can also be read as a critique of the burden of documenting freedom to which all non-White free people were subject to and of which the cobreros constituted a special case. It also seemed to critique legalistic written documentation requirements when access to the archive was difficult – or made difficult – to subordinate subjects such as those considered miserables . Their "misery," stated the Madrid Memorial, had not permitted them to make "the search [*reconocimiento*] of the archives and offices where *undoubtedly* the justification of this *truth* would be found" (my italics).[22] Although access to the archives did become part of the out-of-court battles that the cobreros faced in Santiago to pursue legal action, the issue of the evidence of coartación here was a risky one: what if the archives revealed that no, or few, coartaciones had taken place? The cobreros' lawyers may have thought in good faith that in a *miserabilis* court case summary proceedings and special evidential exemptions were applicable and that the burden of evidential documentation would be passed over, at least initially: "And they hope that Your Majesty will deem to excuse this fault, reflecting with your great wisdom the miserable situation in which they find themselves and the power [*prepotencia*] of

[21] Ibid. [22] Ibid.

some enemies who have the first [say] in the country where they had to be compiled."[23] Here was a typical argument found in the miserable meta-narrative: that the interests and connections of the powerful could obstruct wretched subjects' access to justice, an access that the Crown, as the fountain of justice, must protect.[24] In this case, the reference was to the impossibility of getting access to the archives to make their case properly. But juridically, the strategy of claiming that there was evidence in the archives of their coartación to which they did not have access, was a faux pas since in fact most cobreros had not bought their freedom through the years. The argument also constituted a potential digression from the plaintiffs' collective case since it was based on the excavation of individual evidence of coartación, which could undermine the corporate-based argumentation, as the Council immediately grasped.

The narrative of emancipation intersected with the memorial's story of the formation of the pueblo. It also addressed land claims by conjuring other vague edicts, memories, and, to a lesser extent, actions. According to the Madrid Memorial, the Crown had allegedly made a land grant to the cobreros' ancestors at an unspecified time in the past sometime after the mining estate returned to royal hands: "Since the suspension of work at the mines, for lack of new contractors, *Your Majesty ordered* the distribution to those workers [*operarios*] an extension of four leagues [of land] in the environs of the place [*sitio*] so they could provide for themselves" (my italics).[25] But these "workers" were actually tolerated squatters in the mining jurisdiction's lands. Their possession rights to land were customary, derived from occupation and use of plots of land in the mining jurisdiction, not from any formal grant by the Crown.[26] According to the memorial's narrative, access to land enabled the emergence of a prosperous pueblo: "They made progress and provided not only for themselves but also for the city of Cuba … [and] with time they formed a considerable pueblo of more than 3,000 houses and

[23] Ibid.

[24] Owensby, *Empire of Law*, 49–64. Owensby parses the meaning of "staying powerful hands" through the recourse to amparo writs.

[25] Memorial Madrid, April 4, 1784, AGI-SD 1629.

[26] There is confusion regarding the land issue. The cobreros formerly based their claims to all the land in the mining jurisdiction on their status as royal slaves and their right to be properly sustained by the master, in their case through the king's land that allowed their own self-provision. But there were also claims to a standard minimal land grant as a pueblo and to a land survey in the 1760s that was later suspended and apparently overwritten by another survey sponsored by the heirs in the process of privatization of the mining estate in 1780. See Díaz, *The Virgin, the King*, Chapter 6.

estancias."[27] Here the exaggerated housing and population figures (actually closer to 300) were meant to enhance the magnitude of the pueblo's growth and its utility to the public good.

In arguing the cobreros' presumed emancipation in the past, the memorial's narrative tried to circumvent one of the main potential obstacles to the plaintiffs' freedom argument: namely, the cobreros' former rotational forced labor requisitions in the fortification of San Pedro de la Roca in their capacity as royal slaves (see Figure 1.2). "At the same time, they went to whatever they were ordered in the service of Your Majesty. They worked opening foundations and raising walls of the garrisons of that city ... and they were continuously employed in several occupations without any other gratification than one daily *real* when they were employed and not always."[28] Whereas, in Cuba, royal officials considered this labor a badge of the royal slaves' bondage, in this memorial it was reinterpreted as a service to the Crown and as exploitation given the under remuneration for those services. And in the Echenique memorial of 1793, this labor was explicitly parsed as the service of freedmen (*libertos*) in gratitude for their freedom, a customary form of expected servitude to a former owner and his or her family that extended the dependent relation after coartación.[29]

Given the population increase in El Cobre, the memorial asserted that "the governor of Cuba (*perhaps with the approval of Your Majesty*) decided to establish magistrates from the pueblo for their internal policing regime and councilmen and bailiffs were appointed who were elected every year" (my italics).[30] With this official act based on local memories, the memorial suggested that as local self-government was established the pueblo became institutionalized.

Nothing more is made of this point, however, other than to suggest that freedom must have been attained by then or that by holding such positions the plaintiffs had been treated as free subjects (even though they were still considered royal slaves). Similarly, four military companies were established at some undefined point in the past.[31] Again, in the summary argument quoted above, military service was evidence that freedom must have already taken place sometime in the past, rather than performed by royal slaves as had been the case in two of four companies (see Chapter 2).

[27] Memorial Madrid, April 4, 1784, AGI-SD 1629. [28] Ibid.

[29] Echenique Memorial, Madrid, March 12, 1793, No. 11, AGI-SD 1627.

[30] Memorial Madrid, April 4, 1784, AGI-SD 1629. [31] Ibid.

In the jurisprudence of the Bourbon monarchy, royal edicts – as laws emanating directly from the king – had precedence over other sources of law such as customary law. Other edicts, aside from the Edict of 1673 granting coartación, were also invoked to buttress the plaintiffs' freedom argument. Since the documents were not at hand, they were invoked through hearsay or memory. Their narrative at times seemed to contradict the chronology and argument that had been previously deployed. Although one particular edict would become central to other later briefs made in Santiago, the edicts were undated and fuzzy on the narrative of these memorials. One of them, the Madrid Memorial of 1784 asserted vaguely, was a royal edict that His Majesty dispatched "so that all the descendants of the primitive slaves of El Cobre who were from the fourth or fifth generations be considered free and enjoy all privileges as such."[32] The memorial went on to tell a story that could only have proceeded from the cobreros' own living memory. According to that story, a former dean of the cathedral, Pedro Agustín Morell de Santa Cruz, a protector of the cobreros in the 1730s and '40s, gave the royal edict to the parish priest, Juan Jacinto Silva, to keep and to use "if it became necessary." The priest at the time became the custodian of the edict and "only at times showed it to the natives inside a portfolio [*cartera*] telling them that there lay the shield of their freedom."[33]

Once the priest died, the story went, the edict "was read in the presence of some natives and then it was passed over to the Governor of Cuba, the Marquis of Cagigal, and it should still be in the then Governor's office [*Secretaria*]."[34] The fuzzily recalled hidden edict was actually an edict issued on April 12, 1721. A copy was found in Santiago's archive later and it was cited more clearly and prominently in other briefs drafted in that city especially in 1791 and 1792. The edict had been issued in response to an inquiry by a potential contractor of the mines as to whether he could remove and sell the royal slaves in the mining jurisdiction if he leased the mines. The king responded with the Edict of 1721 prohibiting the removal or sale of the slaves who had reached the third to fourth generation. The rationale to deny removal and alienation was that it would be very difficult to determine if slaves who had passed the first two generations of slavery were still actually slaves. What the elusive edict concretely meant in 1721 was that the natives of El Cobre could only be forced to work in situ in the mines – that they constituted a reserve labor

[32] Ibid. [33] Ibid. [34] Ibid.

pool for the mines, so to speak. That situation was analogous to the recent one raised by the privatization of the mines: did the heirs of Eguiluz have the right to remove and sell cobreros, especially since by then they were beyond the third to fourth generation?

Finally, the memorial invoked yet another edict from September 13, 1733. The edict was issued in response to a local revolt related to lost land and to work excesses in the pueblo during Governor Pedro Ignacio Ximénez's tenure in the 1730s. According to the memorial, the vague edict called for "their treatment according to their misery without punishment [for the revolt], no offensive treatment, not even by words, and that their land be returned."[35] But the land in question, which was part of the royal mining jurisdiction, was never returned because the government of Santiago had rented part of it to vecinos of Santiago and the alleged Edict of 1733 was kept hidden for many years.[36]

These edicts formed a good part of the legal grounds for the cobreros' freedom and land claims in the Madrid memorial. They represented the law of the sovereign, or at the very least, the mindset of the Crown (or the royal master) as favorable to the good treatment and freedom of its royal slaves. Even actions whose origins were lost in the past – such as the alleged land grant and the governor's appointment of magistrates to the pueblo – were attributed to alleged royal edicts, not to local decisions and customary practices developed quietly and out of expediency through the years. Yet the only edict submitted in the brief was the 1673 one granting coartación. The memorial did mention, however, that the other edicts could be found in government offices in Havana or Santiago and that the king could order their retrieval. No evidence of population numbers or of property holdings or taxes and tithes paid were provided in this memorial, so those "facts" could be more easily exaggerated.

The arguments and legal instruments deployed in the Madrid Memorial produced a highly conjectural narrative of the past that

[35] Memorial Madrid, April 4, 1784, AGI-SD 1629.

[36] A 1734 petition narrating the conflict of the early 1730s also recalled a previous conflict around 1708 that took a royal slave to Madrid to report abuses and denounce possible illegal contraband activities by then Governor Joseph Canales (1708–10). This earlier event produced an alleged provision promising their freedom hidden in the city's archive. This episode was not recalled in the Madrid Memorial and its memory was possibly compressed into the more recent memories represented by the edicts of 1720s and '30s. For the earlier episode, see Diaz, *The Virgin, the King*, 289–98. These conflicts point to the recurring contestation of the cobreros' status and customary entitlements throughout the decades culminating in the most serious of all conflicts: privatization and enslavement of 1780.

conjured several juridical routes to freedom. Edicts, coartación, and a mention to genealogical confusion were among those routes. However, yet another bolder, though perhaps more appropriate, legal instrument was also deployed in the memorials: prescription.

PRESCRIPTION

After listing the various ways in which the cobreros had obtained freedom in the past, the discussion cautiously turned to prescription, but only as a last resort. Basically, prescription was a rare statute of limitation that proclaimed that a lapse of property rights occurred after a stipulated period of time.[37] According to the Madrid memorial: "Therefore, even if the heirs of Eguiluz would have had some [possession] right over the 'primitive' slaves of the mines of Your Majesty, a foundation that the natives cannot fathom, it would have prescribed because so much time had passed, especially given a matter as privileged as that of freedom."[38] The Havana Memorial of 1783 made that point more directly: "Even if some slave of that period could be found [in El Cobre] who with the passing of the years would not have [made it to freedom] ... the Law favors them through the right of prescription."[39] The sidelining of prescription in favor of other instruments such as coartación and edicts in the Madrid and Havana Memorials reflected a safer jurisprudential approach to the case: routes less likely to be rejected by the Bourbon court. And yet the cobreros' legal case for freedom – and even for land – basically rested on prescription: in having *lived* in various ways *as free* or quasi free people for decades. These acts of freedom would not have depended on coartación nor on equivocal and hidden royal edicts. They had a force of their own to produce freedom. However, they could also be problematically ambiguous.

Prescription of freedom can be considered a special case of what in Roman law was called *usucapio* and in English common law "adverse possession" (usually in land property). This legal principle states that a person who does not have legal rights to a piece of property, such as land, acquires legal possession by occupying it continuously for a prescribed number of years without the permission of its legal owner. (This is still in

[37] Prescription is a general juridical doctrine that extinguishes rights and produces others from de facto situations. See Scott, "Social Facts, Legal Fictions." For the doctrine's definition in Roman law, see Sherman, "Acquisitive Prescription." For Spain as referring to freedom, see the *Siete Partidas*, Book 4, Title 22, Laws 7 and 8.

[38] Memorial Madrid, April 4, 1784, AGI-SD 1629.

[39] Memorial, Havana December 10, 1783, AGI-SD 1627.

some cases the basis for squatting actions, supported by law in Spain and elsewhere.)[40] In fact, although the Madrid Memorial alluded vaguely to a land grant by the Crown so that the former mining slaves or their free descendants could grow food and provision themselves, their claim to land may have effectively also been based on some *usucapio* or adverse possession of land in the greater mining jurisdiction.[41] Part of that claimed land would have included the *estancias* and *haciendas* and *hatos* (cattle ranches) (again in exaggerated numbers) they had built on the land before 1781. Although it is unclear what claims the cobreros were actually making on land – full possession or usufruct – what they adamantly protested was having to pay rent to the heirs after the privatization of 1781 for what they considered their own land based on their standing as a pueblo and on their long use of the land.

More important here, however, was the application of prescription to the possession of freedom in Spanish law. And freedom was treated as a possession in this formulation. Based on the Castilian medieval code of the *Siete Partidas*, the default code for the jurisprudence on slavery, prescription granted de jure recognition of de facto (possession of) freedom after the passing of a period of time – anywhere between ten and thirty years, but in some cases fifty, depending on circumstances.[42] The memorial claimed that, in the case of El Cobre, the period had been much longer, from 100 years when they became the king's slaves in the 1670s to an exaggerated 150 years: "All of *these acts* exercised constantly for more than a hundred and fifty years *prove* the possession of freedom in which those *natives* have lived" (my italics).[43] Of interest in this comment as well is the association of long-term acts (of freedom) with native standing (as if the mining slaves, or later the royal slaves, had become natives), a point I will discuss below and in Chapter 4. We do not know how common the invocation of prescription as a defense for freedom was in

[40] Modern squatting actions are for the most part urban occupations of land and housing. Although they invoke constitutional principles to the right to housing and the public good, they also use *usucapio*, when retained in civil codes. See Campos and Martínez, "Squatting Activism in Brazil and Spain," 110–29; Cowan and Fox O'Mahoney, "Unlawful Occupation of Land: Squatting and Adverse Possession," 113–33. For a more general overview of modern squatting actions, see Martínez López, ed. *The Urban Politics of Squatters' Movements*.

[41] The adverse possession principle, however, could also be used by citizens in Santiago to encroach on the mining jurisdiction's land.

[42] The *Siete Partidas* recognized ten to thirty years; thirty in the case of escaped enslaved subjects. Book 4, Title 22, Laws 7 and 8.

[43] Memorial Madrid, April 4, 1784, AGI-SD 1629.

the jurisprudence of the time in Cuba or elsewhere in the empire.[44] But too common it was not.[45] Prescription-based arguments and cases are especially significant because they point to acts that can generate freedom with time and they grant public opinion a say in recognizing and validating them. Prescription actions did not depend on official papers nor necessarily on masters' will to manumit. They relied (and still do) on enactment and performance.[46] Perhaps that made prescription uncommon as a legal instrument in the courts of the empire, and perhaps that is why it was used as reinforcement of other weightier legal instruments rather than as a central instrument in the Madrid and Havana Memorials.

Freedom suits, and especially prescription cases, provide glimpses of understandings of freedom in particular historical contexts. All of the memorials made reference to a series of practices that were presumptive of freedom. But they deployed them ambiguously as either the result of a freedom previously obtained through the formal means of coartación and royal edicts or as themselves prescriptive of freedom with the passing of time. What were some of the meanings projected into the abstract concept of freedom in the Spanish Iberian Atlantic world toward the end of the eighteenth century? And, more importantly, what rights were associated with the notion of freedom in the case of El Cobre? The most distinctive and innovative basis of this case is found among some of the prescriptive badges of freedom associated with collective life as a pueblo in El Cobre.

THE GENERAL MEANINGS OF FREEDOM AND THE CONCRETE BADGES OF FREEDOM

Freedom became a central political and politicized notion throughout the Atlantic world in the eighteenth century, especially during the Age of

44 Prescription was retained in Louisiana's legal code from Spanish times. See Scott, "Social Facts, Legal Fictions." Elsewhere, it could be made partly, for instance, as a case of a slave's abandonment by masters as in María Eugenia Chaves' study of María Chinquinquirá's freedom suit in late eighteenth-century Quito. Chaves, *Honor y libertad.*

45 It would be interesting to make a longitudinal study of manumission litigations that used prescription to see how widespread – or effective – this legal instrument was, and if the ambit of criteria used to index freedom in these cases was expanded or reduced over time.

46 Although prescription law seems to fuzzily overlap with customary law, they have a separate status in legal sources. For the notion of custom as a social practice that over time takes the normative power of law within a territorially based community in general and especially of native custom as a dynamic legal category in colonial Mexico, see Yannakakis, *Since Time Immemorial*, especially, 2–4.

Revolutions, but its variable and evolving meanings especially related to personal – or civil – freedom went deep into the past. In the Spanish Atlantic, freedom also had municipal corporatist meaning associated with local self-rule, a notion that was explicitly discussed in one of the memorials and implicitly in others. Yet in general there were no explicit statements in legal sources of the time about what constituted freedom, or the rights, duties, and restrictions associated with that condition beyond some general principles about dominion and some abstractions regarding the judicial capacities of a free subject or in more judicial terms in manumission letters. Despite the important role that the notion of freedom took on as a political concept in eighteenth-century Enlightenment discourse, it did not play a central role in the political discourse of absolutist Spain until the liberal, constitutional, and anti-colonial movements of the nineteenth century. Yet the notion was very much present, if not fully thematized, in various fields of discourse and of life.

Eighteenth-century Spanish dictionaries defined freedom abstractly and negatively or by default, as an absence – that is, as anything that is not banned: "the natural faculty of free will that each person has to do or say what he wants to, except what is prohibited by force or law," a vague definition still used vernacularly today.[47] By then, however, Spanish dictionaries had begun to extend the meaning of freedom explicitly to other areas such as freedom to speak or to worship, even though these were certainly not accepted forms of freedom in Spain's absolute monarchy. But there were other ways in which liberty was thought and acted out in the past. For instance, freedom also had old Christian theological connotations associated with free will, choice, and conscience: a human's capacity to choose virtue or sin, salvation or condemnation. This notion also had personal manifestations such as freedom to make vows (as of marriage, celibacy, poverty, taking holy orders).[48] It was also present in contractual theory as the freedom to enter into legally binding contracts or, later, into more systematic discussions and policies in the late eighteenth century in the Spanish empire about free trade or *libertad de*

47 *Diccionario de autoridades*, 1726–34, https://webfrl.rae.es/DA.html. The *Siete Partidas* defined it similarly, but more carefully, as "Freedom is the power that all men naturally have to do whatever he wants, unless force or right of law [*derecho de ley*] or chartered entitlements [*fuero*] impede it," Book 4, Title 22, Law 1.

48 Seed, *To Love, Honor and Obey*. For a more general discussion of medieval and early modern understandings of liberty, rationality, free will, and natural law through Aquinas and scholastics such as Vitoria, Las Casas, and Suárez, see Tierney, *The Idea of Natural Rights*, 255–315.

comercio.[49] There were also more incipient political ways in which the term could be, and was, deployed regarding municipal self-rule that will be discussed below.[50] These were fractured ways in which notions of freedom appeared in Spanish discourse by the eighteenth century.

Another general and abstract formulation of freedom referred to a relation of personal dominion over others and over things. The 1734 *Diccionario de la Lengua Española* defined it generally as "the condition [*estado*] that does not recognize someone else's dominion [*dominio ajeno*]." Although the most prevalent application of this meaning as discussed below was in relation to servitude and slavery, broader definitions of dominion and power could and were also applied to multiple situations in the Spanish Atlantic in the past. In early modern Castile, for instance, freedom took on a political corporate-based meaning beyond the individual meaning of personal freedom (from slavery or servitude). It referred to liberty from the rule of another municipality. According to Helen Nader, this represented "one of the highest aspirations of Castilian political life" and remained the main way through which Castilians, especially in small towns, thought about and exercised freedom from the sixteenth to the nineteenth century.[51] To be sure, according to Nader, Castilians enjoyed personal freedom, but municipal freedom

49 The dictionary did not make reference to new uses of the term freedom in commercial and economic discourse like, for instance, "*comercio libre*" (free trade), a term increasingly discussed in the late eighteenth century as part of the Bourbon reforms and the pressure of creoles to open up trade with foreigners. The first restricted decree of comercio libre was issued in 1765, followed by another in 1778. But this notion of freedom of trade did not entail liberal laissez faire. The most expansive application of the notion came in the 1789 decree of free trade in slaves with foreigners. See G. Paquette, *Enlightenment, Governance, and Reform*, 99–109.

50 The term "freedom" also appears in Spain's overseas empire in yet another legal and political context that scholars have often overlooked: voting in municipal level government. The *Recopilación de Leyes de Indias*' laws on *cabildos y consejos* (town councils) explicitly stipulated that the alcaldes and regidores (bailiffs and council men) of the cities "vote freely" (*puedan votar libremente*) in their meetings; and again, that (royally appointed) governors and their lieutenants should let regidores "make use of their deputy powers and vote in cabildos [meetings] with total freedom [*toda libertad*]" (Book 4, Title 9, Laws 8 and 9). Yet, there were no specifications regarding general local voting; positions of city cabildos later became monopolized by families often through sale and were claimed as patrimonial property. Liberty referred to the voting capacity of those deputies, to their autonomy from royal jurisdiction, not necessarily to free election mechanisms. Although this kind of political liberty was very limited, it did represent some autonomous attributes of municipal government. For Indigenous communities' invocations to choose freely in their local elections, or of native Indians to stand for elective positions, see Owensby, *Empire of Law*, 224–27.

51 Nader, *Liberty in Absolutist Spain*, 8.

constituted another kind of freedom acquired through corporate belonging. Furthermore, acquiring the status of a town (*villa*), in fact purchasing it, was tantamount to acquiring liberty, or the freedom to self-rule in more powerful ways through one's own cabildo (local council).

Although the sale of townships reached its peak under the Hapsburgs, the Bourbons also engaged in the sale of town charters and titles when pressed for funds.[52] Castilians spoke of "liberation" of a pueblo that obtained a charter of township from the king, or of "enslavement" to another town, or to being under the "tyranny" of a head (*cabecera*) town or of its "despotism."[53] As late as 1790, the Bourbon Charles IV granted township status upon an agreed payment to the village of San Juan del Monte in Castile by formulaically (or ritually) stating that "by virtue of my royal absolute power as king and natural lord, I exempt, remove, and *liberate* you, the village of ... from the jurisdiction of the town of ... and I make you a town by and over yourself."[54] This was a kind of corporate manumission, even a form of corporate coartación or self-purchase, so to speak, one not far from that initially attempted by the cobreros in 1780 (Chapter 1).[55] However, the cobreros' memorials alluded to corporate liberty in other political philosophical ways that I discuss below, not through the purchase of sovereignty.

By far the most prevalent definition of freedom in relation to dominium referred to the relation of personal slavery and freedom, especially in the overseas empire where the institution of slavery had become widespread. The general formulation was already laid out in the *Siete Partidas* where the condition of servitude in contrast to freedom was depicted in a brutally vivid way. Here servitude was portrayed as "the most vile and despised thing that can exist, because man, who is the *most* noble and free creature among all the other creatures that God made, falls by way of it into *the power of another*, so that they can do with him whatever they want, dead or alive" (my italics).[56] There seems to be no restrictions to the

52 Ibid., 10, 119, 128, 222–24.

53 Ibid., 204–5. Yannakakis has found a similar language of "liberty from servitude" in Mixtec Indian pueblos' proposals to secede from their cabecera. *Since Time Immemorial*, 190–91.

54 Nader, *Liberty in Absolutist Spain*, 205.

55 Perhaps the practice of coartación from slavery, which became customary in Iberian slave colonies; constituted an individual practice analogous to the Castilian practice of collective purchase of municipal liberty. In any case, both practices seem like a striking monetarization of liberty, taboo even from our modern hyper commodifying capitalist culture; the same is true with administrative and political position sales in the past.

56 *Siete Partidas*, Book 4, Title 5, Preamble.

master's power over the servant in this formulation. Moreover, "and so *despised* is this servitude that whoever falls into it not only loses the power of doing whatever he wants *with what is his,* but even does not have power *over his own person, unless his master* [*su Señor*] *orders so*" (my italics).[57] Ironically, given the valued place obedience had in a Christian and hierarchical society like the Spanish one, this was a scathing formulation of the degradation of servitude in contrast to freedom. In any case, freedom, by contrast to servitude, consisted in having dominion over one's own person as well as over one's possessions (even after death, presumably through a will). Also implicit in this formulation was the master's power to manumit in the sense that he or she could order that the enslaved person recover "power over his own person." At its simplest, this medieval formulation stated that to be human was to be free and noble and to be able to choose what to do. Terms such as "vile" and "disdain" affirmed the abject character of servitude, a lacerating stigma difficult to bear through life and history. Thus, to act or to be treated publicly as free also entailed manifestations of respect, as if dignity and respect were an intangible right of freedom, as it surfaced in some references in the cobreros' letters; and moreover, as if "good treatment" could ambiguously take on the meaning of freedom, as it did in some passing references in the memorials. To be treated with dignity has become a core principle in current human rights discourse.

Despite these general dicta about freedom, there were some more positively described legal and legalistic definitions of individual personal freedom. These were deployed in the *cartas de libertad*, or manumission certificates given to emancipated slaves. Cartas de libertad had a standard formulation of freedom that seems to have been widespread throughout the empire, with small variations in the formula across time and geographic space. One example comes from the notarized freedom (coartación) document of the cobrero Manuel Vicente de la Caridad, filed in the villa of Santa Clara, Cuba, in 1788: "So that from this date on he may deal and make contracts, provide titles [*otorgar escrituras*] wills and [to carry out] whatever judicial and extrajudicial business [*diligencias*] are permitted to a free person."[58] Freedom in these official formulations was defined for the most part by the capacity to engage in judicial

[57] Ibid.

[58] Autos, Manuel Vicente de la Caridad, No. 59/67/24, 1788, AGISD 1628. See for comparative purposes an unnotarized manumission grant cited by Owensby in seventeenth-century New Spain in "How Juan and Leonor Won Their Freedom," 46.

transactions: to make formal contracts and sell and bequeath property under the protection of the law. No racial restrictions were specified in the listed legal capacities of free status in these freedom letters. They entailed some kind of equality before the law in the execution of these judicial actions as rights (however, the judicial enactments of some of those rights could find gender restrictions, especially in the case of married women).[59] But by including the open phrase, whatever "is permitted to a free person," these letters also recognized that the meaning of freedom was contextual, that it changed with time and place, and that it encompassed extrajudicial actions too. For those without much property to protect in court, the most important distinctions would have been the extrajudicial enactments of freedom or informal transactions. For instance, in El Cobre transmission of personal property (including personal slaves), house plots, and farmland took place among free and royal slaves across generations as informal and customary practices rather than judicially mediated acts.[60] Yet engaging in judicial practices and using notarial services may have nonetheless constituted a symbolic performance of freedom rights or a way to better protect those rights for subjects who could afford the fees. In nineteenth-century Santiago de Cuba, for instance, Adriana Chira has found in the archive relatively poor freedmen and women making notarized wills, perhaps to judicially enact their freedom.[61]

Freedom could take different meanings in time and place for other groups in colonial society too. Indian plaintiffs, both individually and as corporations, filed liberty petitions that, according to Brian Owensby, became common in the Mexican Indian court during the seventeenth

59 There were gender restrictions on judicial transactions. Married women needed permission from their husbands to make judicial transactions but not to make wills. Widows, however, could freely engage in those transactions on their own account. Arrom, *The Women of Mexico City*, Chapter 2. It is unclear if female manumission letters reflected gender restrictions.

60 Díaz, *The Virgin, the King*, 171–78, 187–91. I did not have access to notarial records in Santiago to see how often free cobreros used this kind of formal instrument for their transactions. For internal verbal agreements in Castilian villages for contracts and most business dealings, including inheritance, see Nader, *Liberty in Absolutist Spain*, 22–23.

61 Chira, *Patchwork Freedoms*, 208–23. And yet agreements regarding coartación terms between masters and enslaved subjects did not tend to be notarized in Cuba or elsewhere in the Spanish empire. In the US antebellum South, Kimberly Welch found that free Black people often used the courts to assert property claims, such as collection of debts, successfully even against Whites. The rights of property constituted such an important principle in this society that race did not significantly undercut outcomes if conflicts were formulated exclusively in property terms. See Welch, *Black Litigants*.

century.[62] Claiming they were not slaves, the context-dependent and more explicit references regarding the invocation of "liberty" in Indian cases surfaced in complaints against forced personal service and excessive draft (forced) labor obligations. Freedom was also defined in these petitions as a sort of restricted mobility: not necessarily to be able to move around without restrictions but more narrowly as the right to return to live in their home pueblos after a stint of draft work. Once contracted labor became more widespread, the range of liberty (rights) was expanded and claims were made against forced retention of contracted labor that had been prescribed or for nonpayment of their labor. Indians also invoked a right to choose who they hired their labor to. The meaning of liberty kept expanding with time to encompass other practices and rights such as the ability to sell their goods freely in markets. More significantly, however, Indigenous subjects invoked liberty in corporate and political terms as the right to local autonomy and freedom from outside interference in community life. They also invoked it in political terms as liberty to choose freely in internal local elections.[63] These constituted local struggles with various results.

The badges of freedom deployed in positive terms in the cobreros' memorials included individual and collective forms of freedom too. According to the Madrid memorial, the natives of El Cobre acted as free by "fomenting their own haciendas, working on their own account [*trabajando para sí*] to provision themselves, taking care of themselves in their sicknesses."[64] These acts were concrete encapsulations of the abstract principle of dominion over one's self and one's property that translated into the right to own one's labor and to own property, as well as to own and care for one's body. But then, the memorial shifted to other kinds of freedom practices rarely mentioned in freedom suits and manumission letters, namely, "*exercising justice* in their pueblo" and "serving in *militias*," which wrapped up criteria of freedom into the context-based rule mentioned before: "In short, *executing* peacefully *everything that distinguishes free persons* [*personas libres*] *from those who are not*" (my italics).[65]

Freedom cases based on prescription rules are especially interesting for scholars because, like Indian liberty petitions, they suggested and

62 Owensby, *Empire of Law*, 130–66.

63 Owensby, *Empire of Law*, 224–27. They also deployed it as a right to only allow native Indians to stand for local elections.

64 Memorial Madrid, April 4, 1784, AGI-SD 1629.

65 Ibid.

generated debate on what constituted significant manifestations of freedom in specific contexts, particularly given the ambiguity of some practices. In any given disputed case, there may have been a mix of manifestations of freedom – or freedoms – which could have been argued one way or another. And when acts of freedom coexisted with those of slavery, which ones prevailed in the final reckoning of status? If, in the cobreros' case, for instance, rotating drafted forced labor requisitions coexisted with self-provisioning practices through their own farms, living on their own house and pueblo, and performing military service or exercising local justice, which actions had primacy in defining or prescribing status? Some of these conflicts over what acts counted properly as freedom (and who decides that) will come up in Chapter 5. Suffice it to point out here that many of these freedom badges – often understood as rights – were asserted and made explicit, as in the Indian cases, in the context of dispute and making claims.

COLLECTIVE PRESCRIPTION POLITICAL FREEDOM: THE STANDOUT ARGUMENT

The most significant and far-reaching formulation of the plaintiffs' collective freedom, however, came up in the memorial redacted by Simón Echenique in 1793. That memorial took a slightly different approach to the argumentation in support of the cobreros' freedom; or rather, it amplified the implications of some badges of freedom that remained barely sketched in the previous memorials. More than any other memorial in the dossier, the Echenique memorial parsed the relation between freedom and belonging to a municipal entity. Building on all the badges of freedom that the Madrid Memorial of 1784 had summoned as evidence of presumption of freedom, this memorial reconfigured them into a more powerful proposition based on collective corporate belonging. Furthermore, contrary to previous memorials where prescription played a secondary role to other legal instruments in producing freedom, the Echenique memorial foregrounded the force of prescription especially in relation to constituting a municipal body or pueblo. And unlike the other memorials, this brief distinguished between civil and political forms of freedom. The memorial parsed this distinction in ways that suggested larger questions about freedom rights that could be especially relevant in the case of racialized people of African descent in the colony.

Whereas previous memorials had simply agglutinated a range of acts (or criteria) that were presumptive of freedom, Echenique's brief made finer distinctions among them and ranked them as different kinds of freedom. "The settlement [*población*] of Santiago del Cobre then was composed of *free individuals* who had houses, plots of land, cattle; they had a temple where they went to hear the word of God; *they formed a parish*, paid tithes, were *organized into a municipal body*, *they governed themselves*. In a word, in addition to their *civil freedom* as vassals, they also enjoyed a *political* one" (my italics).[66] Whereas what the memorial called civil freedom entailed individual rights held by free vassals in general (domain over oneself and one's property) and guaranteed by the king's law, other rights manifested domain collectively as municipal bodies – as pueblos, villas or cities. Political freedom entailed self-rule and local sovereignty (however limited) in a municipal body or local republic, a collective actualization of the abstract principle of self-dominion. To some extent that was also the formulation of municipal or "town liberty" that Helen Nader examined in her study of early modern Castile and that I discussed before. Although the Madrid Memorial of 1784 mentioned "civil employments for the governance of their Pueblo" (a reference to cabildo and local self-rule), it listed it among other badges of freedom and did not parse its significance as the Echenique memorial did.

But was El Cobre a proper municipality? The Echenique Memorial indirectly addressed that question by turning aggregate customary practices into a series of specific political and legal criteria constitutive of a municipal entity. The *Siete Partidas* suggested what some of those normative criteria of municipal regime may have been when it specified basic requirements for naturalization or *vecindad* (residence or citizenship)in a locality. Crucial among the listed requirements was long-standing residence in the place, holding land and property in the locality, paying taxes, and performing collective duties such as holding office in a cabildo.[67] Those were the criteria applied in the passage above to El Cobre's case. Thus, beyond badges of civil freedom these were, more importantly, also badges of belonging in a municipal corporate regime. The plaintiffs' legal

[66] Memorial Echenique, Madrid, March 12, 1793, No. 11, AGI-SD 1627. The passage refers only to tithes; and while another in the same memorial also referred to the plaintiffs' payment of "taxes (*derechos*) to the royal treasury," there was no reference to tribute, the colonial tax imposed on Indians and, more erratically, on free Afro descendants in the empire. It is not known what kind of taxes the cobreros paid to the colonial state other than tithes.

[67] Nader also discussed the constitutive criteria of a Castilian pueblo as basically consisting in holding land, paying taxes, having a parish and, especially, establishing a cabildo (municipal government). *Liberty in Absolutist Spain*, 17–40.

action for freedom was entangled with the need to obtain juridical recognition of their pueblo, a particularly pressing requirement given the community's uncertain status as a pueblo of African descendants and royal slaves.

In another passage, the Echenique memorial parsed further the distinction between the two forms of freedom and used it to make an emancipatory argument of freedom that explicitly included political rights.

> In this sense, they [the plaintiffs] could not without the greatest injustice and violence be dispossessed of their freedom ... [because] this is a *political possession that supersedes the civil one* because it favors all in a single body and civil [freedom] only protects each one individually. The former [political freedom] is more encompassing and important attracting as accessory the others. Therefore, even if there were [individual] persons who were really slaves they would be *reputed free by virtue of the municipal body of which they formed part* (my italics).[68]

The argument above worked with corporatist notions entrenched in Spanish political philosophy throughout the Spanish Atlantic world where the municipal bodies were the collective cells of the political body and the center of political life, more important than the sovereign individual as in political liberal notions then circulating in the northern Atlantic world. Echenique's memorial upheld this normative discourse of local municipal corporatism and expanded it to apply to racially mixed colonial subjects and freed people of African descent (second epigraph). This memorial went on to explicitly invoke prescription through pueblo corporate belonging: "If the law only requires ten years for the prescription of individuals, what would it [require] in political bodies that govern themselves as free and [in one that] has governed itself longer in this way?"[69] The argument went beyond any of the softer prescriptive claims made in the previous memorials. Whether Echenique was also indirectly challenging the reach of the absolute monarchy by putting so much weight on an entity of local sovereignty rather than the individual freedom he linked to vassalage is unclear. Suffice it to focus here on the notion of political freedom rights that the argumentation put on the table – or to the court – and its implications for the cobreros and other racialized subjects in the empire.

A possible normative implication of Echenique's argumentation entailed that free people of African descent and racially mixed populations could constitute corporate communities of their own and in doing so

[68] Memorial Echenique, Madrid, March 12, 1793, No. 11, AGI-SD 1627. [69] Ibid.

enjoy political rights of self-rule as had allegedly been the case with the natives of El Cobre. Yet another possible normative implication was that free and freed people of color who were born and lived in other municipal bodies (say in the cities and towns considered Spanish republics) also formed part of those municipal entities and therefore (as natives and vecinos) had – or should have – political rights in them too. The latter formulation jumped in the face of political restrictions and disabilities that subjects of color endured due to *limpieza de sangre* (racial purity) laws in the colony. The Echenique memorial's argument either betrayed ignorance of colonial things or suggested an intentional racial blindness in the application of abstract political and juridical principles. In any case, wittingly or unwittingly, the memorial's argument may be said to constitute a form of judicial activism that presented an expansion or reinterpretation of colonial law and understandings. It remains an open question whether the memorial advocated political rights only for the cobreros as a special case or more generally for people of color in the empire.

To be sure, the notion of local self-government and political freedom in municipal bodies or local republics may have been more a political philosophical formulation than a generalized political practice in the Spanish empire at the time. Echenique's memorial did not make distinctions about the actual internal workings of municipal councils in Spain or its empire. Nor did it distinguish between active and passive local political freedom rights. It simply used the political institution of municipal self-government to expand the notion of freedom theoretically and juridically. And yet, there was possibly more at stake here. In the last decades of the eighteenth century there were debates in Spain and elsewhere in parts of the overseas empire about what modern scholars like Antonio Domínguez Ortiz referred to as the "decadence" of the municipalities and of general decision-making (*consejo abierto*) in these localities in Castile.[70] To be sure, local political rights were enacted in smaller municipalities of Castile where open meetings and elections for municipal office still took place and where even a form of local popular sovereignty may be said to have been at work since early modern times, if not before.[71] But in larger major Castilian towns and cities – and in the empire – local cabildos had long

70 Domínguez Ortiz, *Sociedad y estado*, 461–67; de Castro, *La Revolución Liberal*, especially 37–41, and for the sale of municipal and public office positions, 39–41.

71 Nader asserts that "democratic self-government" was the ideal and often the practice in towns, and citizens made important decisions in general council meetings, but she makes a distinction between small towns and cities. The latter were too large to maintain the democratic town meeting or even run elections. *Liberty in Absolutist Spain*, 8–12.

been controlled or even monopolized by elite families. Positions in these local governments had become proprietary and hereditary running across generations in some families. In effect, what existed were oligarchical forms of internal self-rule in these larger municipalities. Although, in their impulse toward centralization, the Bourbon monarchs tried to undercut municipalities and local institutions in the peninsula as well as in the overseas empire, some Bourbon reformers, among them the Count of Campomanes, wanted some municipal reforms that would at least open up some new positions in the peninsula to be filled by commoners. These minimal municipal reforms would allow the excluded commoners greater participation in local governance and would help break up what he called the "despotism of a few families" and perhaps as well help break local oligarchic power and resistance to other Bourbon reforms.[72] Several modest municipal reforms were mandated from above, starting in 1766, and during the 1790s, with uncertain outcomes.[73] But it was not until 1812, with the liberal Constitution of Cádiz, that a full (but alas short-term) reform of the municipal regimes in favor of local popular sovereignty (and a more encompassing higher level national one) took place in the Spanish empire (see Chapter 9).[74]

In the colonial world, especially in the military colonies of Cuba and the circum-Caribbean, military colonial officials represented a force that could exert more, although not total, control over municipal bodies or republicas. In the overseas empire, aristocratic control of municipalities in the Spanish republics was racialized and controlled by subjects of Spanish descent with *limpieza de sangre*, and members of distinguished families, as in the peninsula, were councilmen in perpetuity. In the Indian republics, these positions were "by ancient custom" often controlled by hereditary lords (*caciques*) and notables (*principales*), a situation in the Andean region that, according to recent scholars, had begun to be challenged from below by Indian commoners or "*el común*," especially since the mid- to late eighteenth century.[75] According to these scholars, this trend

[72] On Campomanes' view, see Domínguez Ortiz, *Sociedad y estado*, 466.

[73] Domínguez Ortiz, *Sociedad y estado*, 461–67. See also Marina Barba, "La reforma municipal de Carlos III," 249–91; and de Castro, *La Revolución Liberal*, 41–43.

[74] For Spain, see de Castro, *La Revolución Liberal*, 57–90. Nader argues that nineteenth-century Spanish Liberals supported the central role of the municipality, *Liberty in Absolutist Spain*, 11–12.

[75] Penry, *The People Are King*, 9–13; Premo, *The Enlightenment*, 159–90. The *Siete Partidas* provides three more general notions of *el común* that may have been redefined with time. It refers to what cannot be privatized, which encompasses the natural resources

represented a radical move toward greater popular sovereignty and local democratization. Premo even conceptualizes this trend as a manifestation of "popular Enlightenment" whereby old regime values such as ascription and hierarchy were called into question by subordinate groups.[76] Thus, despite Bourbon trends toward centralization and what Helen Nader refers to as the undercutting of municipal power and autonomy, reconfigurations of these bodies in a more democratic direction were taking place in some spots of the Spanish Atlantic, a trend that needs further research in all its variations and that may entail conflicts over expansion of local political rights.[77] El Cobre's case may be considered another instantiation of that initial democratization conflict trend in the Iberian world, perhaps an even more radical one given the racial profile of its inhabitants. The cobreros' case pushed letrados, such as Simón Echenique, to summarily theorize the situation and its implications in juridical and political philosophical terms.

In the case of El Cobre, a racially mixed pueblo constituted mostly by Afro descendants, an informal cabildo had existed on and off for almost a century, though its internal workings are unclear. That unorthodox cabildo had been suspended at different points in the past by governors who considered it an anomaly.[78] A request for information or interrogatory meant as evidence of established practices in the running of the pueblo made in 1792, indicated that there had been four perpetual regidores who (as elsewhere) annually elected four alcaldes: two ordinary in charge of internal justice, and two others *del Monte* (the equivalent to the *Alcaldes de la Hermandad* (rural constables) in Spanish republics)

enjoyed by "all creatures, those" to be enjoyed by all humans, and those whose use pertains to all the human inhabitants of a locality, "whether poor or rich," Book 3, Title 28, Laws 2–9.

76 Premo, *The Enlightenment on Trial.*

77 Helen Nader claims that the Bourbon dynasty in the eighteenth century not only tried to dismantle the power of municipal institutions but also to erase their memory as the basis of Castile's democratic tradition. They were successful in imposing new fiscal reforms, establishing intendants in the cities, undermining the jurisdiction of municipal judges and requiring royal inspection of local land management but not in completely undermining municipal administration. It was not until the 1870s that the municipalities were undermined by the creation of provincial level administrative units. *Liberty in Absolutist Spain*, 9–12. In the overseas empire, royal officials had always had a stronger presence in Spanish cities. Nader laments the erasure of the memory of the political significance of municipalities in the historiography of Spain where it is relegated to the medieval period.

78 Díaz, *The Virgin, the King*, 267–76.

who policed the rural surroundings.[79] Records indicate that cabildo members had been for the most part cobreros with the status of royal slaves who were enslaved in 1781 (Chapter 2). Thus, contrary to cities and towns in the peninsula, or Indian republics in the overseas empire, there was no aristocratic control of El Cobre's cabildo since the cobreros' ancestors had been enslaved people, not nobles, and they were also racialized subjects of African descent who were generally banned from holding such positions in the empire. And although there may have been undemocratic tendencies allowing some individuals to be perpetual regidores – among them Gregorio Cosme's alleged father José Cosme or families such as the Cosmes – or to control positions in the pueblo's cabildo due to their economic resources and military service, the crucial point is that all were commoners, in fact, commoners among the lowest commoners in the empire given their race and slave origin. Even if at times like the present crisis, the cobreros' common will lay outside the cabildo properly and was expressed in a parallel way by the apoderados and leaders acting on behalf of the natives of the pueblo, a cabildo of this kind in principle constituted a representation of local sovereignty and citizenship for the usually excluded non-Spanish and non-Indian subjects in the empire. Moreover, in this case the apoderados acting on behalf of the natives of the pueblo represented a common popular will that challenged colonial authorities' backing of the privatization of El Cobre. In any case, the Echenique memorial upheld the viability of this kind of local self-rule regardless of the racial standing of its members.

On a possibly grimmer note, however, these distinctions between civil and political freedoms also seemed to suggest that individual freedom and its attendant civil rights did not necessarily entail political rights of

[79] Interestingly, four cobrero "elders" (including the fifty-one-year-old Justo Cruzata) and four colonial military officials were interviewed. All eight agreed on these points and noted as well that the annual elections took place in the parish priest's house, thereby legitimizing the unconventional practice given the lack of a proper separate cabildo house in the pueblo that institutionalized self-rule in other municipalities. The comment also suggests the possible influence of the parish priest in the cabildo's affairs. As in other colonial localities, per the *Recopilación de Leyes Indias*, elected individuals had to be officially approved by the highest colonial royal official, in this case the governor of Santiago. According to the notary, the only point of difference among respondents was regarding the duties attributed to the two alcaldes del Monte. Three of the four colonial officials reported that they were used to apprehend fugitives or runaway slaves from the village or from private citizens in the city of Santiago, while the cobrero respondents either denied this point or did not mention it. Interviews, ca. 1790–92, Cuaderno No. 5, f. 19–21, AGI-SD 1627.

citizenship. This, of course, became a greatly debated issue regarding racialized subjects (gender was taken for granted) in postcolonial and post-abolitionist societies, especially in the United States during the Antebellum period but also in Brazil and elsewhere in Latin America. In Spain itself, these distinctions, especially in relation to racial identifications, reemerged decades later more explicitly in the Constitution of Cádiz of 1812 and its later iteration in 1821 (see Chapter 9). Whereas in those Spanish constitutions free people of African descent became Spaniards (natives of greater Spain) and their individual civil freedom rights were recognized, in contrast to Indigenous groups (who by law had lived in corporate polities), the former did not receive Spanish citizenship or political rights. In this sense, Echenique's claim that the cobreros (people of mixed racial descent) enjoyed and should be ratified in the enjoyment of local political freedom (as understood in the framework of absolute monarchy) was forward looking and its implications could possibly have extended to the later frame of the constitutional monarchy in a Spanish nation writ large.

The memorials' arguments for freedom show the potential of the cobreros' case for deliberating about freedom at the time. Echenique's memorial pressed farthest the possible implications of the cobreros' customary practices in the past as enactments of civil and political freedom rights. In so doing, it turned an interpretation about the past into a vision of the future using traditional Spanish corporatist political theory.

VIOLENCE AND ENSLAVEMENT

Finally, the third argument used in the memorials was based on the use of wanton violence in the execution of the Executory (Privatization) Order of 1779. Noting the distinct character of the argumentation, the Madrid Memorial of 1784 claimed that the "sacred rights of humanity and of the faithful vassals of the Crown were painfully violated *not* only *in the principal* [substantive] part of the [1779 privatization] orders but [also] in the *violent manner of their execution*" (my italics).[80] The transgression called for the immediate restitution of things to the status quo ante the dispossession before the violators' reasons could be even heard in court.[81]

[80] Memorial Madrid, April 4, 1784, AGI-SD 1629.

[81] This may have been an old juridical principle since it was also invoked separately in a seventeenth-century abolitionist treatise of Capuchin friar Epifanio Moirans, "Just Defense," in López García, *Dos defensores*.

Immediate restitution to the status quo ante 1781 was, at a minimum, what the three apoderado travelers aspired to in 1784, at least while the substantial claims to freedom, land, and pueblo rights were litigated.

The illegality of the violent assault and dispossession was dramatized in the memorial through the depiction of the enslavement of 1781 as a raid. That raid represented the final episode in the narrative of the rise and fall of a pueblo: the ruination of what had once been a prosperous pueblo in the overseas empire. The yoked themes of the violence of enslavement and the destruction of the thriving pueblo combined legal, moral, and policy/political arguments that, intentionally or unintentionally, also represented a potential antislavery critique, though one that could be mitigated in various ways. A brief that wanted to be judicially effective, especially in the Council of the Indies at the time, was not the ideal venue to advance direct antislavery arguments. At most, perhaps, briefs could make sly, indirect allusions to the calamities of slavery or its excesses and to the benefits and utility of freedom. Yet, although the critique could be mollified, the ambiguity of these arguments suggests their potential to become more radical given a more open political sphere or in private contexts.

The Madrid Memorial depicted the enslavement raid of 1781 as an act of spectacular violence, not unlike the accounts of some abolitionists.

> [On Aug. 1, 1781] the militias [of the pueblo] were assembled with the pretext of inspection [*pasar revista*] as was usually done. In the act, arms were cautiously taken away .... Once disarmed the principal heirs of Juan de Eguiluz who are [list of seven names] entered the pueblo backed by a competent number of troops and threw themselves with violence over the houses of those unfortunate ones. They tied all whom they could [*agreder*] and locked them up until little by little they extracted them with tied hands to various places so that in a few days they left no one in the pueblo who regardless of sex, age, or condition was not imprisoned and reduced to a harsh captivity with so much inhumanity that they did not allow them to take from their own houses the clothes of their use [personal property]. Afterwards they have been dispersing them all through other towns [*poblaciones*] of the Island and selling others in exchange for mules, oxen, and even dogs [*mastines*] without many husbands knowing the whereabouts of their wives, nor parents of their maiden daughters. Some have also been transported to foreign Islands to be sold to enemies of our Catholic religion.[82]

The passage portrayed the enslavement as an unexpected and unprovoked military raid led by the heirs against the innocent and unarmed population of El Cobre. Aside from the obvious physical violence of

[82] Memorial Madrid, April 4, 1784, AGI-SD 1629.

assaulting unarmed people in their houses, constraining their bodies, and forcefully removing them from the village, other injuries following the actual raid were also represented as forms of violence. These were all major antislavery themes; and even the use of animalistic tropes was common in antislavery rhetoric. Other critiqued forms of violence in the passage included the commodification of people and their sale as chattel, as well as the separation of families and the deportation of individuals to foreign countries, in this case aggravated by the sale of Catholic subjects to heretics. It is unclear if the latter was actually a legal prohibition that slave subjects could litigate in royal tribunals or if it constituted an innovative line of juridical argumentation for future cases. The separation of families, portrayed here in patriarchal terms, alluded not only to an unchristian dismantling of the family, but also to the hidden dangers of sexual violence unleashed by the enslavement raid and, implicitly, by slavery itself (or, in a mollified view, by unregulated slavery).

What became significant in this passage was the range of acts – many intrinsic to slavery – that were understood and denounced as forms of wanton violence. A possible implication of this line of argumentation was that if enslavement entailed these forms of violence it was a reprehensible, wicked, and even illegal practice. This radical line of argument had precedents in the antislavery treatises of two activist Capuchin friars who preached in Havana in 1681–82 and were deported to Spain due to their radical sermons.[83] A hundred years before the Madrid Memorial, Fray Francisco José Jaca and Epifanio Moirans, partly based their critique of African and Indian slavery on the use of violence. They challenged the legality of African slavery with the tools of scholastic juridical principles and rhetoric that Father Bartolomé de las Casas, sixteenth-century critic of Indian enslavement and treatment, had used before. Suffice it to call attention here to one of the fundamental juridical principles on which these Capuchin friars based their abolitionist critique. Wrote the Capuchin Fray Francisco Jaca: "Know that all this proposal [for slavery] is founded on the sand of the mentioned violence, and therefore should have no value, force, or substance. Because what has secretly or violently or for any other illicit cause been introduced should not be maintained on

[83] López García, *Dos defensores*. This work is a brief biography of these seventeenth-century Capuchin abolitionists and a study of their antislavery treatises argued in scholastic terms based on principles of divine and natural law and *ius gentii*. The work also includes translations of their essays written in Latin.

any firm basis."[84] And similarly Fray Epifanio Moirans: "The principles of law affirm that what has been introduced covertly or by force or in any other illicit way cannot subsist in any stable way."[85] This was also the basis of the Madrid Memorial's argument, if in more restricted terms. Jaca also addressed the issue of unprovoked violence when he asked: "What law gives them faculty to forcibly repel those who do no harm, extort, or do violence and who suffer the blame of a crime with the great inhuman penalty of slavery?"[86]

As mentioned before, the violence linked to enslavement in the Madrid Memorial included other injuries besides violent capture and plunder. Commodification of human beings as animals also constituted a form of deep violence, of the reduction of humans to animal status. Referring to enslavement raids in Africa, Fray Moirans made a similar point regarding the commodification of humans as animals: "At the moment of capture it all becomes like a hunt of animals and after capturing them they are sold like wild animals or beasts from the countryside and receive the treatment of beasts."[87] Enslavement also entailed other forms of violence such as deportation from local native soil and country, the separation of families, and the rupture of the community. The Capuchin friars agglutinated physical, material, social, and emotional injuries in their discourse and Moirans denounced them all as cruelties: "Once transported to the Indies ... [the enslaved Africans] are left without their goods, their parents, their local homeland [*solar patrio*], their freedom, and all consolation. And they are condemned to perpetual work."[88]

Yet subtly hidden in the Madrid Memorial's passage of the raid there were allusions to the indiscriminate enslavement argument raised elsewhere in the narrative. Indiscriminate – and therefore wrongful – enslavement of villagers was signaled through phrases such as capturing and tying up "all whom they could grab" or reducing to "harsh captivity" anyone "regardless of condition." These references could point to other directions. They could provide some ambiguity to the denounced violence in the enslavement scene by referring more narrowly to the indiscriminate use of violence against anyone and everyone in the village, suggesting there could be some who were legitimate slaves and against whom the violence of captivity could be selectively directed. In this formulation,

84 Jaca, "Resolution about freedom," in López García, *Dos defensores*, 145.
85 Moirans, "Just Defense," in López García, *Dos defensores*, 273.
86 Jaca, "Resolution about freedom," in López García, *Dos defensores*, 126.
87 Moirans, "Just Defense," in López García, *Dos defensores*, 210. 88 Ibid., 209.

these forms of violence could be construed only as a violation of a free subject's civil rights and not as a general illicit deployment of violence that could implicitly delegitimize slavery. Similarly, the intrinsic violence of slavery – the original captivity, the physical violence, the commodification and sale, the separation of families and communities – could be construed as extreme forms of "harsh slavery" and of "inhumanity" subject to regulation and mitigation by law and moral suasion. Not unlike calls today for more humanitarian treatment of prisoners or refugees or undocumented immigrants in detention, humanitarian discourse was – and continues to be – important as an invitation for altruistic behavior and as a palliative, but it does not address the fundamental principles and disjunctions at the root of the institution and its practices. In fact, it may deviate attention from them. The passage even provides a trivial instance of this mechanism when it highlighted the prohibition to even "take from their own houses the clothes of their use" as an illustration of the "inhumanity" of the raid. Would the enslavement, removal from the village, separation of families, and commodification and deportation by sale to other towns and countries be less inhuman if the villagers would have taken their personal goods with them?

Spanish ideology tended to mollify the problem of structural slave violence with an often formulaic "humanitarian" discourse using codes that called for the "good treatment" of slaves and other subordinate colonial subjects such as Indians. These were "humanitarian" codes that supposedly created a more bearable form of life in captivity, with the possibility of even breaking free of bondage, especially through self-purchase. The rest was necessary violence linked to the public utility of colonial production, public security, and property rights. And yet this palliative, humanitarian discourse was also important to make claims and to censor the most brutal and insensitive deployments of power. Despite the caveats of an arbitrary and indiscriminate enslavement argument, or of an inhuman and "harsh" use of force in the manner of enslavement, the violence intrinsic to slavery could not be completely mollified in this passage from the Madrid Memorial. Both strong and soft versions of the critique of violence of enslavement coexisted in an uneasy tension, and each could be pushed in either interpretative direction depending on context.

At times, the rhetoric of early abolitionist texts turned into a discourse of passions, heightened affect, and sin. The force of irrational passions could obstruct not only rational human discernment but clear moral action. In this Christian discourse, passions produced sinful disorder, lawlessness, devastation – and enslavement. Bartolomé de las Casas mobilized this rhetoric in his *Devastation of the Indies* and the Capuchin abolitionists also did so in their treatise. The Havana Memorial displayed it prominently too. Passions, according to the Capuchin abolitionists, were a portentous force behind the enslavement of Africans, which helped delegitimize it. "Everything proceeds from frenzied [*desenfrenada*] passion and therefore all slaveries are unjust, iniquitous and impious"[89] wrote Moirans. The Havana Memorial explicitly deployed this moral discourse of blinding irrational passions too: "The plunders are soulless people, they do not observe religion, as it has been seen they let loose their passions and since they are blind the heavenly light cannot penetrate in them and they operate without judgment, apprehending and stealing everything that their greed finds in their way."[90] This constituted a moral and religious indictment of the violence of the privatization and enslavement, a form of despotic and unlawful behavior that the memorial urged the Crown to check in the name of just imperial rule and rational governance.

The Madrid Memorial, using the more sober legal and enlightened language of the royal court, did not use the rhetoric of passions and used that of bestiality sparingly. And yet the language of affect and that of passions was part of the emerging abolitionist discourse in the northern Atlantic, which was also inflected by Christian religion. This rhetoric, in fact, is in some ways still with us today when accusations of hatred, greed, and ambition are linked to modern kinds of transgressions.

OTHER MANIFESTATIONS OF ANTISLAVERY DISCOURSE

Memorials and documents generated from legal actions provide a window into how broader discourses circulating in a locality penetrate into the space of the court. In the section above, I showed how the denunciations of violence against the plaintiffs, wittingly or unwittingly, converged with arguments related to the intrinsic violence of slavery undergirding antislavery discourses in the past and present, and to a potential criticism of the institution at a time that saw the expansion of slavery. This section examines the extent to which a rhetoric of antislavery slipped into this memorial in more modern formulations. Were there any philosophical or political allusions, for instance, to the natural rights

[89] Ibid., 25. [90] Memorial Havana, December 10, 1783, AGI-SD 1627.

of "man" or humanity, rather than to the rights of "free men" (regardless of race)?

Aside from an initial reference to the "sacred rights of humanity" in the memorial of 1784, there was no explicit reference to the progressive discourse of Enlightenment in the Havana Memorial or the Madrid Memorial of 1784. However, beyond the corporatist notions of municipal belonging constitutive of local political freedom discussed above, the Echenique Memorial of 1793 may well have addressed in other ways notions of freedom that may have been circulating among progressive circles in Madrid and trickling down into juridical discourse and briefs like this. Parsing the significance of freedom in concise and critical humanist, if patriarchal gendered terms, Echenique's memorial asserted that "Man without freedom, without the property over himself and of his understanding [*entendimiento*], is not a father, nor a husband, nor is he a relative [*pariente*], nor a friend, nor a citizen [*ciudadano*], nor a vassal, nor anything. He is an animal like any other destined to the labor of his master."[91] These were vivid words, used by abolitionists, that depicted the social death and degradation of the slave as a beast of burden. They contrasted the full life of the free man in society and the polity with the dehumanized, isolated, and depoliticized status of slavery. The "free man" here was not mainly a bounded sovereign individual subject, he was enmeshed in many social and political relations (and in the Iberian world, in corporations), including his family and his municipality. In contrast, a slave was only subject to the will of his master. The latter point was made more narrowly in terms of the dominion principle in the *Siete Partidas* as discussed before, although they could also be deployed in dominion terms as a father and husband, while in more equalitarian, though still gendered terms, as a relative, a friend, or a compatriot.

Echenique's memorial also foregrounded the rational character of "man" (his capacity for understanding) against the sheer brutal nature of animal life. He was making here a powerful foundational humanist argument against slavery, along the binary of (male) human/rational and animal/irrational so central to Western Christian discourse, including antislavery and Enlightenment discourses.[92] In line with modern liberal discourse, the Echenique memorial also placed at the center of its

[91] Echenique, Memorial, Madrid, March. 12, 1793, No. 11, AGI-SD 1627.

[92] This ideology is increasingly questioned today by ecologists and animal rights proponents whose discourses break the boundaries between human and nonhuman agents. See, for instance, Bruno Latour, *Down to Earth*, especially 56–58, 82–90.

formulation of individual freedom, and man's individual "property" rights (rather than a more ambiguous possession or dominium) over his body, his labor, and his self. In this formulation, man as a ciudadano (of a municipal body, as the term was understood then, and perhaps later as citizen of the greater nation) was also a (still gendered) political criterion of freedom and of being human. Was Echenique asserting that free men of color were entitled to political freedom as ciudadanos and to political rights too?

The Echenique memorial's formulations had an antislavery slant that may have reflected views appearing in the late 1780s nascent press of Madrid reporting on antislavery sentiment and organizations in Britain examined at the end of Chapter 2. While this press did not cover Spanish domestic or colonial manifestations of that sentiment, nor cases like El Cobre that could elicit public debate on questions of freedom and slavery in the empire, it shows that such discourses were circulating in some circuits in Madrid and the colony and perhaps merging with Spanish philosophical traditions of municipal corporations and political rights. Judicial briefs like these memorials caught echoes of these views and applied them to cases at hand. They also suggest how concrete cases could trigger further parsing of these notions.

FREEDOM, LAND, AND POLICY ARGUMENT

Finally, the memorials complemented the judicially and morally grounded argumentation for freedom with a policy oriented one too. Using the Enlightened pragmatic discourse of public utility and prosperity central to Bourbon thinking at the time, the memorials also made a case for the cobreros' freedom and their pueblo organization in pragmatic terms. Given the slave plantation regime that was becoming hegemonic particularly in Havana, El Cobre's constituted an alternative model of development and prosperity in the region.

The Echenique memorial, again, stood out by more explicitly emphasizing the benefits of freedom, land rights, and organization as a pueblo in producing benefits and utility to the state. Like other memorials, it noted El Cobre's population growth, its prosperity, and its utility to state and church. But this memorial connected these benefits more explicitly with a freedom-based discourse that subtly critiqued slavery and in fact openly advocated for freedom in general terms. The memorial wove the principle of freedom and its benefits around various episodes of the cobreros' narrative. For instance, in speaking about the pueblo's foundational history, when the ancestors of the present natives were the former mining slaves and Indians, the memorial glossed the alleged land grant their ancestors had received as a manifestation of freedom and corporate status that led to agricultural progress: "Since *the Indians* and *slaves* dedicated themselves to the cultivation of the distributed land; since they *obtained the benefit of being treated as men or attained their freedom* they prospered and formed a pueblo" (my italics).[93] Their civil freedom led to their prosperity and to political freedom. The memorial linked the possibility of acting as free men, with other implicit physiocratic arguments about the benefits and utility of population growth and wealth: "and in short since they began to experiment the *beneficial effects of civil freedom* they *multiplied themselves* in such a way and made such *progress* that in the year 1781, year of painful desolation, the population of that place had reached 6,000 persons of all sexes and ages," adding that "as proof of the *flourishing state* which that settlement [*población*] had attained, with *utility to state and church*, their decimal rents reached in four years, 70,000 pesos."[94] Again, the memorial repeated the same inflated figures presented in previous memorials, which became symbolic "facts" meant to highlight the links between freedom, population growth, material prosperity, and imperial utility. As mentioned before, this blooming prosperity could represent an imagined future under a civil and political freedom regime in the colony.

El Cobre's developmental model was based on free small cultivators creating population and wealth in the empire. In El Cobre's case, according to the plaintiffs' memorials, the wealth developed had been obtained through the industry of people of African and Indigenous ancestry who had built up the village. In this sense, El Cobre represented a different path to "progress" from that currently becoming dominant in the colonies. In fact, implicit in the memorials, and especially in Echenique's narrative of the cobreros' enslavement, there was a counternarrative, namely, that the growing trend toward the expansion of slavery and the heirs' ambition to enslave the cobreros had led to the destruction of the (inflated) "progress" that subjects living in freedom as a pueblo had attained before 1781. Against this imagined formulation of prosperity were the then dominant policies of colonial development based on plantation society and expanded slavery backed by the Council of the Indies, a model that had some critics in Santiago de Cuba and in Havana too.

[93] Echenique, Memorial, Madrid, March 12, 1793, No. 11, AGI-SD 1627. [94] Ibid.

A branch of antislavery discourse based on these ideas was also incipient in the island at the time. The new bishop of Santiago de Cuba in 1793, Joaquín Osés y Alzúa, who became a major advocate of the cobreros, held enlightened reformist ideas about economic development and had antislavery sentiments too. The bishop of Santiago advocated agricultural diversity based on small farmer property owners and the liberalization of trade. Rather than on religious or moral considerations, the bishop's critique of slavery was based on a modern utilitarian view about the inefficient and unproductive character of slave and landless labor.

> The greatest part of this island is composed of black slaves and mercenaries [landless laborers], who do not know any property and cultivate a land that is not theirs and whose fruits pass on completely to the hands of their owners. They only work out of the fear of the rod always raised over their backs [force] and if it disappears for a moment work is interrupted Can land prosper in the midst of the wrath produced by despair and the threats of force, dejection, abjectness and ignominy of slavery and under the raised rod of violence?[95]

Although the bishop did not publicly connect these views with the cobreros' freedom, he did strongly advocate for the preservation of the pueblo of El Cobre. El Cobre would have constituted an alternative model in yet another way. Whereas these physiocratic models based on small and medium farmers relied on the immigration of White *colonos* or settlers, mostly from the Canary Islands, the small and medium farmers of El Cobre were racially mixed natives. Why not grant land to this native population instead to advance this small property agrarian regime model?

The quiet small farming agrarian reformist language and critique in Echenique's memorial, and the critique articulated by the bishop of Santiago, was also present in the writing of the bishop of Havana, Juan José Díaz de Espada y Landa (bishop 1800–32). This bishop favored development based on free small proprietors: "agriculture can be had without slaves and it can be had with perfection. Therefore, slaves are not necessary," he wrote, adding that "so that agriculture flourishes the country must be composed of a greatest possible number of small proprietors and the slave trade is directed to the opposite ends."[96] The bishop did not mention race requirements for this class of agricultural proprietors, however. Did the category include free men of color too? Or mainly White (Canarian) immigrants? Díaz Espada also critiqued monocultural production reasoning that "far from producing utility, the ills [*los daños*]

[95] Cited in Irisarri Aguirre, "El informe del obispo."

[96] Bishop Juan José Díaz de Espada y Landa, "Informe sobre diezmos," 113.

grow each day and with time everything will consist of sugar mills and coffee plantations [*ingenios y cafetales*] with a scarcity of other crops [*frutos*] which will bring about a decadence in population and the island's ruination."[97] These late eighteenth-century and early nineteenth-century voices opposed to slavery and the plantation model were soon after overrun by the forces of the slave plantation regime, however.

Bold judicial and political arguments for collective freedom and political rights for racially mixed Afro descendant natives of municipal entities intersected in the cobreros' briefs with more utility oriented economic arguments for freedom based on alternate models of prosperity to the advancing slavery and plantation regime rapidly gaining ground in the island. The cobreros' unconventional case presented to the imperial court new challenges and novel ways of thinking about civil and political freedom based on Iberian corporate notions that could take on new spins. How the imperial court initially reacted to these and related arguments based on corporate native standing will be addressed in Chapter 5.

[97] Ibid.

4

Native Bonds, Native Rights

> Nativeness is one of the greatest obligations people can have with one another ... [it] converts them into a single unit through the long practice of loyal love. Nativeness is something which resembles nature and assists everything derived from it to exist and be preserved.
>
> —*Siete Partidas*, 13th c.

> El Cobre was composed in its beginnings of Indian *natives* of the country [*Indios naturales del Pais*] and some black slaves [*negros*] that were brought in by account of His Majesty to work in the mines of that place.
>
> —Madrid Memorial, 1784

In 1792, the enslaved cobrera Margarita González had the stonemason José Basilio Maestre summoned by the court in Sancti Spíritus as a witness to answer some questions about her. Although a native of Santiago de Cuba, Maestre was presently a resident (*vecino*) in the town of Sancti Spíritus in central Cuba (see Figure 0.1). Margarita González wanted him to confirm if she was a native of (*si era natural de*) Santiago del Prado El Cobre. Maestre responded that he knew that she "was born in the pueblo of El Cobre where he saw her, knew her, and treated her as a native from there [*natural de allí*]."[1] We do not know just what Maestre's exact words were or what he meant when he said that he "treated her" as a "native" from El Cobre. Encrypted in that phrase were local customary understandings of what nativeness or *naturaleza* meant, perhaps mixed with personal notions closely bounded to context. What the court notary wrote was an abstraction of the exchange. One thing was clear from his

[1] José Basilio Maestre, Sancti Spíritus, September 1792, in Autos Teresa Ramos alias Coba, No. 34, AGI-SD 1628.

statement, however, that birth in the pueblo was an important badge of local nativeness and so was established residence in the pueblo. Margarita González, in a petition of her own, elaborated the notion a bit further. Through her amanuensis, she said that she had been "born, raised and educated in a pueblo in the dominions of our Catholic monarch."[2] Her nativeness was linked not only to birth but to the bonds, relations, and practices that emerged from also being raised and educated since childhood as a member of a pueblo. That is, her subjecthood and her social and alleged legal persona were shaped by belonging to that location and to the community co-residing there. Moreover, Margarita's nativeness derived further legitimacy – and perhaps other rights and protections – from being located in the broader context of the Spanish empire and the Catholic faith, affiliations that were also important to make claims at the time and that may have been emphasized by her *letrado* amaneunsis. Margarita González also asked Maestre to respond regarding whether he had known her as enjoying her freedom, as if establishing a link between her local nativeness and freedom. Maestre confirmed that question too. He said that he "never knew her subject to servitude or slave of any person because generally she was reputed as free and acted as such."[3] Again, he did not specify what this "acting" as "free" consisted of, but it seemed to be linked to his treating her as a native of El Cobre with no private master. Another witness, this one himself a cobrero currently residing in Sancti Spíritus, informed the magistrate that "it is notorious in all the island that there have never been slaves among the natives of El Cobre."[4] Part of the reason may have been that nativeness in a pueblo and slavery did not seem to be compatible statuses and ways of life. The Echenique memorial of 1793, discussed in Chapter 3, parsed in some important ways the basis of that incompatibility. The cobreros and their attorneys played up this contradiction in their arguments in court and alluded to other rights and obligations that came with belonging to a pueblo. Local nativeness mattered – or plaintiffs and their letrados *made* it matter in presenting the cobreros' case.

The identification as natives of a pueblo (here of El Cobre) became a central subject position through which the plaintiffs implicitly claimed rights in court both in the colony and in Madrid. The term roughly corresponded to the vernacular "cobreros," a term of self-identification used by these villagers and also by others in the region to refer to them.

[2] Petition of Margarita González. Ibid.

[3] José Basilio Maestre. Ibid.

[4] Francisco Xavier Quiala. Ibid.

Recall from Chapter 2 Gregorio Cosme's own identification as a cobrero in signing a petition in Madrid with that moniker (see Figure 2.1). Similarly, Rafael Cosme, a leader in the pueblo, closed a letter to an apoderado in Havana by invoking his identity and authority as a native of El Cobre by writing "I bear witness as cobreros [*sic*] [*doy fe como covreros*]."[5] The vernacular local identity of "cobrero" was grafted into the more formal and official term "native of a pueblo" in petitions and court briefs to suggest belonging to a municipal body. In this sense, it was a vernacular identification and standing pressed on the court from life in the ground to make important legal and political claims – perhaps even to make law.

Although nativeness was a common identifier in colonial records, the significance of the category in the Spanish empire, beyond references to a general "Indianness" or a Spanish-American Creoleness, has, for the most part, not been sufficiently interrogated.[6] Assumed to be a mere descriptor of origin, there is little, if any, work examining its local manifestations and uses among racialized subordinate subjects in the Spanish colonial world. This chapter begins to address that gap through the cobreros' use of that identification to make claims as Margarita González's petition suggests but especially through their collective memorials.

The foundational medieval legal code of the *Siete Partidas* provides some basic guidelines to the widespread understandings of nativeness (naturaleza) in medieval Castile and later in the Iberian Atlantic world. Love for patria represented an identity rooted in local place and community that with time (and often simultaneously) could take on an expanded scope when applied to a province, a kingdom, an empire, or later to the modern nation.[7] Although general principles and norms found variations

[5] Rafael Cosme, El Cobre, July 27, 1784, f.1471v, AGI-SD 1627.

[6] On American creoles, see Brading, *The First America*; Cañizares-Esguerra, *How to Write the History*; Lavallé, *Las promesas ambiguas*; More, *Baroque Sovereignty*. On Indigenous communities and nativeness, see among others, the recent work by Penry, *The People are King*; Yannakakis, *Since Time Immemorial*; Herzog, *Defining Nations* and "Colonial Expansion." See Introduction.

[7] Although the main referent was the local pueblo or city, the term "nativeness," in principle, could also apply to broader entities such as kingdom (as Castile or Aragon or later America), province, country, nation (as in the Spanish nation), and even empires. At times, the entities covered by the term overlapped or the use of the term could expand and take on new meanings in different historical contexts. Herzog, in *Defining Nations*, has tracked the changing and expansive meaning of Spanish nativeness. Anderson's *Imagined Communities* is the classic study on the birth of modern nations, a book that has given rise to a vast literature. Today, it may be ventured that the ecological movement can expand or redescribe attachments that bind to dwelling place as a more encompassing

in space and time throughout the Spanish Atlantic, core meanings were retained across these variations and have some resonance, at least rhetorically, to this day. According to the *Siete Partidas*, nativeness was an important category of belonging that created strong bonds of love, loyalty, and obligation among those who shared a living space or territory in a political community (first epigraph).[8] So fundamental were these ties that they were considered to be analogous to other "natural" affiliations such as kinship (consider references to members of a community as "sons of a pueblo"). Nativeness in a locality was acquired primarily through birth and descent, but as Margarita González hinted at, it was also associated to the shared nurturing experience generated by co-residence and conviviality in a place – that is, by shared norms, memories, and practices. Although the *Partidas*' definition naturalized the social and affective ties created by belonging to a locality, the trope of natural bonds tends to conceal the constructed character of the category as well as its political and legal aspects.

Nativeness was linked to different political entities, and it entailed rights and obligations too. The earliest manifestation of this old category of belonging in Castile pertained to local municipal bodies: villages, towns, and cities. As discussed in Chapter 3, Helen Nader has shown the centrality of people's identification with municipal communities in early modern Castile and on into at least the nineteenth century.[9] The notion of the Castilian municipality traveled with Spanish colonizers to the New World model where it took different variations. In the overseas empire, these municipal entities became so-called Spanish and Indian republics.

Legal historian Tamar Herzog has pointed out that the legal and political meaning of categories of belonging such as naturaleza and *vecindad*, (domicile or citizenship) across the Spanish empire was not fixed. Moving beyond Nader's early modern corporate communities in Castile, Herzog focused on the construction of a supralocal sense of "Spanish" nativeness out of earlier medieval and early modern local notions and from the later transatlantic context of Spanish America.[10]

"terrestrial" based nativeness in the biofilm called the "Critical Zone" in Earth. For this kind of bonding metaphor with legal and political implications, see Latour, *Down to Earth*, 52–58, 78–99.

[8] Herzog, *Defining Nations*, 68, from *Siete Partidas*, Book 4, Title 24, Law 1.

[9] Nader, *Liberty in Absolutist Spain*, 8–11, 18, 27–45.

[10] Part of the legal meaning of Spanish nativeness in the overseas empire that Herzog examines through disputes in various localities was related to the rights related to

However, as discussed in the Introduction, in making the (changing) meaning of Spanish nativeness in the Spanish Atlantic the focus of her study, she passes over other non-Spanish racialized subjects' usages of the category of nativeness, especially in its local iterations.[11]

Despite her focus on the broader construction of Spanish nativeness in the empire, I find Herzog's performative approach insightful in other ways. Of particular interest is her methodological point that the actual meaning of these categories, and the rights and obligations attached to them, are best grasped in the context of dispute. I take Herzog's approach as a springboard to examine the customary and political meanings attached to local nativeness by racialized non-Spanish plaintiffs in El Cobre's case. As in the case of freedom, petitions, memorials, and documents generated in legal actions constitute apt venues to study the meaning range of this category and the rights attached to them by historical actors precisely because they constituted customary practices that lay in the interstices of the law. Even though these sources do not catch all the nuances of the vernacular meaning and uses of the term, documents such as the cobreros' memorials and petitions convey the intended legal and political meaning claimed in the dispute. That is, they show the legal "work" the term was called on to perform in the setting of the courts. These legal formulations – or reformulations – could also expand, and not only reflect, the vernacular usages of the term. In this sense, this chapter examines the legal and political uses that "non-Spanish" racialized subordinate plaintiffs such as Margarita González, and more generally the cobreros and their letrados, made of the term local "nativeness." Although my study remains focused on the plaintiffs' and other subjects' usage of the term at the local level of a pueblo, I also examine some supralocal references to nativeness that surfaced on the record. To be sure, the cobreros' case was sui generis, as were some of the rights they claimed through this subject position, but their case raises analogous questions

commerce, residence, and property of Spanish natives versus foreigners in the overseas empire and to the rules regarding how nativeness was determined and acquired. These criteria and rules were not too different from those laid out in the *Siete Partidas* regarding local Castilian municipalities. See the *Recopilación de Leyes de Indias*, Book 9, Title 27: "Of the Foreigners who move to the Indies, their composition and nativeness [*naturaleza*] that they can acquire there to trade and contract."

11 For instance, although Herzog examined what it meant to be a Spanish "native" in the Spanish republic of Caracas, she did not interrogate what it may have meant to be a Black "native" or "vecino" of that city. In playing up the legal significance of nativeness, Herzog plays down its cultural significance. Both kinds of meaning were present as the cobreros' case shows.

about how racialized subjects living in the more common setting of the Spanish republics may have mobilized this category of belonging to make similar or other kinds of claims.

Although Herzog's book examines "nativeness," "vecindad" and "vassalage" to the king, I focus here mainly on "nativeness" with a more cursory look at the plaintiffs' usage of "vassalage." While the first two categories allegedly entailed horizontal bonds of solidarity and obligation among people living as a community, the latter entailed a vertical bond or pact with the king with attendant protections and duties that were often based on an economy of service and rewards. The terms "vecindad" and "naturaleza" were closer to each other and, according to Herzog, by the seventeenth and eighteenth centuries they tended to overlap (though their relation on the ground needs further study). I focus only on nativeness because it was the term mostly used in the cobreros' memorials and petitions and because it referred to a more "primordial" attachment to place through birth and descent than vecindad. In any case, nativeness, in this case, entailed as well vecindad as Margarita González' gloss of her nativeness to El Cobre at the opening of this chapter shows.

But the term "native" had yet another meaning in the context of Spain's American empire where it could also refer broadly to Indian nativeness or Indigeneity in the Indies. The second epigraph, taken from the Madrid Memorial, asserts that in the origins of El Cobre "Indian natives of the country" (indios naturales del país) and "some black slaves [*negros*]" worked and resided in the mines of that place: their descendants subsequently became natives of El Cobre. In this formulation, African slaves became natives of El Cobre. This double ancestry opened other possibilities for anchoring the term in another regime of colonial plural law. In this chapter, I also explore ambiguous references made to Indian ancestry and their use in the briefs to make legal claims to freedom, land, and pueblo within the framework of colonial Indian laws.

Whereas in the first part of the chapter, I examine the social, legal, and political meanings of local nativeness within a Castilian/Spanish discursive framework, in the second part of the chapter I shift the focus to an interrogation of the term's meaning and usage in relation to Indigeneity. Given the cobreros' uncertain standing as a pueblo of colonial subordinate African descendant subjects and former royal slaves, a claim to Indian native standing could secure certain protections and rights for the cobreros that Indian natives had by law. On the other hand, the Indian legal framework also entailed special burdens and constraints in freedom derived from Indian subjects' colonial standing. To be sure, these were legal regimes that were subject to contestation and negotiation on the ground. I argue that the category of "natives of El Cobre" ambiguously straddled the plural Castilian/Spanish and Indian legal regimes in trying to open spaces in the law to accommodate the aspirations of other racialized natives in the Spanish empire. I close the chapter with a brief examination of the vertical and more formulaic category of vassalage to the king that was also politically invoked by the plaintiffs to make claims, in this case in a complementary way.

MAKING CLAIMS AS NATIVES OF A PUEBLO

Although birth and descent from parents in the jurisdiction constituted the main (and most "natural") way to claim nativeness in a place, there were according to the *Siete Partidas* other ways in which naturalization – or acquiring native standing – could be acquired. Herzog pays special attention to the openness of local communities to recognize nativeness through prescriptive actions and their implicit public validation. These naturalization paths, which were also related to vecindad, included marriage, residence for at least ten years, holding land and property in the locality, paying taxes, and performing duties.[12] Particularly relevant to El Cobre's case, and to slave societies in the empire, were two other paths for acquiring local native standing also listed in the *Siete Partidas*: rescue from captivity and emancipation. Although not mentioned again as a path to native standing in subsequent sources, emancipation explicitly

[12] Herzog states that the *Siete Partidas* listed ten ways of becoming a native, with birth at the top. Other paths to the acquisition of native standing included Christian conversion, becoming a vassal of the king, nurture (*crianza*) (in a place and community), and inheritance. It also lists emancipation and rescue from captivity (or slavery), death, or dishonor as ways to obtain nativeness, thus apparently implying it required free status. Birth and prolonged residence continued to be the main criteria in later periods once many of the previous ones that were appropriate in another historical moment faded away. Herzog, *Defining Nations*, 68–70. Similar, if perhaps more stringent, requirements related to naturalization and residence of foreigners (*extranjeros*) in the Indies were explicitly stated in the *Recopilación de Leyes de Indias* (Book 9, Title 27, Laws 10, 13, 15, 27, 28, 31). Law 28, for instance, highlighted the importance given to birth in Spanish territory when it declared that any child (*hijo*) of a foreigner who is born in Spain has a "truly [Spanish] origin [*es originario*] and a native of it [*natural de ella*]." And Law 31 was explicit about naturalization requirements for foreigners. Stipulations (that may or may not have been observed in practice) included having lived for twenty years in the kingdoms of Spain or in the Indies and ten with a household and real estate property. Other possibilities included marriage to a native or to a daughter of foreigners born in Spanish kingdoms or in the Indies.

reappeared as a possible path to Spanish nativeness in the Cádiz Constitution of 1812 (Article 5), this time, however, the reference was to a supra local Spanish nativeness across the empire (see Chapter 9). This point suggests that although enslaved people were not considered natives, freedmen and -women could become natives of a locality and presumably share bonds of solidarity and duty with other members of the place regardless of their tainted past. Acceptance of this norm in earlier times may not have been general though. Although there were general norms suggested by royal legal codifications such as the *Siete Partidas*, pueblos, towns, and cities developed their own local practices and rules (*fueros*), so there were many variations across municipalities in Castile. Communities in the overseas empire (both Spanish and Indian) followed the same general patterns of Castilian ones but had an even wider array of variation regarding natives' rights and obligations.

The term "natives of the pueblo" in the case of El Cobre had been invoked to make claims at an earlier historical moment. Ties to patria and pueblo had surprisingly been claimed by the former mining slaves as early as 1677, soon after the Crown embargoed the mines from the private contractors, when the possibility of sale and removal of the mining slaves initially arose. I have examined the unusual petition of 1677, whereby Juan Moreno, "*negro criollo* [creole slave] and native of the mines of Santiago del Prado" submitted a petition in which his amanuensis made claims to love of patria and pueblo to forestall, at least morally or by custom, the removal, sale, and relocation in Havana of the slaves who had worked in the mining settlement for years.[13] That petition shows how the discourse of "love for pueblo" and patria had already been boldly deployed on behalf of enslaved subjects who claimed to be living as a pueblo – or at least aspired to do so. But the mining estate's slaves – not yet "cobreros" – also asserted that they would seek their coartación in the subsequent years (which only some eventually did).[14] Given political interests behind the scenes, which included retaining a labor force in Santiago de Cuba for public works and fortifications (as well as for the personal use), authorities accepted Moreno's petition and the former

[13] Díaz, *The Virgin, the King*, Chapter 3. For the document where these notions are deployed, see Díaz, "To Live as a Pueblo," 126–41 and especially 135–37.

[14] This petition also listed some services the slaves of the mines had performed for the colonial state. It included services during military emergencies and also mentioned that they had helped return runaway slaves to the colonial state. This last service was not listed in later years and was never mentioned in the memorials of the 1780s and '90s. Nor was it mentioned by "elder" cobreros in an interrogatory in the 1790s (Chapter 3).

mining slaves were not removed from the mining jurisdiction and were incorporated into the Crown's imperial defense and labor system.

That petition and the negotiation that it triggered may be said to have constituted an informal foundation of the unorthodox community that emerged in the midst of this mining jurisdiction. Although freedom through coartación had not been formally obtained yet, but only intended, perhaps the petition cast the mining slaves' request as a variation of the "rescue from captivity" or "emancipation" paths to naturalization listed in the *Siete Partidas* as discussed above. In any case, the invocation of the discourse of love and local patria had first taken place, a century before, in the 1670s, during a transitional and uncertain period regarding the status of the derelict mining settlement, when its 275 former mining slaves constituted a parish in the jurisdiction at most. However, with the passing of years, the vernacular term "cobreros" became associated with birth and descent in the emergent pueblo of El Cobre (rather than to, say, an occupational status as copper workers in the old mining site). As the community grew and consolidated as an informal pueblo, its inhabitants, despite their status as royal slaves, were referred to as natives, and sometimes vecinos, of a pueblo apparently without much ado. In 1745, for instance, the parish priest Juan Jacinto Silva identified Martina Rodríguez in the baptism record of her daughter as a "parda slave of the king, native and vecina of this pueblo."[15] However, the customary compatibility between local nativeness, vecindad, and royal slavery of former times was called into question after 1781. Nativeness in a pueblo was then resignified in the cobreros' judicial petitions and texts, both in the colony and in Madrid as a standing indicative of free status.

Indeed, the reformulation of local nativeness as presumptive of freedom became one of the most remarkable – and controversial – aspects of this case. Nicolás Mancebo, a relative and apoderado of the heirs, protested that judicial move when he complained that by using "*the single* general voice *of being from El Cobre*, and by their refusal of servitude, they all want to destroy an action as real as the transfer of their slavery [to the heirs] which was [legally] made with the intervention of so many [royal] Ministers" (my italics).[16] Whether the imperial state and its courts recognized or denied the cobreros' collective standing as (free) natives of

15 Baptism record of Margarita González, Santiago del Prado, March 7, 1745, f. 317v–18, Autos Teresa Ramos alias Coba, Sancti Spíritus, 1792, No. 34, AGI-SD 1628.

16 Petition of Nicolás Ambrosio Mancebo, Havana, April 25, 1788, Autos No. 39, AGI-SD 1628.

El Cobre is a separate question that will be discussed in Chapter 5. The point here is that the cobreros pressed their standing as natives on the courts to claim freedom and other rights and that collective litigation became one way to juridically enact their communal bonds. The following opening of a petition filed in Santiago by local community leaders acting as apoderados made explicit the kinds of overlapping "natural" bonds that bound the plaintiffs to each other and entitled them to act on behalf of the enslaved: Justo Cruzata, Martín Salazar, Buenaventura Cosme, and Gregorio González "give voice to the miserable enslaved natives of the pueblo of El Cobre, our brothers, relatives, friends, and *compatriots,* claiming their freedom" (my italics).[17] "Compatriots" explicitly referred to the bond created by birth and co-residence in a local patria (homeland). But this manifestation of primordial bonds of love and solidarity as natives of El Cobre, this collective act of assertion in court that attempted to overwrite official distinctions between slaves and free in the community, became a strongly contested issue.

The heirs disputed the cobreros' collective standing as natives to make claims in a petition to the governor of Santiago: "Is it not possible [to stop] the impudence and boldness [*atrevimiento y osadía*] with which they represent and the perverse influence and corruption of our slaves?" And added, "What right, action or standing [*Qué derecho, acción, ni facultad*] does Martín Salazar [the cobrero apoderado in this case] has to come or go or contradict in his cited [brief] the possession or dominion of our slaves, nor what motive does this tribunal have to permit him with so much impunity to go, pass and contradict [*que vaya, pase y contradiga*] our rights so many times mandated [*executoriados*]?"[18] The heirs basically claimed that their property rights forfeited the cobreros' right to act in common based on their "natural" communal bonds of "love" as a pueblo, a social and ideological formulation that went to the heart of the conflict.

The resignification of native standing in El Cobre took on other important legal and political implications after 1781. As discussed in Chapter 3, Simón Echenique's memorial of 1793 made a collective prescriptive case for freedom based on the legal and political incompatibility

17 Petition of Justo Cruzata, Martín Salazar, et al. Santiago de Cuba, February 3, 1792, No. 33/41, f. 271–75, AGI SD 1629.

18 Petition of Manuel Garzón, Bernardo Mancebo, Santiago de Cuba, August 31, 1791, Autos Cuba, No. 6, f. 1010v– 14, AGI-SD 1629.

of slavery with belonging to a municipal entity. According to that memorial's argumentation: "If man individually is presumed to be free, with how much more reason should [freedom] be presumed in [the case of] a villa, community, political body, or municipality composed of many governing themselves and forming within the state a civil society [*y forman en el estado una sociedad civil*]."[19] Native standing in a pueblo both entailed and produced freedom. But this freedom was also contingent on juridical recognition as a pueblo.

The juridical rationale for the claim that the cobreros constituted a pueblo became explicit in a petition drafted in Santiago in 1791. In this document, native apoderados of El Cobre protested "reverently once and as many times as *derecho* [the law] allows us to claim ... our damage [*perjuicio*] ... of having been despoiled of our Pueblo acquired by force of our labors, [and] by law and custom [*derecho y costumbre*]."[20] The petition grounded the pueblo's legitimacy and right to exist juridically in a combination of customary law, the social practices of living together as a community, and the labor invested in the cultivation of land and the creation of the material infrastructure of a pueblo.[21] These actions, rather than, say, any royal charter or edict granting official permission to establish a municipal entity, had the force to prescribe possession of land and settlement through occupation. Especially interesting here was the allusion to the pueblo's legitimacy based on *costumbre* (custom) and their own work, implicitly an argument of prescription, although without specific reference to time limits nor to "ancient" or "immemorial" custom. This petition was redacted in Santiago, possibly in the bishopric of that city, and was directed to the captain general, not to the Council in Madrid. Although the Madrid Memorials made references to possessing the land in the pueblo and working it with the sweat of their labor, they also suggested that the land had been granted by a vague royal edict (Chapter 3).

Gregorio Cosme understood well the importance of obtaining judicial recognition as a corporate entity in tandem with obtaining civil freedom.

19 Memorial Echenique, Madrid, March 12, 1793, No. 11, AGI-SD 1627.

20 Petition of Gervasio de Castro et al, Santiago Cuba, August 25, 1791, f. 257v–65v, AGI-SD 1628.

21 Some of these precepts may have been based on old scholastic jurisprudential views. For instance, the influential seventeenth-century Spanish jurist Francisco Suárez held that usage ensured possession rights by natural law so that anyone who occupied a plot of land could possess it as his own while he used it. See also Suárez's view on the constitution of political corporate communities in Tierney, *The Idea of Natural Rights*, 308–12.

In Madrid, he pushed the claimed status of "pueblo" to one of "*villa*" or town. The title of villa referred to a corporate jurisdiction entailing even greater autonomy and prestige than a pueblo, at least symbolically.[22] Although racial disabilities to obtain villa status (or for that matter pueblo status) were not explicitly mentioned (they were overlooked or bypassed), the upgrading effectively ratified El Cobre's standing as a municipal body constituted by Afro descendants and racially mixed natives and vecinos. Cosme highlighted the significance of the shift to villa status when he reminded the community: "And who has been the cause that the Villa [of El Cobre] is given value? I, because if any other among you would have come would have never gotten Pueblo nor Villa nor would he have gotten or attained freedom, because there is no Author who can convey the work it has cost me."[23] We do not know what kind of negotiations he faced to obtain the title or what all the work he mentioned entailed. Aside from the central role he assigned to himself in this juridical achievement, this comment shows not only his awareness of the augmented "value" that the status of villa conferred upon the community but also that his political and legal activism in Madrid consisted in obtaining both freedom and official recognition of the cobreros' informal and customary corporate status. References to El Cobre as the "villa of El Cobre," instead of the "pueblo of El Cobre," began to appear in legal paperwork, in informal references, in plaintiffs' petitions, and in the parish priest's letter below. It is not clear if, when, and how that title was formally granted, however.[24]

This upgrading of nativeness in a pueblo to a villa provided a firmer ground for the cobreros' freedom (and according to Nader it constituted an important actualization of corporate emancipation or liberty in Castile for which pueblos were willing to pay the Crown considerable sums). The villa title also offered a more prestigious identity to the cobreros, particularly given their racially vulnerable status as villagers of African descent.

[22] This upgrading to town status (*villazgo*) through a collective purchase to acquire greater autonomy or liberty in Castile was the focus of Nader's study in *Liberty in Absolutist Spain*. See also Domínguez Ortiz, *Sociedad y Estado*, 455. In Mexico, this aspiration for autonomy was also reflected in Indian pueblos legally seeking separation from the jurisdiction of their cabecera towns, although whether purchases were involved is unclear. For examples, see Yannakakis, *Since Time Immemorial*, 191.

[23] Gregorio Cosme, Madrid, October 6, 1795, No. 75, f. 195–207, AGI-SD 1629.

[24] Although there is no extant record, it is possible that the cobreros had to purchase the title of villa (perhaps through loans). Sales of "villa" title, according to Nader, went on until the late eighteenth century under the Bourbon regime when the Crown was strapped for cash. *Liberty in Absolutist Spain*, 119–20.

The apoderado of the nearby Indian pueblo of El Caney, who years later petitioned for the title of villa for that pueblo, parsed the significance of such an upgrading of collective status as follows: "Nothing has so much interest for a humble and dejected pueblo than a new title ... because it produces a certain noble disposition with which extraordinary advantages are obtained for political matters (*la política*) and for education and from this surges a certain self-pride (*amor propio*) that makes many fathers of families remain in the place of their birth who perhaps would abandon it due to contempt for the name of pueblo."[25] A grant of villa "contributes to make it more considerable in the [public] opinion and acquire thereafter even more honorable titles."[26] In the case of El Cobre, the initial aim of obtaining recognition as a pueblo mutated into the stronger one of being promoted to a villa (of free people of color), an even more significant corporate claim in the case of African descendants. In principle, the status of villa would have even emancipated El Cobre from subordination to the cabecera of Santiago de Cuba (a doubtful proposition in this case), or more likely in this case, from the heirs' claims of domain, as the parish priest noted below.

Linked to the resignification of their status as free natives of El Cobre and to the defense of their communal bonds as a villa, there were other concrete political and material concerns. There was, for instance, an aspiration to protect the villa's control over resources such as land and its local sovereignty from private appropriation by the heirs. The following memo written by the new parish priest, Father Paz y Ascanio, to the bishop upon taking possession of his new ministry in 1793, almost twelve years into the conflict, made reference to some of those local concerns. In the letter, Father Paz eschewed the question of collective freedom of all the natives of El Cobre (although behind the scenes he aided the cause of freedom), but he was adamant about the conservation of what he considered to be the community's corporate rights as a villa:

Among the things I am learning in this my new parish that should be put under your consideration is the following. The gentlemen Garzones and Mancebos [the heirs] consider themselves *absolute lords* not only over the neighboring *land* but over *the plots of the houses in the pueblo too* and therefore they expect the cultivators of any class and condition to pay them a *high rent* [for land and house

[25] Letter to the Governor of Santiago de Cuba, El Caney, February 28, 1817. f. 81v–82. AHN-Ultramar 1647. The letter claimed it benefitted the Crown through the income derived from purchases.

[26] Ibid.

> plots]. I do not recognize the [possession] rights of these gentlemen ... [given that] the same settlement is recognized *as a villa*, and [as such] should be *realenga* [public] and therefore have *right to its own soil* and oxygen (my italics).[27]

The parish priest's views about the villagers' rights to land, autonomy, and control over resources illustrates well the meaning of corporate liberty and rights. In this formulation, villas were not private holdings: access to land for its members should be as free as air (a natural right necessary to preserve life). In that sense, Father Paz challenged the legitimacy of the privatization of the village and its land asserting the municipality's corporate sovereignty over its resources. The priest did not, however, refer to how land was held internally by villagers, as private property (alongside some common pasture and forest land) as in Spanish republics or in full communal usufruct as in Indian pueblos. He only alluded to corporate holding rights vis-à-vis any private external contender such as the heirs. He also unyoked villa autonomous land rights from racial considerations. Paz y Ascanio even insinuated that the king could not legislate against those established corporate rights. Although the priest did not use or base his claims on "nativeness" per se (he referred to "inhabitants" and "cultivators" instead), at stake were major issues that were part of the cobreros' vernacular claims through municipal corporate belonging as natives of El Cobre.

Finally, the Madrid Memorial of 1784 also alluded directly and indirectly to other rights that it associated with nativeness. Suggested in the memorial was also the right to reside and stay put in one's local birthplace. The memorial protested that in their wrongful enslavement, the cobreros had been "*extracted from their patria*, dispossessed of their goods which they had acquired with their own sweat and that of their parents, and *dispersed through foreign countries*."[28] In decrying the cobreros' forced removal from the village and calling it an "expatriation," the memorial asserted the cobreros' native standing and the natural right to live in their local patria, the pueblo and land of their naturaleza. Forced removal from one's local patria meant disruption of all the "natural" bonds of love and local territory that constituted them as a community and the political rights that such a corporate standing entailed. Furthermore, local expatriation and deportation from the larger native country to "foreign countries" were regarded here as violations of the

[27] Alexandro Paz y Ascanio to Bishop Osés, El Cobre, December 25, 1794, AGI-SD 2229.
[28] Memorial Madrid, April 4, 1784, AGI-SD 1629.

plaintiffs' natural rights as natives, as free subjects, and as royal vassals too.[29] This natural right (based on natural bonds of love) to stay put as a native of a locality (or even a country) seems to have been an important right in the Spanish Atlantic that free, racialized subjects were able to claim, a point, however, that may merit further research regarding how the right was invoked in concrete situations.[30]

Larger questions about native and citizenship rights emerged years later in discussions leading to the Cádiz Constitution of 1812 in Spain, to the Brazilian constitution of 1820, and to those of other postcolonial Spanish American republics too.[31] In some southern slave states of the American Republic, emancipation laws became particularly harsh in the antebellum South when requirements began to be imposed stipulating deportation from the state as a condition for individual emancipation.[32] These laws refused to recognize basic natality rights to newly emancipated African descendants in the state polity. Furthermore, a large-scale movement for colonization of Sierra Leone advocated the self-deportation of free Afro-Americans not only from the state but from the greater nation too. Native standing and its related rights, therefore, constituted a legally and politically charged category of belonging throughout slave societies in the Americas at the local municipal level and at times in larger more encompassing configurations of the polity such as states and nations.[33]

29 In some abolitionist discourse, bonds of nativeness and natural freedom barred enslavement and removal from Africa. The seventeenth-century abolitionist Capuchins Moirans and Jaca discussed in Chapter 3 alluded to this point. Similarly, in 1786, the British abolitionist Thomas Clarkson also alluded to the significance of social ties to homeland when referring to the deportation of Africans. He parsed the general meaning of nativeness in moral terms as follows: "What then must be their sufferings, to be forced forever from their country, which includes them all? Which contains the spot in which they were born and nurtured; which contains their relations and friends; which contains the whole body of people, among whom they were bred and educated." Clarkson, *An Essay on the Slavery*, 35.

30 Indigenous subjects, for instance, were subject to temporary removal from their villages for mita and repartimiento purposes. Owensby finds that in their amparo petitions the right to return to their home villages after excessive time was framed as a freedom right and only in one case did he find a reference to "patria" that would allude to a patria discourse, *Empire of Law*, 147–51.

31 Grinberg, *A Black Jurist*, 41–54. More generally, see Andrews, *Afro-Latin America, 1800–2000*, 85–115.

32 De la Fuente and Gross, *Becoming Free, Becoming Black*, 148–53, 158–71.

33 For a thorough study of this point in Antebellum Baltimore, see Martha Jones' book, *Birthright Citizens*.

NATIVES, COUNTRYMEN, AND IMPERIAL SUBJECTS

Other categories of native belonging beyond the local municipal level also surfaced in memorials and depositions. This did not mean that more capacious notions of belonging dislodged or displaced local ones associated with pueblo or villa, however. On the contrary, they could coexist or be alternately invoked in different contexts. The case of El Cobre brings up some examples of how scaled-up identifications could work and be politically mobilized along local ones by subordinate "non-Spanish" colonial subjects or on behalf of them.

Broader meanings of native belonging beyond the local level were politically mobilized, for instance, in the Havana Memorial of 1783. Drafted in the colony, and the original probably in Santiago, the Havana Memorial reflected local usages of terms better than other briefs produced in Madrid. In this case, the scope of local nativeness and the solidarities it entailed was scaled up to the broader category of *país* (province or country). Terms like *circumvecinos* (neighbors) and *paisanos* (countrymen) made their appearance in this memorial and were used to denounce the moral, social, and perhaps legal offense of enslaving people construed as "neighbors" or natives of the same país (despite racial differences): "All of these [heirs' names] ... are cubanos, [natives of Santiago de Cuba] and as powerful people they have adjudicated to themselves the people of El Prado [aka El Cobre] as theirs."[34] The memorial posed questions about the proper political, moral, and legal relation between natives of neighboring municipal communities: "In view of such an assault [*atentado*], can the most stupid [*estólido*] understanding conceive as proper and legal the pretended right against the natives of El Cobre by the cubanos, their neighbors and paisanos?"[35] In this formulation, nativeness-based bonds at any scale trumped status and racial divisions where they existed. Despite the implicit racial status of the natives of El Cobre, paisano solidarity bonds could not be ruptured, especially through captivity.

An even more significant example of a supra local claim to nativeness, but in this case to Spanish nativeness, was mobilized by a racialized non-Spanish colonial subject. The reference came from Valentín Saavedra during a deposition in favor of the cobreros. Saavedra, a free Black tailor native of Havana who resided in El Cobre at the time of the cobreros'

[34] Havana Memorial, December 10, 1783, AGI-SD 1627. [35] Ibid.

mass enslavement, volunteered a memory about the day when Governor Zéspedes went to El Cobre to officially hand over the cobreros to the heirs.[36] "That day," Saavedra recalled, "seemed as if a trial [*de juicio*] was taking place and he heard Governor Zéspedes say publicly that he was handing Spaniards over to Spaniards [*estaba entregando españoles a españoles*]."[37] To Saavedra, and allegedly to Governor Zéspedes, the cobreros, were not (African) aliens and stateless people, but imperial subjects, like other Spaniards, protected by the Spanish Crown and laws who could not be enslaved. It is interesting that Saavedra attributed those words to Governor Zéspedes, the interim governor of Santiago who had initially put a stay on the enslavement orders (see Chapter 1). What the governor or Saavedra meant politically, legally, culturally, and perhaps racially by "Spanishness" is left unsaid. But minimally, to be a Spaniard was to have legal and political immunities that precluded forced removal from patria and the degradation of enslavement. The governor's comment may have also referred to the cobreros as *españoles* by analogy: as people living in a municipal body like Spaniards did in their own republics. In this formulation, the cobreros were explicitly inserted in a Castilian/Spanish framework of nativeness. "Spanishness" may have also referred in Zéspedes' (and Saavedra's) conception of patriotic loyalty and military service, as well as to natality rights, and perhaps to other belonging criteria such as Christian affiliation and other shared cultural traits like language. The reference to Spanish status by the Black tailor Saavedra may have also been a vernacular claim by a free subject of color to equal standing with Spaniards, here authorized by placing the remark in the mouth of a governor. (The comment seems to have previewed the 1812 Constitution of Cádiz' extension of Spanish nativeness to all subjects born in the lands of the Spanish empire, including freed people of African descent.) Contrary to the prevailing norm in the colony where Spanishness entailed *limpieza de sangre* (purity of blood), Spanishness in this formulation did not have a racial marking nor did it depend on purity of blood. Saavedra, or Zéspedes, either intentionally elided racial markings from the larger category of españoles and thereby made a political assertion of a de-racialized meaning of Spanish nativeness or perhaps suggested that, as light pardos, the cobreros were sufficiently "whitened"

[36] José Valentín Saavedra, 1793, in Autos Teresa Ramos alias Coba, No. 34, AGI-SD 1628.
[37] Ibid.

to be considered españoles.[38] The invocation of native standing by racially marked subjects could perform political and legal work in different contexts as this example shows.

NATIVE INDIAN STANDING IN COLONIAL PLURAL LAW: ANOTHER POSSIBILITY?

So far, I have examined the meanings and usages that letrados and cobreros gave to the category of natives of El Cobre, mostly through a generic Castilian/Spanish framework of municipal belonging that took on many variations throughout the empire. However, there was yet another notion of nativeness subtly conjured in the memorials that was based on the colonial notion of Indianness. Indigenous subjects in the Spanish Indies were ruled through special colonial laws and organized into separate Indian republics. These republics were based on a Castilian corporate municipality model hybridized with pre-Columbian and post-conquest *usos y costumbres* (usages and customs) that Spanish law allowed Indian subjects to maintain or recreate as long as they did not conflict in fundamental ways with Spanish law.[39] In any case, the mobilization of the "natives of a pueblo" identity in the cobreros' case also alluded to an Indigenous genealogy and a separate legal regime of municipal belonging that could also be deployed to make claims, in this case as colonial subordinate subjects.[40] Although the Indian ancestry argument constituted a subtext more than a main line of argumentation in the memorials, the allusions to Indian ancestry were there (and may have represented the tip of an iceberg). That genealogy – or, as I argue, that colonial subject

[38] Recall from Chapter 2 that some cobreros were depicted or depicted themselves as "white and free mulatto" or as "pardo of white color and free" thereby deserving of honor and respect. Martín Salazar, El Cobre, August 21, 1792, No. 1, AGI-SD 1627.

[39] See Penry, *The People are King*, for a pointed account of the historical transformations of Indian republics in the Andean region and more generally for her discussion on appropriation and her redefinition of the colonial. For the legal category of ancient Indigenous custom as a colonial construction and a discursive terrain that could take on shifting and diverse meanings, see Yannakakis' *Since Time Immemorial*. For a more contemporary global iteration of the construction (or reconstruction)of Indigeneity as a cultural and political process, see Clifford, *Returns*.

[40] Herman Bennet, in *Africans in Colonial Mexico*, has called attention to the appropriation of the Indian category by Afro descendants in Inquisition cases to obtain exemption from a jurisdiction that excluded Indians as neophytes. See also Graubart, "Pesa más la libertad."

analogy – would eventually become more significant in the final outcome of the case (see Chapter 8).

It may sound strange to suggest that there were allusions to Indian nativeness undergirding the cobreros' case for freedom given the established view that the Indigenous population of Cuba, and more generally of the Caribbean, was obliterated in the holocaust of the Spanish conquest during the early sixteenth century. But Indigenous people resided and worked in the jurisdiction of the mines of El Cobre at least until the 1620s. And a couple of communities recognized as Indian pueblos established in eastern Cuba, near El Cobre, did survive into the nineteenth century, although not without conflict and controversy. Memories and stories of Indian ancestries survived in the region and in El Cobre too. And they could be tapped and pressed into arguments if needed.

All the memorials made reference to an Indian presence in El Cobre's past. The Madrid Memorial placed Indian natives at the very beginning of El Cobre's story, preceding or alongside the arrival of African slaves to work in the mines (second epigraph).[41] The Havana Memorial went even further back, into a brief boilerplate account of conquest days that praised the docility of the Indians and the facility of their evangelization, traits that alluded to their right to retain land and minimal self-rule if they submitted to the "requirement" of Spanish rule and Christianization – a reference that the Madrid Memorial saw fit to delete.[42] Instead, the Madrid brief compressed the Indian ancestry theme into a brief passage that encapsulated two versions of a genealogical confusion argument. The first suggested that racial mixture between Indians, Black slaves, and even some Spaniards had taken place across several generations, so that slave maternal lineage by then was impossible to retrace. In this formulation, racial mixture also helped dilute Blackness, Africanness, and slavery in El Cobre.

> The procreation of *Indians* and *blacks*, mixed as well with *many whites as* evinced in the *color of their descendants*, multiplied in such a way that at the time of their recent dispersion, the inhabitants of that pueblo included more than 6,000 souls and many of them *so equivocated* [*tan equivocados*] in the accidents of the race with that of criollos [white American born] that *their primitive origin could not be distinguished* (my italics).[43]

[41] Memorial Madrid, April 4, 1784, AGI-SD 1629.

[42] Havana Memorial, December 10, 1783, AGI-SD 1627. For a similar but more expanded argument in the memorial of four Afro descendant plaintiffs in seventeenth century Lima, see Graubart, "Pesa más la libertad."

[43] Memorial Madrid, April 4, 1784, AGI-SD 1629.

The passage established that the natives of El Cobre were racially mixed subjects (or *castas*) and that evidence of miscegenation was inscribed in the color of the plaintiffs' bodies. To be sure, the color/racial based argument was more common in US freedom suits than in Spanish ones, but it was found in incipient form here although it was not probed further or pursued with evidence.[44] The memorial insinuated that due to the racial and genealogical confusion, many present-day natives of the pueblo had been wrongfully enslaved. Although the racial mixture theme also emphasized whitening, it highlighted the cobreros' partial Indian ancestry to claim presumption of freedom (and other rights). Perhaps there was a further normative claim that partial Indian ancestry was sufficient cause for Indian standing before the law – a disputed issue in the case of subjects in two Indian pueblos discussed below.

It is difficult to know to what extent Cosme contributed to these Indian mixed-blood narratives through familiarity with vernacular ideas running through the pueblo or if these arguments were concocted by the letrado authors of the memorials. To be sure, it is possible that these Indian ancestries were informally recognized in the pueblo and the region and concealed under informal vernacular categories of racial mix such as "chino." The term "chino" was a category in the *casta* racial regime that in some places referred to a mix of Black with Indian blood.[45] The term was sometimes applied to individual cobreros. For instance, the alcalde of Santiago drafted a complaint against the "the insolence [*atrevimiento*] of a *chino* cobrero" named Eusebio Quiala.[46] And the cobrera Rafaela Sánchez was inscribed in a bill of sale made in Sancti Spíritus as "a china named Rafaela," but in the court records of a hearing she was recorded as a "parda natural del Cobre" and in yet another as the "morena Rafaela

44 . For the United States, see Gross, *What Blood Won't Tell*; de la Fuente and Gross, *Becoming Free, Becoming Black*, 95–98, 121; Sachs, "Freedom by a Judgement"; Wallenstein, "Indian Foremothers"; Ablavsky, "Making Indians 'White'"; Vandervelde, *Redemption Songs*, 39–56.

45 Hernández Cuevas, "The Mexican Colonial Term 'Chino' Is a Referent of Afro descendant." Racial mixture labels were also "unpacked" in a 1774 treatise from Mexico: "Negro and Indian produce a lobo; a lobo and Indian, a chino; and a chino and Indian an *albarazado*; all of which incline towards the mulatto" in Katzew, *Casta Painting*, 192. Juan P. Morlete Ruiz in his 1761 series has "de Indio y negra, chino *cambujo*" and in Andrés de Islas' 1774 series, the tableau No. 10 represents a "chino" as the offspring of a Lobo and a Black, both in Katzew, *Casta Painting*, 108 and 117. Other artists also included this mixture too. However, it is unclear if this was the way in which the term was used in eastern Cuba too.

46 Expediente de Ramón Vizente de Hechevarría y Garzón, n.d., received in Aranjuez, June 25, 1798, AGI-SD 1627.

Sánchez."[47] All three racial categories applied to the same cobrera. The category of chino, however, did not appear in the local household censuses of the village where chinos would have been swallowed up by the more generic rubric of pardos or Mulattos. Gregorio Cosme's own stepfather, Ignacio Solís, was inscribed in the census of 1739 as a free Mulato; yet depositions at the time capturing vernacular voices referred to him by the moniker of the "Indio" Ignacio Solís. Solís was elsewhere identified as a native of Cartagena de Indias.[48] He would have become a vecino of El Cobre by marrying Cosme's widowed mother and growing a family in the village. Cosme's younger siblings then were cobreros with Indian ancestry, if not of a local Indian lineage. The category "pardo" or "Mulatto" elided Indian ancestries but could contain them too. Although the narrative of the natives of El Cobre's Indian ancestry by blood mixture in the briefs was vague and speculative, it was also suggestive of stories that could have circulated below the official radar in the pueblo. It is not possible to know to what extent Indian blood ancestries were acknowledged by cobrero families in the 1780s. What is significant here is that that possibility was turned into an argument for freedom in the Madrid Memorials.

A second variation of the genealogical confusion argument based on Indian ancestry among the natives of El Cobre surfaced in the same memorial of 1784. This variation was based on co-residence in the pueblo, rather than on blood mixture. The passage read: "[the heirs] have *indistinctly* appropriated more than 6,000 souls [comprising the pueblo] ... who, *without being descendants from female* [*mining*] *slaves*, were *descendants from free* [*female*] *Indian* [*indias*] *and* [*female*] *mestizas who resided* [*avecindadas*] in El Cobre" (my italics).[49] Although in this formulation the racial groups were kept separate, the descendants of Indians and Mestizos living in El Cobre had by birth become natives of El Cobre and had allegedly been wrongfully encompassed in the general enslavement of all the village's natives in 1781. Looked at from another angle, the passage suggested that collectively, either by blood or co-residence, the natives of El Cobre had Indian and Mestizo along with African (and Spanish or European) ancestry.

[47] Case of Rafaela Sánchez, 1792, in Autos Teresa Ramos alias Cobas, No. 34, f. 347v–53, AGI-SD 1628.

[48] Household census of El Cobre, 1739, AGI-SD 385; Depositions, Claudio Alcántara, f. 16–24 in Autos Salvador Borzaga, 1737, AGI-SD 451.

[49] Memorial Madrid, April 4, 1784, AGI-SD 1629.

The allusion to nativeness based on Indigeneity had other bolder political and legal implications beyond a simple genealogical confusion argument. What claims were implicit in this line of argumentation? Imperial law was plural, and Indians had a special standing as conquered but free people in the colonial legal regime. The New Laws of 1542 had declared Indians free, and their emancipated status was firmly reiterated in the colonial code of the *Recopilación de Leyes de Indias* of 1681. Colonial laws encouraged the reduction of Indians to live in their own corporate communities called Indian republics with partial local sovereignty and their own common land.[50] Colonial laws of the Indies gave Indigenous people a special protected status and jurisdiction as *miserables* constantly invoked in their prolific litigation and petitions.[51] On the other hand, whereas naturales had rights to separate corporate Indian Republics and land, they were burdened with tribute taxes and were subject to draft labor obligations, especially in the mines and in other public works – the infamous *mita* or *repartimiento* (rotational labor draft) systems. Those were major manifestations of coloniality: and they resonated with the cobreros' own forced labor arrangements in the fortification projects of Santiago (Figure 1.2).

Laws pertaining to Indian standing and governance, however, could also be invoked to claim prerogatives of freedom, land, and corporate status for the natives of El Cobre by suggesting that they were related to or like Indian natives, even if this kind of native standing also entailed subaltern colonial status and obligations. This would not be the first time that such a proposal was made. A full century before, in the distant city of Lima, in the viceroyalty of Peru, four enslaved Afro descendants, "natives of Lima," made a case for their freedom by functional analogy with Indian legal standing (not by blood ancestry) in a memorial that went up to the Council of the Indies.[52] In the brief, they claimed that pardos as a class and Indians were all natives and vassals of the Crown, and the former, by analogy with the latter, were deserving of freedom. This line of argumentation, like that of the cobreros implied bridging colonial legal pluralities and reconfiguring the law.

The legal analogies between native Indian pueblos and El Cobre, had, in fact, models on the ground, close to El Cobre. There is no need to make trans-regional jumps to the mainland where Indian communities were

50 *Recopilación de Leyes de Indias*, Book 4, Titles 2 and 3.
51 Owensby, *Empire of the Law*, 56–58; de la Puente Luna, *Andean Cosmopolitans*, 148–53.
52 Graubart, "Pesa más la libertad."

more prevalent, and awareness of the related legislation was widespread. In the jurisdiction of Santiago de Cuba there were two pueblos with the special protected standing of *pueblos de Indios*. San Luis del Caney (El Caney) near El Cobre, for instance, got its title of pueblo de Indios, quite late, in 1697, right around the time when El Cobre was taking shape as a pueblo of royal slaves and free Afro descendants in the Real de Minas' jurisdiction. The other Indian pueblo in eastern Cuba was San Pablo de Jiguaní (or Jiguaní), near the town of Bayamo (see Figure 0.1). In 1778, El Caney had a total population of about 959 inhabitants and Jiguaní had 1,332 souls. With a count of 1,482 souls (not the incorrectly reported 6,000 in the memorials), El Cobre's population in 1778 was slightly higher than those of these two Indian pueblos but in the same range of large pueblos (Table 1.1).[53]

Like other Indian pueblos in the empire's mainland, El Caney and Jiguaní had a communal land regime, a cabildo, and less clearly, a *caja de comunidad* for communal funds and expenses. By the 1830s, it was questioned that either of them had ever had a caja de comunidad, although they rented out communal land to *colonos* (settlers) to fund communal expenses that included the salary of a teacher and funds to sponsor the annual festivities of patron saints.[54] Although villagers had taken up arms in case of invasion, they did not seem to have been subject to forced draft labor in public works, at least not in the fortification works where many cobreros were forced to toil on a rotating basis. One important feature of El Caney's and Jiguaní's legal standing as Indian pueblos was that the villages had – or were subject to – a p*rotector de Indios* (advocate of the Indians), an appointed position by the Audiencia of Santo Domingo held by prominent citizens in Santiago de Cuba who were not always looking after this population's best interests. (The position had first started in the Indies with Bartolomé de Las Casas, considered the first official protector.)[55] Given Indians' status as minors, the Protector was charged with the improvement of the pueblo and its native residents and with representing them in judicial matters when needed.[56]

53 General Census of Cuba, 1778, AGI-Indiferente 1527. The regional Census of Santiago of 1780 (AGI-Cuba 1272), gave different population figures: El Caney, 778 souls; Jiguaní, 1,883; and El Cobre, 1,406 (corrected) souls.

54 Expediente Jiguaní and El Caney, No. 31, AHN-Ultramar 1647.

55 For the position of the Protector de Indios in the Recopilacion de Indias, see Book 4, Title 6. See also Cutter, *The Protector de Indios of Colonial New Mexico.*

56 The existence (and need) of a Protector was a symbol of the Indian standing of the natives of these communities. Other criteria deployed on either side were the existence of separate

The position in Cuba had become controversial due to abuses and inaction of some protectores. No such formal position existed for El Cobre and its natives, however. Instead, Santiago's bishopric seems to have informally taken up some of those functions, at least in the 1730s–40s, under Dean Morell de Santa Cruz, and again in the 1790s under Bishop Osés y Alzúa. Although the cobreros paid for annual festivities to the Virgin and perhaps other expenses, apparently through rental of some pueblo lands, they had no formal communal funds, nor any was mentioned, to pay, for instance, for collective litigation, nor did they have a formal communal land grant either; instead, they had for the most part long used and claimed rights to land pertaining to the mining jurisdiction as royal slaves. But like the Indian native population, they had the standing of miserables or wards of the Crown.

Local records referred to the inhabitants of El Caney and Jiguaní as naturales or natives, and more commonly as Indios. But the actual meaning and status of these natives and these pueblos de Indios by the late eighteenth and early nineteenth century was fuzzy, and this confusion may have enabled the analogy with the natives of El Cobre's own standing and claims. For one, these Indian pueblos were said to be no longer inhabited solely by Indian subjects, as the Laws of the Indies called for, but their dwellers were racially mixed and diverse. In fact, debates regarding their character and standing as Indian pueblos given the mestizaje of its inhabitants went back in the case of El Caney to the 1730s when the parish priest stated the population of the "community of the Indians (by now only in name) of the pueblo of El Caney" were all "mulattos, *grifos* and other mixtures."[57] In this view, there was African ancestry in this Indian pueblo, whereas the argument in the cobreros' case became that there was Indian ancestry among the African descendant natives of El Cobre. The issue reemerged in relation to El Caney and

baptism records for Spaniards and Indians (a discarded former practice) and the existence of a caja de comunidad (communal funds), which a witness said in the case of El Caney did contain papers and documents that alcaldes safeguarded during their tenure in office. In the case of Jiguaní, a witness declared that its natives did not pay tribute or *alcabala* (the former constituted the kind of taxes required from Indian and the latter were sales taxes required from non-Indians) while another said they paid "all kinds of derechos [taxes] and did not use special legal paper [*papel sellado*] for their judicial causes." Some referred to lack of *propios* (community assets), though there is reference to the reliance on renting land to *colonos* and *forasteros* or at other times of collecting funds for litigation and other projects. Most of these criteria pertained to legal and governance practices. Expediente Jiguaní and El Caney, No. 31, Interrogatories, 1837, AHN-Ultramar 1647.

57 Father Juan Rivero Arause, El Caney, May 20, 1731, AGI-SD 520.

Jiguaní in the nineteenth century: in 1814, and most extensively in 1837, when pressure to suppress the standing of Indian pueblos arose in the context of liberal tendencies under the pretext that there was no "pure race of Indians" left in these villages. In an investigation made in 1837, one official recommended that "it would be convenient that the pueblo *se españolizase* (become [legally considered] Spanish) and the privileges granted to the Indians suppressed because there are none [left] and because all the *forasteros* (foreigners or outsiders), whites, pardos and morenos enjoy the benefit of the community's land."[58] In this comment, natives of Jiguaní were counterposed to outsiders of different races who had displaced or replaced the original Indians and settled in their communal land. The witness, a royal tobacco agent, put the issue in terms of miscegenation: "I have never known in this pueblo [Jiguaní] any real Indian [*verdadero como tal*] ... [and] if some *naturales* descend from the founders, they have degenerated from that [Indian] race due to the mix [*mezcla*] they have had with whites and pardos."[59] A merchant who had resided eighteen years in Jiguaní even noted the presence of cobreros there: "Real Indians [*verdaderos indios*] do not exist in this pueblo [of Jiguaní] and only the descendants of the first founders like the Calsadas, Fonsecas ... and some are linked [*enlazados*] with whites and others with pardos *and cobreros*" (my italics).[60] Perhaps in El Cobre there were similar ties with Indian descendants and similar racial mixtures as in these two official Indian pueblos.

In fact, the erasure of Indians from Jiguaní and El Caney (and perhaps El Cobre too) went back further. Despite their title as Indian pueblos, the first island censuses of 1778, 1780, and thereafter did *not* use the category of Indians to inscribe subjects in these localities. Contrary to censuses in the mainland, general censuses in Cuba used a formulaic breakdown of the population by race and status based on the fundamental binary of White and Black lineages and went into considerable detail classifying the population of African descent as Mulatto or Black, free or slave. Thus, there was no room for Indians or even Mestizos in these island-wide censuses, a factor contributing to the "invisibility" of the Indigenous population in the island's official record. In this case, people of Indian descent were reclassified as Whites, or if very racially mixed, perhaps as pardos. The population of El Caney and Jiguaní, for instance, was

[58] Expediente Jiguaní and El Caney, No. 31, Interrogatories 1837, Jiguaní, f. 41v–52. AHN-Ultramar 1647.
[59] Ibid. [60] Ibid.

recorded in the general regional census of 1778 as White (*blancos*) in the majority, suggesting that Indians were officially classified as Whites, and not so much that White vecinos had taken over the pueblo (Table 1.1). Whitening or transformation into españoles took place here by officially imposed classifications.

However, local household censuses (*padrones*) from pueblos, when available, gave a different sense of the inhabitants of these villages, although those local counts had a political basis too. A household census of El Caney from 1836, for instance, did inscribe the majority of local inhabitants as Indians, showing that, at least internally, the category still mattered. As mentioned before, at this time, these classifications took on strong political meaning as the natives (or some of them) wanted to retain their protected corporate status as an Indian pueblo in the face of (liberal) attempts both in Madrid and the colony to dissolve these communities and their protected communal land regimes, a struggle that was taking place as well in other new republics in postcolonial Latin America (see Chapter 9).[61] Whereas in 1778, 69 percent of El Caney's population was reported in the general census as White, in the local household census of 1836 the proportion of españoles or Whites, was only 6 percent and that of Indians 70.6 percent (another 7.8 percent were free of color, mostly pardos, and 1.5 percent were slaves).[62] There were no racially mixed categories in the Indian line such as Mestizos: there were only Indios, as if to affirm that racially mixed subjects could have Indian standing. El Caney and Jiguaní, like El Cobre, constitute ideal sites to study the local meanings and political uses of the category of nativeness in racially mixed pueblos where nativeness may have had several overlapping racial, social, legal, and political connotations related both to Indian ancestry and to local birth.[63]

But if the memorials of El Cobre alluded to an Indian ancestry among the natives of El Cobre to suggest that El Cobre was like an Indian pueblo with attendant rights and obligations, were there any local vernacular allusions to this ancestry? Vernacular stories about the Indian presence in El Cobre's foundational past did circulate in El Cobre and Santiago at the

[61] Expediente Jiguaní and El Caney, No. 31, AHN-Ultramar 1647. See also Sartorius, *Ever Faithful*, 35–38.

[62] Household census of El Caney, 1837, No. 31, AHN-Ultramar 1647.

[63] For instance, by the early nineteenth century, distinctions were also made in El Caney between *naturales*, *colonos* (settlers) and *extranjeros* (foreigners, mostly French refugees). These terms were also found in El Cobre's land distribution lists in 1842 (see Chapter 9). Who belonged to these categories? And what were the implications?

time. At least two stories from collective memory surfaced in the archival record (and Cosme would have been very familiar with the first). We do not know what others may have circulated in oral lore.

The first was about the finding of a miraculous statue of the Virgin of Charity, who later became the patroness of the village and whose sanctuary in El Cobre had regional fame. The widely diffused oral story, originating in the early seventeenth century (and transcribed from oral memory in 1687), was also set down in the Havana Memorial of 1783, but it was edited out of the Madrid Memorial of 1784 as too local and perhaps out of place in a legal brief cast in sober Enlightened Bourbon regalist culture. According to the original story, the miraculous image was found floating in the waters of Nipe Bay – and this is the relevant part – by two Indians and a Black slave boy from the mining settlement who took the image with them back to El Cobre. The Havana Memorial emphasized that those who found the image at sea were "of the natives [of El Cobre]" and that "two of them were Blacks [slaves] and two Indians" thereby augmenting to four the original three seers for greater balance and making them all natives and adults with the same symbolic surname "de la Caridad."[64] Thus, Indians and Black slaves entered the collective memory yoked together as foundational figures in a Christian Marian cult that became iconic of the pueblo of El Cobre. (The figures in the story today have mutated into an Indian, a Black, and a White, symbolizing the three races that make up the Cuban nation.)[65] In this memory, they once lived and worked together in the mines of El Cobre. Although the seers of the story constituted two different groups, in this telling they were all considered natives of El Cobre and chosen sons (and therefore brothers) of the Virgin mother and patroness of the pueblo. But theirs was not just a symbolic presence in the story. In the early seventeenth century, there were Indian men and women living and working in the mines of El Cobre.[66] Although they eventually faded as "Indians" from the record, their descendants may have well lived on in the village and kept the memory of that lineage identification. Others may have mixed with cobreros to be later termed "chinos." And ultimately all became natives of El Cobre (born in the pueblo of El Cobre).

64 Havana Memorial, December 10, 1783, AGI-SD 1627.

65 See Díaz, "Rethinking Tradition and Identity."

66 Report of Captain Francisco Sánchez Moya, Santiago del Prado, November 30, 1608, AGI-SD 451.

The second vernacular story was even more interesting. It was based on a local pre-Columbian oral tale about three Cacique brothers who supposedly ruled over three localities in eastern Cuba before the Spanish conquest: Santiago, El Cobre, and Baracoa. This story was not recounted in any memorial. It was deposed by a cobrero in response to a question posed by a notary. Asked in 1790 to recall everything he knew about the history of El Cobre, a cobrero elder named Francisco Sánchez recounted a tale about "the first beginning and foundation" of El Cobre that may have circulated locally but that the notary dismissed as nonsense not bothering to write it down fully. The scribe did jot down that Sánchez "mentioned the lands the cacique Cobe [of El Cobre] had owned at the time, and that His Majesty had granted to its natives [the cobreros]."[67] The point of this local story was that the cobreros were the legitimate heirs of the lands belonging to the cacique Cobe and of the ancient pre-Hispanic Indian community over which he ruled: a land and village that had passed into the Spanish Crown after the conquest and the king had given to the cobreros. Temporalities overlapped in this repurposed tale. This was a layered story that basically ratified the cobreros' standing as the new natives of the pueblo with a right to its land and perhaps to other prerogatives that eluded the scribe.

Both stories made the standing of Indians and cobreros of African descent as natives of El Cobre socially, legally, and politically analogous, without necessarily fusing or confounding one group with the other in blood terms. These vernacular stories niftily conveyed some of the lawsuit's strategic arguments based on the relation of natives of El Cobre and Indians. They seem to point to a collective genealogy whereby El Cobre was originally an Indian locality that after the conquest became a mining settlement and then a racially mixed pueblo. That ancestral framework could be reclaimed in the legal action at the end of the eighteenth century to assert rights for the new natives of El Cobre. The claims made from this subject position constituted an attempt to bridge plural colonial legal regimes between Indians and free and enslaved Afro descendants and racially mixed people in the empire: a way to anchor and legitimize long-standing customary arrangements through the written legal regime of colonial corporate Indian law. However, the move went against the increasingly dominant trend in the colony to erase Indigeneity (and its attendant legal regime) from the island's social and legal order, a trend

[67] Interview of Francisco Sánchez, El Cobre, ca. April 4, 1790, No. 6, AGI-SD 1629.

that became stronger after the liberal turn that found expression in the Cádiz Constitution of 1812 but that would not reach a final implementation until the 1840s (see Chapter 9). In the 1780s and '90s, there was still room to invoke Indian nativeness within a plural regime framework to make claims to corporate rights, land, and freedom, even if in colonial limited terms (that could be subject to further negotiation and contestation in the ground).

VASSALAGE TO THE KING

Finally, a brief look at the subject position of vassals of the king completes the major parameters from which the cobreros made claims in the memorials. Vassalage to the king was a pervasive but more standard and formulaic category that subjects across the Spanish empire used to claim protection and seek higher justice.[68] At times, it even entailed an economy of rewards for services rendered to the Crown. Recall how Gregorio Cosme had used the military services of his father and himself to claim rewards from the king when he arrived in Madrid (Chapter 2). Whereas nativeness represented a more autonomous horizontal relation among members of a locality linked by bonds of love and loyalty to each other, vassalage to the king referred to a direct vertical pact between sovereign and plaintiffs based on a relation of subordination, loyalty, and obedience to the king.[69] The distant king was usually used as a proxy for justice while conflicts were usually displaced to lower officials of the state. Scholars of colonial Latin America have shown the primacy of that imagined relation among subordinate subjects.[70] Whether real, opportunistic, rhetorical, or plainly formulaic, the invocation of the subject position of loyal vassalage to the king was central in an absolutist monarchy and almost de rigueur when petitioning for favors or sometimes in seeking justice in royal courts. Historian Marcela Echevarri has recently drawn attention to the royalist identifications and political strategies of both Indians and Afro descendant slaves in the Popayán (Colombia) in the

[68] Owensby, *Empire of Law*, 257–60.

[69] Although slaves, in principle, were not imperial vassals because they were either under private jurisdiction of a master or more crassly because they were private property, at times the standing of enslaved people as imperial subjects is more ambiguous and some historians have accepted that enslaved persons were vassals of the Spanish Crown. See Bennet, *Africans in Colonial Mexico*, 32–33, 41.

[70] Owensby, *Empire of Law*; Echeverri, *Indian and Slave Royalists*; Penry, *The People are King*; Díaz, *The Virgin, the King*.

judicial system and in extrajudicial actions.[71] Subordinate subjects, such as Indians and slaves, widows, children, and, to a lesser extent, free Blacks, were also considered wards of the king subject to special protection as miserables. The Madrid Memorial of 1784 opened with the usual formulaic rhetoric of these writings professing complete loyalty to the king: "The natives of the said pueblo of El Cobre … dare to humbly claim to the highest justice and the paternal clemency of Your Majesty the sacred rights of humanity and those of loyal vassals of the Crown [that have been] sadly violated."[72] Claiming loyal vassalage was a way of claiming protections owed by the king to its imperial subjects. Frederick Cooper has pointed out that in the study of empires it is important to understand how subjects made political claims on the state by invoking belonging to empire.[73]

The cobreros, in former times, often invoked a special relation to the king as His Majesty's royal slaves, but that relation often veered into one of vassalage to the king instead. Their briefs now asserted vassalage unambiguously. Especially in the memorial of Havana, and to a lesser extent in the Madrid ones, loyal vassalage was linked in a gendered way to the cobreros' active militia service in former times and to bearing arms for His Majesty.[74] The memorial's strong remonstration on this issue went as follows: "By any chance, has it ever been heard that military [persons] serving the King since *immemorial time* … that these *vassals of the King* would have been made to give up arms with deception, take them away so that they should follow such an unequal destiny as that of serving private subjects as it has recently happened?"(my italics).[75]

[71] Echeverri, *Indian and Slave Royalists.*

[72] Madrid Memorial, April 23, 1784, AGI-SD 1629.

[73] Cooper, *Colonialism in Question*, 32. For nineteenth-century colonial Cuba, Sartorius argues that many Black subjects made claims as loyal subjects of the Spanish Crown. See *Ever Faithful.*

[74] For reward and naturalization petitions made in Spain by foreigners claiming distinguished service as loyal vassals to the king, especially through military actions, see Herzog, *Defining Nations*, 134–35.

[75] Havana Memorial, December 10, 1783, AGI-SD 1627. The memorial appealed in this case to the force of custom as normative. Yannakakis has examined the pliable trope of "immemorial time" as applied to and invoked by Indigenous subjects in colonial Mexico to make different kinds of claims. In this case, the phrase refers more generically to a local customary practice going back decades, not centuries, but that despite its shorter span had allegedly acquired normative power (without referring to the law of prescription itself). The *Siete Partidas* defined *costumbre* or customary practice as "non written right or privilege [*derecho o fuero*] which men have used for a long time," but it did not specify duration. Book 1, Title 2, Law 4.

Military service and veteran status were male badges of royal vassalage and freedom used in the memorials to reinforce and complement nativeness (although once, before the Bourbon military reforms of the 1760s dissolved them, the militias of El Cobre also had a local corporate referent).

The comment of the cobreros' local apoderado Justo Cruzata in a letter to Cosme illustrates the separate but complementary relations of loyalty to which a subject in the Spanish empire was committed. Informing Cosme about his recent arrest and about the increasing persecutions and violence the cobreros were enduring, Cruzata affirmed that he was "ready to die for God, the king, for my pueblo, and for six children that God has given me" (but apparently not for his wife, unless by then he was a widow).[76] His patriarchal local (natural) bonds and alignments were to his family and to his pueblo. The vertical ones were those of a subordinate vassal loyal to a patriarchal Crown and church. Corporate pueblo figured prominently in these loyalties. There was nothing over that alignment and that of family except the king and his God; alignments to colonial royal officials did not figure here. Chapter 6 discusses Cosme's royalist proclivities and how he could deploy them as a shield to stridently critique colonial officials and colonial rule. Justo Cruzata's stated alignments were those of a free man in the Spanish empire at the time. But, of course, those alignments could also be subject to rupture – or redefinition – especially in an Age of Revolutions.

[76] Justo Cruzata, El Cobre, December 27, 1795, No. 135. AGI-SD 1627.

5

The Council's Ruling and the Politics of Litigation

> All [cobreros] insist on their freedom under the false assumption that His Majesty has declared them free indistinctly.
>
> —Don Nicolás Mancebo, Havana, 1788

> Everything is turned into disputes, contradictions and impediments that employ malice, prepotency, and complicity to keep [the plaintiffs] in oppression and make them die in slavery.
>
> —Echenique Memorial, Madrid, 1793

September 22, 1784. The Council of the Indies issued its ruling almost six months after the three *apoderados* from Cuba filed their Madrid Memorial on behalf of the natives of El Cobre's freedom.[1] How did the imperial court respond to this unusual freedom case in view of the ascendant pro-slavery policies of the Council itself and of the state's interest in the mining revival project? How did it address the various challenges that this composite case posed? Were the arguments for freedom – or rather, for collective freedom and implicitly for local native rights – presented in the memorial of 1784 persuasive? The imperial court's response sounded elusive at best, and to some, ambiguous and confusing. As the epigraphs suggest, the ruling created considerable controversy and enkindled further conflicts in the colony. In addressing the initial outcome of the plaintiffs' action and its impact in the colony, this chapter turns to what scholars call the law in action as well as to the politics of litigation both at the imperial and the colonial level.[2]

[1] Council of the Indies' ruling, Madrid, September 22, 1784, f. 24v–26 (hereafter Council's ruling of 1784) in Autos, AGI-SD 1629.

[2] The "law in action" refers to the messy operations of the law in practice as opposed to the "law in the books," which refers to the law in its ideal prescriptive form. See McKinley, *Fractal Freedoms*, 240–43.

Basically, although the Council's Gracia y Justicia (Justice) division's ruling in 1784 opened a narrow window to further dispute, the Council rejected the arguments for freedom put forward in the Madrid Memorial of 1784 and effectively foreclosed further dispute on collective terms as natives of a pueblo. But ambiguities in the language led the cobreros and their legal advocates to push for an alternative interpretation of the Council's ruling.[3] The publication of the Council's writ as an edict in the colony in 1786 made the cobreros' conflict public throughout the island. Ordinary male and female enslaved cobreros, and not just their apoderado representatives, directly entered the legal arena at this point, claiming freedom in colonial lower courts based on a collective interpretation of the ruling. Paradoxically, while the Council tried to judicially contain the conflict over freedom, it effectively spread it beyond Santiago into the tribunals and streets of other cities in the colony where it was disputed and discussed by a broad range of people including the cobreros, their counsels, allies, and friends as well as slaveholders who owned cobreros, notaries, apoderados, first instance judges, royal officials, and perhaps a more general public who heard about the case.

The Council's decision came down on September 22, 1784. It took yet another year and nine months for the Council's ruling to be ratified by royal edict on June 11, 1786, and dispatched to the colony. An additional three months went by before the edict arrived in Cuba for enforcement. There, it took about four to five years to play out in local courts with the usual holdups and deferrals of judicial battles that, as the second epigraph suggests, were also part of the politics of litigation. The wheels of Justice, wittingly and unwittingly, moved slowly in the administrative apparatus of this vast empire.

The first part of the chapter examines the specific requests (not the arguments) made in the plaintiffs' Madrid Memorial of 1784. While I argue that the collective requests in and on themselves were consequential, the memorial's cautious wording introduced a loophole regarding the affected plaintiffs which had the potential to undermine the collective case. The second part turns to the state and its use of slave law.

[3] At this point of the game, Echenique's 1793 memorial, with its bolder and more explicit collective and pro-freedom argumentation had not yet been filed. In fact, that memorial entered the fray as a response to the Council's elusive judicial ruling of 1784.

It analyzes the Council's ruling itself: what it conceded and what it rejected as well as the basis of the writ's apparent ambiguity. The third part turns to the politics of interpretation of the king's voice or edict by different sides. While the official (and intended) interpretation of the Edict of 1786 seemed to reject any recognition of collective freedom, as the first epigraph suggests, many cobreros and their counsel interpreted the edict otherwise. I first examine Cosme's testing of the Council's ruling of 1784 in the Council's own tribunal through an individual freedom suit he filed on behalf of a cobrera he ran into in Madrid in 1787. Then I move to the responses to the ruling in the colony and to the politics of litigation unleashed in various colonial courts. Ironically, at this point, individual cobrero plaintiffs found more room for maneuvering in colonial courts than in Madrid. The actions that ensued allow me as well to examine the existing tensions between the operational procedural rules of a centralizing Bourbon state and the discretionary ambit of lower courts and related issues regarding the force of customary norms and the written law. Battles over procedural rules and the interpretation of edicts and the law pervaded the litigation at all levels, if in different ways.

THE REQUESTS OF THE MADRID PETITION OF APRIL 4, 1784

The Madrid Memorial of April 4, 1784 was basically a collective *amparo* petition requesting royal protection for the plaintiffs as *miserables*.[4] These petitions required that plaintiffs present specific requests that the court could address with a writ. If these remedies failed to work, the plaintiffs could pursue other forms of legal action such as a formal suit, as it happened.[5] Before analyzing the Council's ruling, it is worth reviewing the specific requests the plaintiffs made in their memorial of 1784, which were by no means insignificant. But there was a seed of ambiguity and conditionality in that memorial's redaction that wittingly or unwittingly produced a loophole in the case.

The Madrid Memorial petitioned that "the governor heretofore protect the plaintiffs in the possession of their freedom and in their use of the land that His Majesty had granted them for their establishment [implicitly

[4] Madrid Memorial, April 4, 1784, AGI-SD 1629.

[5] Writs of *amparo* were executive summary rulings granted to plaintiffs who fell in the legal category of "miserables." See Owensby for Indigenous cases in New Spain, *Empire of Law*, 51–53.

as a pueblo]" and requested from the court the restitution of "houses, haciendas [estates], and other land and movable goods that they possessed in the pueblo before they were extracted from it."[6] In so doing, it asserted their rights to property as free imperial subjects.

However, a dangerous ambiguity obfuscated the petition's requests when it specified who were to be its beneficiaries: "All those who were inhabitants of El Cobre and descendants of that pueblo *who were in possession of freedom until the 1st of August, 1781 and who have been dispossessed of it* by those who call themselves heirs of Juan de Eguiluz, be returned *to their previous state* in the very act of claiming *this right* before any justice in whatever place they currently are" (my italics).[7] The equivocal qualifying clause that I highlighted inserted an escape clause in the petition that the Council would grasp and use to ground its own ruling. Did it suggest that all cobreros (in collective terms) were free before the privatization as the Madrid Memorial (and the other memorials argued) or did it concede that there had been a distinction between free and non-free cobreros before 1781? I suggest that the qualification may have been intentionally inserted by the Madrid attorneys out of caution so that the petition would pass muster in the court. But that very qualification had the potential to undermine the Madrid Memorial's collective narrative of prior emancipation in the past and, more importantly, the prescription-based argument. In fact, it could have undercut the claimed rights based on the plaintiffs' nativeness and weakened the memorial's corporate-based claims. The equivocal phrase incubated ambiguities in the Council's verdict and subsequently in the disputes in the colony over the ruling's reach and meaning.

Aside from the restoration of freedom, land, and property, the Madrid Memorial of 1784 made other important requests too. It asserted the plaintiffs' right to be heard as an affected party in any deliberation involving their (collective) interests as a pueblo and it asked that they be cited and heard in any subsequent action that the heirs may want to take, a procedure that had not been followed in the 1770s when the heirs negotiated the privatization of the mining estate in the Council of the Indies. This equity-based request to be recognized as a subject with rights (in this case as a collective subject) with the right to speak and be heard effectively constituted an assertion of their corporate standing and rights: a community had a right to be heard before the state made any decision

[6] Madrid Memorial, April 4, 1784, AGI-SD 1629. [7] Ibid.

regarding "persons and land" that concerned them. This claimed right is perhaps not far from what some pueblo communities today call the right to "previous consultation" with regard, for instance, to the state's mining concessions to private (often foreign) companies that may affect their common welfare.[8] Furthermore, denouncing the complicity of highly placed colonial royal officials with the heirs, the Madrid Memorial petitioned that, due to their partiality, those officials be recused from investigating or adjudicating the cobreros' claims in the colony. Specifically included among those colonial officials were the island's intendant, the governor of Santiago de Cuba, and other justices "who have cooperated in the ruin of that pueblo or permitted the *sale* of its individuals" (my italics).[9] Although Spanish law recognized litigants' right to disqualify a person or a judge in proceedings for conflict of interest and partiality, what is significant here is that the request criticized the sale or commodification of the cobreros that these highly placed royal officials had sanctioned, effectively accusing them of corruption, collusion, and cronyism with the heirs. But the petition stopped short of explicitly denouncing the Council of the Indies for issuing the Executory Order of 1779. In addition, the Madrid Memorial called for an investigation of "the excesses that have been committed against the lives, honesties, and estates [*haciendas*] of the said natives [*naturales*] by their pretended owners and their cronies since the day in which they were dispossessed of their freedom in the Pueblo and elsewhere."[10] All the *autos* (proceedings) resulting from an investigation of these events were to be immediately remitted to Madrid for final vetting, a request that would be particularly subject to the politics of litigation through delay tactics.

[8] Prior consultation issues are today very much part of Indigenous (and other local) communities' struggles with their national states and with foreign mining and extractive companies over policy regarding control of resources. The principle applies to the right to have a say on national deliberations regarding decisions that affect their pueblo. This right has already been inserted, for instance, in Colombia's progressive 1992 constitution. International conventions and organizations such as the 1989 International Labor Organization (ILO) Convention 169 on the Rights of Indigenous and Tribal Peoples endorse prior consultation regarding mineral or sub-surface resources and other resources pertaining to land. The Inter-American Commission and the Inter-American Court of Human Rights have heard legal cases regarding mining concessions, land, and resources filed by Indigenous communities in Latin America since the 1980s. See Sieder, "Legal Cultures in the (Un)Rule of Law," 164–68. For a more general account of this type of requests by Indigenous organizations and their backing by international organizations, see Van Cott, *The Friendly Liquidation of the Past*, 257–65.

[9] Madrid Memorial, April 4, 1784, AGI-SD 1629.

[10] Ibid.

Finally, the petition went as far as promising to present at some undefined future a "useful *asiento* [contract] proposal" to the Crown to extract copper from the mines of El Cobre.[11] The projected offer addressed the state's public utility concerns regarding activation of the dead mines and provided an alternative to the privatization of the estate. This mining proposal was a bold suggestion whereby the natives of El Cobre would take control of the jurisdiction as active mining contractors and developers of the mines, rather than as slaves working for a White private owner or contractor. This effectively constituted a right to contract with the Crown or at least to engage in artisanal mining as they had been doing for decades on their own account. Were they making an implicit claim that nativeness entailed rights over resources other than land and water in their territorial jurisdiction?

Freedom, land, physical security, protection of property, the right to be heard collectively, impartial justice, recognition as a corporate entity, and even contracting with the Crown over exploitation of resources in their local home territory were not inconsequential demands. They constituted a package of freedom rights claimed by subordinate colonial subjects on the basis of their standing as free natives of a pueblo and vassals of the Crown. How did the Council of the Indies respond to these explicit and implicit requests?

THE COUNCIL'S RULING OF SEPTEMBER 22, 1784

The Council's ruling of September 22, 1784, basically offered a limited and confusing solution to the deeper questions and challenges that the cobreros' memorial pressed on the imperial court. Although it indirectly recognized the legitimacy of the pueblo and the right of its free inhabitants (of color) to exist as a pueblo as they customarily had, the Council rejected the plaintiffs' collective standing as "natives" of a pueblo and that category's power to override distinctions between free and slaves – a claim implicit at the heart of the cobreros' memorials.

The Council's ruling basically upheld the Executory Order of 1779 and condemned only the excesses that may have been incurred in its implementation. In line with legal rules that recognized a slave's right to contest wrongful enslavement and the Crown's protection of these cases as *casos*

[11] Cosme brought this issue up in a separate petition requesting a loan of 8,000 pesos that would be repaid in 500 quintals of copper mined by the cobreros. Cosme to Minister José Gálvez, Madrid. December 13, 1784, AGI-SD 1628. See Chapter 2.

de corte (royal protected cases), the Council allowed *individual* legal recourse to those cobreros who had grounds to dispute their enslavement.[12] But, by dictating the evidential standard in these cases, the Council's writ went further: it effectively had a better control over the outcome of cases. The Council stipulated that the Royal Treasury's lists of royal slaves – the very same official lists used to adjudicate the 1,065 former royal slaves to the heirs – were to be considered the decisive evidential instrument to determine the legitimacy of slave status. In setting this procedural condition, the Council basically foreclosed the use of other criteria to contest status in courts and it undercut the Madrid Memorial's arguments. Prescription and long-standing customary practices associated with living as free, for instance, were suppressed as judicial means to contest the cobreros' enslavement. The memorial had presented alternative criteria to determine freedom that would have challenged and overwritten official criteria. In fact, at a deeper level, the memorial had called into question the state's possession rights over these emancipated subjects and therefore its right to adjudicate them to the heirs in the first place. The Council's evidential mandate constitutes an example of what may be called the politics of adjudication.[13] One cynical slaveholder noted the redundancy of the Council's 1784 writ asserting that it had done nothing but reiterate that "those [cobreros] who had been free [before 1781], were free, and those who had been slaves, were [to remain] slaves."[14]

And yet the meaning and reach of the Council's ruling (and the Royal Edict of 1786 that was based on it) was not clear to everyone. A gem of obfuscating legalese, the Council's verdict, intentionally or not, created further confusion and controversy. Capitalizing on the Madrid Memorial's ambiguous qualifying phrase discussed above, the Council's ruling also created other ambiguities. Like many other state documents, it cut and pasted phrases from various documents, including the plaintiffs'

[12] *Casos de corte*, or royal court cases, were cases subject to special royal protection under the doctrine of miserables. They applied to cases of orphans, widows, slaves, and Indians too.

[13] An example of this relation can be found in the evolution of evidential rules in Maryland. Given a greater ideological openness toward emancipation at the onset of the American Revolution, evidential rules allowing hearsay facilitated emancipation outcomes. However, Maryland's Supreme Court raised the bar on evidentiary standards in 1813 regarding the hearsay rule making it more difficult for enslaved plaintiffs to win their freedom suits. Thomas, *A Question of Freedom*, 4–5, 181–90.

[14] Brief by Domingo García, in Autos Marcelina Antonia de los Reyes, 1787, No. 35/43, f. 408–541, AGI-SD 1628.

memorial, and rearranged them in new configurations, at times deftly inverting their original meaning. With the right dose of artful negative and conditional constructions, these convoluted texts could become dizzyingly disorienting. Basically, the main confusion in the convoluted passage stemmed from the ruling's legalistic maneuver to suspend retroactively the Executory Order of 1779, only to subsequently reiterate the order in positive terms with the explicit clarification that the enslavement of cobreros only applied to those listed in the Treasury's official records, not to the whole pueblo. The revision was meant to address the charge of indiscriminate enslavement of all cobreros raised in the Madrid Memorial of 1784 (see Chapter 3). What the legal rephrasing stipulated was that the pueblo and its free inhabitants would retain the customary status they had before the Executory Order was issued in 1779, but this would not be the case for those considered royal slaves. Thus, the clarification implicitly rejected the claims of the Madrid Memorial that all had been emancipated long ago in the past. The cobreros and their attorneys, however, gave a broad interpretation to the ruling, claiming that the call to suspend the Executory Order and return things to the status quo ante 1779 applied indistinctly, or collectively, to all the enslaved cobreros – some even believed that the Edict of 1786 (based on the Council's writ of 1784) ordered a general emancipation of all the cobreros (first epigraph). But others read that edict more narrowly.

The Council's writ of 1784 did not object to the heirs' sale of the enslaved cobreros either. That silence effectively recognized the heirs' full property rights to legally alienate and dispose of their claimed human property and ignored any stipulation that the possession of slaves was made conditional to their use in the revival of copper mining. The Council's ruling also completely ignored the question of who had a right to the pueblo's land, for which the heirs had begun collecting rent payments. Also significant was another (intentional?) confusion regarding runaway cobreros. Apparently singling them out for judicial hearings, the Council's writ asserted that "and so that this restitution [*reposición*] has its rightful and due effect in the case of all the fugitives [*prófugos*] who have been aggrieved so they can be reintegrated in the possession of their freedom and all their goods."[15] Many cobreros had indeed run away after the enslavement, and the Madrid Memorial briefly addressed these actions (see Chapter 7). But those who fled were not so much the free

[15] Council's Ruling, Madrid, September 22, 1784, f. 24v–25v, AGI-SD 1629.

cobreros (who remained in the village) but those targeted for private enslavement. The Council's writ's explicit reference to the fugitives was meant to deal with the public security concerns that cobreros who fled enslavement in the mountains posed. Was the offer to hold individual hearings of fugitive cobreros a maneuver to attract and placate them with the promise of freedom and resettlement in the pueblo or to capture them once they presented themselves if their name appeared in the Royal Treasury's records? More ambiguity, or duplicity, in the Council's writ.

Finally, addressing the memorial's grievances regarding brutality and wanton violence, the Crown's *fiscal* (attorney), Minister Antonio Porlier, manifested skepticism about these accusations but did not dismiss them outright. Taking up the lapidary language of justice, he stated that "if the [violent] event was committed on the pretext of an executory order [*Executoria de 1779*] given to the governor of Cuba ... the culprits should be severely castigated [*escarmentados*] and the injury to the offended should be redressed [*reparada*]."[16] But, he added, "because the latter did not offer proof through which the abuses [*atropellamientos*] could even be made credible, their exposition could only serve to investigate the truth."[17] In other words, while the charges seemed farfetched and no evidence had been provided for them in the Madrid Memorial, the fiscal considered that the accusations should be investigated and, if proven true, redressed in justice. Fair enough. That was the role of due process. But did this injunction apply to all cobreros or just to those deemed free?

The Edict of 1786, which ratified the Council's writ of 1784, opened the doors of lower tribunals to individual enslaved cobreros, especially to fugitives, to dispute their status in the courts. Multiple battles of interpretation over the edict's meaning and reach took place in lower colonial courts, but one took place in Madrid as well. I turn to this case first to compare it with those that took place in the colony.

TESTING THE RULING IN MADRID

The opportunity to test the Council's writ in Madrid, in the Council's own tribunal, came up in August 1787 when Gregorio Cosme found out that two young enslaved cobrera women were in Madrid and tried to liberate them using his broad interpretation of the Council's ruling of

[16] Relator's report, Council of Indies, April 24, 1790, No. 27, AGI-SD 330. [17] Ibid.

1784. The women's masters were powerful people in Santiago de Cuba. One was a prominent merchant, Don Juan Francisco Creagh, and the other was Doña Josefa de Moño, the wife of then Governor Nicolás Arredondo (1781–88) who had overseen the privatization and distribution of cobreros to the heirs and had permitted their removal and sale. Creagh had been a legal advisor of the governor. Both had brought the captives to serve them during their stay in Madrid. Citing a collective interpretation of the Council's ruling of 1784, Cosme sued the powerful masters asking that the cobreras be set free and their repatriation costs be paid by their alleged masters.

The opening petition went right to the heart of the interpretation conflict. It stated that despite the Council's ruling of 1784 ordering that "the freedom and usurped property and haciendas" of the *vecinos* (citizens) and naturales of that villa "be returned [*sean restituidos*] to the state in which they were prior to the events of 1781,"[18] Don Juan Francisco Crea [*sic*], vecino of Santiago de Cuba, and Governor of Santiago, Don Nicolás de Arredondo, had "appropriated as slaves" Damiana Ortiz and Bárbara Rodríguez with "clear contempt of court [*con desacato*]."[19] Asserting the native (and vecino) status of all the cobreros, the petition attributed a collective reach to the Council's mandate. The petition added that not only had the alleged masters "not returned them to their previous freedom, but they had even brought them to this court ... where they are treated with the greatest inhumanity."[20] The case of Bárbara Rodríguez held captive in Madrid by the governor's wife thereafter disappeared from the record, perhaps handled separately or settled out of court. The case of Damiana Ortiz then became the focus of the suit.

Creagh responded with a different interpretation of the Council's ruling. He contended that Damiana "*has never been free* and is one of the many slaves that through Executive Order of His Majesty [1779] were handed over to Don Juan Manuel Garzón and partners" (my italics).[21] Explaining how he had obtained legal ownership over the enslaved cobrera, Creagh claimed that the heir Garzón allocated her to Don José Nicolás de Quiroga (another heir) who in turn gave her with "judicial authority" to Creagh as payment for a debt of 7,000 pesos that Quiroga owed him. In his view, his deed of ownership and notarized transfer were

[18] José Uruñuela, Madrid, August 8, 1787, in Cosme vs Creagh, f. 1–1v, AGI-SD 1627.
[19] Ibid. [20] Ibid.
[21] Juan Francisco Creagh, ca. August 9–14, 1787, in Cosme vs Creagh, f. 3–4, AGI-SD 1627.

sufficient legal evidence to invalidate Damiana Ortiz's wrongful enslavement claim. But while the deed may have proved the proper transfer of property, it did not show if the acquisition of the slave at its source had been legal. Although Creagh was familiar – even complicit – with the controversial enslavement and alienation of the cobreros, by using the deed as evidence of Ortiz's legitimate slavery, he was claiming a neutral role as a third party in a proper market transaction, thereby eliding the previous history of how Ortiz had become a commodity or whether she had been wrongfully enslaved and sold in the first place. For some reason, Cosme's attorney, the court's Procurador of the Poor, failed to challenge the evidence in procedural terms. Instead, as a fallback, the procurador and Cosme concurrently filed more conventional accusations of mistreatment and cruelty against the master.

The case went to trial mostly on the grounds of cruel treatment (*sevicia*). Ultimately, the Council ruled that Damiana Ortiz was a legitimate slave of Don Juan Francisco Creagh. According to the judgment, Ortiz "was not among those comprehended in the Council's Provision of 1784 with respect to the natives of the Villa of Santiago del Prado."[22] Creagh's word that she had never been free and his written title of possession prevailed as evidence. The Council did not even follow the evidential rule it had created. No Royal Treasury lists from the colony were sent for and consulted as the ruling of 1784 stipulated, nor was Ortiz deposed on any matter other than her mistreatment claims. Perhaps given the fact that the state's lists that were stipulated as evidence of Ortiz's pre-1781 status were in Cuba favored Creagh's case, but the court did not apply the ambiguous rule of favoring freedom in cases of uncertainty either. Furthermore, in accepting Creagh's deed of Damiana Ortiz as evidence of property, the Council also upheld the heirs' right to alienate and sell the enslaved cobreros. The court also ruled against the accusations of mistreatment due to insufficient evidence given the lack of proper witnesses.

The verdict of this individual case manifested the Council's intent regarding its own (confusing) ruling of 1784. It effectively confirmed the Council's ratification of the Executory Order of 1779 and the heirs' property rights over the enslaved cobreros and did not admit a collective interpretation of its writ of 1784. The judgment on Damiana Ortiz's case constituted a major blow for Cosme and for the cobreros' case in general.

[22] Sentence, Madrid, November 28, 1787, in Cosme vs Creagh, f. 59, AGI-SD 1627.

Was this a preview of the future of their lawsuit? If this was the Council's interpretation of its own ruling, what interpretations could be expected in the colony? Ironically, the Council's writ, ratified by the Royal Edict of 1786, received a more extensive life in the colony than in the Council's tribunal.

THE POLITICS OF LITIGATION IN THE COLONY AND AMPLIFICATION OF THE CONFLICT

The Edict of June 11, 1786, arrived in the colony on October 6 of that year. As the epigraphs suggest, it elicited considerable controversy, much of it related to what I term the politics of interpretation and of procedural rules. Although the main evidential rules dictated by the edict foreclosed or limited the possibilities of claims to freedom by individual plaintiffs who accessed colonial tribunals, it is important to show how these rules operated in actual cases. And yet, judicial battles in some of these colonial tribunals produced wider openings for dispute than those displayed in Damiana Ortiz's trial in Madrid. In any case, these hearings allow us to get closer to ordinary enslaved cobreros' experience of the judicial system.

Charged with the execution of the edict as special judge (*juez privativo*), Captain General José Manuel de Ezpeleta (1785–89) ordered the publication of the edict throughout the island.[23] Town criers in plazas and priests in churches announced that the natives of El Cobre could dispute their enslaved status through judicial hearings. Notices were also posted on church doors, and priests must have announced the orders in Sunday masses as they usually did throughout the empire.[24] The dispute thereby became visible to a general public beyond its epicenter in Santiago de Cuba. Yet, although the king's voice was heard everywhere, it was heard differently by different people. Some read collective freedom into the edict, others, closer to the edict's intent, read its confirmation of the cobreros' enslavement.

A disgruntled slaveholder commented on the edict's impact on the cobreros and on the interpretative disputes it gave rise to in the colony:

> As soon as the Royal Edict of 1786 was published inserted in the *bando* [proclamation] there was a general commotion [*una conmoción general*] in the cobreros' spirit. The free believed that the sovereign's disposition showered him with benefits and privileges; and the slave that it took away his slavery and put

[23] Relator's report, No. 3, Madrid, April 3, 1799, AGI-SD 1627. [24] Ibid.

> him in the state of freedom. And due to this mistaken [*errada*] idea, they immediately saw themselves surrounded with unjust, contrived and impertinent litigations [*litigios*]. Not only the heirs of Eguiluz, but all of those [slaveholders] they sold slaves to became part of this convulsion.[25]

Another slave holder noted with approval that "the Governor of Cuba, witnessing the disquiet and disorder that the royal edict was taking hold among the cobreros, prudently declared in its order of enforcement that it did not protect in any way the slaves that had been handed over through the Royal Treasury's mediation."[26]

The fiscal of the Royal Treasury in Havana, a key player representing the Crown's interests, also intervened in the controversy over the edict's interpretation. By parsing the various aspects of the dominant jurisprudence of slavery at the time, he provided guidelines on how the edict should be interpreted by colonial tribunals on the island. The fiscal's account may be regarded as the official colonial interpretation of the controversial edict based on a strict reading of slave law and property rights at the time. According to this official, the Edict of 1786 upheld the Executory Order of 1779: the mining estate belonged to the heirs of Eguiluz "whose possession right should be protected."[27] Taking the high ground of imperial slave law, he added that, however, "this possession should not overstep one point [*no debía pasar un punto adelante*] with respect to the natives of that pueblo whose condition as freeborn [*ingenuos*], freed [*libertinos*] or slaves may be doubtful"[28] The fiscal focused on the determination of status based on only these three categories. His parsing of the law did not include any intermediate category such as *coartados* (enslaved persons in the process of purchasing their freedom), *status libero*, or any other form of in-between status of conditional freedom. His was an either free or slave clear status question. People in these in-between statuses abounded in the island and their disputes over their status or the conditions of that status constituted a good number of the slave-based litigation throughout the empire. Many cobreros' own former status as royal slaves was arguably one such in-between or undetermined status.

Although the fiscal used the term "natives," he rejected the category's alleged force to override individual free or slave status, as the memorials had claimed. In fact, the fiscal explicitly rejected any collective or

[25] Autos Marcelina Antonia de los Reyes, 1787, No. 35/43, AGI-SD 1628. [26] Ibid.
[27] Fiscal of Royal Treasury, Relator's Report, No. 3, April 3, 1799, AGI-SD 1627.
[28] Ibid.

corporate claim to freedom asserting that the dispute should be over "their personal freedom in particular and not in common [*en común*]." The restitution order, he asserted, "only applied to those native individuals of El Cobre whose status [*condición*] was doubtful."[29] In this formulation, he unyoked official individual status from native status. That reading rejected the Madrid Memorial's formulation of the cobreros' case. The colonial state spoke by backing the heirs' case and providing a small individual margin for mistaken condition.

The fiscal also parsed the uncertainty principle signaled in the edict's phrase that only in the cases where it had been determined "without doubt, contradiction or controversy" that persons were in "actual slavery" should they be considered legitimate slaves. Wrote the fiscal: "Given the pious [*piadosa*] and privileged character of these [freedom] cases, mere doubt is sufficient cause to open a hearing."[30] Whereas the fiscal's reading of the uncertainty principle found in the *Siete Partidas* elicited only a judicial hearing to adjudicate status, in other more liberal formulations, this rule was carried further to the presumption of freedom at point of sentence in cases of doubt, not unlike presumption of innocence unless irrevocably proven guilty today.[31] The variable interpretation and application of this rule suggests the malleability of the law in practice.

I turn now to the actual hearings and to the legal actions that the Edict of 1786 generated in the island. What becomes interesting in these cases is not so much how colonial courts conducted their proceedings and interpreted the edict's mandate as the use that ordinary cobreros, both men and women, immediately made of these openings in the lower courts and the networks they employed in this legal mobilization.

THE HEARINGS

A number of legal actions took place in some cities in the island where enslaved cobreros were to be found. These actions were all interconnected through the Edict of 1786, which opened the doors of the courts to individual cobreros. Arguably, this surge took on the aspect of a

[29] Ibid. [30] Ibid.

[31] The notion of uncertainty in freedom cases was later invoked in the final deliberations regarding the adjudication of the cobreros' case, but in a different way, see Chapter 8. This issue was also invoked in freedom suits in nineteenth-century Brazil. See Grinberg, *A Black Jurist*, 55–57.

sprawling legal movement since networks of communication and support developed among plaintiffs in different cities. Contrary to Santiago, where the bishopric (and covert private citizens) provided legal advice to the cobreros' apoderados, in Havana and other cities, clergymen or the church played no role in advising individual cobreros. In Havana, the Spanish merchant Espinoza de los Monteros, who sponsored Cosme's trip to Madrid in 1784, acted as apoderado of the cobreros in the island's capital. Espinoza oversaw the cases of minors and provided legal recourse through a private attorney to cobreros who wanted to pursue further judicial action beyond the hearings.

Espinoza had his own communication line to Madrid that bypassed Cosme. The Spanish apoderado in Havana may have provided a check on the captain general's compliance with orders from Madrid. In other cities, the cobreros used other intermediaries to access the courts. In the town of Trinidad, for instance, there was a *padre de pobres* (advocate of the poor) who acted as a magnet attracting a number of cobreros from Sancti Spíritus who needed a defense. Elsewhere, there may have been a friendly notary, or lawyer, and/or judge who offered compensated or uncompensated aid. But nowhere in the island, or for that matter in Spain, were there abolitionist organizations or activists as in Britain and some northern American cities, where they were beginning to play an important role in taking slave cases to court.[32]

[32] The most prominent early British activist working through the courts was Grenville Sharp, especially given his role in filing the Summerset case (and others) in London in 1773. In some slave states in the United States, enslaved plaintiffs made use of private legal practitioners in their freedom suits who had no ideological antislavery commitment. In northern states where abolitionist associations were legal, these organizations sponsored freedom suits. Although abolitionist societies sponsored many freedom suits, many slave plaintiffs hired attorneys on their own. For a discussion on the many motives other than antislavery views that lawyers in Maryland (often themselves slaveholders) had to take up freedom suits, see Thomas, *A Question of Freedom*, 61–63. For the Upper South and Louisiana, Schweninger argues there were no monetary incentives since fees for these cases were low, but lawyers, most slaveholders themselves, and few if any holding antislavery views, represented slaves *pro bono publico*. He estimated that more than 1,000 lawyers in these slave states took up those cases, *Appealing for Liberty*, 241–45. Lea Vandervelde states that in Missouri there is little evidence of "cause lawyering" among lawyers representing slaves. In that state, slaves were declared paupers and were assigned an attorney, though some slaves did approach lawyers who were then assigned to represent them, *Redemption Songs*, 8–9. For Brazil, Grinberg argues lawyers took cases for slaveholders and slaves, and that there were no "freedom activist" lawyers in the lower courts (appeal court cases were assigned) until about the 1860s, and not until later did lawyers with abolitionist views take to the courts to defend freedom suits. See *A Black Jurist*, 115–25.

Given that the captain general was appointed special judge (juez privativo) to oversee the cobreros' hearings, most of these extant records are from Havana. Local judges were to oversee the initial hearings and send them at point of sentence to the captain general for final adjudication, from where they were to be remitted to Madrid for vetting. The captain general presided over at least twenty-seven cases in his own court in Havana. Although the Edict of 1786was published in major cities and towns, only the records of five judicial actions from other tribunals went far enough to make it to Havana for final adjudication. These were the tip of the iceberg.

Others were sent back to the tribunals where they originated for further evidence or were dismissed outright at the first instance level or not reported to the captain general regardless of outcome. Some may have been settled out of court. Whereas there was an initial cascade of hearings in 1786, some cases were unresolved as late as 1790, and four even as late as 1794; others were begun but never further pursued or adjudicated. And although records of these hearings and legal actions were supposed to be remitted immediately to Madrid, they were retained in the island's archives until 1797. Part of Cosme's task in Madrid was to keep protesting in court the alleged nonenforcement of the edict and pressing the Council to order the remittance of local proceedings and documentation to Madrid. Simón Echenique denounced in 1793 the delaying tactics and emphasized the political motives behind it (second epigraph).

The initial hearings in Havana took place during November 1786, eight months prior to Damiana Ortiz's court case in Madrid.[33] Confusion reigned from the beginning. Captain General Ezpeleta ordered all vecinos owning slaves from El Cobre to report them in court within five days, not just the doubtful cases. His published order initially sounded misleading as it suggested that the king had granted freedom collectively to all cobreros. Don Francisco and Don Dionisio Luis Jorge, two brothers who had purchased the cobrero Norberto Norate, declared that "it has arrived to our notice the bando published as a result of a Royal Order whereby His Majesty declares free from all servitude the natives of El Cobre ordering all those who have purchased them to present them [to the magistrates] in order to comply with the royal resolution."[34] But whereas Ezpeleta made an open call to masters and

[33] I do not have the record of the *bandos* (orders) he published and their actual text, only what was reported in the hearings is available.

[34] Autos Antonio Vicente Norate, Havana, 1786, No. 55/63/20, AGI-SD 1628.

cobreros suggesting the edict was a royal grant of collective freedom, in practice he applied a narrow interpretation of the edict in line with the fiscal of the Royal Treasury's pronouncement discussed above. Basically, Ezpeleta tried to sort out the cases of slavery that seemed doubtful and merited further investigation from those that he termed "legitimate" slaves. How did he go about this sifting task?

A few key questions in the hearings were meant to initially determine, on a case-by-case basis, whether the examined cobrero had been a royal slave or not prior to 1781. While this process allowed some initial space for determination of status through performance and oral evidence, Ezpeleta, as judge, decided on the relevant evidential rules and actions that defined legitimate slavery in the cobreros' case. Royal Treasury lists were only consulted in the last instance.

Those cobreros who were considered legitimately enslaved were inscribed in a notebook as "legitimate" slaves. Others (those who could not "without doubt, contradiction or controversy" be considered slaves before 1781) were given an order of *resguardo*, a legal document showing court protection that allowed them to go about temporarily as free while their case was investigated, a process that could take days or months to the cobrero's advantage. In other cases, they were returned to their master with the proviso that time be given to them to collect evidence to pursue their case. The initial hearings could result in further legal action if a cobrero's status was uncertain or if the cobrero pressed further charges. None of these protocols were followed in Damiana Ortiz's case in Madrid, however. In this sense, Ezpeleta opened up the contestation procedure somewhat, but ultimately the state records and the fiscal's recommendations were the decisive factors in each case.

Hearings in Havana opened with a short account by slaveholders of how they had obtained possession of the cobrero they claimed to own. They were asked to produce their legitimate deed; if they did not have it on hand, they were given a grace period to submit it. The state wanted to know if it had been a legal transaction and if sale taxes to the state had been paid. Ezpeleta gave powerful citizen Don Sebastián Peñalver three days to present his property title over the enslaved cobrera; since MaríaJosefa was a minor, Ezpeleta passed over the case to Espinoza, as the cobreros' apoderado in that city. The outcome of her case is unknown.

Many owners presented their enslaved cobreros and were willing to comply with orders provided their economic interests were not affected. Doña Bárbara Hernández presented her two slaves, Isabel Cruz, eighteen to twenty years old, and María Francisca, twelve years old, whom she had purchased in 1783 for 350 and 300 pesos, respectively. Hernández said she was willing to return them "if their price is returned to her [*si se le devuelve el precio*]."[35] Some masters requested a certificate of presentation in case they needed to claim indemnification for a freed cobrero. The city's solicitor general (*síndico procurador general*), Don Antonio Basilio García Menocal, another distinguished citizen who also owned a cobrero, sought indemnification for the 400 pesos he had paid for the enslaved cobrero. He filed a claim stating that "since as a consequence of the sovereign order he has become free, I must immediately demand the possession title against my predecessor [*repetir contra mi causante*]."[36] Lurking over the proceedings were, in principle, chains of reclamations that went back to the heirs as the original sellers. But whereas some slaveholders were willing to comply with the court's decision as long as they were reimbursed, others were adamant about not returning their slaves even with payment and these cases evolved into longer legal disputes. For example, whereas Rafael de los Reyes' master let him go while reclaiming reimbursement from the heirs, his sister, Marcelina de los Reyes, faced a different master. Hers hunted her down through four tribunals, blocking her claims when it probably would have been easier for him to give her up and claim reimbursement by passing back the dispute over her status to the heirs.[37] Thus, some slaveholders entered the fray of the general dispute letting their cobrero slaves go free (at least temporarily) while others put up a staunch resistance.

Following the master's presentation, the cobrero in question was summoned and submitted to a short interrogation to preliminarily determine his or her status as legitimate or doubtful. At this point, cobreros had no legal counsel. They walked in perhaps thinking that the king had granted them freedom and the interview was a pro forma requirement; or they answered candidly without much thought about the implications of their responses. When deposed, cobreros were first asked to name their masters: the enslaved cobreros' memory thereby became a living archive of the sales and property transfers that had taken place from slave owner to slave owner. While the questions were structured and the court scribe transcribed the responses in an abridged formulaic manner, at times, some pushback from savvier cobreros could be heard in the recorded

35 Autos Isabel Cruzata and María Francisca, Havana, 1786, No. 43/51/8, AGI-SD 1628.

36 Autos Pedro de Cárdenas, Havana, November 7, 1786, No. 46/54/11, AGI-SD 1628.

37 Autos Marcelina Antonia de los Reyes, 1787, No. 35/43, AGI-SD 1628.

responses. Sometimes an indignant phrase or choice of words either from the scribe or the deponent slipped into the transcript. For instance, María Josefa Sánchez declared that her present master "obtained her [*la tuvo*] from Doña Josefa Angulo who [in turn] got her in the distribution made when all the *sons of El Cobre* were imprisoned [*todos los hijos del Cobre fueron aprisionados*]" (my italics).[38] In using words such as "sons [and daughters] of El Cobre" and the loaded term "imprisonment," María Josefa hinted in her testimony her view of the enslavement as a violation of the cobreros' native status. But what did Maria Josefa in fact say? How did she describe this harrowing collective event of captivity in her own words during the interrogation? Did she elaborate on the significance of this memory further whereas the scribe abridged (and interpreted) her account simply with this phrase?

Next came the more potentially incriminating questions. The deponents were asked about their genealogy: personal histories that their masters had no way of knowing. Intimate questions about personal kinship bonds became evidence of the transmission of captive status. Most responses were self-incriminating. Cobreros were asked to identify their parents, grandparents, brothers and sisters. No questions were asked about spouses or children. Twenty-seven-year-old Mónica Cruzata remembered well the names of her deceased paternal and maternal grandparents. Although she did not say so, Mónica was the niece of one of the most important local apoderados of the pueblo, the freedman Justo Cruzata. Whereas Cruzata's immediate family, his wife and children, were all free born, he had relatives like Mónica Cruzata in his extended family who had been enslaved. This may have driven him to take up the defense of all the natives of El Cobre.

At times we hear more heart-wrenching testimony in these hearings. For instance, the young cobrera María Francisca, aged fifteen and a minor, responded that "since she was young when they caught her, she only remembers that her parents were named Manuel y Antonia, she does not know what else [surnames], and that she had four siblings named Emilio, Bernardo, Angela, and Juan José, but that she ignores the names of their owners, [and] that her parents and siblings and *all the pueblo* were sold without her knowing to whom" (my italics).[39] Hers was a glaring case of family and pueblo dismemberment. María Francisca had lost contact with her family and her identifying markers eluded her. Her

38 Autos María Josefa Sánchez, 1786, No. 53/61/18, AGI-SD 1628.

39 Autos Isabel Cruzata and María Francisca, Havana, 1786, No. 51/43/8, AGI-SD 1628.

memory made it difficult for the court to trace her lineage and status. Hers became a doubtful case in need of further review and was not included in the "legitimate slaves" notebook. Instead, her file was remitted to the apoderado Espinoza to charge him with following up on her case and providing the necessary evidence of status to the court. Meanwhile, the girl returned to her alleged master. Whether or not Espinoza, in his duties as apoderado, followed up on her case, or in others remitted to him, we do not know.

The most compromising question, however, was one meant to determine enactment of slavery to the king. This was done by inquiring whether parents or siblings were required to do temporary labor for the state or provide personal service to royal officials. Performing this type of work met the criteria for determining "actual" slavery to the king and, therefore, legitimate proof of enslavement. In other words, contrary to the Madrid Memorial of 1784 where these requisitions were transformed into a service, or in the Echenique's Memorial of 1793 where they were transformed into the service owed by *libertos* to their former masters, in the captain general's tribunal this corvée labor was considered a badge of royal slavery and no prescriptive acts were considered by the court. The question was posed indirectly as follows: "Were your parents among the people of El Cobre who went to [Santiago de] Cuba to serve the Señor Governor and other Ministers for some time each month [*algún tiempo en el mes*] or among those who were exempted from this? Or do you know anything about the freedom of your parents?"[40] María Francisca, like Gabriel Vicente, was keen enough to answer that her parents were not among those who went to serve "but among those who were as if free in their houses [*los que estaban como libres en sus casas*] and that she does not know about the rest [of the question]."[41] That response made her slavery potentially dubious and required corroboration of her name with the Royal Treasury lists. María Francisca also introduced in her testimony a vernacular notion of what she – and other cobreros – invoked as the major criteria of freedom: living autonomously in their own houses in the pueblo. Was this an acceptable performative of freedom? If so, it should have applied to all cobreros, as the memorials argued. Yet the state's draft labor criterion overruled other possible freedom criteria.

At other times, the questioning was more direct, and cobreros were asked if they went to serve in Cuba "as a slave of the king [*esclavo del*

[40] Ibid. [41] Ibid.

Rey]" Most cobreros, unaware of the incriminating side of the question, candidly answered that their father and siblings were among those who served the governor and ministers in Santiago de Cuba or were slaves of the king. For instance, Simón de la Paz, a fugitive who presented himself thinking the edict granted freedom to fugitives, responded that "his mother and siblings were among those who went to serve in Cuba as the king's slaves." Ezpeleta ordered that "since the *pardo* Simón de la Paz confesses to be among those who went to serve in Cuba as the king's slave and the same happened with his siblings, he is hereby declared a legitimate slave."[42] Many cobreros understood that they had once been the king's slaves, but that this status did not imply private slavery; rather, it constituted some kind of privileged status closer to royal vassalage. That was precisely the vernacular understanding that had prevailed among many cobreros in the past and the new collective legal actions were trying to upend. But many of these enslaved and dispersed cobreros, out of contact with matters in the pueblo, were perhaps unfamiliar with the main litigation based on presumption of freedom in the past.

Significantly, no questions were asked in the hearings about the performance of military service to the Crown or holding cabildo positions in the pueblo, which were among the criteria that the plaintiffs' memorials advanced as signs of gendered merit, honor, and freedom. Yet, the sixteen-year-old Manuela Borrero managed to slip into her testimony that "her father was a soldier and served the king, and also her brothers [who] carried water and firewood, and around this time they were imprisoned [*apresados*] by the Cubans [*los cubanos*] [from Santiago] and sold there."[43] Her recorded testimony was the only one that made reference to militia service, and she framed the labor draft of her brothers as militia service, not as a performative of slavery. In this formulation, that kind of work should count as service to the king and not as servitude What else was said or claimed by deponents and left out of the record we cannot know.

Captain General Ezpeleta provided some margin for the disputation of status for individual cobreros. He started with genealogy and performative criteria. Yet, by restricting questions and dictating the performative criteria of slavery to be corvée labor, he foreclosed other ways of arguing for freedom and undermined the plaintiffs' argumentation in the Madrid Memorial. However, he did open the possibility of using baptism records

[42] Autos Simón de la Paz, Havana, 1786, No. 65/57/22, AGI-SD 1628.
[43] Autos Manuela Borrero, Havana, November 7, 1786, No. 37/45/2, AGI-SD 1628.

as evidence. These procedures, however restrictive, were not even followed in the case of Damiana Ortiz in Madrid. Although some cobreros obtained temporary reprieves, no case on record was adjudicated as free by the captain general of Havana.

BEYOND THE EDICT: OTHER CHARGES PRESSED ON THE COURT

Conflicts spilled over from the courts into everyday life outside the courts as some cobreros defied their current masters citing implications of their edict-given rights. The masters of the enslaved cobrero Antonio Vicente Norate, who worked in the tobacco farm of the Jorge brothers, complained to the captain general that "the said slave resists to work invoking the royal edict."[44] When the enslaved cobrero Bartolomé Rodríguez, a rented slave working in the construction works of "Casa Blanca" in Havana announced to his mistress, Doña Nicolasa Mancebo, that he had heard that all the enslaved people of El Cobre were free, she allegedly responded that "she did not object to my freedom and said she was happy about the news."[45] But the amicable attitude dissipated when Rodríguez made his alleged edict-based freedom retroactive and pressed claims against her to pay him for the work he had done during the past year at five *reales* a day. Cases like this showed the potential of the edict and the hearings to fight slaveholders' appropriation of their labor and to claim freedom rights – and compensation – retroactively. If it did not pass muster, at least temporary reprieves could be gained.

If most of the extant hearings in Havana were initiated by masters presenting their enslaved cobreros in compliance with Ezpeleta's order, there were also cases initiated by the cobreros themselves. A private counsel working with the apoderado Espinoza took these cases to court. Cobreros who had fled since 1781, and even years before, presented themselves in court to officially claim the alleged edict-based freedom for fugitives (*prófugos*). The brothers Juan Agustín and Juan Salvador Cruzata, tobacco farmers in El Cobre, had run away (*profugamos*) in 1781 during the raid "leaving behind our goods [*bienes*]" which they now wanted to recover.[46] They had been able to escape to Havana where they

44 Autos Antonio Vicente Norate, Havana, 1786, No. 5/62/19, AGI-SD 1628.

45 Autos Ana and Bartolomé Rodríguez, Havana, October 8, 1787, No. 36/44/1, AGI-SD 1628.

46 Autos Juan Agustín and Juan Salvador Cruzata, 1786, No. 48/56/13, AGI-SD 1628.

had been hiding and working in the *partido* (district) of San Antonio until they heard the news about the edict. A grapevine of cobreros in the Havana region helped the two brothers bring three other cobreros as witnesses to testify that the brothers were natives of El Cobre and that they had escaped during the raid (*rebato*) when "the cubanos [natives of Santiago de Cuba] apprehended the cobreros" and they had fled to Havana.[47] Here, again, implicit accusations of transgressive violence by their neighbors, natives of Santiago, entered the record through these hearings. Reacting to the published edict, the Cruzata brothers requested a court certificate to allow them to return to Santiago de Cuba to claim their property in the governor of Santiago's tribunal. Ezpeleta granted them the *resguardo*. The cobrero brothers may not have been aware that it was more difficult to press claims in Santiago's tribunal where cobreros were not even being heard. But then a license to travel to Santiago may have given them the opportunity to return to the island's eastern region where they could escape and settle in the village's environs as many other cobreros did (see Chapter 7).

More combative suits against masters were pursued by another group of cobreros. They pushed further the edict's implications, as understood by the cobreros and their supporters. Cobreros who had initiated coartaciones after their enslavement in 1781 or purchased their freedom also sued their former masters – now their *causantes* or vendors – to recover the amounts paid for their freedom. These cobreros were acting as free subjects claiming possession rights over themselves per the royal edict. The cobrero Manuel Vicente de la Caridad filed a petition demanding that "the apoderado of [the heir] Don Bernardo Mancebo in this city return to me the 250 pesos [that I paid for my freedom] immediately and without being heard to avoid delays [and] to do so within one day."[48] Don Nicolás Ambrosio Mancebo, the apoderado in question, indignantly called Manuel Vicente's claim a "distorted [*dislocada*] petition guided by the same error as his compatriots."[49] In another case, Ana del Rosario, a cobrera slave who had partially purchased her freedom from Doña

[47] The three cobreros witnesses that the two fugitive brothers presented were Bartolomé Rodríguez, who worked in the garrison and was suing his mistress for his back wages, Pedro de Cárdenas, and Gabriel Vicente Oquendo. The last two had once been fugitives themselves and were now also suing for reimbursement of their coartación payments.

[48] Autos Manuel Vicente de la Caridad, Havana, January 25, 1788, No. 59/67/24, AGI-SD 1628.

[49] Petition of Don Nicolás Ambrosio Mancebo, in Autos Manuel Vicente de la Caridad, February 6, 1788, No. 59/67/24, AGI-SD 1628.

Nicolasa Mancebo, insisted on getting reimbursed for the 275 pesos she had already paid for her freedom (she had 50 pesos still pending to complete the payment for her freedom certificate). Her attorney used strong combative words in her petition: she was to be allowed to enjoy the possession of her freedom peacefully and "not suffer the extortions that the said Doña Nicolasa Mancebo wants to make and that she be ordered to return to me the amount [of 275 pesos] within a day."[50] By 1790, there was still no resolution to Ana del Rosario's case. Although perhaps no longer washing clothes for Doña Nicolasa, or making further payments, Ana del Rosario was probably still waiting to recover the money she had invested in her own emancipation.

The presence of Espinoza and his lawyer may have facilitated the initiation of these legal actions based on their interpretation of the Edict of 1786. Even if in restricted terms, the edict meant the opening up of the courts to battle masters and to press claims as far as possible. Don Nicolás Mancebo, the heirs' apoderado, suggested that these hearings were inciting cobreros in Santiago and elsewhere to flee their masters to seek protection in the tribunal in Havana. Allowing their claims to continue would effectively mean "that there will be no one left among freedmen and slaves [of El Cobre] who will not come [all the way] from [Santiago de] Cuba to claim freedom [in Havana], and under this system they will all live and die free, and their masters, and all of those who have bought them across the island, will be left without their service, beyond what the royal intention [entailed]."[51] Although this complaint suggested the dreaded potential of slaves suing masters en masse, it was also an example of the hyperbolic rhetoric all too common in legal battles. Whereas some enslaved cobreros moved around pushing their cases in various tribunals, there was also a strong pushback from the courts to block these cases. Mancebo's protest, however, illustrates how affronted the heirs felt by the mere act of the cobreros' use of the courts to pursue their freedom and how entitled they and other slaveholders felt to slave servitude. This may have been the tenor of Havana's slaveholders' opposition three years later to the 1789 slave code promulgated in the Council of the Indies.[52] And they had a point.

[50] Autos Ana and Bartolomé Rodríguez, Havana, October 8, 1787, No. 36/44/1, AGI-SD 1628.

[51] Petition of Don Nicolás Ambrosio Mancebo, in Autos Vicente de la Caridad, February 6, 1788, No. 59/67/24, AGI-SD 1628.

[52] Guide to the Education, Treatment and Occupation of Slaves, 1789, AGI-SD 2588. On planters' refusal to its publications in Havana, Venezuela and other localities and

COLLECTIVE INTERPRETATION OF THE EDICT AND ALTERNATIVE PROCEDURES IN THE COURT OF SANCTI SPÍRITUS

Not all lower tribunals in the island followed Captain General Ezpeleta's procedural rules nor the even more perfunctory ones used by the Council of the Indies in Damiana Ortiz's case in Madrid. At least one tribunal in the island took a different path that led to provisional freedom in the case of four cobrera plaintiffs in the town of Sancti Spíritus (see Figure 0.1). A brief look at their hearings shows how a case based on the same edict could be differently processed and contested in another lower tribunal. Not only was the edict's interpretation at stake, but the evidence admitted and the procedural rules in use could vary, especially where there were no official lists at hand since the lists were only available in Havana and Santiago. Without them, lower courts had to decide how to filter and provisionally decide cases. Proceedings and outcomes in lower colonial tribunals could depend on various factors: friendliness of the tribunal and its judge; adopted procedural protocols, competence and commitment of counsel; the masters' inclination to dispute the case; the enslaved plaintiff's own tenacity in pressing the case; and, to some extent, the plaintiff's networks. These contingent factors gave some unpredictability to the outcomes of court cases. The Bourbon policy of centralizing the judicial process, in this case through the appointment of the captain general as special judge, and of providing guidelines for adjudication from the top aimed to control the discretionary power of lower courts.[53] The case of four cobrera friends enslaved in Sancti Spíritus – Rafaela Sánchez, Margarita González, Teresa Coba, and María del Rosario Rodríguez – illustrates the tension between local discretionary rules and the centralized control.[54]

The four plaintiffs were allowed to file their case jointly (*en sociedad*) as cobreras in 1792, five years after a first wave of hearings had taken

their reasons, see Ferrer, *Freedom's Mirror*, 26–29; Lucerna Salmoral, *Los códigos negros*, 108–19.

[53] Although according to historian Adriana Chira the tendency to rely on customary norms remained judicial practice in Cuba until the 1850s and '60s, the Council seems to have set in motion here a procedural centralization, at least in a major special case like this. Chira, *Patchwork Freedoms*, 143–44, 2339–41. See Yannakakis, *The Art of Being In-Between* for similar conflicts in Mexico in the case of Indian litigation.

[54] Autos Teresa Ramos alias Coba, Sancti Spíritus, 1792, No. 34, f. 306–407, AGI-SD 1628.

place in 1787. Their cases had made it to the Havana tribunal during that first round of legal actions. However, Captain General Ezpeleta returned their cases to Sancti Spíritus' court recommending that the women be given time to compile further evidence to pursue their cases, as had happened to others in Ezpeleta's court.

The Sancti Spíritus tribunal returned the women to their alleged masters and their cases subsequently stalled, as may have happened to many other cobreros. The women's first round of legal mobilization, therefore, had been effectively countered. Five years later, however, one of the women, Margarita González, was able to revive her case with the help of new counsel and had greater luck this time around. In her opening petition, González offered the reason why she – and probably other cobreros – had not pressed her case again on the court until then. She said that she had lacked counsel to direct her but that a "letrado professor, out of sheer charity," had advised her recently, pointing to the work of allies behind the scenes. She requested that the court name Licenciado Isidoro Rensoli, presumably her secret advisor, as her father defender (*padre defensor*) to revive her cause. Court and counsel costs would be paid by the defeated party. The presiding judge that year readily accepted her petition. After González won the case under Rensoli's counsel, the other three cobreras contacted each other (one was ensconced in a rural hacienda) and filed jointly (*en sociedad*) so they could use the same attorney and witnesses and follow the same procedures, given the similarity of their cases as cobreras. The joint action would also be less costly. More importantly, the same favorable judgment passed on González's case would presumably apply to them too since their case was based on a collective reading of the edict. The friendly acting alcalde and judge again readily accepted. An accommodating judge, an encouraging counsel who backed the cobreros' collective interpretation of the edict, friendship, and native-based solidarity networks among the four enslaved cobreras facilitated the renewed legal action.

Pressing a collective interpretation of the edict on the court, Rensoli argued that procedurally the royal edict only called for a summary hearing to determine origin and standing as a cobrera since the edict applied generally to all natives of El Cobre. Counsel argued that four witnesses could orally confirm some basic facts that were presented as prompt questions in an interrogatory. Witnesses' depositions constituted the sole evidence an attorney would need to make the case for freedom per the Edict of 1786, he argued. Origin, public reputation, and performance were the significant sources to determine status (not labor services to the king, as in Ezpeleta's court, or royal records and lists, as prescribed in the edict). Rensoli was ready to argue that living as free constituted the basis of freedom. Witnesses were asked if they could confirm that each of the plaintiffs was a native of El Cobre, if they had known the plaintiff living publicly as a free person in El Cobre, if the plaintiff had been among the enslaved and sold (*enagenadasy vendidas*) after 1781 and, thus, were among those encompassed by the edict. Rensoli did not shy away from facing the more controversial question of royal slave status. Contrary to Ezpeleta in Havana, for whom (forced) service to the royal officials in Santiago was the mayor index of royal slavery, and, thus, of legitimate enslavement and sale, Rensoli turned the question around, arguing that royal slave status was not incompatible with freedom since it did not entail private dominion. The last fact to be confirmed in the interrogatory reflected what had customarily been the case in previous decades and what constituted a conundrum of the legal case: "Declare how before the alienation and sale those belonging to the pueblo were considered and treated as slaves of His Majesty without any other person having dominion over us, living openly [*francamente*] as free."[55]

Rensoli proposed that the main criteria of living as free that should be considered by the court was autonomy and its related manifestations. The witness Francisco Xavier Quiala stated succinctly that the cobreros "each lived in his own house, serving their parents, without other known master than the king."[56] Mobility and leisure seemed to count as a vernacular badge of freedom too. Pedro Moreno, native of El Cobre but vecino of Sancti Spíritus declared that he knew Rafaela Sánchez in the pueblo "and in the city of Cuba when she went to visit [*iba de* paseo] enjoying her freedom openly [*francamente*] and without any impediment."[57] Gender, in this case, precluded the use of criteria such as military service or holding official positions in the pueblo's cabildo. Although Margarita González did not bring up this point, Jose Valentín Saavedra volunteered that her husband "was *regidor* (council man) in the pueblo," thereby highlighting another criteria of freedom, having and being member of the local cabildo, and she, as wife and cobrera, partaking of that standing.[58]

[55] Ibid., f. 336. [56] Ibid., f. 344.

[57] Pedro Moreno, Sancti Spíritus, October 23, 1792, in Autos Teresa Ramos alias Coba, f. 357, AGI-SD, 1628.

[58] José Valentín Saavedra, Sancti Spíritus, September 22, 1792, in Autos Teresa Ramos alias Coba, No. 34, f. 342v, AGI-SD, 1628.

The same four witnesses gave testimony on behalf of the four women. They included two cobreros (one of them freed in the court of Sancti Spíritus and still residing in the town), a Black tailor from Havana who had once lived in Santiago and often visited El Cobre, and a White mason and militia soldier from Santiago de Cuba who was also familiar with the cobreros. They represent the social networks that the cobreros were able to tap into for their legal actions. The use of witnesses, including friends and free people of color, gave procedural priority to reputation, performance, opinion, and the word of even lower status subjects over written documents or state records as evidence of freedom. These kinds of evidential rules were more favorable to the cobreros' ability to make a case for freedom and they were a more inclusive tool that allowed a wide range of people to participate in the legal action.[59]

Yet Rensoli also made use of written records, the kind of documents, precisely, that were given preference in proceedings in other tribunals. However, he used them differently. Rather than as evidence of slavery, Rensoli used bills of sale as proof of wrongful enslavement and sale. Similarly, he mollified an incriminating baptism record where the plaintiff was inscribed as slave of the king, a record that was used in other tribunals as evidence of slavery, to show instead that there was no private owner at the time of the plaintiff's birth. Margarita González, wrote Rensoli, claimed that her baptism record showed that "I was baptized seven days after being born as slave of His Majesty, and not of Don Manuel Garzón nor of Don Tomás, his brother, who were the ones who sold me, despoiling me of the freedom I enjoyed."[60]

The *alcalde ordinario* (bailiff) acting as judge quickly issued a favorable sentence of freedom for González and the other three cobreras and charged court costs to their former masters. But, and here lay the caveat, the freedom was qualified as *por ahora* (for the time being) pending a final sentence by the captain general who was the special judge in these cases.[61]

59 In other lower instance tribunals, oral hearings denied further process outright and in yet others there seem to have been out of court settlements that never reached Havana. Thus, despite the edict's procedural and evidential centralization guidelines, first instance colonial courts seemed to be inconsistent in how they approached the individual cobreros' cases. Similarly, whereas some gave greater weight to written documents, such as the slaveholder's title of ownership or baptism records, others allowed for witness testimony as evidence of freedom, but only one seemed to favor the latter over written documents.

60 Petition Margarita González, September 22, 1792, Autos Teresa Ramos alias Coba, No. 34, f. 337, AGI-SD 1628.

61 The assessment of court and personnel fees, including the cobreras' private attorney added up to a substantial 125 pesos. Private counsel's fees amounted to 25 pesos. The

The cobreras could have remained indefinitely in the limbo of a "for now" freedom. But three months after their temporary freedom verdict was issued, their four alleged masters filed a petition in the captain general's tribunal in Havana criticizing the proceedings in Sancti Spíritus and demanding the restitution of their four slaves. By then, Ezpeleta's term had expired. The new captain general, Don Luis de Las Casas (1790–96), referred the case to the fiscal of the Royal Treasury for a recommendation, presumably based on the state treasury's records. In July 1794, more than a year and eight months after the temporary freedom verdict in the tribunal of Sancti Spiritus and a year and a half after the master's petition to the captain general for the revocation of their alleged slaves' temporary verdicts, the case was still on the fiscal's desk awaiting his recommendation. Whether the fiscal's delays were intentional or not it is difficult to say, but the cobreras' case, like others before them, remained dormant at point of sentence. The four friends, like some of the luckier cobreros who received reprieves, may have been able to live in freedom during the *por ahora* period. But the masters' pressure and a new alcalde magistrate in Sancti Spíritus may have put them back under their alleged masters' dominion until Las Casas gave sentence, which he apparently never did. By then, however, Madrid was repeatedly sending orders that cobreros be returned to El Cobre and that all proceedings and papers be remitted to the Council of the Indies for adjudication, which may have motivated the fiscal to delay taking action in the cases referred to him for consultation.

Thus, what became, in the best of cases, a possible favorable temporary outcome and reprieve for these four plaintiffs was subjected to further

alcalde ordinario who served as judge charged standard fees for his signatures in documents of 4 pesos and for his presence during the depositions (115 pesos and 6 reales) and since like most first instance judges he had no legal training he received legal assessment (for 19 pesos and 6 reales). Fees were to be paid among the defendant slaveholders who lost the case, but they refused to pay. Non-payment would block access to the file, and therefore to further litigation, until fees were paid. Autos Teresa Ramos alias Coba, No. 34, f. 392–93v, AGI-SD 1628. In the case of Marcelina Antonia de los Reyes, who lost her case, the costs of litigation in three tribunals ascended to a hefty 153 pesos and 3 reales. Although she did not have to pay for the services of the Father of the Poor's counsel in Trinidad, the only city that seemed to offer such service, she paid for private counsel in Havana and ultimately was assessed other fees, including the expenses of the opposing party, her master. De los Reyes's master, however, was responsible for paying his slave's litigation costs, but these costs would be added to her assessed value (between 350 and 400 pesos) in case she was to be sold to another master or if she wanted to buy her freedom. Autos Marcelina Antonia de los Reyes, 1787, No. 35/43, f. 523–24v, AGI-SD 1628.

contestation and reversal. To be sure, there were some cobreros whose masters freed them and used the edict to claim indemnification from the heirs. But even in these cases, the heirs could eventually reclaim possession of the returned slave, as happened in the case of Rafael de los Reyes.[62] For the most part, cases found impediments in the court, but a number of so-called doubtful cases may have slipped through. In other places, as in Santiago de Cuba, enslaved cobreros did not even bother showing up for hearings at the governor's tribunal knowing what the outcome would be. These cases show a range of interpretations and of procedural approaches used in first instance colonial tribunals that the Council tried to reign in and control by dictating the definitive evidentiary procedural rule to be employed in the adjudication process. Ultimately, these individual court disputes were not effective in bringing about a resolution to the cobreros' claims. Cosme and the cobreros' apoderados kept pressing the court in Madrid for a collective resolution to the case. Echenique's bold argumentation for collective prescriptive freedom and political rights in the memorial of 1793 represents this continuing judicial pressure in the royal court (Chapter 3). However, by the early 1790s, things began to turn around in Madrid, if not in the colony.

[62] Autos Marcelina Antonia de los Reyes, Havana, 1787, No. 35, AGI-1628.

6

A "Pernicious" Communication

Gregorio Cosme's Letters from Madrid

> [Cosme] assures them each day more and more of the certainty of their freedom, and I understand that if a solution is not found to this pernicious communication . . . your purposes will be impossible to carry out.
>
> —Governor Quintana, Santiago, 1796

In 1795, Gregorio Cosme Osorio wrote to an old cobrero friend back home: "Friend, Sale Cruzata, if you could see me you would not recognize me because with these battles of papers I have become very thin, and with the illnesses even more so, and with the disappointments and setbacks [*desasones y sinsabores*] because five times I have had to appeal [the case]."[1] There was weariness in those lines. His words provide a rare glimpse of the mighty toll that protracted litigation had taken personally on his body and spirit. Other matters, such as his precarious economic situation and money troubles, the reprimands and attempts at marginalization he had endured, the prolonged limbo in court and perhaps loneliness mây have also scarred him. The following passage echoes a similar frustration and fatigue in collective terms as Cosme shifts to an inclusive "we": "How can it be possible that so much time or such a long time has gone by during which *we* have been in these matters and contests [*contiendas*], *working with our pueblo*, standing in its defense to see *if we can obtain the privileged right of freedom*" (my italics).[2] By the time Cosme wrote those lines, he had been pursuing an elusive justice in Madrid for more than a decade. The interpretation of the Council's ruling of 1784 (and Royal Edictof 1786) was still being contested in the colony. Cosme

[1] Gregorio Cosme, Madrid, March 16, 1795, f. 11v–14, AGI-SD 1631.
[2] Gregorio Cosme, Madrid, October 6, 1795, No. 75, f. 195–207, AGI-SD 1629.

had not been able to free the cobrera Damiana Ortiz in the lawsuit he filed on her behalf in the Council in 1787. In Cuba, few enslaved cobreros had been freed and returned to El Cobre, although a number had fled back to the village. And, regardless of repeated orders, hearings from the colony had not yet been remitted to Madrid. Letters from the village did not bear good news either; some conveyed a desperate urgency. In 1792, the cobrero Martín Salazar asked Cosme to do "everything that can be done on your part . . . before they destroy all the cobreros, so many enemies are persecuting us, and in this city no one heeds orders."[3] In fact, local conflict in Santiago had been escalating since the early 1790s as Chapter 7 will discuss.

And yet, by 1795, the grim situation had begun to turn around in Madrid, if not in the colony. In letters from this year, Cosme wrote, though not without some defensiveness, that victory and collective freedom were around the corner. A change in policy does seem to have taken place at the imperial level by then. The subordination of the Council of the Indies to a centralized Council of State overseeing governance matters in the empire and other internal court politics gave rise to a shifting jurisdiction over the case.[4] New channels of communication directly to the Crown through *vía reservada* (confidential direct channels) seemed to cut through the prevarications of the case in the Council's Gracia y Justicia (Justice) section.[5] The involvement of new prominent figures such as the Bishop of Santiago de Cuba, Joaquín Osés de Alzúa (1792–1823), brought weighty and active sponsorship of the cobrero litigants. Even an alleged audience of Cosme with the king may have may have helped bring about the shift on the case in Madrid. In addition, the plaintiffs' claims had been better substantiated with evidence compiled with some difficulty in Cuba. Above all, the heirs' failure to restart mining operations in El Cobre by the ten-year deadline raised a flag in the imperial

[3] Martín Salazar, El Cobre, August 21, 1792, No. 1, AGI-SD 1627.

[4] Major imperial administrative changes took place in 1790 under Charles IV that led to the subordination of the Council of the Indies to the centralized Council of State integrating imperial governance matters. Gracia y Justicia, the judicial branch of the Council of the Indies where the freedom case of El Cobre had been filed, was retained. This restructuring went along with factional court politics. See Burkholder, "Council of the Indies," 404–23; and Johnson, *The Social Transformation*, 122–24.

[5] The direct *via reservada* channels were an early Bourbon reform but on the use of direct communication channels by royal officials and other subjects to Madrid see Johnson, *The Social Transformation*, 159.

administration. Finally, the geopolitical situation of war with France and revolution in Saint Domingue seems to have raised security concerns in Madrid (passed over in the colony) regarding the status of the case.

Cosme's extant letters from 1795 allude to some of these factors, but he lacked the inside perspective on the imperial state to make a proper assessment of the politics informing the shift in Madrid away from the Council's ruling of 1784. Except for a cryptic reference in passing to France, Cosme did not mention the larger geopolitical conflagrations unfolding at the time that could politically affect the case. But the reference suggests that despite the strong censorship of news in the metropolis, there were rumors about the anti-monarchical and regicidal disorders in France and perhaps even of the uprisings and violence in the French colony of Saint Domingue near eastern Cuba. In that sole reference, Cosme compared the magnitude of the imbroglios and crimes of the heirs in Cuba to those in France: "[The disorders [*embrollos*] of your opponents] are compared here in this court with the event of the French [*el suceso de los franceses*]."[6] Perhaps the analogy referred to the disruption of order or to the anti-monarchical disregard for royal law and order. Regardless of how aware he was about those events, Cosme did not discuss them in the extant letters. What he did write about and criticized bitterly from his perch in Madrid was colonial politics and the corruption of royal justice both by colonial officials and private interests in the colony. Cosme's letters constitute an invaluable source to plumb his views and activities as an apoderado along with the challenges and difficulties he faced in performing that role, especially as a colonial subject of color in the royal court. He also wrote about the juridical basis of the case, about royal law, and about the meaning of freedom among other issues. Citations from his letters dot the pages of this book and constitute epigraphs to some chapters.

In general, private letters especially by or between subordinate subjects tend to get lost in time since few make their way to official repositories where diligent historians can exhume them.[7] Cosme's extant correspondence with the cobreros back home constitutes an exceptional primary source by one of the few colonial subjects of color who may have crossed the ocean to the royal court. New research has uncovered the active role

[6] Gregorio Cosme, Madrid, October 6, 1795, No. 75, f. 195–207, AGI-SD 1629.

[7] Lockhart and Otte, eds., *Letters and People of the Spanish Indies*, Preface, ix–xi. For a recently digitalized trove of 1739–48 undelivered private letters to the Indies that made it to British archives by chance after Spanish vessels with mail were captured at sea during war, see the "Prize Papers" Project, Case Study: Spanish Ships at www.prizepapers.de/case-studies/case-study-spanish-ships.

of Indigenous intermediaries and apoderados in lower colonial courts and at the Audiencia level in Mexico and the Andean region.[8] More recently, Juan Carlos de la Puente Luna has located a number of Andean travelers to Madrid, some of them seeking personal and communal redress, but any correspondence between them and their constituents has been lost. Nor has de la Puente been able to document the kind of work they engaged in Madrid. Similarly, Alcira Dueñas also found a handful of cacique and Mestizo travelers from Peru to the "lettered" city who submitted petitions in Madrid, but again, no personal correspondence is available from them nor much on their activities in the royal court.[9] Cosme's extant correspondence with the cobreros begins to fill that gap.

Some of Cosme's correspondence made it to the archive because the Governor of Cuba was able to seize a sliver of letters from 1795. Ironically, the paucity of Cosme's correspondence in the state's archive is a sign of how private and autonomous the cobreros were able to keep their written communications for years. There is also on record an important letter from Cosme's counterpart in the village, the also literate Justo Cruzata, that further illustrates the character of the back-and-forth communication between Cosme and the community. Other letters to Cosme written by amanuenses in El Cobre also occasionally appear in the record. Cosme encouraged leaders in the village to keep him abreast of local news and channeled some of these letters into their dossier in Madrid. Avoiding surveillance and keeping the correspondence flowing secretly across the ocean was a difficult task as the letters show. Were it not for Cosme's presence in court, local news would not have reached the higher court since the other apoderado, the Spanish merchant José Espinoza de los Monteros, resided in Havana and was only connected to cobreros residing in that city. Nor would copies of royal orders and other news have reached the community to keep them abreast of their case in the imperial court. Thus, Cosme's role as intermediary between Madrid and El Cobre was crucial to the legal struggle and, I will argue in Chapter 7, to extralegal mobilizations in the pueblo as well. As Chapter 7 suggests, once colonial authorities uncovered some letters, they found this communication pernicious. Although Cosme's role as apoderado depended on writing and maintaining communication with his distant constituency, it may have also been important to keep

[8] Yannakakis, *The Art of Being In-Between.*

[9] For the earlier Hapsburg period, see de la Puente Luna, *Andean Cosmopolitans*, especially 7–8; for a later mid- to late colonial period, Dueñas, *Indians and Mestizos*, especially 2–7, 59–62.

personal contact with his homeplace from where friends sent greetings and news. Writing kept local bonds of nativeness alive across the ocean.

Finally, through his letter-writing, Cosme enacted the role of "author" producing a narrative where he played the protagonist role in the cobreros' legal struggle for freedom in Madrid. We cannot know if that is how he saw his role in the royal court or whether that is how he portrayed it to the cobreros back home to shape his own legacy. In any case, his account re-centers narratives about judicial mobilization that usually focus on *letrados*' voice and work into one where subordinate colonial litigants played a central role. In his narrative, Cosme even obliterated the role of more powerful figures or pushed them to a barely perceptible background, unfortunately now difficult to unravel. I want to recover here the cobreros' apoderado's voice, his opinions and views, his possible influences, his actions, and his relation to the community he came from and represented. Attentiveness to tone modulations in his written voice can also reveal glimpses of the person penning those letters.

This chapter turns again to Madrid, to Cosme's actions as apoderado in the royal court as reported by himself and enacted in the correspondence itself. It also moves events in this book to the 1790s and to the developments of the case in this period. I argue that Cosme's role as liaison between El Cobre and Madrid was crucial in keeping the case alive in the royal court, although less significant than what he thought it to be. Whereas his presence in Madrid gave the community a greater direct control over the litigation process at this level, it also gave force and legitimacy to the judicial and extrajudicial resistance taking place at the local level. The extreme effort and the costs of this judicial emancipation battle could cast a shadow over the endeavor, however.

AN APODERADO'S WORK IN THE ROYAL COURT

In his role as the cobreros' apoderado, Cosme had power of attorney to act on the plaintiffs' behalf in court, sign papers, and take out loans. The cobreros seemingly had a great trust in him since any missteps on his part could lead to considerable expenses for the signatories. Cosme claimed an exclusive role in coordinating the community's legal battles in court. In one of his letters to the cobreros, he wrote, "the Council does not recognize any other to follow this case and defense but me."[10] Cosme

[10] Gregorio Cosme, Madrid, n.d. (ca. 1795), f. 102–7, AGI-SD 1631.

may have felt the threat of displacement by rivals, particularly by White Spanish rivals with a higher social position, and was effectively affirming a political right to officially represent his constituency as a native of El Cobre despite his lower racial and colonial status as he had done eleven years before vis–à–vis the Spanish merchant José Espinoza in Madrid (Chapter 2). Although Cosme did not mention any possible current rivals in his extant letters, Espinoza had kept the role of apoderado after his return to Havana from the joint trip to the royal court, though apparently he did not correspond with Cosme after their falling out in Madrid in 1784.[11] Cosme had also recently worked closely with Sergeant Valentín Sánchez, another White apoderado stationed in Havana, whom he had met in 1783 during his first stay there. Valentín Sánchez apparently had spent some time in Madrid between 1793 or 1794 and March 1795 and reported that he had seen Cosme almost on a daily basis during that time.[12]

Gregorio Cosme emphasized his autonomy and efficacy as apoderado, almost always portraying himself as actively engaged in all aspects of the litigation: "You will see how much I have worked without the help of anyone except the attorney [*abogado*], the solicitor [*procurador*], and the moneylender [*prestamista*], Señor Pedro Sedano."[13] Those three figures constituted major pillars in the support structure of the litigation process. Cosme's role complemented that of the two letrados in charge of the technical aspects of the judicial proceedings. Whereas attorneys usually presented and dispatched cases in court and in principle formulated the legal argumentation presented in the briefs, solicitors coordinated the filing process, compiled the documentation and evidence, prepared the file, and tracked its progress. Cosme would have worked most closely with the solicitor. Both attorneys and solicitors in the royal court were letrados and legal specialists with university degrees and professional licenses from the guild association in Madrid.[14] The third figure, the moneylender, provided the economic resources needed to finance the

[11] José Espinoza de los Monteros, Havana, June 22, 1796, No. 7, f. 1097–98, AGI-SD 1629.

[12] Valentín Sánchez, Havana, June 23, 1796, No. 7, f. 1098r–98v, AGI-SD 1629.

[13] Gregorio Cosme, Madrid, March 16, 1795, f. 11v–14, AGI-SD 1631.

[14] Although by 1795 Cosme seemed to be working with a private counsel team, he had worked with a court assigned Protector of the Poor in Madrid before, specifically when he filed Damiana Ortiz's case in court in 1787 and perhaps in previous occasions in the 1780s after he found himself stranded in court. José Uruñuela, Madrid, August 8, 1787, in Cosme v. Creagh, f. 1–1v, AGI-SD 1627; Petition of Cosme, Madrid, January 14, 1785, AGI-SD 1627.

judicial business. Cosme's mention of the moneylender raises some ominous questions about the costs and risks of litigation that could stifle the pursuit of justice. The moneylender Cosme had secured in court using his power of attorney was effectively an alternative to Espinoza who had informally lent money for the trip to the royal court at a high interest rate in 1784.

Letter writing was fundamental to maintaining the flow of information about the case and local news from Cuba. Cosme wrote regularly to update leaders in El Cobre on the progress of the case, sometimes at extreme length. One extant excerpt of a letter written on October 6, 1795, ran to more than seven double-sided folios (some fifteen pages). Mail was sent to the Indies once a month, so perhaps he stayed secluded in his room, as a spy reported in 1786, busily writing letters and copying documents to send out on the next ship. The cobreros' apoderado must have eagerly awaited the notices of arrival of mail from the Indies and despaired when communications broke down. The correspondence between El Cobre and Madrid consisted of news, accounts of recent events in both locations, and documents obtained from the court.

Cosme transcribed excerpts of orders and sent notice of edicts issued to governors and asked for confirmation of receipt. Wrote Cosme in his most businesslike voice: "I give notice to the public in general that I am forwarding orders in this mail, one for the Governor of Cuba and the other of Havana and I am giving you notice so that you can claim them if they delay them and can inform me about their enforcement."[15] Such documentation sent through independent channels provided checks to ensure colonial authorities' compliance with royal orders. But Cosme also requested official documentation from his counterparts in the colony. As the legal battle escalated, the cobreros had to struggle even to receive basic notarial services in Santiago to make official copies of documents. Cruzata informed Cosme, "I cannot send you the paper that you asked me for because none of the notaries will do it, the opponents have blocked everything so that no one can do anything for us."[16] Every aspect of the judicial process became a contested issue. But as the legal process became increasingly politicized, its most basic activities opened new fronts in the battle of papers.

Cosme also requested letters from the community to counter the reports that his opponents were filing about events in Cuba: "I advise

[15] Gregorio Cosme, Madrid, n.d. (ca. 1795), f. 102–7, AGI-SD 1631.
[16] Justo Cruzata, El Cobre, December 27, 1795, No. 135, AGI-SD 1627.

you not to stop writing to me, do not let any mail go by without letting me know everything that happens, since letters are very useful, and on these occasions all the more."[17] Some of these "dispatches" also became part of the written record of the community's past in the dossier that Cosme curated. Local missives expanded the scope of the legal archive to include the cobreros' voices, narratives, and counternarratives. A letter by Martín Salazar stands out among the accounts that Cosme received. It denounced recent atrocities perpetrated against members of the community by their alleged "new masters." Despite years of judicial action, the heirs to El Cobre were still making violent incursions into the pueblo to capture enslaved cobreros and to collect land rents. Salazar wrote of beatings, extortions, and even a shooting. He asked Cosme to transmit the news to His Majesty, emphasizing that these were but a sampling "of what we are currently enduring since the insults have been outright so enormous and boundless that a whole ream of paper would be needed to explain them."[18] Such accounts recording the community's memory were routed into the archive of the state as testimonial evidence and legal ammunition – and more than two centuries later, they resurface in this book.

The importance of alternative information inputs to contest official and opponents' narratives sent from Santiago, or simply to fill a vacuum of information, is reflected in a memo from a high minister, by then entrusted to oversee the case: "The Governor has not responded to this order [querying the state of affairs of El Cobre], but His Majesty knows through other venues that the harassment [*vejaciones*] against those vecinos continues ... and, the rapid remedy to so many injuries being necessary, His Majesty wants to know in what state are the affairs of El Cobre."[19] Revealing the source of his information, the minister then added "for their general apoderado Don Gregorio Cosme Osorio has informed me in truth of the many damages that impinge on his party [*perjucios les impelen a sus partes*]."[20] The reference to Cosme as "Don" reflects the honor and status of an apoderado – and suggests the minister had not met Cosme, whose racialized body would have precluded such a title. The persistence and pressure of the plaintiffs began to show some results. Cosme wrote in 1795, "I have already said that the King and the Council have been informed of the infamies that have been executed

[17] Gregorio Cosme, Madrid, October 6, 1795, No. 75, f. 195–207, AGI-SD 1629.

[18] Martín Salazar, El Cobre, August 21, 1792, No. 1, AGI-SD 1627.

[19] Eugenio Llaguno, Aranjuez, January 15, 1795, f. 16r–16v, AGI-SD 1631.

[20] Ibid.

against these miserable ones."[21] Orders were sent repeatedly to the governors in Cuba to send the local *autos* (proceedingss) on the case to Madrid, orders that were deliberately delayed for at least a dozen years, until 1797.

However, direct communications between Madrid and El Cobre presented many hurdles for a subordinate community like El Cobre and called for networks of allies and alternate channels to keep it flowing. Although the state-supported transatlantic mail service had been reformed since the mid- to late 1760s, mail could be lost or intercepted, so the cobreros had to seek more reliable methods of communication.[22] Whereas the apoderado in Havana had his own mail channels and the cobreros had used it in the early years (Chapter 2), perhaps due to the fall out between Cosme and the Spanish apoderado in Madrid in 1784, Cosme established a direct line with the cobreros. But securing confidential communications between El Cobre, Santiago, and Madrid became problematic since the conflict's epicenter was in that city. Finding reliable contacts and couriers to deliver mail became part of the work outside the courts. Back in 1786, Cosme began to covertly receive his mail from Cuba in Madrid by way of the widow of a former royal official in Cuba, "because he had been losing the letters from the Indies."[23] The cobreros' correspondence itself was full of references to the means of transmission and receipt of mail and to interruptions in these epistolary flows. In one instance, Cosme asked villagers to send their letters to the treasurer of the Spanish city of Córdoba, Don Juan Mayoral, because via him "[the correspondence] arrived safely."[24] There must have been a local contact person on the island, another royal official, probably in the Royal Treasury office, who could discreetly pass letters to the treasurer. The use of such channels suggests that the community had allies and supporters at high levels of the royal bureaucracy.[25]

[21] Gregorio Cosme, Madrid, October 6, 1795, No. 75, f. 195–207, AGI-SD 1629.

[22] The imperial communication system was reformed in 1763. See Jensen, *Children of Colonial Despotism*, 3. A central Royal House of the Post Office was built in the 1760s in the Puerta del Sol plaza where people could drop and pick up mail. See Gómez de la Serna, *Historia de la Puerta del Sol*.

[23] Report of Pedro Muñoz de la Torre, Madrid, October 9, 1786, Expediente Crímenes Cosme, AGI-SD 1529.

[24] Gregorio Cosme, Madrid, October 6, 1795, No. 75, f. 195–207, AGI-SD 1629.

[25] By 1795, the cobrero leaders seem to have had a secret contact in the *Auditor de Cuentas* in Santiago, Don Pedro Antonio Esaguirre, who reportedly passed on information to Justo Cruzata but his role is unclear. Testimony of Francisco Ojeda. Interrogation, ca. 1795, f. 86, Autos Cuba, AGI-SD 1631.

Due to its immunity privileges from state oversight and its own mailing venues, ecclesiastical intermediaries were also tapped to send mail.[26] Cruzata asked Cosme in 1795 to write the parish priest's name on letters to him to ensure their arrival.[27] And Cosme found some bishops willing to send mail for him. In 1789, documents were sent in person to Madrid by way of a courier from Santiago de Cuba, the literate mulatto Santiago Barrera, who also traveled illegally to the court.[28] There seems to have been secret mail channels through other people in Santiago too. The governor of Santiago informed the island's captain general that "for their security they send the letters to people in this city who secretly forward them to them."[29] But the cobreros apparently also received letters from a cobrero, Cristobal Salas, in Havana who may have updated them of the business carried out by the Spanish apoderado who represented them in Havana.[30] Horizontal and vertical social networks, both secular and ecclesiastical, were important to keep communication circuits open when the mail service was inadequate or intercepted by enemies. Other oral and written communications took place across the island passing the word on where and how to best press legal actions and find witnesses as suggested in some of the actions discussed in Chapter 5.

COSME'S LEGAL CULTURE AND VIEWS

As the case moved forward in Madrid, Cosme announced in his extant letters of 1795 that a freedom verdict was imminent (though it would still

[26] Gregorio Cosme, Madrid, October 6, 1795, No. 75, f. 195–207, AGI-SD 1629.

[27] Justo Cruzata, El Cobre, December 27, 1795, No. 135, AGI-SD 1627.

[28] Barrera seems to have been stranded in the court for at least three to five years and asked for state alms to survive. However, he seems to have accessed the king and queen to whom he took his plight in Madrid. He even wrote some verses to the monarchs. His relation to Cosme is not clear but they must have shared travails together. Upon his arrival in Madrid, Cosme met yet another colonial man from Havana, an officer named Captain Vicente Blanco, Captain of the Black militias of Havana, who may have fought under General Bernardo Gálvez. It is not clear if he entered the peninsula illegally. Although ordered to leave Madrid, he was either stranded or waiting for some petition to resolve when he befriended Cosme. In any case, there seems to have been more travel to the royal court of free colonial of African descent than scholars had imagined. See Petitions of Santiago Barrera, Aranjuez, May 20, 1790, and Madrid, October 12, 1792, both in AGI-SD 330. For Captain Blanco, see Expediente crímenes Cosme, Madrid, October 12, 1786, AGI-SD 1529.

[29] Governor Juan Nepomuceno Quintana, Santiago de Cuba, May 30, 1796, AGI-SD 1629.

[30] Testimony of Matías Quiala, ca. 1795, Interrogation, Autos Cuba, f. 88–88v, AGI-SD 1631.

take five additional years for the final sentence to materialize). As he proclaimed the good news, the self-taught apoderado elucidated what he took to be the juridical basis of the community's freedom thereby displaying the legal culture and values that he had absorbed in the imperial court. Cosme cited – and celebrated – general principles of justice that he considered applicable to their case and extolled the virtues of royal laws stressing aspects about it that were of special interest to enslaved and subaltern subjects in general. In line with the Bourbon Crown's regalist ideology, Cosme grounded the legitimacy of the cobreros' freedom case almost exclusively on royal law and the will of the royal sovereign: he did not directly make reference, at least not in these few letters, to divine law, moral rules (other than those related to the principles of justice), or policy considerations as even complementary grounds for freedom. In some ways, his discourse was more legalistic than that of the memorials. More importantly, although Cosme alluded to notions of pueblo, villa, and collective freedom, he did not elaborate on rights based on their standing as natives of a pueblo, as, for instance, his counterpart back home, Justo Cruzata, did (see Chapter 7). And although he must have been familiar with that subtext in the memorials, no reference to Indian ancestry is to be found in the extant letters. How then did he explain to his constituency the legal basis of their freedom?

Even though local apoderados in El Cobre were also familiar with Spanish legal culture through their engagement with the courts in Santiago, Cosme enacted his role as apoderado in the highest court of empire by deploying his knowledge of royal law and his interpretation of tenets of justice favoring the community: "The legitimate laws are those of the King our Lord, which are the ones he has founded, which are as much for the *poor as for the rich, and slaves* are only burdened with the law that requires them to present an express license from their master, but if [the master] does not give it, *right* [*derecho*] allows them to present themselves to the royal justices *to obtain their rights*" (my italics).[31] In this passage, Cosme used several related notions of juridical discourse such as laws (*leyes*), rights (*derechos*), and right (*derecho*) in the abstract.

Whereas laws referred to the concrete commands and rules mandated by the sovereign; rights referred to the juridical faculties that law and principles of justice gave to subjects to do or claim something; and derecho was the more abstract faculty of subjects to bear rights by justice.

[31] Ibid.

The notion of right and rights is strongly present in Cosme's discourse, as it was in Spanish legal culture going back to the early modern scholastic jurists, but it is difficult to unravel the deeper meanings the terms may have been taking in Cosme's discourse or in the legal culture of the royal court at the time or in other more progressive juridical circles.[32] However, Cosme's use of the notions of right did not refer to the discourse of the rights of man then circulating in important regions of the Atlantic world, including neighboring France or Saint Domingue, yet he could put his own spin on more traditional and still important notions of right present in Spain's jurisprudence.

To the allusion of the primacy of royal law above other sources of law in the centralized Bourbon regime, Cosme added further relevance by inserting a comment on the equity principle informing royal laws that protected all royal vassals without distinction of class or status. Even the lowliest in the social hierarchy – the poor and the slaves – he asserted, were entitled to royal justice in the empire. In this formulation, legal protection and justice took on the character of a fundamental right, a natural right that even enslaved persons had the right to enjoy (and that was continuously disputed by the cobreros' adversaries in Santiago). So fundamental was this right to be heard and get justice that it could override a master's opposition to his slave's use of it and thereby it could overwrite the master's (private) dominion over his slave. In this formulation, presumably of great interest to Cosme and his constituents, the enslaved subject was a bearer of rights; and furthermore, his (natural) right to justice, according to Cosme, enabled the slave to claim yet other specific rights. Cosme may have derived some of these views from the doctrine of "miserables," a doctrine that offered special royal judicial protection to the "weak" and "wretched" in the empire: to indigent and disabled people, women, orphans, Indians, and slaves.[33] But regardless of the sources for his legal culture, in Cosme's eyes, these rights and precepts of justice endowed royal law with enormous legitimacy.

Cosme offered his readers another example of this natural or universal precept of justice noting that "another ancient law says that even if the *reos* [felons] are imprisoned under iron grills and chains, it is ordered that

[32] For a history of the evolving juridical notion of right (*ius*) and natural rights in medieval and early modern Europe and in Spain with Las Casas, Vitoria, and Suárez, see Tierney, *The Idea of Natural Rights*, Chapters XI and XII; for a somewhat different account of new legal Enlightenment notions of derecho and law in the eighteenth-century Spanish Atlantic, see Premo, *The Enlightenment on Trial*, Chapter 2.

[33] Borah, *Justice by Insurance*.

all reos be heard in justice."[34] This question was discussed by Thomas Aquinas and seems to have been a common topic of dispute in scholastic approaches to law and rights, a reference that may point to Cosme's influences.[35] If incarcerated subjects accused of crimes, another category of abject subjects, were entitled to be heard through a judicial process, Cosme implied, how could enslaved captives not have that right as well? By drawing on this ideology of law and fundamental rights, Cosme legitimated the cobreros' standing to pursue judicial recourse, as well as their right to challenge hierarchies of power in the colony.

The community's apoderado in Madrid also addressed the question of freedom, the cobreros' main concern. Cosme did not broach this question as a fundamental inalienable human right as much as one obtained through just royal laws and through principles of justice favoring freedom. Putting a particular optimistic spin on his interpretation of the legal regime underpinning emancipation paths, he wrote that "the laws were not unjust but very clear and openly declare any right to freedom, and in this I have founded all my defense in your favor."[36] (Note Cosme's implication that he had assembled the arguments for freedom himself, rather than in collaboration with letrados.) The apoderado explained that "a Castilian adage of the law says that all the Laws aspire to the question [*negocio*] of freedom, especially when they are graced and based on some true facts, and even if there were some ambiguities … it is undeniable that … the vecinos and pobladores and hacendados of the villa of Santiago del Prado are all favored by these rights, because of the antiquity of their possession [of them]."[37] In this formulation, Cosme seemed to be alluding to a *natural* right of liberty that all *human* laws or legal regimes should aspire to bolster as well. More concretely, the apoderado may have been referring to the rule also stated in the *Partidas* that in cases of uncertainty, the law should favor freedom, a juridical principle that could be given different interpretations: from a strong presumption of freedom in cases of uncertainty, as Cosme seems to be using it, to the more narrow sense of a legitimate cause for a hearing as the colonial fiscal of the Royal Treasury defined it (Chapter 5). Although Cosme claimed that there were

[34] Gregorio Cosme, Madrid, October 6, 1795, No. 75, f. 195–207, AGI-SD 1629.

[35] Tierney, *The Idea of Natural Rights*, 87. Scholastic sources, however, had the potential of anchoring fairly radical ideas and policies against slavery as the case of Las Casas and the abolitionist Capuchin friars Francisco José Jaca and Epifanio Moirans discussed in Chapter 3 show.

[36] Gregorio Cosme, Madrid, October 6, 1795, No. 75, f. 195–207, AGI-SD 1629.

[37] Ibid.

"true facts" (or evidence) grounding the cobreros' freedom, he also suggested that there was some ambiguity and doubt regarding their status, in which case presumption of freedom should prevail.

Furthermore, although he did not invoke the category of "natives" here, by referring to the cobreros as former "vecinos," "pobladores," and "hacendados" of the "villa" of Santiago del Prado (aka El Cobre), Cosme attributed freedom status to them since only free subjects could inhabit the categories of original settlers, landed property owners, and citizens of a villa, indirectly echoing here the Echenique Memorial's municipality-based argument, which was discussed in Chapter 3 (though not the Indian-based argumentation). And in referring to the "antiquity" of the practices and rights linked to the enactment of those categories, Cosme implicitly invoked the force of custom or even the law of prescription, a statute of limitations that prescribed freedom after ten, twenty, or thirty years of de facto or reputed freedom (Chapter 3). Cosme may have acquainted himself with that legal source by discussing it with letrados working on his case. This statute was also invoked in the memorials as an argument of last resort. Comments like this suggest the interaction between Cosme (as direct oral conveyor of the pueblo's past) and letrados (translators of vernacular notions and situations into legal and philosophical discourse). Cosme communicated to the cobreros in his letters this juridical reworking of their aspirations, anchoring them in legal culture.

Elsewhere, however, Cosme explained the basis of the cobreros' freedom in more royalist and regalist legal terms by referring specifically to royal edicts found in the state's archive. Taking on his apoderado and letrado voice, he wrote: "You are free by all rights [*por todos derechos*] because I have it well justified and proven in many ways and also by the maritime ordinance and by the ordinance of the Royal Service of all of you and of your ancestors who served the Catholic monarchs in the constructions of fortified castles."[38] To be sure, though Cosme interpreted them as such, these were not edicts of freedom. They were rather documents pertaining to the cobreros' recruitment as laborers (as royal slaves) in the region's royal fortification projects. Contrary to Captain General Ezpeleta's reference to these labor practices as criteria of royal slavery (Chapter 5), Cosme repurposed them as signs of simple labor services to the Crown, as the memorials also had. Yet he did not mention

[38] Ibid.

here the more important Edictof 1721 allegedly recognizing the freedom of third- and fourth-generation cobreros.

Further informing the cobreros of other juridical grounds in which their freedom was based, Cosme amplified his interpretation of royal edicts as evidence of the Crown's recognition of the cobreros' freedom when he referred to their former military service: "And in effect I have justified it [freedom] by Royal Edicts found in several old dossiers, as in effect I found in one the noble thanks that the King Philip V [1700–46] gave all of you for guarding the Port of Guaycabón and Cabañas and Agüadores ... and the four urban militia companies that [were formed] ... and he ordered by Royal Edict to thank you in his royal name with his seal for the loyalty they [the cobreros] had to their sovereign."[39] Cosme implicitly translated the king's gratitude to his loyal subjects for their military service into a sort of pact whereby the cobreros were rewarded with freedom for that service. However, no claims or documentation seem to have been included regarding military participation in the more recent event of the British occupation of Havana in 1762 that Cosme himself had earlier invoked claiming the veteran status of his alleged father Commander José Cosme and himself in that key event (see Chapter 2).

Overall, Gregorio Cosme claimed that his activism in court had clarified the legal foundations of the cobreros' concealed freedom. In terms of evidential requirements, Cosme pointed in a self-enhancing way to his own legal work of compiling documents from state archives to support the cobreros' freedom. Invoking his bonds of love with the community in somewhat paternalistic terms, he reminded them: "But my beloved, all of this was hidden [in the archives] and no one has been able to move it [*moverlo*]; only me due to my efficacy and my paternal charity, and my zeal."[40] Ultimately, then, according to this legal reasoning, the basis for the cobreros' freedom lay in written documents and royal edicts buried in the archive and Cosme's legal work, to a large extent, had consisted of removing the fog of the past by extracting the king's written voice stored in the archive.

COSME'S ALLEGED MEETING WITH THE KING

Despite the bleak picture of local corruption and indifference to royal orders, Cosme's narrative asserted that royal justice and power would

[39] Ibid. [40] Ibid.

prevail over local mischief and contempt of the law: "and so the King [Charles IV] says that whoever does it to him will pay for it [*el que la hiciere que la pague*] and notice will be given of this superiority for the determination of the King."[41] What he meant by this cryptic colloquialism was that anyone who broke the king's laws would eventually pay for the transgression and that eventually royal justice would be done. Cosme's king was not stately or majestic; he was forthright and plainspoken. Nor was he distant and detached. His was a king personally involved in the affairs of the colony and the protection of his loyal vassals – or wretched subjects – the cobreros. Cosme may have tested the limits of contemporary (and modern) credulity in another remark meant to reassure, and undoubtedly impress, his readers. Insinuating close contact with the king, he boasted: "And I let you know that the King, our Lord, has already been informed of what each one does in those countries. The King has dumbfounded me [*me ha dejado tonto*] with the things he told me to my face."[42] Cosme left it up to his readers to imagine what those stunning words may have been and on what kind of terms he was with the monarch.

Gregorio Cosme gave a more sober account of his face-to-face encounter with Charles IV elsewhere in the same letter:

> I was compelled to find a way of speaking to the King himself in person [and] a great friend placed me where I did not expect to find myself, and I spoke to him and presented him the memorial that you sent me and the testimony of the Church where the generations of slaves were [recorded], by means of which he found out all the untruth [*todo lo incierto*] and the King offered to me that if what I said in favor of them [the cobreros] was true, that he would keep me and all [of you] in his mind, and just as he offered, he has executed it. But it takes us so much effort [*pero mucho nos cuesta*].[43]

This episode suggests a brief encounter with the king for the purpose of putting documentation related to the lawsuit in royal hands and acquainting the king with the community's plight. In it Cosme seemingly transformed a vague, formal, and conditional promise of reward (if his claims "were true") to a direct commitment of protection from the king thereby converting what may have been a spontaneous meeting with the king into a winning diplomatic move. Were those the words that left him dumbfounded?

How a direct encounter with the king took place – if it happened – is not clear, but there were ceremonial royal audiences where brief

[41] Ibid. [42] Ibid.

[43] Gregorio Cosme, Madrid, March 16, 1795, f. 11v–14, AGI-SD 1631.

encounters could take place.[44] However, the encounter, as Cosme described it, does not seem to have been a formal audience. It is not clear either who his great friend was, if a powerful courtier or perhaps a lowlier servant in the palace, but the vague account suggests a casual meeting to offer papers or a petition, as it sometimes happened.[45] Networks in court, however, seem to have enabled this brief encounter, which had pragmatic and symbolic implications.

The aura of an audiencia with the king and its potential for mythologization were enormous, particularly in the ideology of an absolutist monarchy where the figure of the "king" was the repository of divine will, the symbol of justice, and, at least in principle, the most powerful figure in the polity. There were some precedents of royal audiences being granted to subordinate subjects from Cuba and elsewhere in the colonies. Charles III had granted the lieutenant of the Black militias, Antonio Soledad, and the second lieutenant, Ignacio de Alvarado, an audiencia where he had decorated them for their brave defense of Havana during the British occupation of 1762–63.[46] The memory of Charles III's audiencia with these two Black militiamen from Havana was so powerful that it was rendered in 1812, almost fifty years after its occurrence, in José Antonio Aponte's famous book of insurrectionist drawings. In that picture, one of the most analyzed by scholars, Charles III was depicted placing his right hand on the heads of the two Black soldiers in a gesture that signaled his respect for them.[47] The image conveyed the message that the king did not make racial distinctions among his vassals, at least not among distinguished loyal vassals; or that the king, as the fountain of justice, was above racial differences and was color blind. While that faith in royalist ideals may have sustained Cosme's loyalty to king and the Spanish empire, the case of Aponte also shows how those loyalties could turn once disillusion set in – or perhaps when other more radical alternatives emerged.[48]

Cosme's critiques of official corruption in the colony and his personalized accounts of the king's support for the cobreros impacted the

[44] Cosme seems to have had one such a personal encounter with General Bernardo Gálvez in Aranjuez soon after his arrival in Madrid in 1784. See Chapter 2.

[45] Perhaps it was Santiago Barrera who did have some open audiences with the monarch.

[46] Childs, *The 1812 Aponte Rebellion*, 80–81. For alleged encounters with the king by Andean subjects in Madrid, see de la Puente Luna, *Andean Cosmopolitans*, 6, and 204n11.

[47] For other interpretations of that image, Ferrer, *Freedom's Mirror*, 299–328; and Palmié, *Wizards and Scientists*, 100–103. For its importance and memory among free militias of color in Havana, see Schneider, *The Occupation of Havana*, 304–6.

[48] Childs, *The 1812 Aponte Rebellion.*

cobreros' resistance in the ground. Having seized some of Cosme's letters, Governor Juan Bautista Vaillant (1788–95) and later Governor Juan Nepomuceno de Quintana (1796–98) grasped the danger they represented. Quintana wrote to the captain general in Havana that "this concern is born from some lies with which Gregorio Cosme Osorio, who calls himself their apoderado in the court, hallucinates them in the papers he sends ... and continues sending them from the court with the same tenor."[49] Quintana warned him of the political influence that Cosme's letters had on the community: "He assures them each day more and more of the certainty of their freedom, and I understand that if a solution is not found to this pernicious communication that Osorio has established with another of the free cobreros who resides in the pueblo named Justo Cruzata ... your purposes [of reducing the slaves to their masters] will be impossible to carry out."[50] Indeed, Cosme's writings legitimized other forms of extrajudicial mobilization among the cobreros in Cuba as Chapter 7 will discuss.

FINANCIAL SUPPORT AND CONCERNS

The financial exigencies of litigation, particularly across such a distance, cast a deep shadow over the legal action in Madrid and posed great challenges for Cosme and the community. Even under the reduced fees for "miserables," and despite fixed fees for legal services, justice was not cheap. Cosme was pragmatic about the financial demands underpinning the justice system: "Even though [royal] orders may be issued, if there is no money to deliver them, Justice is not done."[51] His letters of 1795 betrayed a defensiveness that seemed motivated by the mounting costs of litigation and the loans that he anticipated the community would have to face once the case was resolved.

We do not know what the costs of legal services in Madrid were, what interest rates the moneylender charged, or what kinds of deals the latter made with Cosme. These loans, however, had to be guaranteed with collateral from the community, specifically from the co-signing power granters; members of the pueblo may not have had any idea of the potential costs of protracted litigation. In 1792, a group of twenty-five

[49] Governor Juan Nepomuceno Quintana, Santiago de Cuba, May 30, 1796, AGI-SD 1629.

[50] Ibid. Governor Vaillant before him also archived some letters that Justo Cruzata handed over. Vaillant to Las Casas, Santiago, September 14, 1795. AGI-SD 1631.

[51] Gregorio Cosme, Madrid, October 6, 1795, No.75, f. 195–207, AGI-SD 1629.

cobreros had given Cosme proxy powers to spend 6,000 to 7,000 pesos or more to pursue the case in court.[52] But accumulated expenses may have been much higher. Although in Madrid Cosme was sustained by periodic remittances from the community, we do not know either how much individual cobreros contributed or how much was sent, through what channels, or at what intervals.[53] But irregular remittances from his home community led to a precarious existence in Madrid. Reprimanding his constituency for neglecting to send him his due, Cosme complained that "you have not remembered that he [your apoderado] needs to eat and dress or [pay] for anything that may be possible to obtain the welfare [*el bien*] that is solicited for the *common good of all* ... for you have not aided him or sent him the natural sustenance" (my italics).[54] There was an understood pact in cases of collective litigation whereby working on behalf of the common good bound the community to sustain him as a natural obligation. Cosme had faced economic hardship since his early days at court. In 1795, economic distress still haunted him, aggravated perhaps by his bouts of illness and other setbacks. It is not clear what produced the abrupt cut in remittances, perhaps the war with France had made communication and money transfers more difficult or perhaps there was anger back home at the slowness of the judicial process by then into its eleventh year with little progress to show.

Cosme seems to have been uncomfortably aware that the accumulated debt may have caused discord in the community: "I have not received a single letter from anyone in that villa [El Cobre]," wrote the distressed apoderado, "I do not know if the motive [for your silence] may be *the debts contracted in your cause*, but I do not think so because you well know that I have executed it by virtue of the powerful capacity and faculties that you have conferred upon me and have deposited your greatest trust as the true and loyal general apoderado of that villa of Santiago del Cobre" (my italics).[55] Cosme here addressed a disturbing issue: did the community think he had abused their trust and had mis-spent their funds?

In a perturbing comment on what may lay ahead, he wrote, "I give notice to the public in general that all are free already and free from

52 Francisco Mancebo, July 1792, "Escritos presentados," No.7, f. 100v–101, AGI-SD 1627.

53 José Emigdio Maldonado, Santiago de Cuba, July 11, 1796. No. 73, f. 204–11, AGI-SD 1629.

54 Gregorio Cosme, Madrid, n.d. (ca. 1795), f. 102–7, AGI-SD 1631.

55 Ibid.

captivity and we give notice to all those who are present and absent and fugitive [*prófugos*] so that the news reach all, [and] so that they can start collecting the money with which to pay so many debts and costs that have come up [*que se han causado*]."[56] He added that "although I judge that the opponents will be made to pay, this is what I do not know" and could not know, he said, until the final verdict. Cosme based his hopeful presumption on the fact that "they [the heirs] were the ones who caused everything [*los causantes de todo*]."[57] Mixing good with not-so-good news, he excitedly wrote, "Señores, this rushes out to let you know this great news of your freedom" only to add in the next line, "Friends, you have much to thank me for and pay me" for having won freedom and the title of villa.[58] Clearly, Cosme was expecting compensation for his many years of service to the community. He located his service somewhere in-between that of a professional advocate and an affected party. Cosme and the cobreros may have faced these costs pragmatically and literally as the price of freedom, what they would have had to pay anyway if they had been allowed to purchase their freedom in 1780 or individual coartaciones thereafter.

But Cosme suggested that the suit had other kinds of intangible value too: "I let you know that you are all free and that it has cost me great quantities [*grandes cantidades*] but that is nothing, in order that they [the opponents] do not get away with what they want, I would even give my life."[59] As passions escalated, the legal battles may have taken on other cultural and social dimensions. In a strongly hierarchical society like the Spanish one, the courts could effectively provide a protected arena in which to fight and defy social superiors and play out issues of honor. Nonetheless, Cosme's notices must have been sobering for a decimated community in fear of being overburdened with loans and payments for their emancipation and autonomy as a villa. The prospect must have cast a deep shadow on the good news of imminent freedom.

A LEGACY NARRATIVE

As the case approached resolution, Cosme shaped a narrative about the legal and political significance of his advocacy in the royal court. In portraying his labors, sacrifices, and triumphs as apoderado, he cast

56 Gregorio Cosme, Madrid, October 6, 1795, No. 75, f. 195–207, AGI-SD 1629.

57 Ibid. 58 Ibid.

59 Gregorio Cosme, Madrid, March 16, 1795, f. 11v–14, AGI-SD 1631.

himself as protagonist of the cobreros' story of emancipation. Although at times he included himself in the community's collective travails, as when he lamented how long they had been "working with our pueblo, standing in its defense to see if we can obtain the privileged right of freedom," at other times, he assigned to himself an exclusive leadership role.[60] Wrote Cosme: "And who has been the cause that the Villa [of El Cobre] is given value? ... I, because none [of you] would have been able to obtain as much,"[61] or "there is no Author who can convey the work it has cost me," (although to all effects he became that Author through his letters).[62] Lamenting that "you erase from your memory he who is doing so much good and has done in your favor, who is your Apoderado, who has given you life and plenitude and who puts you in the great privilege of your so desired and appreciated freedom," he set himself to remind them about his legacy.[63]

In shaping his legacy as emancipator of the cobreros through his work as apoderado, Cosme called attention to the notoriety and support their case had attained in the royal court. Not only did he flaunt the support that the king had personally promised him after learning about the wrongful enslavement and persecution that his loyal vassals had been subjected to for years, Cosme also intimated contact and approval from the most powerful ecclesiastical figure in Castile: "The Señor Archbishop of Toledo tells me I have won in life the gates to heaven for the great work I am doing, so pleasing to the eyes of the sovereign creator who is the King of Heaven."[64] Although he had elucidated the basis for the cobreros' freedom in legalist and regalist terms, here Cosme added religious and moral extrajudicial legitimacy to their freedom cause.

According to this lowly colonial apoderado, God, church, and state had vindicated the justice of the cobreros' collective emancipation and, in his telling, their freedom lawsuit seems to have gained notoriety in the court: "Many people praise me [*me hacen corte*] for having justified the uprightness [*hombría de bien*] of so many wretched innocents."[65] Portraying himself as the champion of poor ignorant but noble victims and as vindicator of their honor, a proud Cosme here tapped the paternalist discourse of "miserables" to signal social distance from his constituents.

In another passage, Cosme mythologized himself in Christian biblical terms as the community's liberator and savior. Was he justifying the expenses of litigation? Or carving out his legacy?

[60] Gregorio Cosme, Madrid, October 6, 1795, No. 75, f. 195–207, AGI-SD 1629.
[61] Ibid. [62] Ibid. [63] Ibid. [64] Ibid. [65] Ibid.

I have given myself to this great defense that is the pretended freedom . . . and it has been through the providence of our omnipotent and merciful God, so wise and powerful, who has thrown me over the face of the earth, so that I was born [and] through me you could have your freedom. And if not, look at how many years it has been since this villa was founded and no one has asked for freedom, nor obtained it from Kings for you. I think no one, and if some had it [freedom], it was because of their money [self-purchase]. These are very substantive reasons that will reach your hearts and you will come to know what I have insinuated in my pages.[66]

Cosme inserted his legal battles and the cobreros' story into a larger Christological story of redemption based on New Testament tropes with which he was quite familiar. In this narrative, he portrayed himself as a God-sent emancipator of the community bringing them life and plenitude through freedom. In so doing, he depicted emancipation as a watershed moment of salvation in local history. He also differentiated the prestige and dignity of a collective emancipation based on royal law from the more prosaic commodified freedom obtained through individual monetary transactions (self-purchase or coartación).

Although Cosme's emancipation as redemption narrative has a self-laudatory, and perhaps self-serving, hagiographical character, this was a narrative based on an ancient popular rhetorical archetype often used in the Catholic Spanish empire to memorialize even secular figures and to this day to enshrine their significance in communal memory.[67] Ultimately, the local acceptance of Cosme's self-portrayal as chief emancipator of the cobreros through the judicial path he advocated hinged on the final outcome of the case – and perhaps as well on who was burdened with the litigation's expenses. But time engenders its own ways of erasing and rewriting memories and legacies. Perhaps Cosme's seized letters buried in the archive can lead posterity to remember him in more complex human ways: as a bold man with big dreams who was part of a remarkable communal struggle for freedom in which he played a very significant part. He can also be remembered more modestly as a scribbler who unwittingly left a rare testimony of an Afro descendant apoderado's activities in Madrid along with his interpretation of Spanish legal culture and justice on the question of freedom.

[66] Ibid.

[67] I'm thinking here about iconic figures such as José Martí and Antonio Maceo who are seen as having self-sacrificed for a political cause they thought would bring freedom and redemption to the Cuban people, namely independence from Spain and the establishment of a republic. Arguably, the more recent figure of Ernesto "Che" Guevara is portrayed in a similar way even if the "cause" he represented is different.

7

Violence, Marronage, and Litigation

> They [authorities and heirs] are threatening them that if they do not return to their masters they will catch them with fire and blood [*a fuego y sangre*]. The pueblo responds that they will not go [back] to [Santiago de] Cuba, that they will only go back in pieces [*hechos cuartos*], that the King ordered that they be returned to their native pueblo [*pueblo de su naturaleza*] under his royal protection [*amparo*].
>
> —Justo Cruzata, El Cobre, 1795

Right about the time Gregorio Cosme's letters from Madrid announcing the cobreros' imminent freedom were arriving in El Cobre (Chapter 6), the cobreros' local apoderado, Justo Cruzata, wrote back with alarming news: an impending carnage in El Cobre. His words were chilling. The epigraph is an excerpt of that letter.[1] More than at any other moment since the heirs began conducting private raids in the village to collect rents and capture escaped cobreros, the community faced spectacular violence – this time from government troops rather than from the heirs' private raids. Enslaved cobreros in Santiago had recently fled en masse believing the king had ordered their return to what Cruzata explicitly termed their "native pueblo" (*pueblo de su naturaleza*). In doing so, Cruzata highlighted the nature of the enslaved cobreros' relation to their local place of birth as if to legitimize their escape and return to El Cobre as a natural right confirmed by the king. Packed into that phrase was the idea of "natural" belonging and of native rights that had been violated by enslavement and expatriation in 1781.Wittingly or unwittingly, Cruzata was conjuring in his letter the notion of nativeness (discussed in Chapter 4) that undergirded the cobreros' identification as "natives of

[1] Justo Cruzata, El Cobre, December 27, 1795, No. 135, AGI-SD 1627.

El Cobre" in the memorials that they filed in the courts of the colony and in Madrid. Interlaced social, legal, and political notions of identity and rights traveled back and forth between judicial and vernacular contexts.

Cosme's letters and a recent confusing order from the island's captain general fed the cobreros' belief in the legality – and not merely the legitimacy – of their claims to freedom and to live as a pueblo. Cruzata informed Cosme that the pueblo – and he expressly gave the pueblo a single voice – was prepared to resist enslavement and another forced removal at the cost of shedding blood. El Cobre was at risk of becoming a place of death rather than of life and freedom. In that same letter, Cruzata assured Cosme that he was also prepared to die "for God, for my King, for defending my pueblo, and for the nine children that God has given me."[2] To him, all these loyalties were bound together in the present struggle.

It was December of 1795. Spain's war with revolutionary France was technically over per the Treaty of Basel of July 1795. But revolution in neighboring Saint Domingue was an ongoing event unfolding close to home: abolition of slavery had been declared and full French citizenship for all Black people proclaimed. People were fleeing the French colony and refugees were beginning to arrive in Santiago. Although pro-slavery lobbyists tried to play down the danger, there were fears of contagion in Cuba as well as in other slave societies in the hemisphere. A new war with Britain and the possibility of an occupation of the island in 1796 triggered yet another round of anxieties. This Atlantic geopolitical context of inter-imperial warfare and revolution added new dimensions to the escalating local violence and to the pueblo's litigation in Madrid.

Historians have long debated the impact of Saint Domingue's revolution in slave societies of the Atlantic world and especially in the Caribbean region. Whereas some scholars have argued that the fear that the revolution triggered in neighboring slave societies produced a backlash against the emerging antislavery movement and failed to contain the expansion of slavery in subsequent years, others have argued that dissemination of news about the revolution correlated with an increase in slave revolt and conspiracies and that it generated a more radical horizon for subsequent slave mobilizations.[3] The Haitian Revolution's impact, like that of any other grand historical event, was in no way uniform. It varied across

[2] Ibid.

[3] Geggus, "Slavery, War, and Revolution," in Gaspar and Geggus, *A Turbulent Time*, eds., and that anthology in general. See also the various chapters in Geggus, ed., *The Impact of*

societies in the hemisphere depending on a combination of contextual factors. I argue that in the case of El Cobre, it had an indirect impact. The cobreros' conflict preceded the revolution in the neighboring French colony by a decade and had a sui generis character. Bourbon policy in the Spanish empire in conjunction with broader Atlantic trends linked to an increased demand for slaves generated the immediate tensions that produced the conflict at the center of this book (see Chapter 1). Moreover, the notions and arguments that were deployed on the ground and in the courts in El Cobre's case were also largely based on legal and political discourses long widespread throughout the Spanish Atlantic world. Royal officials became aware of the danger that Saint Domingue's Revolution posed in the 1790s, but there were different reactions to its possible threat. Paradoxically, in this case, the imperial state acted with greater caution than the colonial state: colonial authorities, especially in Santiago, were willing to make fewer concessions to resolve El Cobre's conflict than Madrid began to call for.

This chapter returns to the colony: to the epicenter of the political conflict in the villa of El Cobre and the city of Santiago. But its scope becomes trans local as it expands to Havana and other towns where cobreros could be found, as well as to the periphery of the *monte* (forest, mountains) where many other cobreros sought refuge especially after 1795, as the epigraph shows. Moreover, the chapter provides another angle to the story of legal action that I have pursued so far in this book as it turns attention to other individual and collective forms of extrajudicial mobilization that the cobreros engaged in alongside litigation to resist their enslavement. Thus, this study rejoins here the story of marronage that has dominated the narrative on El Cobre since Luciano Franco's book *Las minas de Santiago del Prado*. Yet, as I argue, extrajudicial political actions and insurgencies such as marronage were not separate or antithetical to judicial actions and should not be compartmentalized as it is often done in the historiography of resistance.[4] In fact, they had a ricochet effect on each other as the epigraph also suggests. Flight and violence alongside litigation were sometimes concurrent forms of political action in Indian communities throughout the empire too.[5]

the Haitian Revolution; Ferrer, *Freedom's Mirror*. 10–13, 229–34. A foundational work in this controversy was Genovese, *From Rebellion to Revolution*.

4 Bryant, "Enslaved Rebels, Fugitives, and Litigants."

5 For litigation, flight, and riot in the case of Indigenous people, see Yannakakis, *The Art of Being In-Between*, 167–69; Owensby, *Empire of Law*, 260–63.

In some formulations, marronage has become a normative expression of freedom itself, an assumption that has been called into question by some scholars.[6] Although important as a form of defense and exit from the penuries of slavery and oppression or, as in the case of El Cobre, as a political strategy to exert pressure, marronage represents an unsettled and precarious state of fugitivity rather than an ideal form of freedom or of attained autonomy in itself. Marronage may be approached as a movement toward freedom, rather than away from slavery, though not as freedom itself. Fugitivity represents a negative movement – a reaction away from. Freedom, on the other hand, requires a more positive assertion or enactment of a project, so to speak. I argue that in the case of El Cobre, several forms of marronage took place: flight to the periphery of the monte as immediate reaction to violence and threat of enslavement (in this sense flight away from El Cobre too); flight as a means to other provisional options (such as access to the courts); and flight from sites of slavery *toward* El Cobre, as an act of returning and reclaiming a collective place of belonging and of (civil and political) freedom within the wider imperial framework. In this sense, there was a concrete local political project on the near horizon, one that, to be sure, called for further refining and struggle in the process of its actualization on the ground, since freedom is an evolving notion. Aside from fugitivity, the cobreros' extrajudicial actions to assert claims to freedom and native rights also included civil disobedience in various forms and armed ambushes – all of which became especially prevalent in the 1790s. But these actions were also informed by positive notions of legality and by vernacular views of justice as Cruzata's letter cited in the epigraph suggests.

Besides examining the use of extrajudicial actions such as marronage and ambushes, I also probe how these actions were portrayed and justified in judicial and vernacular narratives. Accounts of escape and violence also became part of the dispute and made their way into the legal dossier. Those accounts appeared in the plaintiffs' memorials and became prominent in letters from the pueblo. The heirs and colonial authorities countered with their own narratives of the cobreros' fugitivity, violence, and subversion of the law. The relator who summarized the voluminous dossier for the magistrates in Madrid wrote: "Representations from the natives of the pueblo and the heirs have poured in, the ones protesting the

[6] For a discussion of this formulation, see Roberts, *Freedom as Marronage* and his critics: Gordon, "The Limitations and Possibilities of Freedom as Flight"; and Wilder, "On Neil's Freedom as Marronage."

abuses [*atropellos*], usurpations, and incredible cruelties they suffered, and the others the insubordination, uprising and forays [*alzamiento y correrías*] of those they called their slaves."[7] Violence was at the center of both kinds of narratives. But their legal constructions were different. In one kind, the cobreros were unjust victims of violence; in the other, they were its perpetrators. Questions of right were intrinsic to the rhetoric of these narratives and metanarratives (then and now) and as such constituted forms of legal mobilization too.

The first part of the chapter examines the various individual and collective responses by the cobreros to the enslavement of 1781. Flight and use of violence went back to the moment of privatization (and even before), but these actions reached new levels in the 1790s. The second part focuses on a failed attempt at brokering an out-of-court settlement between cobreros, heirs, and colonial authorities that took place in 1795: the event discussed in Justo Cruzata's letter in the epigraph. Failure to negotiate and impatience with local obstructions to alleged royal orders and law propelled political mobilization and marronage to new levels, ahead perhaps of the slow-moving litigation, but never separate from it. The mobilization this time took place against the background of war, which gave a new urgency to the resolution of the conflict on the ground and to the protracted litigation in Madrid. Political issues on all sides steered the litigation process until the very end.

EXTRA-JUDICIAL RESPONSES TO PRIVATIZATION AND ENSLAVEMENT

As this book has argued so far, collective legal action as natives of a pueblo may have been the most distinctive – and potentially seminal – response of the cobreros to the privatization and enslavement of 1781. But it was not the only one. Individual actions were also part of the repertoire of actions the cobreros made use of to fight enslavement. After the initial bid for a collective coartación with land was denied in 1780, a few cobreros initiated individual coartación processes, even as the costs of self-purchase had become more onerous (Chapter 1). Historian José Luis Belmonte has uncovered thirty-seven coartaciones of cobreros in the notarial records of Santiago between 1780 and 1804, a not insignificant number, although the number of enslaved cobreros ranged between

[7] Relator's summary, Madrid, 1799, AGI-SD 1146.

800 and 1,065.[8] Other enslaved cobreros were able to individually negotiate hiring out arrangements with their new masters, paying the latter "wages" (*jornales*) while they worked and lived on their own.[9] Bartolomé Rodríguez worked in the construction projects of Casa Blanca in Havana earning a wage of five reales a day from which he paid a daily wage to his mistress while saving for his coartación.[10] Some cobreros seem to have gone back to El Cobre under similar arrangements, especially during the 1790s.[11]

But other cobreros took riskier individual paths. A number of them had run away years before the privatization of the mines. The heirs reported that they had received "through Royal Hacienda 1,041 slaves of all sexes ad ages, effectively about 800, because 200 and more did not present themselves, and the Royal Hacienda gave them to us as deserters or fugitives [*desertores o prófugos*] of the mines."[12] That number represented a considerable 20 percent of the slaves targeted for enslavement according to the Royal Treasury's records. They were considered lost or hard to recover assets and therefore assessed at much lower prices in the valuation lists. The heirs later tried to hunt them down in different cities by contracting slave hunters throughout the island. Pedro de Cárdenas, for instance, had run away some two decades before, when he was still a young man of about fifteen years. Sent by the governor of Santiago to deliver some horses to Havana during the British occupation of that city in 1762, Pedro stayed in Havana and went about as free until the heirs captured and sold him as a slave.[13] Others, resisting re-enslavement when located, were able to make arrangements to purchase their freedom. Manuel Vicente de la Caridad, a fifty-year-old disabled man with a ruptured groin, had run away many years before and was also inscribed in the hacienda lists as a "deserter." When recaptured in the Villa of Santa Clara in 1782, Manuel Vicente paid 250 pesos for his freedom papers, a considerable amount given his age and disabled condition.[14]

[8] Belmonte, *Ser esclavo en Santiago*, 233.

[9] The arrangement involved paying the master a daily predetermined fixed wage (instead of buying freedom) in exchange for working and living autonomously and keeping a surplus of earnings.

[10] Autos Ana and Bartolomé Rodríguez, No. 44/36, AGI-SD 1628.

[11] Martín Salazar, El Cobre, August 21, 1792, No. 1, f. 209–10v, AGI-SD 1627.

[12] Francisco Mancebo and Bernardo Mancebo Fernández Aguado, Rosa Antonia Garzón, Santiago, de Cuba, February 19, 1796, AGI-SD 1630.

[13] Autos Pedro de Cárdenas, Havana, 1786, No. 6/54/11, AGI-SD 1628.

[14] Autos Manuel Vicente de la Caridad, 1788, No. 59/67/24, AGI-SD 1628.

Still other cobreros ran away soon after the privatization in 1781. The brothers Juan Agustín and Juan Salvador Cruzata, tobacco farmers in El Cobre, fled during the actual enslavement raid (*rebato*) of 1781. The two brothers ended up in Havana where they worked incognito for about five years and came out of hiding to reclaim their freedom when the Edict of 1786 was published.[15] Similarly, three other cobreros escaped "immediately" after a purchaser bought them and their buyer "was never able to recover them."[16] Others, including women, ran away to the surrounding mountains where they formed or joined *palenques* (maroon communities). Marcelina Antonia de los Reyes ran away with her free husband and two toddler children to a palenque called Loma del Gamuco where they lived for two years. De los Reyes later declared that while she and her two children were captured in a slave hunting raid of the palenque, her husband was killed. Two other children that she gave birth to while living in the palenque "died (*se me murieron*) without baptismal waters," she lamented as if suggesting the loss and violence that marronage represented to a mother and wife.[17] Mother and children were then sold in Puerto Príncipe. When the Edict of 1786 was published and judicial paths were opened up for enslaved cobreros, Marcelina de los Reyes fought her way through four different tribunals in the island seeking freedom, albeit eventually without success. Throughout the three to four years de los Reyes pursued freedom in the courts, she was also concurrently engaging in another form of marronage: urban marronage, escaping from one city to another, all the way to Havana, seeking court protection in different tribunals by invoking the Edict of 1786's protection. She and other cobreras used the courts when the opportunity came up and fled at other times.

The initial cascade of runaway actions unleashed the first persecutory expeditions by the heirs in the district of Santiago. The following passage shows the way in which Santiago de Cuba's cabildo portrayed the conflict with runaway cobreros in 1785 during the organization of one slave hunting expedition. The expedition was headed by Tomás Garzón, a relative of the heirs, who had been elected constabulary (*alcalde de la Hermandad*) that year. Note the language used to criminalize the

[15] Autos Juan Agustín and Juan Salvador Cruzata, 1786, No. 8/56/13, AGI-SD 1628.

[16] Autos Luis González, Bernabé Martín, Bernardo de Soto, and Francisco Quiala, 1786, No. 56/64/21, AGI-SD 1628.

[17] Autos Marcelina Antonia de los Reyes, No. 5/43, 1797, AGI-SD 1628.

runaways and the (racialized) legal terms based on the legal source *Recopilación de Leyes de Indias* (1680) used to legitimate the persecution.

> A high number of the slaves that by order of His Majesty were given to the heirs [of Eguiluz] ... are currently fugitive and insurgent [*sublevados*], robbing and insulting the haciendas, wounding and ill-treating persons, and making resistance to the ministers of justice with weapons of all kinds, to the point that they have congregated [the slaves] of other citizens of this city. Therefore, the number of the insurgent slaves [*esclavos sublevados*] increases and it will be very difficult to reduce them, and without any loss of time, a remedy prescribed by the laws of the Kingdoms, of Book 7, Title 5, in relation to mulattos, blacks, *berberiscos* [Berbers] and children of Indians, should be provided.
>
> Black slaves of other vecinos, other idle free people and thieves are linking up with the insurgent slaves. And *cuadrilleros* [slave hunters] are going out with the Alcaldes of the Santa Hermandad in their persecution.[18]

A month later, however, the owners of slaves who may have initially supported the expedition were protesting and refusing to contribute to "the sustenance of the *cuadrilleros* persecuting fugitive slaves, because they say that those who have been apprehended are not fugitive slaves, but were [slaves] earning a wage in the *campos* [countryside]."[19] This follow-up note pointed to the muddled persecution that the sensationalized threat had triggered.[20]

Countering the criminalizing discourse of marronage could present serious, though not unsurmountable, challenges, however. Recognizing its potential for tarnishing the cobreros' freedom case, the Madrid Memorial of 1784 tackled the problem of marronage by mobilizing available jurisprudential philosophical notions related to natural and civil law. The cobreros' attorney in Madrid framed the runaways' actions as follows:

> Since nothing is easier to confuse than the *natural* love of freedom with the desire of shaking off the yoke of civil subordination because one resembles the other the opponents will surely attempt to paint *these and other efforts that the natives have made to free themselves from an unjust slavery with the dark colors of sedition, uprising or lack of obedience to the government* But the wisdom of Your Majesty will know how to discriminate the flight [*fuga*] *that nature dictates* from any kind of evil [*mal*], and the humble docility with which an immense *pueblo* has allowed

[18] Bacardí, *Crónicas de Santiago*, 237. [19] Ibid., 238.

[20] Although Luciano Franco in *Las minas de Santiago del Prado* adopts the language of insurgency used in this passage, he does not qualify its shrill and criminalizing character, the context in which it was used, and by whom. The cobreros did not use this language, at least in their writings.

> itself to be put into chains inside their own houses due to the profound respect they feel to superiors who exercise justice in the name of Your Majesty in those countries (my italics).[21]

The passage cautiously distinguished legitimate and illegitimate forms of resistance, drawing a fuzzy line between them. The moral and political justification of these acts of running away were cast in the common law medieval philosophy of natural law. According to this view, the love of freedom constituted a state of natural existence before men lived in rational society (a sort of instinctual state of being in present-day parlance); running away was also constructed as a defensive natural reaction in case of danger or attack. These "natural" (universal) reactions, rather than any intentional act of defiance of governmental orders or any refusal to obey, motivated these acts. Basically, they were acts of self-defense. But there was also a more significant allusion to moral reason in the passage above: the assertion that these natural (or transgressive) acts were also motivated by a sense of injustice. An "unjust" enslavement constituted a profound act of aggression against the plaintiffs that conferred moral and political legitimacy to their actions. Ultimately, however, the passage returned to a concept of passive subordination and complete victimhood as the ideal state in which justice could be easily discerned and dispensed. Today, we face similar juridically inspired notions. Any kind of active resistance risks tainting the image of perfect victimhood in the portrayals of people or events in tribunals and in the media's court of public opinion.

An even greater wave of cobreros absconded to El Cobre in the 1790s. Some escaped cobreros went back to their family houses and farms in El Cobre where relatives sheltered them; others discretely opened up land to establish small estancias and tobacco farms in the peripheral region, within a radius of twenty miles from El Cobre. Records from 1796 showed that 129 cobreros, labeled *prófugos* by authorities, were living in El Cobre and its environs at the time: 78 males (60 percent) and 51 females (40 percent). About 70 percent of these returnees had fled captivity – or negotiated a hiring out arrangement with masters – sometime in the early 1790s.[22] Among this wave of returnees were Martina Josefa Norate, Gregorio Cosme's wife, and their daughter María Candelaria Osorio. Although all were labeled prófugos, some seemed to have contracted with slaveowners to pay "wages" (jornales) for the

[21] Madrid Memorial, April 4, 1784, AGI-SD 1629.
[22] List of fugitive cobreros, El Cobre, September 23, 1796, AGI-SD 1627.

option of living on their own in El Cobre, which they may not have paid regularly as the heirs claimed. These informal returns to El Cobre can be considered individual acts of self-restitution to the pueblo: enactments of what the cobreros considered to be their legitimate rights to live in their native pueblo, which, in their interpretation, the Royal Edict of 1786 had sanctioned and Cosme's later letters from Madrid had confirmed.

Violent confrontations and raids escalated in the early 1790s. As the cobreros began to take refuge in El Cobre, or refused to pay wages and land rent, raids to capture them and to collect rents became increasingly directed toward the village. In 1791, a petition by the cobreros turned the "outlaw bandit" trope around: "We are seeing in front of our eyes the arming of formidable *cuadrillas* under the direction of the alcalde de la Hermandad Don Tomás Bravo with express orders to finish them [the cobrero runaways] with *pólvora y bala* [gunpowder and bullets] committing so many iniquities that they sacked the whole pueblo like bandits breaking the doors of locked houses and taking all they could find inside [and] they punished a lot of free people."[23] Although financed with private funds (in 1792, the heir Francisco Mancebo claimed he had spent about 1,300 pesos in the persecutions and "*cojeduras*" or seizures of cobreros),[24] the heirs carried out these raids with the governor's authorization and the city's cabildo backing. Yet the cobreros proved elusive. Mancebo protested that "I have worked [hard] but without the [material] support of the governor I cannot do anything; he is the only powerful one to stop this torrent because he has under his orders more than 1,200 armed men."[25] Mancebo's proposed strategy was to "raid them constantly and by surprise, on holidays when they least expected it ... and on the days of bad weather."[26] Francisco Mancebo proposed that his brother Fernando Mancebo head these raids, describing the latter in militaristic gendered jargon as "a brave, arrogant caudillo and a good man ... who could have put into practice these healthy operations with optimal efficacy and saintly zeal."[27] Yet the governor of Santiago held back, granting the heirs only licenses for their private slave hunting expeditions to the pueblo but not providing troops for private slave hunting operations.

Although the cobreros represented themselves in their letters and petitions as passively enduring the violence, these raids did produce defensive

[23] Petition of Buenaventura Cosme, Justo Cruzata, et al., Santiago de Cuba, February 3, 1792, f. 271–75, AGI-SD 1629.

[24] Francisco Mancebo, Santiago de Cuba, October 16, 1792, AGI-SD 1627.

[25] Ibid.

[26] Ibid.

[27] Ibid.

and retaliatory violence by some cobreros who took on a gendered role of armed defenders of their pueblo. Violence and retaliation for these incidents of physical abuse were backed by a strong feeling of community solidarity and by a desire to uphold family honor. Ignacio Ramos, who the heirs referred to as the "principal leader of the insurgent ones" (*principal cabeza de los alzados*), was shot to death (*murió a balazos*) in 1790. His brother vindicated him two years later in the most violent local ambush on the record. In that incident, Tomás Ramos, one of the three cobrero attackers, reportedly said to the wounded heir, Don Fernando Mancebo: "I am the brother of Ignacio, the one who died in one of your campaigns."[28] The ambushing cobreros insulted Mancebo with expressions like "this bully is over" (*ya se acabó este guapo*); "we will no longer have anyone harassing us" (*ya no tendremos quien nos incomode*); and, most significantly, "how have you dared to come here with two men where there are so many of them?" (*¿Cómo has tenido el atrevimiento de venir aquí con dos hombres en donde hay tantos?*).[29] Male honor was a strong motivator in the armed defense and protection of kin and pueblo.

This ambush resulted in the wounding of the raiders, the heir Fernando Mancebo, and the death of another associate in 1792. The three cobreros accused of the crime escaped and were tried in absentia. Since the event involved the death of a White man, the sentence was brutal but not unusual for the time: hanging and quartering as exemplary punishment. The body parts of the quartered bodies were to be displayed at the entrance to Santiago and along the road leading to El Cobre. The state's scripted sentence and its virtual display of spectacular violence was publicized throughout Santiago's jurisdiction. The community of El Cobre closed ranks around the three cobreros, now turned into fugitives of the law. Four years later, a petition to commute the sentence of the three cobreros, probably written by the parish priest or prepared in the bishopric, explained that the prófugos had taken refuge in a hill known as Loma de la Cruz in the environs of the pueblo and that although, the petition admitted, at times they had been forced to "take what is not ours for our subsistence," at other times they had been able to farm and "sell the produce through the mediation and help of our *compatriots,* free and slaves, who pained with our misery, gave us the necessary help" (my italics).[30] Their compatriots also "brought news about government orders

[28] Francisco Mancebo, Santiago de Cuba, August 14, 1792, f. 135, AGI-SD 1627.
[29] Ibid.
[30] Petition of Dionisio Torres and others, El Cobre, March 25, 1797, AGI-SD 1630.

and thanks to those news we had the luck not to be arrested since at the slightest movement of troops ... we abandoned the sweat of our labor and took refuge in the *monte* at the expense of suffering hunger and need to the most inexplicable degree."[31]

The use of the term "compatriots" in this narrative invokes the language of solidarity bonds of *patria* and corporate *comunidad* among all cobreros, in this case manifested in yet another kind of practice, one that effectively constituted a show of defiance against the state. The pain and compassion rhetoric softened the illicit complicity with the three condemned cobreros and mitigated what could have been depicted as criminal behavior – theft, threat of attack, defiance of the law, fugitivity – by portraying it as motivated by bare (natural) necessity to survive and thus an expression of natural law. While emphasizing the three fugitive men's weakness and precarity, the petition also suggested their redemption as industrious subjects.

Although this Christian humanitarian rhetoric of charity and clemency sought to tame the violence and severity of the sentence, at the bottom of the negotiations for the commutation were political and security urgencies of the time.[32] In the end, the three fugitives changed their mind and did not turn themselves in. The alternative of deportation and forced labor for life away from their community, or perhaps distrust of authorities, broke the negotiation. At this point, the three fugitive cobreros disappeared from the record.

Ambushes and threats became part of the direct actions of local villagers' intent on freeing fellow cobreros. These actions can be considered another form of extrajudicial activism. A government spy named Don José Emigdio Maldonado, who visited El Cobre in 1796, reported that "among the *slave cobreros* who are inseparable from the pueblo there is one who belongs to Don Manuel Garzón named Bartolo Vicente who, I am informed, is one of the most *revolutionary*" (my italics).[33] By revolutionary, the informant meant seditious, defiant, rebellious, wayward. He noted: "At any news he receives that Your Señoría has ordered the extraction of a slave by petition of their owners, he [Vicente] convokes those of his faction and they station themselves at the exit of the pueblo to

31 Ibid.

32 Governor Quintana to Captain General Las Casas, Santiago de Cuba, October 14, 1796, AGI-SD 1627.

33 José Emigdo Maldonado to Governor Quintana (hereafter Maldonado's Report), Santiago de Cuba, July 11, 1796, No. 73, f. 204–11, AGI-SD 1629.

impede it."[34] Vicente must have also had communication networks that alerted him of these slave hunting expeditions. In any case, far from the portrayals of the cobreros in some memorials as wretched docile subjects (or bandits), these accounts wittingly or unwittingly depicted them as actively engaged in forms of direct action to defend freedom and pueblo. These men protected the boundaries of the pueblo from trespassing heirs and defended the villagers' physical integrity and the honor of native men and women. They also defended their property, their homes, their families, their neighbors and friends, their land, and the right to bear arms. One may say that these cobreros were enacting the sovereignty of family and pueblo that their apoderados defended in the courts. They did so from within the village itself, not from the monte. These actions were defensive, but they could be risky if they went too far, as the hanging and quartering verdict of the three cobrero prófugos demonstrated.

A PROPOSED OUT OF COURT SETTLEMENT AND CRISIS: CONFLICT AND THE SPECTER OF SPECTACULAR VIOLENCE

Although interim Governor Vicente de Zéspedes (1779–80) had unsuccessfully questioned the privatization and especially the enslavement of the cobreros in 1780 (Chapter 1), conflict had been thereafter continuous in subsequent administrations from Governor Nicolás Arredondo's (1781–88) to Governor Sebastián Kindelán's (1799–1810). Local tensions with the cobreros reached a peak in the summer of 1795, and thereafter never tapered off until the final resolution of the case.

Captain General of Havana Luis de las Casas (1790–96) took it upon himself in 1795 to put an end to the "longstanding disturbances" in Santiago and preempt the litigation in Madrid. A strong ally and enabler of Havana's plantation sugarocracy and a strong supporter of slavery and the deregulation of the slave trade, his aim was to resolve the cobrero prófugo problem while preserving the heirs' and other private slaveholders' property rights in enslaved cobreros.[35] Had he not intervened, he claimed later, the heirs "would have very probably not recovered the considerable capital [in slaves] that has been restituted to them through

[34] Ibid.

[35] Captain General Luis de las Casas, Havana, October 13, 1795, AGI-SD 2229. Recall from Chapter 5 that captain generals had been appointed special judges (*juez privativo*) of the cobreros' case. On Luis de las Casas' association with sugar and slave interests, see Ferrer, *Freedom's Mirror*, 29.

the efforts of the government and without their having to pay for anything."[36] Things became more complicated, however, and the captain general was not only unable to restitute captives or capital to the heirs, but in fact he precipitated a crisis: the loss of many more cobreros who fled en masse to their native pueblo.

Unbeknownst to Cosme or to the local apoderados of El Cobre, in July of 1795, Las Casas negotiated an out-of-court settlement with the cobreros' apoderado in Havana, Don José Espinoza de los Monteros, and with the heirs' apoderado in the city, Don Nicolás Ambrosio Mancebo. The deal would enable enslaved cobreros to purchase their freedom at half their assessed value, and the prófugos (fugitives), always the main concern of colonial authorities, would be granted amnesty. On July 16, 1795, Las Casas published in Havana a *bando* (order) with the coartación offer giving prófugos six months to present themselves to authorities. He remitted the order to the governor of Santiago, Juan Bautista Vaillant (1788–96), for publication in that city and El Cobre.[37] As nine years earlier with the Edict of June 1786, the cobreros' conflict came again to public attention. This time around, however, the published order created a stronger reaction than before, though mostly in the Santiago region. After reading the bando to the community, Don Alejandro Paz y Ascanio, the pueblo's parish priest (1794–1832), described its reception in the pueblo: "I cannot explain the delight and happiness that the first [published order] produced with many long live the King [*muchos vivas al Rey*] ... especially among the fugitives who came down to the pueblo leaving the *palenques* and the forest [*el monte*] where they had taken refuge."[38] The long sought-after freedom and the aim of returning to their native pueblo seemed to finally be within reach.

The heirs in Santiago, however, vehemently protested the order calling it a "most exorbitant and corrupting [bando]"[39] Las Casas later admitted that the bando "produced serious damage since the cobreros who were living peacefully with their masters fled, against my orders, with great injury to their masters."[40] Revoking the original order, Las Casas issued a second bando qualifying the first. The coartación offer, the new bando proclaimed, applied only to the fugitive cobreros, not to those who were

36 Report of Captain General Las Casas, Havana, November 24, 1796, AGI-SD 1627.
37 Ibid.
38 Alexandro Paz y Ascanio to Bishop Osés, El Cobre, May 25, 1795, AGI-SD 2229.
39 Representation of Bernardo Mancebo and Francisco Mancebo, May 15, 1799, AGI-SD 1549.
40 Las Casas to Bishop Osés, Havana, October 13, 1795, Autos Bishop Osés, AGI-SD 2229.

"peacefully serving their masters." Las Casas admitted that "the point of the policy was to reduce the *cimarrones*" who were "roaming the region" and presenting a threat to public order.[41] The heirs were apparently prepared to surrender half the value of the runaways, whose full value they had effectively lost anyway, but stopped short at accepting an agreement that would have entailed losing half the value of all the slaves still under their or other slaveholders' power. The initial order opened the gates to a new flood of runaways to El Cobre and to a more general and active mobilization by enslaved cobreros in Santiago.

In the letter that opened this chapter, a bewildered Justo Cruzata informed Cosme about the commotion that the captain general's bando had produced in the pueblo and updated him on other events. Cruzata told Cosme, for instance, that he had been recently arrested following denunciations that he was misguiding cobreros with the news that Cosme was sending from Madrid. Cruzata seemed particularly puzzled by the unexpected coartacion offer, however:

> Friend, I cannot but participate you the events and troubles [*trabas*] in which I find myself They [colonial authorities] say that the King's order [of return to the pueblo] is for those who have been in the monte, not for those who have been serving [masters].
>
> They [enslaved cobreros] say that why those who have been in the monte should have more merit than those who have served fourteen years and are all from the same origin [*cepa*]. They [authorities] are threatening them that if they do not return to their masters they will catch them with fire and blood [*a fuego y sangre*]. The *pueblo respond*s that they will not go to [Santiago de] Cuba, that they only go back in pieces [*hechos cuartos*], that according to the bando that the captain general sent, the King ordered that they be restituted to the pueblo of their *naturaleza* under his royal protection, although now they say that His Majesty orders that they buy themselves [*los coarteen*] at half their value, and that this is just for those in the monte, and about those in servitude nothing is said.
>
> And that is why they want those who have left [servitude] to return to their masters. Those who remain in [Santiago de] Cuba are [still] there because they are imprisoned [*lo tienen preso*]. We find ourselves very afflicted and puzzled that you have not informed me about that *coartadura* [self-purchase deal], because I do not understand how it works since you have not informed me about it [*no me da razón de eso*]. I let you know that they do not allow me to read them the letters that you send me, because with those letters the slaves do not want to serve them (my italics).[42]

[41] Ibid. The two bandos were included in the Bishop's autos forwarded to Minister Eugenio Llagunas Amirola in Gracia y Justicia, AGI-SD 2229.

[42] Justo Cruzata, El Cobre, December 27, 1795, No. 135. AGI-SD 1627.

Cruzata's chronicle shows the political agency of cobreros outside the judicial sphere as they made use of complementary forms of extralegal action: self-restitution to their local birthplace, unified civil disobedience by refusing to return to their masters, willingness to die as slaughtered victims of state violence. Yet protest and resistance were cast in the language of the law. By invoking royal protection and the higher law of the sovereign as official law, the cobreros squarely challenged the orders issued by colonial officials, in this case the island's captain general and the governor of Santiago. The triangulation of power at play served to pit imperial officials against colonial ones.[43]

However, the cobreros invoked not only the higher royal law (communicated through Cosme's letters) and the captain general's initial order. Vernacular notions of justice also undergirded their claims. They decried the penalization of those who had patiently obeyed the order of enslavement and endured captivity while the case moved through the higher court in Madrid (i.e., performed the docile victim's role), while those who had run away were rewarded. A possible split emerged in the pueblo with the divisive order. Cruzata papered over these possible divisions by stressing unity as a pueblo ("the pueblo responds") and the fearless willingness of all to endure a massacre to defend their freedom and the right to live in their pueblo.

The standoff also provoked a major conflict between the colonial state and the church that had been incubating since Bishop Osés took office in 1792 and since his appointment in 1793 of a new parish priest, Father Paz y Ascanio. Both the bishop and the new priest became supporters of the cobreros' cause during this crisis.[44] The governor accused them of

[43] The conflict over the bando of 1795 (and perhaps going back to the Edict of 1786) may have reached other regions into where cobreros had been trafficked. In July 1795, a small and short-lived rebellion took off in a small hacienda in Puerto Príncipe. Among the two leaders was a twenty-year-old cobrero named Romualdo, (and a French slave perhaps from Saint Domingue). It is uncertain what the aims of the revolt were, if they were influenced by events in Saint Domingue or of other internal rumors from the cobreros' conflict and the belief that the king had ordered their freedom. Although it was originally reported that words to the effect that "all men were equal" were uttered, another official investigation did not mention those words and revealed the cobrero had heard a circulating rumor of the arrival in Puerto Príncipe of a royal edict emancipating slaves. The two leaders reported their intention to go to the governor of Puerto Príncipe to demand the freedom he was hiding from them. Other slaves claimed they were recruited by force. The case of was eventually transferred to the Audiencia of Santo Domingo for trial but the outcome is not known. Geggus, *A Turbulent Time*, 133–36.

[44] Among other forms of support, the church provided secret communication venues between El Cobre and Madrid. Also, Bishop Osés had training in canon and royal law

advising the cobreros that they were free, of distributing land plots to the returnees (along with Cruzata), and of encouraging their civil disobedience.[45] In Bourbon regalist political culture, these interventions of the bishop were construed as improper interference by the church in state governance matters. This kind of church and state conflict echoed throughout the empire as Bourbon policy had sought to reduce church power by expanding the state's jurisdictional reach. Yet the state also sought and accepted church aid to mediate conflicts when convenient.[46]

When Las Casas and Governor Vaillant ordered Bishop Osés to immediately remove the parish priest from the village, the bishop squarely refused to follow the captain general's directive.[47] He justified his refusal by stating that the priest's removal would be a "notorious injustice to which I would never consent" and that it would be considered "cruel, reckless and unfair to defer."[48] In the pueblo, some cobreros also mobilized to protest the priest's removal using yet another kind of political tool. Some thirty-six cobreros (a note at the end stated they were all free) petitioned the bishop for the priest to remain in his post: "Don't take him away for we will not admit another one."[49] Although the petition initiative was organized by Justo Cruzata, and possibly the priest himself (with a nod from the bishop), it was nonetheless an unusual claim of the right of cobreros, as parishioners, to have a say on their priest and their parish.[50] Signing a petition was a political act, effectively an act of citizenship. Although addressed to church authorities, the petition was indirectly directed to the colonial state that had ordered the priest's removal. The clarification that they were all free constituted an assertion of a right based on free status regardless of race or gender. Still, thirty-six free cobreros represented a fraction of the free adult cobreros, although a

and became a powerful ally of the community in the litigation efforts sending reports up to Madrid and providing legal aid. His intervention provided a powerful counterweight to colonial official actions in Madrid.

45 Governor Juan Bautista Vaillant, Santiago de Cuba, December 9, 1795, AGI-SD 2229.

46 In neighboring Santo Domingo, Bishop Fernando Patillo was helping reduce the maroon community of Naranjo in the 1790s. See Yingling, "The Maroons of Santo Domingo."

47 Bishop Osés to Las Casas, December 15, 1795. AGI-SD 2229; Report of Captain General Las Casas, Havana, November 24, 1796, AGI-SD 1627.

48 Bishop Osés to Las Casas, Santiago de Cuba, May 13, 1796, AGI-SD 2229.

49 Petition of free cobreros to Bishop Osés, Santiago del Prado, December 5, 1795, AGI-SD 1630.

50 This petition in support of the parish priest was allowed because the bishop in this case supported the priest. Had the bishop not approved of him, the parishioners' petition would have meant little.

considerable portion if counted as heads of households still living in the village.

While Governor Vaillant threatened the use of force to restore the cobreros to their alleged owners, accusing them of disrupting the public peace and defying orders, the bishop reminded the governor of his responsibility to preserve public peace and warned him of possible bloodshed if force was used: "I think it will be quite difficult to reduce them to the service of their masters without shedding blood; and it can be feared that from that venture no other result would be obtained except pushing them to take to the forest [*monte*] and take the place left by the others [the previous runaways]."[51] Bishop Osés shrewdly added that according to ancient governance policy it was "a priority that no pueblo be abandoned or that any trouble should lead to a popular unrest [*desenfreno popular*] that disturbs the Government," thereby placing the blame on the governor for any upheaval.[52] Familiar with the development of the cobreros' case in Madrid, Bishop Osés calculated that the final resolution of the litigation would take no more than eight months and that, for now, it was better to take a hands-off policy with those who refused to return to slavery. The rift between colonial state and church grew so strong that, before stepping down at the end of his tenure in November 1796, Las Casas invoked regalist arguments to recommend to the Crown that both the priest and the bishop be deported from the island for interfering with state matters, a recommendation that Madrid did not heed.[53]

Governor Juan Nepomuceno de Quintana (1796–98) succeeded Vaillant and overlapped with Captain General Las Casas for several months. The new governor inherited the standoff with the cobreros. Since he was unsure of how to handle the conflict, Las Casas suggested that he send a spy to El Cobre to "acquire all the possible knowledge related to this people" and find out "their hideouts, trails, ways of life, number of relations, understandings, and subjects who advise them or have influenced over them [*los sugieren*]."[54] Governor Quintana recruited a young upstart clerk from Santiago named Don José Maldonado for the surveillance mission. Maldonado's report, however biased, constitutes a valuable glimpse into the internal happenings of the pueblo. Ironically, historians can sometimes benefit from the state's stratagems, the very

[51] Bishop Osés to Las Casas, Santiago de Cuba, November 15, 1795, AGI-SD 2229.

[52] Bishop Osés to Las Casas, Santiago de Cuba, May 13, 1796, AGI-SD 2229.

[53] Report of Las Casas, Havana, November 24, 1796, AGI-SD 1627.

[54] Las Casas to Quintana, Havana, June 15, 1796, AGI-SD 1629.

instruments that were used to penetrate and undermine the community's struggle.

Maldonado went to El Cobre sometime around early July of 1796 with the excuse of visiting the Marian sanctuary in the village. Whether they believed him or not, Maldonado talked to people there pretending to have friendly intentions. The informer singled out the cobrero Juan Rafael, observing that he is "very well armed, with a long machete, and seemingly with handguns and a dagger in his belt." In fact, he noted that "all [the cobreros] carry the long machete" and that the blades were the kind banned by the governor after one of the ambushes turned deadly.[55] Maldonado also tracked Vicente Santa Clara whom he identified as a "free mulato" from Santiago de Cuba who "is a tailor and resides there with two young women and has his main residence in the miserable rancho where he lives with one of them."[56] He added that Santa Clara "does not work, and his only entertainment is going from house to house, lying to all about the news that his slyness [*bachillería*] invents to have a good time among those *miserables*."[57] Although not a native of El Cobre, Santa Clara was a vecino in the pueblo where he lived with a cobrera. He was an example of the friendship between some free people of color from Santiago and El Cobre, or rather, of the internal solidarity bonds that also included vecinos in the pueblo. In fact, Santa Clara was among the power grantees to Cosme and among the latter's correspondents in the pueblo. His visits "from house to house" may have been an early example of political canvassing. Vicente Santa Clara's political involvement in the village affairs was so important that the governor issued orders for his and Justo Cruzata's arrest in December 1795. Whereas Cruzata may have felt it beneath him to flee, Santa Clara did not. Cruzata informed Cosme that "Vicente is fleeing, I am not capable of fleeing for many reasons," including his willingness to die for God, his king, the defense of his pueblo, and for his children.[58] Divisions in the pueblo or among its leadership regarding proper strategies of political resistance – either running away, waiting patiently for a possible legal resolution of the case in Madrid, taking local legal actions, ambushing trespassers, or even, as Cruzata suggested, confronting the state directly in the pueblo – may have formed part of the internal politics creating divisions in the pueblo during those critical years. Bigger splits and betrayals had emerged in the

[55] Maldonado's report, Santiago de Cuba, July 11, 1796, No. 73, f. 204–11, AGI-SD 1629.
[56] Ibid. [57] Ibid.
[58] Justo Cruzata, El Cobre, December 27, 1795, No. 135, AGI-SD 1627.

pueblo too, however. Cruzata told Cosme that they had found who had been informing the governor about their activities: the Ojeda brothers who had been appointed alcaldes by the governor. Old enmities and memories internal to the village may have resurfaced during this crisis. Regarding the Ojedas, Cruzata commented to Cosme: "It seems to me that from their generation or their descendants nothing good will come, because bitter seed cannot produce sweet fruit, [and] their great grandfather was the one who [once] sold out [*vendió*] the pueblo."[59] It is impossible to know what event in the past Cruzata was referring to, but memories of enmities and factionalism resurfaced in the present conflict.

During his visit to El Cobre, Maldonado carefully mapped the landscape and the manmade features that reflected the tense military situation the pueblo was living through. He drew attention to the many trails that led from the roads around the pueblo into the neighboring hills "where in case of an attempt to invade them they would all scatter making it difficult to block their way into the density [*escabrosidad*] of the immediate hills through which they know their way so well."[60] Maldonado speculated that all the trails may have been made intentionally "because the constant fear that they have of being surprised has possibly made them live with all these precautions."[61] The carved landscape of hidden arteries connecting the community with the monte reflected the cobreros' use of the environment not so much as a conduit for flight from the carceral regime of the plantation as in the case of other slaves but as a means for temporary flight from a terrain claimed as home whenever outside forces threatened occupation. Other hidden byways to Santiago and across the island and the sea connected communications of dispersed cobreros in other towns with the community and the community with Cosme in Madrid. These communication circuits were trans-local and transatlantic.

Maldonado raised another security issue in his report, one that had been especially troubling to colonial officials lately. The governor's spy noted with some alarm that two soldiers from the Second Battalion of Havana, who had recently fought in Saint Domingue and were currently stationed at the garrison of Santiago, had visited El Cobre on their day off while Maldonado was still in the village. When he tried to find out what brought them to El Cobre, the two soldiers responded that they had

[59] Ibid.

[60] Maldonado's report, Santiago de Cuba, July 11, 1796, No. 73, f. 204–11, AGI-SD 1629.

[61] Ibid.

simply come to visit [*a pasearse*]. Maldonado found their visit dangerous because

> having just returned from the Island of Santo Domingo, the individuals were versed in those depraved maxims of the colony, [and] their conversations [with the cobreros], even without any determined intention, can trigger some movement among those natives who do not lack any other ill than their desire for freedom; and if they, or any of their companions, were to desert, they could, through the friendships they now make [in the pueblo], settle there and produce unfavorable consequences.[62]

Although there had been utmost official silence regarding the revolution in nearby Saint Domingue, it is highly unlikely that the cobreros would not have already known about the war given that two battalions from Santiago de Cuba had gone to Saint Domingue and had lost 573 men (Havana's regiments had lost more than half their men).[63] The campaign in Saint Domingue had resulted in the death of 1,800 Cuban soldiers and many others had fallen sick with fevers, a fact that would have been difficult to conceal in a relatively small city like Santiago. Some of these soldiers or their relatives may have even brought personal vows to the allegedly miraculous image of the Virgin in El Cobre's sanctuary. Also, refugees from Saint Domingue – White and of color, free and slave – had begun to arrive in Santiago, although it is difficult to know what kind of stories about Saint Domingue they circulated in the region.[64] French slaves were also illegally imported and they came with stories, even though perhaps in French.

When Las Casas' term came to an end in November 1796, the cobreros' conflict was still unresolved although a sort of detente had been achieved whereby cobreros who refused to return to slavery were allowed to stay in El Cobre paying jornales (wages) to their masters. However, Madrid eventually annulled the negotiated out-of-court settlement on June 16, 1797, and suspended arrangements of jornales that allowed

[62] Ibid.

[63] Johnson stated that Governor Vaillant sent 1,224 soldiers from Santiago as troop reinforcements to fight in Saint Domingue in 1794. *The Social Transformation*, 157. See Ferrer for the regiments sent to Saint Domingue, the French slaves illegally smuggled to Cuba, the refugees, the "excess of news" circulating despite the state's attempts at silencing the news from Saint Domingue, *Freedom's Mirror*, Chapters 2 and 3.

[64] Scott and Hébrard tell the story of one such refugee from Saint Domingue who arrived in Cuba a few years later, in 1804, but the flow had begun before. By 1809, there were some 10,000 refugees from Saint Domingue in Santiago's jurisdiction. *Freedom Papers*, 49–64. Other estimates give 10,000 to 18,000 in Santiago in 1803. Geggus, *A Turbulent Time*, 25.

captive cobreros to reside in El Cobre.[65] Orders were reissued to colonial officials – and again ignored – to send to Madrid all documentation related to El Cobre and to return the cobreros to their pueblo. A quiet conflict between imperial and colonial officials (based on the old "I obey but do not comply" strategy) in support of slaveholders and heirs kept any official judicial resolution of the case stalled and fed the fire despite the political dangers of a revolt in the broader geopolitical context of the decade. The political pressure from human property owners was stronger than the risk of public disorder in the colony.

A new war, this time with the British, loomed on the horizon. The British invasion of Trinidad in February 1797 and the rejected attack in Puerto Rico on April 17, 1797, brought the British threat frightfully close to the domestic scenario of hostile cobreros in the island's eastern coast. Governor Juan Nepomuceno de Quintana revealed his anxieties to Las Casas' successor, Captain General Conde de Santa Clara (1796–99), when he informed him that "certain rumors [*especies*] have reached my ears that [the cobreros] may be awaiting this event [a British invasion] to take sides against the Governor."[66] Quintana, by his own admission, found himself in a dire predicament and did not dare to act. On the one hand, he felt "distressed with the cobreros" because "once more they are carried away [*arrebatados*] with the false idea of freedom if the Government's determination does not agree with their own … their character is insubordinate and stubborn."[67] Yet, in another letter to the captain general, Quintana acknowledged that "I assure Your Excellency that these men will never be useful if they remain in servitude to the heirs … who they look at with horror and if in any way they have withstood slavery it has been with the hope of being restituted to their pueblo."[68] Governor Quintana was torn: "If I order their return [to El Cobre], the heirs would clamor that they were being stripped of their legitimate rights and it would be difficult to placate a commotion. In such critical circumstances I don't dare to take a decision without a superior determination."[69] Feeling paralyzed, the governor of Santiago passed on the decision of how to act to the island's captain general in Havana. Political pressure came from all sides: cobreros, heirs, Havana, Madrid, and the context of another inter imperial war.

[65] Las Casas' report, Havana, November 24, 1796, AGI-SD 1627.
[66] Quintana to Conde de Santa Clara, Santiago de Cuba, May 30, 1797, AGI-SD 1628.
[67] Ibid. [68] Ibid. [69] Ibid.

An autonomous and direct communication line to Madrid through Cosme became crucial for the cobreros at this point. Cosme's letters not only played a political role in motivating and legitimizing the cobreros' resistance to colonial authorities. His missives also provided documentation from Madrid that otherwise would have been kept secret under royal officials' control. Governor Quintana told Captain General Santa Clara that "all the warnings are in vain; [the cobreros] are convinced that the King is protecting them in their freedom by means of certain Royal declarations that they have the audacity to believe are in the power of Your Excellency and this government, and have been suppressed."[70] He added that "this concern is born from the lies that Gregorio Cosme Osorio, who calls himself their captain and apoderado residing in the court, has them deluded [*alucinados*] with some frequent papers [*papelorios*]."[71] The governor may not have found Cosme's letters credible, but he was well aware of royal orders by then backing the cobreros' restitution to the pueblo. In another equivocating letter to the captain general, Governor Quintana admitted that he kept "a royal order of October 16 ... which deals with the return of natives to El Cobre to continue peacefully in their labors."[72] Yet he disclosed that "I have tried to keep it in *Secretaría* [government office] under the greatest reserve," but he had realized that its content was out.[73] The governor thought that "the Apoderado that the said cobreros have in Madrid [Cosme] had informed his counterpart Justo Cruzata about it."[74] Here was another reiteration of the powerful theme of a hidden royal edict of freedom that often circulated as rumor through slave societies. But this time the royal order was real – even if still provisional until the final adjudication of the case was made in Madrid. Cosme's liaison role in Madrid was crucial to keep the local community informed of what decrees had been issued on their behalf and sent to the colony.

A new and striking element of political action emerged then in the crisis. *Pasquines* or anonymous leaflets were nothing new in the colony or the empire. They appeared throughout the Atlantic world, but they were especially significant in polities with no open civil societies where other voices could organize or be heard. Pasquines popped up in Havana against Captain General Las Casas in the 1790s and had recently done so in Santiago attacking Governor Vaillant's policies.[75] They reappeared

70 Ibid. 71 Ibid. 72 Ibid. 73 Ibid.

74 Quintana to Santa Clara, Santiago de Cuba, November 1797, No. 69/77, AGI-SD 1628.

75 Johnson, *The Social Transformation*, 162.

now during Governor Quintana's administration, this time directly targeting the governor's handling of the cobreros' crisis and indirectly accusing him of tyranny. A pasquín with a strident message written "in imitation of letterpress" appeared in a street corner of Santiago de Cuba.[76] Its fake letterpress calligraphy was meant to hide the handwriting that could betray its author. It was also intended to subvert official control of communications in a city with no press or freedom of the press. The leaflet would have required graphical skills to produce it, a sign of intriguing covert alliances in the city. The pasquín's message consisted of a proclamation directed to the people of Santiago that publicized the orders that the governor wanted to keep secret. A few days later, two other leaflets with the same message were slipped under the office doors of a government scribe in the *Secretaría* and another under a clergyman's door in the Cathedral. It is not clear why these specific individuals were targeted. Governor Quintana speculated that Justo Cruzata may have been behind the composition of the flier since he knew about the hidden edict, but it is unlikely that Cruzata had the graphic skills to compose the pasquín. Its author remained a mystery.

The pasquín's message went beyond civil disobedience and bordered on the seditious. It proclaimed that if the governor defied the king's law, citizens were entitled to enforce it with lethal force if necessary. It was effectively a call for violent resistance against local tyranny. The leaflet proclaimed that:

> THE KING ORDERS that every cobrero can move to reside in El Cobre and that no one can impede it and whoever hinders it can be killed.
>
> Freedom by the Sword [Libertad y hierro en medio][77]

The message sounded like an ultimatum. It was a reminder of the volatility of the cobreros' unresolved situation and of the potential for violence lurking over the city. The anonymous pasquín also suggested the existence of networks in the city strongly supporting the cobreros' freedom and their return to their pueblo. Could the cobreros' aspiration to

[76] Quintana to Santa Clara, Santiago, May 31, 1797, No. 69/77, f. 17. AGI-SD 1628.

[77] "El Rey manda que todo cobrero pueda pasarse a residir al Cobre sin que nadie lo pueda embarazar, y si alguno lo impidiere se pueda matar. Libertad y 'hierro en medio.'" The translation of "hierro en medio" is difficult. *Hierro* (iron) in Spanish can refer to a weapon. The context of "can be killed" in the message reinforces this translation. I am also basing the translation on the Spanish saying, "el que a hierro vive, a hierro muere" and its English equivalent "he who lives by the sword, dies by the sword."

freedom legitimized by royal edict contain the seed of a possible conflagration in the Santiago region?

After all, the uprising in the French colonies had started with rumors about a royal order too.[78] The combative message may have even given advanced warning of what could happen if the cobreros' case eventually had a negative outcome in Madrid. Would such a verdict turn the cobreros against the king and not only against colonial officials? Moreover, although the proclamation referred to the cobreros' case, the final phrase could be more general. Given the current geopolitical situation in Saint Domingue, its call for liberty was not to be taken lightly.

At the end of 1797, Captain General Conde de Santa Clara finally complied with superior orders and remitted all the government's documentation related to the cobreros to Madrid. Scribes made notarized copies of the material in the colonial archives, including of the thirty-one hearings and proceedings from the captain general's tribunal dealing with the Edict of 1786. After sixteen years of enslavement and thirteen of litigation in Madrid, the case was finally on its way to adjudication. Yet it would still take three more years before a final verdict came down. Meanwhile, new petitions and complaints from the cobreros' apoderados and from the heirs kept engrossing the legal dossier in Madrid. The battle continued on both fronts, in the ground and in the imperial court, pitting colonial officials against the Crown. In 1798, Justo Cruzata kept the pressure up protesting lack of enforcement of superior orders. In his role as local apoderado and activist, he sent a series of sharply worded representations directly to the king (using technical language written by a secret amanuensis, probably from the bishopric) accusing Governor Quintana of ignoring the latest edict of restitution to El Cobre. Cruzata said he had no hope left that the edict would be enforced or justice done adding that his power granters (*poderdantes*) were back in the monte due to the rigor and threats of Governor Quintana and the heirs, a way of exerting pressure on Madrid to move on the case and to denounce the governor. Finally, Cruzata wrote that he was sending his complaints directly to Madrid because "The petitioner is too fearful and does not dare to present himself in the Governor's tribunal because having done so

[78] On the rumor of a royal edict granting emancipation, or partial freedom, to slaves withheld by colonists in Saint Domingue and Martinique in 1789 and the "emancipation rumors" trend elsewhere in the Caribbean into the nineteenth century, see Geggus, *A Turbulent Time*, 8–12. Geggus calculates that false rumors of an official emancipation that had been hidden by local officials occurred in about one-third of slave conspiracies and rebellions between 1789 and 1815.

on some occasions in use of his power [as apoderado], he has been threatened and persecuted and insistently questioned about the person or persons who make him the charity of directing the writings and recourses to His Majesty, and he feared being a victim of vindictiveness."[79] The politics of litigation unfolded not only inside the courts, in substantive and procedural battles but also in the space around and outside the courts where access to the judicial arena, to legal personnel, to the instruments of the law, and eventually to enforcement of the law were also part of the battles that had to be waged, at least in a major case like this. Although the cobreros acted with great autonomy, allies, powerful ones like the bishop of Santiago, were also important as guarantors and advocates.

But there was yet another broader political context involved in the politics of litigation. Cruzata in his complaints to the Council accused colonial officials of disobeying royal orders, of misgoverning, and of exposing the colony to danger given the situation of war with the British enemy at the time. He was also affirming his right to protest through judicial venues – the proper and legal way of protesting and doing politics in the context of an absolute monarchy. Raising the specter of marronage as a legitimate reaction to the governor's or the colonial state's breaking the law by not enforcing royal decrees, he conjoined legal and extralegal actions in a powerful and directed way.

It was now Madrid's turn to give closure to the protracted litigation. The conflict could not bear further equivocation during times of turbulence in the Caribbean. The empire was already on the brink of bankruptcy at the time and aware of its precarious situation. And the cobreros were fatigued and angered with the legal stasis. The threat of a conflagration in the city that the pasquines intimated loomed large, especially given the regional and global context of inter imperial warfare and revolutions nearby.

As late as April 1799, the parish priest, Father Paz y Ascanio, "in the name of the aggrieved natives of the Villa of El Cobre," sent to the king a letter deploying what had become the community's recurring self-narrative. Paz informed the king that "despite the inhuman persecutions we have experienced since 1780 into to the present," for the royal orders issued in 1796 and 1797 had not yet been enforced, and despite "the destruction of this Villa, [and the] houses, personal property [*alajas*],

[79] Representation of Justo Cruzata, Santiago del Cobre, November 14, 1797, AGI-SD 1630.

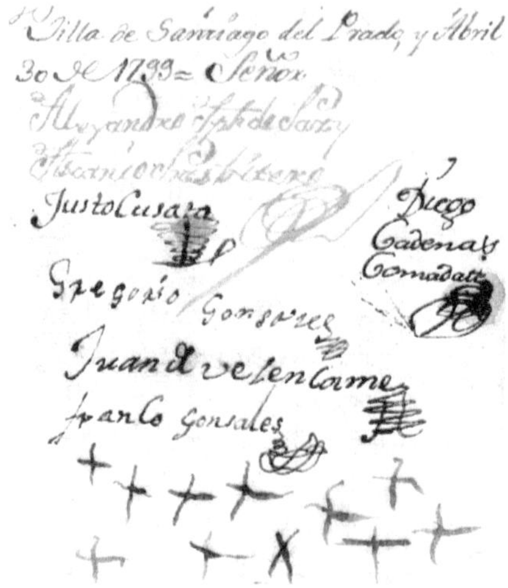

FIGURE 7.1 Petition and signatures of natives of El Cobre, 1799.
A petition to the king by the parish priest on behalf of the natives of the Villa of Santiago del Prado. It contains the autographs of the priest, Alejandro Paz y Ascanio, and the cobrero apoderado, Justo Cruzata, followed by the signatures of four other literate cobreros and the anonymous crosses of eleven illiterate villagers. Ministerio de Cultura y Deportes. Archivo General de Indias. Carta del Presbítero Alejandro Paz y Ascanio, AGI, Santo Domingo, 330

haciendas and animals [of the natives] in different occasions, and the lack of a parish church for nine years" they had just finished building a new one in December 25, 1798, "in the midst of many travails and opposition by the heirs."[80] They were offering this accomplishment to His Majesty hoping he would grant "this sad villa" some privileges. A new parish church raised almost heroically through the collective labor and efforts of villagers confirmed the Christian and corporate credentials of the community that they hoped the king would protect and recognize. It was signed by a few literate cobreros, including Justo Cruzata, and three others who had acted at one or another point in the past as local apoderados too. Most powerful perhaps were the crosses of illiterate natives of the villa representing the living community looking forward to a generous outcome of the case (Figure 7.1).

80 Letter of Father Alejandro Paz y Ascanio on behalf of the natives of El Cobre, El Cobre, April 30, 1799, AGI-SD 1627.

8

The Final Outcome of the Case

> The 1,065 persons who are said to be descendants of the primitive *siervos* [serfs or slaves] that existed in the past in those mines and were handed over as such in August of 1781 to those said to be heirs ... all, without distinctions of occupation, age, or sex, be declared free, so that at no time, nor with any pretext, can they, or their descendants, be troubled [*molestados*], nor any demands be brought-up against them regarding their condition or status.
>
> —Special Junta's Opinion, Madrid, 1799

> The royal edict issued by His Majesty in Aranjuez on April 7, 1800 whereby the slaves were declared free was published in this city on March 18, 1801. And with it, I had the great upset [*disgusto*] to see the only slaves that served us walk out through my and my children's doors.
>
> —Doña Ana María López Navia, Santiago, 1805

Success finally arrived in 1800. It materialized in the royal Edict of April 7, 1800, that emancipated collectively more than 1,000 enslaved cobreros and all of their descendants. Victory came after a protracted battle of two decades against heirs, slaveholders, colonial officials, and even the Council of the Indies. The edict reached the colony almost a year later. One can only imagine the cobreros' elation when, on March 19, 1801, El Cobre's parish priest, Father Alejandro Paz y Ascanio, read the royal edict in front of the sanctuary of the pueblo's patroness, the Virgin of Charity of El Cobre. One wonders where Justo Cruzata and other cobrero leaders who had acted as apoderados were standing during the priest's public reading of the royal edict.[1]

There are no accounts memorializing that official event that can provide a sense of the local alignments symbolically played out during that

[1] Franco, *Las minas*, 131.

festive occasion. A better record has survived of the edict's proclamation in the capital of Santiago de Cuba three days before. On March 16, 1801, state and church officials, natives and vecinos of the city, and perhaps enslaved people came together in the Plaza de Armas to hear the king's voice. The city's White militias and its militias of color, in which some free cobreros may have served, were deployed for the ceremonial occasion. The members of the city's and the cathedral's councils were present in their official capacity. Present as well was Bishop Joaquín Osés y Alzúa who had been the city's most prominent supporter of the cobreros' freedom in the 1790s. Conspicuously absent from the ceremony (no mention is made of him) was Governor Sebastián Kindelán (1799–1812), who, as other governors before him, had backed the heirs' rights to the mining estate and to the enslaved cobreros. The royal edict was not read by the governor. It was read by the government's notary, Gregorio Félix Quiroga.[2] The public reading counteracted previous maneuvers by colonial authorities to keep royal edicts hidden. Likely absent from the event as well would have been the former beneficiaries of the privatized mining estate, the heirs of the original contractor Don Juan de Eguiluz, now perpetually dispossessed of the mines, land, and slaves of El Cobre. The cobreros' victory and the heirs' humiliating public defeat provided a dramatic denouement to the protracted conflict: a theatrical finale to a memorable upending of the usual colonial order of things. One can imagine the jubilation with which enslaved cobreros walked out of their captors' houses after hearing the news of their emancipation. Scenes like those represented by the heir and slaveholder Doña Ana María López Navia (Figure 1.3 No. 31) may have played out in many houses in Santiago and elsewhere in the colony (second epigraph).[3] The liberation news would also travel orally through the cobreros' networks to reach relatives, friends, and compatriots enslaved in other cities and districts.

The Edict of 1800 deviated from the Council of the Indies' initial ruling of 1784 suggesting that there had been a shift in the imperial state's position on the case during the intervening years. Whereas, in 1784, the Council had rejected the collective and corporate basis of the plaintiffs' legal action and basically upheld the privatization and enslavement

[2] My account is based on Franco, *Las minas*, 129–30.

[3] Petition of Doña Ana Maria López Navia y Quiroga, Santiago, December 3, 1805, No. 131, AGI-SD 330.

Executory Order of 1779 (Chapter 5), now the king ruled in favor of the cobreros' freedom, revoked that executory order, and divested the heirs in perpetuity of any property rights over the mining estate they had aspired to. Gregorio Cosme had written about an immanent freedom at least since 1795 (Chapter 6). What considerations guided the final outcome of the case? What motivated the shift in the state's position in the 1790s? I must rewind a couple of years back to document the factors that informed the final outcome of the cobreros' long and grueling lawsuit eventually resulting in the Freedom Edict of April 7, 1800, proclaimed a year later in Santiago de Cuba and El Cobre.

In the first part of this chapter, I probe the considerations informing the final adjudication of the case and analyze their significance. Magistrates did not write opinions on their rulings at the time and thus rationales for court decisions are not generally available to the historian.[4] In this case, however, there is a rare document that provides invaluable insight into the imperial state's political and juridical considerations undergirding the final adjudication of the case. The document in question is a *consulta* or report with the recommendations of an ad hoc ministerial junta composed of three jurists appointed in 1798 to deliberate on the "age-old disputes [*pleitos*] and disturbances between the free and slave natives of the pueblo of Santiago del Prado [El Cobre] and the heirs of Juan de Eguiluz ... who call themselves Owners of the copper mines."[5] Using the junta's consulta (recommendation report) as my main source, I examine how the imperial state tackled the challenges raised by this controversial case and how it grounded the opinions that resulted in the Royal Edict of April 7, 1800. The document illustrates the entangled dynamics of law and reasons of state at work in the meting out of justice in the Bourbon imperial regime, especially in a major case like this.

In the second part of the chapter, I address the question of the edict's immediate afterlife. Aftermath-related questions often deal with enforcement politics in the short run; though less so with an edict's long *dureé* afterlife. In most judicial cases the record ends with the judgment (if at all). But, if the archive allows it, the possibility of tracing the verdict's actualization in the social world constitutes an opportunity to breach gaps between law and society in our studies and to better understand

[4] Premo, *The Enlightenment on Trial*, 78, 274n85.

[5] Report of Marqués de Bajamar (Antonio Porlier), Francisco Gutiérrez de Piñeres, and Ramón de Posada y Soto to the king (hereafter junta's report), Madrid, October 31, 1799, AGI-SD 1146.

the political aspects involved in enactments of the law. And more simply, following a ruling's future outside the courts provides a more effective closure to the story – even as it begets new questions. I will address the immediate aftermath of the Freedom Edict of 1800's proclamation first and sketch its longer-term afterlife in a changing historical context in Chapter 9.

THE JUNTA'S OPINION AND REPORT

Once Madrid received the long-awaited documentation from the colony in 1798, it took the ministerial junta another seventeen months to produce its sixty-page consulta or report. Covering a period of more than one hundred and eighty years, the gargantuan dossier contained thousands of documents from the archives in Cuba and Madrid.[6] Ministers acting as jurists did not read a case's dossier directly, especially not a file as thick as this (only historians do). Instead, they relied on summaries of the documents made by an official *relator* (reporter) divided, as if in chapters, into various *cuadernos* (notebooks).[7] The junta's final report represented yet another layer of narrative carved out from the relator's own summaries. The junta members would have discussed the case orally and made their main recommendations, and a scribe would then produce the final document with a shorter narrative that substantiated the ministers' recommendations. That working procedure is manifest in the report itself, which laid out the regalist principles guiding the junta's deliberations in defense of the Bourbon Crown's interests. Although political concerns regarding governance had top priority, they also had to be anchored in some juridical justification, lest the state be open to accusations of arbitrariness and despotism. But there was considerable room for maneuvering within the law in a complex case like this.

In any case, the junta's mandate seems to have been preordained. The three ministers were called upon to examine the file and "propose to His

[6] The junta went back to examine the Crown's contract with the first contractor Don Juan de Eguiluz (ca. 1614).

[7] Summarizing the contents of the dossier was an enormously demanding task especially in a dossier containing thousands of documents as this one did. *Relatores* were letrados. Their task was to organize the documentation and make a short summary of the major points in the documentation for a discussion among magistrates. The role of relatores has not been properly studied, but arguably they had the power to shape (or confuse) the narrative that supported a case as officials relied on their summaries. See the *Recopilación de Leyes de Indias*, Book 2, Title 22.

Majesty the means to ensure the freedom of those vassals and satisfy the Justice of the interested [parties] [*los interesados*]."[8] That is, this selective group of jurists was entrusted with the task of determining the best way to substantiate the cobreros' freedom and the opponents rights within the wide framework of the law, while simultaneously safeguarding the Crown's and the imperial state's interests. Their deliberations were guided by policy considerations explicitly summarized at the end of the junta's document. The top priority for the imperial state at this time (as it had been in the late 1770s) was to insure copper mining production. According to the junta's report: "It is very convenient that the mines of Cuba be worked and this is not going to happen [*no se va a lograr*] under the heirs' dominion [*poder*]. This has been, and should have been, the primary consideration [all along]."[9] The imperial strategic character of the mines was directly stated in the following passage:

> Señor, these mines, close to the sea, and to the port of Guaicabón, close to the [port] of [Santiago de] Cuba, can produce a sweet metal in abundance, and as it was said, with a high grade of silver and gold [*con mucha ley de plata y oro*]. Your Majesty has such a great need for copper that it has it brought from Chile and other more distant parts, even when it is bitter [*agrio*] and of bad quality. [The copper] is transported on the backs [of workers] [*a lomo*] from New Spain and its minerals from Santa Clara and Maravatio, more than 160 leagues inland from the port of Veracruz [Mexico], at great costs and it is then embarked to these kingdoms in compliance with very precise orders of Your Majesty.
>
> Therefore, it is very convenient that the mines of Cuba be worked and that it be recognized that this will not happen with these heirs.[10]

The advice was completely focused on the imperial demand for the metal, which may have been especially urgent at a time of war. Although this fell under the principle of "utility" linked to the defense needs of empire, there was no mention of copper's commercial utility in relation to the needs of the island's sugar industry (see Chapter 1). Thus, the main concern of the Bourbon state's ministers here was to recover possession over the mineral deposits in this locality to insure the extraction of an imperial strategic resource. The state recognized the enormous value of the mines, even though it lacked the means and even the technology, to fully exploit them at the time. (That task would fall three decades later to mostly British companies that would convert El Cobre into a world producer of copper.) For now, the Crown just wanted to recover the

[8] Junta's report, Madrid, October 31, 1799, AGI-SD 1146. [9] Ibid. [10] Ibid.

mines from idle private hands. The junta's top recommendation was "that the heirs of Eguiluz and Salazar be declared without any right to continue the lease [*asiento*] of the copper mines near the Pueblo of Santiago del Prado and that their dominion [*su dominio*] has been and is His Majesty's, as were the lands and their usufruct as well as the slaves."[11] In using of the term "lease" rather than property over the estate the junta was defining the terms of the conflict. Everything should revert to the Crown.

The second point guiding the junta's opinion fell under the principle of security, which the report linked directly to the need to pacify the cobreros through the recognition of their freedom. Threats to internal political stability in the context of geopolitical inter-imperial conflicts were a major policy concern, what today may be termed a national security issue. Once an issue is placed under this rubric, it can trump other considerations of right (then and now). Ironically, this security concern in the context of war was, unwittingly, an acknowledgment of the political effect that the cobreros' acts of marronage and other extrajudicial forms of resistance had on the final decision.

The third point guiding the junta's deliberations was related to the question of how the cobreros' freedom would affect the rights of slave owners who had bought enslaved cobreros from the heirs and stated that "their property rights must be protected," though it never addressed how any indemnification should take place and who would pay for it.[12] The junta also considered whether the heirs had any rights to compensation. Policy considerations related to governance and recovery of a strategic resource touched on issues related to civil law that the junta had to address too.

How were these policy-based recommendations juridically grounded in the junta's report? I turn first to the question of the possession rights over the mining estate that were at the heart of the conflict between Crown and heirs – and only indirectly touched the cobreros. The junta justified the Crown's possession rights over the mining estate and its right to de-privatize and recover them on the basis of three related legal arguments. At the most general level, it invoked the mining law that recognized the Crown's royal right or *regalia* over all the subsoil minerals in the empire (a notion that many Latin American national states retain to this day). Second, the junta asserted the conditional character of the

[11] Ibid. [12] Ibid.

possession of mines and slaves granted to the heirs by the Executory Order of 1779, which had not been met as the mines were not revived. Third, the junta opined that the heirs had never enjoyed property rights to the mines as they had claimed, only leasing rights that had expired in the seventeenth century after they ceased producing copper for the Crown. At a more fundamental level, at stake was a proto liberal conflict between royal prerogatives and the private sector's conditional or absolute property rights particularly over the mining estate's slaves. The conflict was not turned into an eminent domain issue. Rather, it remained a matter of mining law and of misinterpreted confusing contractual terms. But larger lines between regalist and private sector rights were being drawn or asserted through the adjudication terms. These tensions, however, call for a separate story.

Embedded in the charge of failure to activate the mines and dereliction of contract were also insinuations of the heirs' criminal attempt to defraud the Crown and of bribing royal officials to enable the alienation of the mining estate's slaves. These allegations also made in the plaintiffs' memorials may have been behind the covert support that other imperial officials in the colony and the metropolis gave to an investigation of the heirs' actions, especially at a time when the state was desperate for funds to pay for the current imperial wars and no copper was forthcoming.[13] Thus, the Crown reasserted its regalist prerogatives and power against the heirs' overreaching claims to private property rights and over colonial officials who had supported the heirs' rights to alienate and sell the enslaved cobreros, arguably as part of the frenzy in slave trading and official policy backing the expansion of slavery in the colony.

In short, de-privatization of the mining estate to recover royal control of the mines and reactivate production under new private contractors was the main policy consideration guiding the adjudication of the case. The junta went on to recommend the publication of a new lease or asiento for the reactivation of the mines. Yet, in supporting the Crown's recovery of

[13] Royal officials of the Royal Treasury seemed to be part of Cosme's network in Madrid. In the mid-1780s, he received correspondence safely through the widow of a former royal official in Santiago de Cuba. Expediente Crímenes Cosme, Madrid, 1786, AGI-SD 1529. And by the mid '90s he asked cobreros to address their letters and documents for safe conduit to Don Juan Mayoral, the Royal Treasury official of the city of Cordova. Gregorio Cosme, Madrid, October 6, 1795, No.75, f. 195–207. A cobrero reported that Cruzata in Santiago had communication with the Auditor Don Pedro Antonio Esaguirre, but Cruzata denied it. Interrogatories. 1795, Autos Cuba, f. 85–87, 92–92v, AGI-SD 1631.

the mining estate, the junta also invoked mining, contractual, and property law to ground its recommendation. But, if in the junta's opinion, the Crown had never lost its legitimate possession rights over the mining estate's assets (including its slaves), how did its report substantiate the cobreros' freedom?

THE JURIDICAL AND POLITICAL BASES FOR THE COBREROS' COLLECTIVE FREEDOM

The junta's ministers were not so much asked to independently decide on the plaintiffs' freedom, as to properly justify it in juridical and governance or policy terms. I will focus first on the juridical grounds it used to justify the cobreros' freedom and secondly on the governance-related reasons informing its recommendation in favor of that freedom. Significantly, the juridical deliberations on the cobreros' freedom were more cursory than the extensive effort the junta invested in justifying the Crown's possession rights over the mines and the estate. My brief summary above by no means reflects the long cumbersome discussion dedicated by the junta to the topic. My interest, however, lies more on the junta's justification of the cobreros' freedom, and on the possible reasons for the shift in the Council's previous stance on that important matter, or rather the shift in jurisdictional venues in which the case was resolved.

The junta based its juridical support of the plaintiffs' freedom mainly on one of the royal edicts cited in the memorials, the Edict of April 12, 1721, and on the principles that undergirded this edict. This edict played a more central part in some briefs filed in Santiago than in the Madrid or Havana Memorials where it was fuzzily sketched. That royal edict had been issued as a result of an unsuccessful bid made by a contractor interested in the early 1720s. The junta cited the legal principles undergirding that edict as proper legal precedent for the plaintiffs' freedom.

> Among the many and grave grounds [*fundamentos*] spread out through the relator's extraction ... these miserables have opportunely invoked the edict of April 12 of 1721 ... where it was wisely said that it was very difficult to consider [as] slaves those who belonged to the 3rd and 4th generation since to do so it was necessary to establish that all had been born of slave mothers and to find out how long those living as free had been doing so, because the freedom of some may have been prescribed and that of others bought. And not being just that these rights depend on the decision of a contractor [*arrendador*] who was an interested party, it was the will of His Majesty that the governor of [Santiago de] Cuba investigate so that he would hand over to Delgado [the possible contractor of the mines in

1721] only the number of slaves that were necessary [for the work in the mines] finding out first if they were really slaves (underlining in the original).[14]

Asserting that the plaintiffs had noted that none of those said to be slaves by 1781 belonged to anything less than the fifth or even sixth generation, the junta opined that "given the *uncertainty and doubts* noted before, reason and equity dictate that freedom be granted to those who had not obtained it so as not to reduce to slavery those who obtained it fairly [*justamente*] and legitimately by those means" (my italics).[15] This was basically an ample invocation of the juridical rule of presumption of freedom in case of uncertainty applied to the final judgment.

But this was not the restricted interpretation of the uncertainty rule parsed by the fiscal of Santiago de Cuba in 1787 or used in the island's tribunals. The uncertainty principle in the island's jurisprudence seemed to have merely implied the opening up of a judicial hearing or the granting of temporary reprieves to plaintiffs to shore up their cases – but it was not used to decide a case (Chapter 5). Here is another example of the elasticity and interpretative possibilities of some principles of the law, in this case of slave law. This ambiguous jurisprudential rule from the *Siete Partidas*, when liberally interpreted, was a powerful tool that could have strongly impacted many freedom suits.

Moreover, the imperial jurists' opinion echoed the edict's rationale regarding the validity of *coartación* and prescription as juridical tools conducive to freedom. It reinforced the tool of prescription by citing laws from the *Siete Partidas* and other written sources as a basis for freedom: "For more than 100 years all have been in possession of freedom at least in fact [*de hecho*] which is sufficient to induce freedom."[16] This was an assertion of the force of custom and customary practices associated with freedom rather than formal written title. The junta's report also cited even more obscure medieval laws such as the *Ley del fuero* (law of customary privileges) and the *fuero real* (royal privileges) that proclaimed prescription using different statutes of limitation, all under thirty years.[17] Yet these citations seemed like a pro forma legal grounding of freedom. The opinion merely asserted that the plaintiffs had lived in freedom (or in de facto freedom) for more than a century, but there was no further discussion of what kind of actions constituted significant criteria of freedom in this case. This was, wittingly or unwittingly, a lost opportunity to discuss

[14] Junta's report, Madrid, October 31, 1799, AGI-SD 1146. [15] Ibid. [16] Ibid.
[17] Ibid.

the meaning of freedom in positive terms and perhaps to set up precedents and guidelines for prescription cases; or perhaps it was an uncharacteristic Bourbon recognition of the importance of local customary norms that could provide flexibility and discretionary space to lower instance judges in the interpretation of freedom badges. Although the junta's deliberations on the Crown's legal rights to the mines and the heirs' possession claims were extensive, its discussion of prescription and slave law in the cobreros' case was too cursory to engage in significant jurisprudential work on this matter.

In fact, the junta's judicial justification for freedom may have been considered flimsy or inappropriate by the Council's branch of Justice where the case had sat and stalled for years. When asked to issue the edict, the Crown attorney of Justice (Gracia y Justicia)refused to acknowledge the judicial interpretation of the case, regarding it as a matter of governance overseen by the Council of State and Governance [Consejo de Estado y Gobierno]. In doing so, the fiscal disavowed the juridical grounds invoked in the junta's opinion, which were not only cursory but probably too divergent from the interpretation of slave law and property rights given by the Council in 1784 and by royal officials in the colony after the Edict of 1786.[18] The fiscal added that in 1795, impatient with the slowness of the case (in Justicia), which was "of interest policy, justice and humanity," the king declared that it should be treated as a matter of governance. This shift in jurisdiction partly explains the policy shift in the cobreros' case in the 1790s when the

18 Crown attorney's report, Madrid, February 5, 1800, AGI-SD 1672. The fiscal stated that "the resolutions [of the ministerial junta] categorize this matter as pertaining to Governance and it was resolved in governance terms [*gubernativamente*] and therefor the Governance section [*sala de Gobierno*] should issue the edicts for its enforcement. Nonetheless the Council in its three sections has determined that it pass to the Justice section. But there is no sufficient reason [*fundamento*] for this decision because although this matter has been heard there since its beginning, the main royal decisions have been based by their character and progress in the said section [of Governance]." Antonio Porlier had been the fiscal of the Council's Gracia y Justicia division in the 1780s and although semiretired by the late 1790s he was appointed to the ministerial junta. The weak pro forma juridical parsing of the case's freedom issue may have been a way of resisting the royal mandate to ground juridically the predetermined decision to grant freedom to the plaintiffs. Portlier would have been the minister called on to do the juridical work on that matter since he had been responsible for civil cases on slavery and freedom in the Council from the late 1770s to the late 1780s, had seen the case, and had even been responsible for compiling the slave code of 1789. In principle, after justifying the reversal of the estate to the Crown, Porlier could have used the master's power and will to manumit his slaves as the justification for freedom, but perhaps that would have seemed too arbitrary as a justification.

jurisdictional conflict began to take place.[19] Finally, although the legal grounds for the decision to dispossess the heirs of the mining estate was extensively conveyed in the Edict of 1800, those for the cobreros' freedom were suppressed. No one listening to the Freedom Edict's proclamation in the colony in 1801 would have heard any mention of prescription, uncertainty, or even the Edict of 1721. As the first epigraph shows, the pronouncement sounded simply as a royal declaration of the cobreros' emancipation.

Ultimately, this was not any kind of substantial (secret or public) juridical reflection on slavery and freedom as, say, Lord Mansfield's on the Sumerset case of 1773. Except for an incidental pro forma reference from the *Siete Partidas* to the freedom of man as an "invaluable good," there was no philosophical reflection on natural law, on rights of freedom, or nativeness versus property. To be sure, there was an indirect assertion of the non-perpetual character of slavery in the Spanish Empire, of prescription, on the imperative to favor freedom, and on human concerns pertaining to miserable subjects, but the decision was based on the precedent of an amply read royal edict. Although the junta effectively recognized the collective freedom of all the plaintiffs, it did so by categorizing them as descendants of the original slaves of the mines (first epigraph), not as natives of a pueblo, thereby avoiding the question of the relation of native standing to freedom posed in the memorials. For the most part, the consulta referred to the plaintiffs as "persons and descendants of siervos," or as "negros" (slaves), vassals, people (*gente*), although two references were made to "vecinos" (despite the dossier's title as "free *and slave natives of a pueblo*"). The predominant legal persona category running through the junta's opinion was the more ambiguous one of miserables or wretched wards of the Crown, effectively the colonial category applied to slaves but also to Indian natives in the legal arena.

Using the discourse of miserables, the junta condemned "the scandalous abuse that has been made at all times of the condition and labor of these miserables."[20] The miserable victims alluded to were those cobreros formerly considered slaves of the king who had been subject to draft and personal labor. The junta decried that "of the 40 or 50 who were requested for the fortification works of El Morro and were paid by the

[19] Ibid. For the administrative restructuration and the downgrading of the Council of the Indies that took place in the early 1790s and also may have affected the case, see Burkholder, "Council of the Indies," 404–23.

[20] Ibid.

Royal Treasury ... they were distributed [as personal labor] among the governor, royal officials, engineers, vecinos, and employees of some rank in that capital [Santiago de Cuba]."[21] It is unclear who the junta considered the injured party in this imputation of abuse: the miserable cobreros whose labor was exploited or a Crown defrauded of its access to the cobreros' labor by royal officials and other groups who appropriated their labor as personal service. Despite the injunction that the doctrine of miserables placed on the Crown and the royal court to protect the interests of the weak and disempowered from the prepotency and abuse of elites, the junta seemed more concerned with the violation of the Royal Treasury's own interests.

Ultimately, then, the junta's recommendation of the plaintiffs' freedom was not based primarily on juridical reason, as the mentioned conflict with the fiscal seems to confirm. The kind of freedom the cobreros were granted was mainly driven by the imperial state's mining policy and production concerns. As in the heirs' dispossession of the mining estate, reasons of state were entangled with juridical ones in the junta's deliberations. If the heirs' possession rights to the mines and the slaves had been contingent on the working of the mines, the cobreros' freedom was also made conditional to the state's mining policy concerns. In this case, the plaintiffs' freedom was encumbered by labor impositions similar to those burdening Indians in the mainland: "This declaration of freedom should be understood with the qualification [*calidad*] of having to attend in *mita* [draft labor] of 20 of 100, or a fifth [per turn], counting only the vecinos of the said pueblo from 18–50 years of age ... to be paid at the current wage by His Majesty, or by those who exploit the mines."[22] The state's interest in reactivating the mines drove the policy of securing a reserve labor pool near the mines and the imposition of *mita* obligations on the (freed) cobreros.[23] Bourbon reforms in Mexico and Peru had included a tightening of mita service on Indian subjects, so this condition was in line

[21] Ibid.

[22] Junta's report, Madrid, October 31, 1799, AGI-SD 1146. The junta's recommendation specified a fifth of the pueblo's vecinos (as had been the rule in the past with royal slaves) were subject to each *mita* turn. It stipulated that they had to be paid the current wage according to the work or the skill of each in cash, not in credit or in effects. In former times, they had been given one or two daily reales, half of the current wage, to cover their bare subsistence ration. Díaz, *The Virgin, The King*, 242–43.

[23] This condition was based on the Indian based laws in the *Recopilación de Leyes de Indias*, Book 6, Title 3, Law 10: "That Indian pueblos be established near places where there are mines."

with general policy elsewhere in the empire where it was increasingly contested.

Furthermore, aside from possible mita service, the cobreros would be subject to other kinds of public service at the discretion of the governor of Cuba: "They should turn out to everything that is required of public service, and to the defense of the land whenever the governor of Cuba deems it convenient."[24] Thus, not only did the junta ignore the possibility of indemnifying the plaintiffs for labor exploitation in the past, it may have reopened the way for the same kind of violations by royal officials to take place again.

Thus, although the emancipation of more than 1,000 plaintiffs represented a considerable victory for the cobreros, it did not represent a recognition of full or absolute freedom. Theirs became a compromised notion of freedom rooted in deeply conservative assumptions of servitude and colonial subjection, as well as on degrees of freedom that depended on race, ethnicity, gender, and age, but one that could in practice be subject to contestation on the ground as part of the politics of freedom rights. Although the junta never referred to the plaintiffs as "natives of a pueblo," it effectively applied colonial Indian law when imposing mita (draft) labor requirements on the freed plaintiffs. Although the mita service was not fully forced labor, in that payment at current wages was prescribed, the performance of this kind of labor was obligatory. No Spaniards or Whites, nor even free vassals of color, seemed to be subject to such labor requisitions, at least in Santiago.[25] And though labor impositions could also be viewed as the customary obligations expected from freed slaves – to be available to render labor to their ex-master – all these expectations and impositions represented a restricted notion of emancipation. Freed cobreros who had purchased their freedom in the past had enjoyed fuller freedom rights in that they had not been required to do draft labor in the fortification works or forced to do personal service once they became free (Chapter 2). The cobreros "freed" by royal edict in 1800 were now to be subjected to a less dignified and more onerous freedom. Moreover, given that Gregorio Cosme had offered to make an asiento (contract) to work the mines with the cobreros, and therefore to

[24] Junta's report, Madrid, October 31, 1799, AGI-SD 1146. However, tribute impositions were not mentioned.

[25] Sherry Johnson noted that Captain General Las Casas did impose labor requisitions for the maintenance of bridges and roads on White commoners in Havana in the early 1790s, a policy that was strongly resented and resisted. *The Social Transformation*, 130–35.

become co-contractors, producers, and partners in mining production (a farfetched proposition to be sure), the imposition of mita requisitions was a humiliating downgrading of that aspirational status to one of semi-forced laborers. Fortunately, since no mining revival offers came through in subsequent years, mita mining service did not become an inconvenient reality. It is unclear, however, whether governors eventually requisitioned freed cobreros for other kinds of public service and under what payment arrangements.

Aside from mining considerations, state security reasons were also a top governance concern informing the junta's opinion over and above juridical ones: "even *if* [*their freedom*] *was not just and legal*, as it is, it would be *indispensable* to avoid ... the regrettable consequences that could be feared by the continuation and day by day escalation of the subsisting ancient and pernicious fermentation [of the conflict]" (my italics).[26] The junta summarized its assessment of the situation in the following pragmatic terms: "Your Majesty should not overlook [*desentenderse*] the protection of so many *useful vassals,* who, well governed, can multiply themselves much for the benefit of agriculture, the increase of security and defense of the Island, and conversely, *exasperated with a private, unjust and harsh servitude, it is to fear, because of their propensity to run away to the mountains*, that one day they will form a *palenque* [runaway community] or strongholds difficult to penetrate, as in other places, and it may be necessary to annihilate them to reduce them" (my italics).[27] The problem of runaway cobreros became a major security concern that in fact put political pressure on the state to recognize the cobreros' freedom. In this sense, the cobreros' direct actions on the ground and the threat of violence had an impact on the legal outcome. Furthermore, actions that in another context had been censured as acts of bandits, *alzados* (insurgents), and fugitives of the law (the "terrorist" categories of the time) were portrayed in the junta's report instead as the defensive (perhaps even self-preserving) actions of potential useful vassals against an unjust and brutal private slavery.

Moreover, given the international context of war in 1799, during the junta's deliberations, and during the decade of the 1790s, the specter of local violence and disorder pragmatically required the preemptive concession of freedom to the plaintiffs: "It can also have fatal consequences that in times of war this people were not to be happy and calm, [since if]

[26] Junta's report, Madrid, October 31, 1799, AGI-SD 1146. [27] Ibid.

dispersed through the mountains they could, in case of invasion, join the enemy and serve them as guides and spies."[28] Whereas at other moments the specter of violence by runaways and disgruntled subjects could spark strong military, political, and legal measures of repression, the cobreros' conflict led to a cautious, even constructive, state policy.[29] The imperial junta displayed a keen sense of realpolitik at this time, whereas colonial authorities dragged their feet and resisted orders from above to return cobreros to El Cobre, despite the dangers of the broader geopolitical context. The fever for slaves in the colony and the rights of slaveholders trumped the risks or imperial security concerns.[30]

More significantly, the specter of abolition of slavery in neighboring Saint Domingue, buried deep in the papers of the dossier, surfaced in the deliberations of the junta too. The alluring prospect of freedom for the enslaved, hailing from so near, was a matter of political concern for imperial ministers: "And at the very least, once they have lost hope that their clamors will be heeded, they would move as families to the neighboring islands [*sic*] where there is no slavery."[31] Spanish imperial policy called for prudence and preemptive concessions in the face of more radical options appearing in the horizon of at least one island. Despite the avowed monarchist affiliation of many cobreros, and especially of leaders like Gregorio Cosme and Justo Cruzata, the junta implicitly recognized that their political alignments could flip if their aspirations for freedom were not recognized or if proper protections as free vassals of the Spanish Crown were not forthcoming. At the least, discontent could lead to the emigration of useful vassals, and at worst, it could produce disorder or an uprising.

Four years earlier, in 1795, the revolution in Saint Domingue had raised similar admonitions from Don José Antonio Urizar, the regent of the Audiencia of Santo Domingo who was then also heading the military government of Spanish Santo Domingo. Right before the end of the war

[28] Ibid.

[29] I'm thinking of the security recommendations against runaway slaves drawn up in Havana in the 1790s, or of the measures taken a few years later as a result of the Aponte conspiracy of 1812, or in the aftermath of the alleged Escalera conspiracy of 1844. In the United States, legal regimes became more restrictive especially after Nat Turner's rebellion. Childs, *The 1812 Aponte Rebellion*; Reid-Vazquez, *The Year of the Lash*; de Tomlins, *In the Matter of Nat Turner*.

[30] Ada Ferrer suggests a similar attitude on the part of colonials in her discussion of the illegal entry of slaves from revolutionary Saint Domingue in Cuba despite imperial prohibitions. *Freedom's Mirror*, 60–82.

[31] Junta's report, Madrid, October 31, 1799, AGI-SD 1146.

with Saint Domingue and the cession of Spanish Santo Domingo to France, Urizar wrote a policy recommendation report (a consulta) entitled "Treatise about the modification and limits of slavery," which he directed to Minister Eugenio Llaguno in the Council of the Indies, who was also directly overseeing the case of El Cobre at the time. In it he warned Llaguno and the Council that "if the French colony subsists with its system of general liberty, ours [Santo Domingo] cannot remain as it is presently without evident risks."[32] Urizar added that "[our slaves in Santo Domingo], excited with the captivating ideas and friendly reception of our neighbors [in Saint Domingue], will want to go there since there are no barriers that would impede their transit to enjoy the honored title (as they call it) of free and French citizen with active and passive voice equal to that of the whites. This is a consideration in my opinion calling for the greatest attention."[33] Urizar even stated that after the war, if Spain still retained Santo Domingo, it would be difficult to maintain slavery on the Spanish side of the island. He wrote that "Justice and equity inspire us to look for some plan [*declaración*] for the benefit of these wretched ones [*infelices*] to draw them out from the dejection and sadness that they suffer [as slaves]."[34] The situation called for new policy and legal thinking.

As a countermeasure, Urizar made a proposal for gradual emancipation that, he suggested, could be narrowly applied for now to the slaves of Spanish Santo Domingo "where the necessity is more urgent" and, according to him, could be extended to the Caribbean islands and even more generally to all Spanish America if the Council saw fit.[35] His emancipation plan was severe, however, making sure slaveholders' interests were not unduly affected. It required twenty-five years of full "service" starting at age fifteen (therefore, forty years of slavery). After that period of servitude, "well behaved" slaves, whose twenty-five years of coerced labor would have covered slaveholders' investment in them and provided an ample surplus, could be emancipated without further compensation to masters by the state. Their labor basically would have purchased their freedom, a reasoning that Bishop Osés also made to argue away the difficulties that compensation to slaveholders for the dispossession of emancipated cobreros potentially represented.[36]

[32] José Antonio de Urizar, "Discurso sobre modificación y límites de la esclavitud" (hereafter Discurso de Urizar), Santo Domingo, June 25, 1795, AGI-SD 1032.

[33] Discurso de Urizar, Santo Domingo, June 25, 1795, AGI-SD 1032. [34] Ibid.

[35] Ibid.

[36] Through a series of calculations, Bishop Osés y Alzúa claimed that in almost two decades of enslavement, the to-be-freed cobreros had paid off their cost and even yielded a surplus

More significantly for our purposes was Urizar's post-emancipation proposal. Following the model of Indian law, emancipated African descendant slaves could thereafter be settled as pueblos under Crown jurisdiction. He explicitly stated that the best guidelines and rules for this work could be found "in our legislation and in the many royal edicts and orders that His Majesty has issued for Indians."[37] Urizar explained that, like Indian pueblos, the new pueblos of Afro descendant freedmen and women would have a fund for communal expenses, a Protector de Indios, and a resident parish priest, but he left the issue of local self-government with a cabildo implicit. Members, he suggested, would have the standing of miserables and pay an annual tribute to the Crown like Indians, Blacks, and Mulattoes already did elsewhere in the empire.

Urizar framed his emancipation scheme in imperial language suggesting security and public benefits that would be attractive to the state and slaveholders. According to him, the hope for eventual freedom and settlement as a pueblo would "inflame their spirit, and would stimulate them in good undertakings, deviate them from revolutions and thinking about suicide and would turn their attention to their duties."[38] The emancipation and settlement proposal was a far-fetched possibility in its broader contours at the time, yet not far from what became the junta's recommendation in 1799 for the case of El Cobre.

Urizar's proposal was not far from a subtext that, as I argued in Chapter 4, ran through the memorials on behalf of the natives of El Cobre's standing. But El Cobre's proposal was earlier: whereas the plaintiffs of El Cobre's freedom memorials insinuated Indian ancestry and the bridging of plural legal regimes in 1783, 1784, and again in 1793, Urizar's proposal based on analogy and the bridging of plural law circulated in high imperial circles in 1795. The revolution of Saint Domingue, as reflected in Urizar's proposal, pushed Spain to look for some alternatives within its own plural legal tradition to counter the more radical schemes of emancipation that were produced at the time in Saint Domingue (albeit eventually more restricted in practice).

Moreover, to the proposal of colonizing with emancipated slaves invoking the legal regime of Indian republics, Urizar added another

to the slaveholders who had purchased them, therefore the latter need not be compensated. In this formulation, the cobreros not only had purchased their freedom with their labor; they had also already compensated and yielded profit to slaveholders for the investment in them. Bishop Joaquín Osés y Alzúa, Santiago de Cuba, 1795, AGI-SD 2229.

[37] Discurso de Urizar, June 25, 1795, AGI-SD 1032. [38] Ibid.

consideration that went against the grain of colonial thinking, especially in Havana. Rather than importing (White) Spanish and European Catholic colonists as had long been the ideal policy, and continued to be so in the nineteenth century, Urizar suggested populating the still sparsely populated island of Hispaniola (and implicitly elsewhere) with pueblos of freed Afro descendant people.[39] According to him, Europeans could not resist the rigors of the climate in that region; but freed people were more suited to work under harsh environmental conditions. Although this had been – and would continue to be in the next century – an environmentally based ideology to justify the necessity of slavery, Urizar turned it on its head to argue for the utility of colonizing the land and developing pueblos with emancipated small agricultural producers presumably controlling their own corporate pueblos.

Thus, in Urizar's imperial formulation and proposal for new policy – and laws – local republics could be turned into an option for Afro descendants in a distant future without much cost to the slaveholding private sector and with much public utility. The plan was never realized (except partially perhaps in the case of El Cobre). Other forces in the nineteenth century, including liberal ones, closed off the possibility of this Indian-based corporate model. Indeed, the communal corporate model more generally came under increasing contestation for established native Indian communities like El Caney and Jiguaní in Cuba and elsewhere in the Spanish Empire during the nineteenth century (see Chapter 9). At the end of the eighteenth century, however, this still seemed a possible option that could take on expanded meanings of municipal belonging and limited local level autonomy.

RECOGNITION AS A PUEBLO? WHAT KIND OF PUEBLO?

The junta recommended the formalization of the pueblo and a land grant, as the plaintiffs had requested. Again, policy considerations, especially those regarding mining, guided the recommendation: "Although in the dossier there is reason for the apprehension that the growth of this pueblo may have once produced, for now, all those declared free should settle in it within a period of three months until the governor informs if some inconvenience could follow [from this order] or if it would be convenient

[39] For some whitening plans through immigration, see Sartorious, *Ever Faithful*, 43–46; Chira, *Patchwork Freedoms*, 191–92.

to form another pueblo, also subject to the *mita*, near the mines."[40] Years later, the Council's fiscal reiterated that "the declaration of freedom [in 1800] in their favor was made *under the condition* that they would work in them by *mita* divided into five parts" (my italics).[41] There was no reference to long-established attachments to place and municipal community or to the rights that nativeness allegedly conferred. Return to the pueblo, from the imperial perspective, was now mandated for mining policy considerations, a condition that potentially could dissuade many cobreros from returning.

Aside from collective freedom and formal recognition of pueblo – or villa – standing, the cobreros' legal action had called for recognition of their corporate possession of land. The junta recommended a corporate land grant to the pueblo and to cobrero families from available *realenga* (public) land or from private land and ordered that a land survey be made to establish legal boundaries and possession rights of the pueblo.[42] Yet the land grant came with stipulations. In line with the colonial Indian standing effectively given to the plaintiffs, the corporate land grant insured communal ownership and usufruct rights to the community's land. The governor was to order a land survey and allocate the land that should be set aside for "buildings, pastures, and [communal] needs" and that which would be divided into "plots of land and assigned to each *vecino* for his family that could not be sold, divided, or alienated."[43] This arrangement was comparable to the corporate land regime of the old Indian republics in the empire, including El Caney and Jiguaní in Cuba. In old regime Spain, pueblos and villas enjoyed more hybrid land tenure regimes – and so did the Spanish colonial towns with not only private ownership and alienation rights but also with the sharing of forest and assets (or *propios*). The cobreros had customarily enjoyed usufruct rights to an ever-shrinking part of the royal mining jurisdiction's territory for which they claimed possession now not as royal slaves but as natives of a pueblo. A corporate communal land arrangement of the sort granted by the Edict of 1800 would ensure them land, but that kind of arrangement was also beginning to be challenged by liberal-inspired notions of individual private property for commercial agriculture.[44]

[40] Junta's report, Madrid, October 31, 1799, AGI-SD 1146.

[41] Council of the Indies, response to Representation of Justo Cruzata, Madrid, June 6, 1815, AGI-SD 330.

[42] Junta's report, Madrid, October 31, 1799, AGI-SD 1146. [43] Ibid.

[44] In 1800, for instance, a royal edict broke up the hereditary possession of land held as *señoríos* and permitted their ownership and alienation. The Edicts of 1815 and 1816 gave

Although the main policy concern motivating the recognition of the pueblo and its formalization through a land grant was the securing of a labor force for the mines, the junta mentioned other complementary, if secondary, reasons for the preservation of the pueblo. For instance, El Cobre's strategic military location: "Because it is located in the southern coast and the Port of Guaycabón, it is like a frontier to the Island of Jamaica and the western part of Santo Domingo."[45] Although this passage made an old allusion to the strategic utility of this pueblo for imperial defense purposes, references to this point in the junta's opinion were no longer central. To the imperial state, the cobreros' militia service did not seem to play such a prominent role anymore. Its more immediate concern was the reduction of the runaway cobreros and their transformation into useful future workers in the mines and agriculture. Gregorio Cosme, however, had placed great significance in his petitions on his military credentials and continued presenting himself in Madrid as an officer of the pardo militias of Santiago and of the former militias of El Cobre to the end.

Another productive concern, if only secondary to mining ones, was tobacco production, a small-farmer agricultural activity in which many cobreros had once engaged. Given its monopoly on tobacco production and the quality of the island's crop, this productive activity also represented an important form of utility to the Crown. The junta's report acknowledged the significance of its population and the pueblo's agricultural development (or at least its potential) when it noted its "fertile tobacco farms [*vegas*] and immediate lands, the quality of its inhabitants [*moradores*] closeness to the capital of Santiago de Cuba."[46] Closeness to Santiago was an ambiguous reference to either markets in the city for the cobreros' produce or for the city's access to labor from the cobreros. As argued in Chapter 3, the small farmer model endorsed by the junta in the above passage represented an alternative model to the advancing slave-based plantation regime gaining ground on the island. Could a flourishing community be possible in the future with the returning cobreros? Could free people of color form their own communal,

landowners the right to parcel, use, and alienate their land without legal intervention. See Knight, *Slave Society in Cuba*, 17. In Santiago, French refugees had been buying up land in the jurisdiction of El Cobre, as well as in El Caney, after 1802. For the French refugee Prudencio Casamayor's purchase of land in the jurisdiction of El Cobre in 1802 and its resale to French compatriots, see Ferrer, *Freedom's Mirror*, 180–81; Chira, *Patchwork Freedoms*, 80–84.

[45] Junta's report, Madrid, October 31, 1799, AGI-SD 1146. [46] Ibid.

autonomous and prosperous town despite the plans of the imperial state for them?

THE EDICT'S IMMEDIATE AFTERMATH

As can be expected, the Freedom Edict of 1800 created political resistance among colonial slaveholders and their supporters, thereby opening up another round of conflict on the ground and in the courts. Affected interests were considerable in terms of the number of people impacted and the fortunes involved. The reconstitution of the cobreros' community, even in its compromised terms, constituted a logistical and political challenge too. Hundreds of enslaved cobreros and their children had been sold over the years. Governor Sebastián Kindelán, who supported the rights of slaveholders and heirs, pointed out "the fermentation of litigation [*pleitos*] that will take place is undeniable, with grave damage [*perjuicio*] to the common [good] and the destruction of families of [Santiago de] Cuba."[47] Kindelán was concerned about the compensation demands that slaveholders who had purchased cobreros would file in court: "The resolution of the chain of legal recourses [*encademaniento de recursos*] that will unfold until the principal source where the contract was born is identified will create great difficulties for the government and therefore trials will be interminable."[48] A first rehearsal of what this process could entail had occurred during the hearings related to the Edict of 1786 examined in Chapter 5.

But if compensation claims could involve long and complicated chains of buyers and sellers across the island and beyond, tracking down enslaved cobreros to emancipate them could be a daunting operation for the cobreros too. The story of the cobrera Damiana Ortiz, who was taken to Madrid by her masters in the mid-1780s, is a case in point (see Chapter 5). Five years after Ortiz's alleged owners, the Santiago merchant and councilman Francisco Creagh and his wife, won the freedom suit that Gregorio Cosme filed against them in 1787, the couple moved to Puerto Rico in 1792, taking the captive cobrera in tow.[49] Isolated in Puerto Rico,

47 Governor Kindelán to Somersuelos, Santiago de Cuba, August 15, 1800, No. 6, AGI-SD 330.

48 Ibid.

49 The case of Damiana Ortiz Villavicencio in Madrid is briefly covered in Chapter 5. Her embarkment visa to Veracruz as a servant of the Creagh couple is in Expediente de licencia de pasajeros a Indias, Juan Francisco Creagh, July 2, 1792, No. 189, AGI-Arribadas 516.

would Damiana Ortiz ever hear about the Edict of 1800 that set her free? Or would her family be able to trace her and claim her back? And who would pay for her repatriation? Furthermore, what about cobrero children sold in Havana when they were three-, five-, or eight years old? Did they even remember where they came from? Would their families be able to trace them and claim them? How would their identities be established? This case, and others like it, hinted at incipient labyrinthic suits as well as to those enslaved cobreros who may have never felt the emancipation edict's reach. But it also hints at fascinating histories of post-emancipation efforts by individual cobreros at family reunification and the revival of bonds of nativeness.

By 1802, the liberation of enslaved cobreros had stalled or faced obstacles in the colony. The cobreros sent a petition to the Council saying that those who had been handed over in 1780 and the generation whose parents were still alive had been freed, but that "they had no hope left that the rest would [*los demás*] [be freed] or that the land distribution would take place."[50] The comment suggests that those whose parents had passed were having trouble being claimed and that the children of enslaved cobreros, whose names were not in the official lists, were also having problems reclaiming freedom. Another question suggested by the complaint was over the reach of the freedom edict: just who were the cobreros to be emancipated? The Council responded that the "declaration of freedom included all the natives [*oriundos*] of the pueblo, even those who had been sold before 1781."[51] This clarification was in some ways a victory. It linked freedom to local nativeness, and it meant that birth in El Cobre, a municipal-based criterion, produced freedom retroactively. It also meant that freedom applied to those who had been forcefully separated from the village and also to *ausentes* (absent), deserters, and runaways prior to 1781, who had settled elsewhere in the island. But were they now obliged to return to El Cobre or could they remain in the localities where they had been residing for years, now as free vecinos? Was the right of mobility a freedom right to be respected? Or what would their new identification as vecinos entail in other localities?

As Governor Kindelán suggested, the edict potentially triggered a cascade of claims and suits among buyers and heirs regarding compensation. But the cobreros had claims of their own too. The heir Tomás

[50] Council of the Indies, response to Representation of Justo Cruzata, Madrid, June 6, 1815, AGI-SD 330.

[51] Ibid.

Garzón suggested as much when he complained that "also producing feuds are the issues that they [the cobreros] bring up regarding the price of the freedoms [*libertades*] that had been acquired [through coartación] ... although the edict does not say anything about this."[52] Some of these issues had popped up before. Among them were the claims of cobreros who, due to their liberal interpretation of the Edict of 1786, had sued at the time for reimbursement of their coartación price (Chapter 5), now broadened to those who had purchased it in the 1790s, before the collective emancipation of 1800. This issue seems to have created serious divisions inside the cobreros' pueblo. In 1805, the parish priest, Father Paz y Ascanio, reported to the governor of Cuba and to the captain general that discord between two factions in the pueblo had produced a *motín* (riot) in which he had to intervene. Governor Kindelán had ordered the cobreros to appoint an apoderado in Santiago to conduct affairs related to the Royal Edict of 1800, but there was disagreement as to who should be appointed. By now distrusting their parish priest as too lame, some cobreros had been consulting with a Don Manuel González y Pereira in Santiago who, according to Father Paz y Ascanio, was trying to "embroil and retain [*enredar y retener*] the sovereign orders dealing with the amount of the freedoms [*importe de las libertades*] (a point that the royal edict does not touch) and many other things he was making them see."[53] González y Pereira may well have been one of the cobreros' old covert allies in the city. Paz y Ascanio thought this man was deceiving them about how far they could press claims so that he would be chosen to represent them. Wondering why he was no longer trusted, Paz y Ascanio asked "if in the times of their slavery they had not come to me and consulted me and I received them and consoled them with my words, why did they not come to me now?"[54] Paz y Ascanio, who aspired to the lucrative chaplaincy of the Sanctuary to the Virgin in the pueblo, did not want to rock the boat or perhaps he had other agendas.[55] Conflicts

[52] Petition of Tomás Garzón, Santiago de Cuba, ca. 1802, AGI-SD 330.

[53] Father Alejandro Paz y Ascanio to Somersuelos, El Cobre, July 14, 1805, AGI-Cuba 1549.

[54] Ibid.

[55] Father Paz y Ascanio eventually obtained the desired chaplaincy of the El Cobre's Marian Sanctuary and even edited and published an early history of it in 1829. By the time he died in 1836, the once lowly Canarian priest had prospered leaving an estate worth almost 14,600 pesos that consisted of a small hacienda in El Cobre and a house in Santiago. Whereas the diversified agricultural hacienda worked by five male slaves was assessed at 9,664 pesos, his residential house with marble floors in Santiago was valued at 4,907 pesos. After more than four decades of ministry in El Cobre, Paz initially

regarding the interpretation of vague points or silences in the Freedom Edict of 1800 had penetrated deep into the pueblo. These became now disputes about the standing and rights of free – or freed – people deriving from the freedom edict.

Yet one wonders how far González y Pereira and some cobreros were willing to force the compensation issue or how far it could be taken in the jurisprudence of the time. For instance, what about the hundreds of injured plaintiffs who had unjustly endured private captivity after 1781 for so many years especially since the junta's opinion had recognized their freedom by virtue of the Edict of 1721 and by prescription long before 1781? And, if the cobreros had long been free as the junta recognized, were they not entitled to compensation? Who would pay them for the wages (*jornales*) and land rents many of them had paid their alleged masters, for their lost labor and income, and for the property the heirs took from them in the raids? Were their rights as free persons to be protected too? Here were the seeds of another jurisprudential legal and political battle. Perhaps this was a reason why the edict did not make public its rationale for adjudicating freedom.

To be sure, the *Recopilación de Leyes de Indias* (1608), the early seventeenth-century body of laws governing affairs of the colonial New World, explicitly stated that Indigenous populations were not subject to enslavement, but it also explicitly refused them compensation for wrongful enslavement when freed.[56] Since Indian colonial law was applied to the cobreros' case, this may have been an assumption in their situation too. And yet, there were other truly radical possibilities in the Spanish tool kit from medieval canon and civil law that could have been mobilized. For instance, the seventeenth-century Capuchin abolitionists Francisco José de Jaca and Epifanio de Moirans mentioned in Chapter 3, explicitly raised the question of indemnification, especially in the case of African slaves, in their antislavery sermons and treatises produced in Havana in the early 1680s (for which they were detained and deported).

Using scholastic argumentation and medieval contract (tort) law, Moirans asked: "Are masters obliged to manumit them [African slaves],

bequeathed the hacienda to the Sanctuary of El Cobre, but before dying changed his will and bequeathed the property to his nephew (or illegitimate son as often was the case). He bequeathed the house to the Cathedral of Santiago for the erection of an altar to the Assumption of Our Lady but with the caveat that if that wish was not possible, the house would pass to his nephew too. Testimonio Expediente Legado Presbítero Paz y Ascanio, Santiago, 1848, No. 472, AHN-Ultramar 702.

[56] Recopilación Leyes de Indias, "Of the Freedom of Indians," Book 6, Title 2, Law 15.

restitute them for their labor, and pay them indemnification? Because of having unjustly possessed them, their labor is also unjustly possessed, and consequently in restituting their freedom to them it is necessary to restitute them and pay them the price of their labor."[57] The rule was based on a moral principle of justice that said: "No one should enrich himself through injury or damage done to another."[58] This rule was invoked almost verbatim as a principle of law (*principio de derecho*) with a different application in a 1791 brief on behalf of the cobreros drawn up in Santiago, probably in the bishopric where the local apoderados of El Cobre found legal support for their actions. A passage in that petition asserted that "No one should become rich with detriment to another. How could the Prince (the king) issue an order [the Executive Order of 1779] in which doing good to the heirs harmed us and their enrichment be based on our detriment?"[59] There must have been awareness of this legal and moral principle at least among letrados as well as jurists also familiar with canon law, at least in the bishopric, as this citation shows. Could it have also been applied to the compensation issue as the Capuchin friars had argued more than a century before?

In an even more radical formulation based on St. Thomas Aquinas, the Capuchin friars extended the issue to inheritance rights. The friar Moirans wrote that "the descendants of negros ... whom the Spaniards call criollos should receive the price of their labors [*trabajos*] and be freed and all the consequent damages should be repaid; and not only this, but since they are heirs and successors of their deceased parents and of their labors and fruits they should be compensated for their damages, according to the opinion of the prudent [magistrates]. Because all of that belongs by right to the negros that descend from the former."[60] Moirans added that "according to the doctrine of St. Thomas who says 'when it is not possible to restitute what has been taken away giving back the same thing, the restitution should take place in any way possible, for example, in money or in some kind of honor, taking into consideration the condition of both, according to a prudent man.'"[61] This kind of argument was suppressed in the cobreros' case as well as in most future discussions of emancipation in the Spanish Atlantic world since new liberal arguments

57 Epifanio Moirens, 268, in López García, *Dos defensores*. See also 277.

58 Rule 48 *iuris in* VI, Moirans, 268, in López García, *Dos defensores*. This principle is also cited as a "rule" in the *Siete Partidas*, Book 6, Title 33, Law 13.

59 Petition of Gervasio de Castro, Justo Cruzata, et al., Santiago de Cuba, August 25, 1791, No. 40/32, AGI-SD 1628.

60 Moirans, 286, in López García, *Dos defensores*.

61 Ibid., 286.

were strongly rooted in property rights of slaveowners but did not tackle the principle of property as applied to the formerly enslaved individual, her body and labor.[62] The compensation issue to the formerly enslaved is at the heart of the discussions on reparations to this day in the United States, the Caribbean, Colombia, Ecuador, and Brazil, although not yet in other Spanish Latin American countries (including Cuba).[63]

The issue of non-compensation leads to other questions. Were the plaintiffs also burdened with the final costs of years of litigation in Madrid, the loans Cosme took and fees for his services, and those of the apoderado José Espinoza de los Monteros and Sergeant José Valentín Sánchez in Havana? These were ominous questions lurking over the outcome of the case. The junta did not make recommendations regarding who would bear the costs of the litigation (perhaps that was not part of its purview). Cosme expected in 1795 that the opponents would be burdened with the costs due to their culpability in triggering the conflict (Chapter 6).[64] I have been unable to find the decision on what party would carry the costs of the legal action nor the *tasación* (appraisal) of the legal services. Unfortunately, this missing piece of information prevents a more probing analysis of the impact of legal mobilization on the community. Resources among the free in El Cobre or the even more meager ones of emancipated cobreros returning to the village would have been depleted by these fees. This hemorrhage of funds and material

[62] Quakers raised the issue of compensation as did some abolitionists. Sinha, *The Slave's Cause*, 66, 107.

[63] For the largest reparation amount ever won by a former enslaved individual in a US court (in 1878), see McDaniel, *Sweet Taste of Liberty*. Calls and movements for reparations have been taking force since the late twentieth century. In the United States, the denunciation of a massive slave sale by the Catholic Jesuit Order in 1838 to fund Georgetown University led to reparation talks that resulted in one of the largest funds to benefit descendants of former enslaved persons. The reported rationale for the reparations is formulated in religious terms as "atonement for sin" and "betrayal of human dignity," terms different from those advanced by the seventeenth-century Capuchin friars Jaca and Moirans. For *New York Times* reportage of the case, see Rachel Swarns "Catholic Order Pledges $100 Million to Atone for Slave Labor and Sales" (March 15, 2021). For other models of tort law compensation, moral atonement, and restorative justice, see Brooks, *Atonement and Forgiveness*; Beckles, *Britain's Black Debt*; Araujo, *Reparations for Slavery*; Coates, "The Case for Reparations." For an organization working on reparations and literature on the topic, see N'COBRA.org. Movements have also appeared in some Latin American countries and reparation provisions made in their constitutions based on global discourses on human rights. For Colombia and Ecuador, see the wonderful anthology compiled by Mosquera Rosero-Labbé and Barcelos, *Afro-reparaciones*.

[64] Gregorio Cosme, Madrid, n.d. [ca. 1795], No. 6, f. 102–7, AGI-SD 1631.

resources would have affected their ability to reconstruct their pueblo and consolidate their land grant as suggested in Chapter 9.

Although by 1800 Cosme seems to have been honored and rewarded with the title of "don" and that of "Captain of the Volunteer Militias of Pardos of the Villa of Santiago del Prado," he may have never returned to his village, nor perhaps to the island. Burdened with illnesses and debts, as he mentioned in 1795 (Chapter 6), he may well have died in Madrid with at least the satisfaction of having accomplished his mission of helping liberate his local compatriots from the tyranny of slavery (hopefully he did not die in prison for non-payment of litigation debts).[65] The last time I found him in the archival record, a strong-willed Cosme was revoking the power of his attorneys and petitioning to be one of the three recipients of official copies of the forthcoming freedom edict in order to be its bearer to the community.[66] Perhaps he was fighting rivals in the court to assert his status as the cobreros' legitimate representative as he had done before. His race, slave origin, and colonial status had made him an atypical apoderado in the imperial court. Thereafter, his name disappeared from the archive. Justo Cruzata's in El Cobre survived, however. In 1815, right after the Napoleonic crisis of 1808–14 was over, and Fernando VII was restored to the Spanish throne, Cruzata was still writing petitions to the Council regarding nonenforcement of the Edict of 1800's land provision.

Although the collective emancipation of more than 1,000 subjects was undoubtedly a major victory for the cobreros, it was not an unencumbered one. The freedom came saddled with a rotational forced (mita) labor burden that although not enforced due to lack of mining contractors, may have been expected in other kinds of public works at the discretion of the governor. Furthermore, compensation for almost twenty years of wrongful private enslavement, loss of their own labor, and other injuries was not even considered. Ultimately, the liberated cobreros could be said to have paid for their emancipation with their own forced labor

[65] In a petition of 1798, and again in 1800, Cosme was presented as "Don Gregorio Cosme Osorio," "native and vecino of the Island of Santiago de Cuba," "General Apoderado of the Villa of Santiago del Prado Real Minas de Cobre," and "Captain of the Militias of Volunteer Pardos of it." Madrid, October 29, 1798, AGI-SD 330 and Madrid, ca. March 8, 1800, f. 585–86. AGI-SD 1627. Even before, in 1794, a creditor referred to Cosme as "Don Gregorio Cosme" and as "Captain of the Regiment of Pardos" of the Plaza of Santiago de Cuba. Petition Antonio Saez, Madrid, October 22, 1794, Archivo de Simancas SGU. Leg. 6852, 87.

[66] Petition of Don Gregorio Cosme Osorio, Madrid, ca. March 8, 1800, f. 585–86, AGI-SD 1627.

during almost two decades of private enslavement. If they were also encumbered with litigation debts, the costs of their judicial freedom may have soared.

The cobreros were eventually able to return to their pueblo and their standing as a pueblo or villa was officially recognized with a corporate land grant. Furthermore, the natives of El Cobre won the litigation battle at the highest level of empire. The symbolic power of such a signal judicial victory must have generated an enormous sense of vindication and empowerment among the cobreros. That victory also meant an inversion of the usual colonial order of things through the humiliating judicial defeat of the powerful heirs, other slaveholders, and colonial authorities made public through the proclamation of the Freedom Edict of April 7, 1800, on March 16, 1801, in the Plaza de Armas of Santiago de Cuba. Whether the exhilaration of victory, the public kudos, or the joy of reunification with family, neighbors, and compatriots could have compensated for the accumulated material costs of the protracted legal action and other injuries through the years, it is difficult to say. Litigation battles involve intangible factors, passions, and satisfactions that cannot always be quantified. They also can open possibilities for further contestation of unsatisfied claimed rights as seems to have been the case.

In any event, individual and collective civil freedom constituted the cobreros' main and most immediate victory. That freedom was achieved through the common efforts, resources, and mobilization of a whole community that envisioned itself as a pueblo and made claims as natives of one. In doing so, they invested that local identitarian category with social, political, and legal significance that would continue to take on new meaning in different historical contexts.

9

The Nineteenth-Century Afterlife of the Freedom Edict of 1800

Where to end a story or a book often constitutes a dilemma for the historian. Historical accounts should not end with proclamations. Wars end, emancipations take place, pronouncements are made, cases are adjudicated: but what actually happens in their aftermath? The actualization of the Edict of April 7, 1800, became the focus of the cobreros' politics for the next four decades. This chapter works as a postscript to the main story at the center of this book. Although the crisis of empire and the liberal Cádiz Constitution of 1812 mark the beginning of a different period in the Spanish Atlantic world, it is not until the 1830s that the cobreros' story takes a major turn into a different kind of future world. I briefly examine the Freedom Edict's afterlife in the new global and local historical context that emerged with the Cádiz Constitution of 1812.

Although state records are available for the changes that took place in the long aftermath of the Edict of 1800, I lose sight of local voices and actions, especially those of cobreros, as my local archival documentation begins to taper off after the first decade of the nineteenth century. Digging out those voices from the archive would require another round of research in other archives, a search for new legal actions, and another book. But this sketch opens new questions and broadens the comparative frame. Developments in eastern Cuba had points in common with issues and discussions unfolding in other regions of the Spanish Atlantic then and even beyond the anti-colonial wars which did not irrupt Cuba. The arrival of new players to the region – French refugees and later British mining companies – globalized El Cobre and the region in the nineteenth century in ways that have remained unexamined, isolating the island from other Latin American historiographies. El Cobre was at the center of many of the social, economic, and cultural transformations taking place at the time. The Indian pueblos of El Caney and Jiguaní also fell into the vortex of change that threatened their corporate formation and the meaning of Indian nativeness. Finally, in a leap into their far future (into our own present), we glimpse the emergence recently of scenarios for Afro descendants and Indian communities elsewhere in Latin America that were adumbrated in the cobreros' legal action and the Edict of 1800. The past reemerges in the future in new guises and places.

FREEDOM AND RETURN TO EL COBRE?

I turn first to questions about the cobreros' formal reconstitution as a pueblo or villa – to the promise of land and to the kind of freedom and corporate rights that they were able to secure as natives of El Cobre for the future. As this book has shown, after the 1780 privatization of El Cobre, different notions of place came into conflict with each other: the Crown's project of mining revival in this former mining site, the heirs' view of the place as a private estate and a repository of human commodities for sale and land for lease, and the cobreros' vision of pueblo as a human community constituted by bonds of solidarity and duty to each other and based on common land and territory. Enslavement had constituted a violation not only of personal freedom but a rupture as well of the "natural" bonds and rights that held them together as natives of a pueblo, leading to the removal, sale, and dispersion of enslaved cobreros throughout the island and beyond. Chapter 8 suggested some of the challenges at hand in the tracing down, reclamation, and emancipation of dispersed cobreros and in the reunification of families and community. Did cobreros return to El Cobre after their emancipation was proclaimed in 1801? Did they recover any rights to land and did a reconstruction of the pueblo take place as expected or at least as mandated by the Edict of 1800? What challenges (old and new) did the emancipated cobreros face especially as they entered a new historical period where the rising voices of liberalism and of new stakeholders came into play? Did the flourishing villa conjured in the memorials come about with collective freedom?

In 1803, Bishop Joaquin Osés y Alzúa, in his role as informal protector of the cobreros, informed the Council of the Indies that after 1802 "a regular settlement [*población*] has been taking shape [and] a number of tiled houses have been built where none existed before since they were all thatched roof ones."[1] But the bishop did not mention who owned the new tiled houses that suggested some affluence nor if emancipated cobreros were settling back in the village. He noted other infrastructural improvements related to the pueblo's reconstitution as well. The new parish church that had been finished in 1798 had already been expanded. A road (for carts) from Santiago to the village and to the center of the island had been opened, and villagers had constructed a bridge and roadway (*calzada*) across a mire (*atolladero*) thereby reinserting the pueblo into the communication and commercial arteries of the region.[2] These were the kind of communal projects required in a municipality that were usually paid for by communal assets (*propios*) such as rented land, local taxes, or labor obligations from vecinos. By 1803, the bishop, not the king, had established a parochial grammar school in the village, the school some cobreros had asked Cosme to get royal funding for in 1784 ("the teacher [*el maestro*] Gervasio wants you [Cosme] to try to get the school from His Majesty").[3]

A count of the parish population in 1810 suggests that the population had grown back to some 1,529 inhabitants and that it had surpassed the population of 1,482 inhabitants in 1778 by 47 people (see Table 1.1).[4] A handful of White vecinos were now living in El Cobre: 49 (3 percent) of the village's population consisted of White men, women and children, up from 19 persons in 1778. Another 69 (or 4.5 percent) in 1810 were enslaved persons privately held by various vecinos.[5] The overwhelming majority of the population, however, 1,411 or 92 percent of the pueblo, still consisted of free people of color – and almost all were labeled racially mixed pardos (1,342 or 95.1 percent) with only 69 or 4.9 percent categorized as Blacks.[6] Although some of the population may have been due

[1] Report of Bishop Joaquín Osés y Alzúa to José Antonio Cavallero, October 31, 1803, AGI-SD 2230.

[2] Ibid. [3] Salvador Quiala to Cosme, El Cobre, August 19, 1784, f. 48, AGI-SD 1627.

[4] Moradores of the parish of Real Minas del Cobre, 1810, AGI-Cuba 1689; General Census of Cuba, 1778, AGI-Indiferente 1527. The population count of El Cobre in 1780 was lower at 1,406, suggesting a larger population increase of 123 souls. Census of Santiago, 1780, AGI-Cuba 1272.

[5] In the eighteenth century, there had been some private slaves in the village that a few royal slaves and other free cobreros had owned, but there was no mention of them in the memorials. Díaz, *The Virgin, the King*, 179–83. Private slaves were not distinguished from royal slaves in the regional or general censuses, but they were in the local household censuses. The 1739 local family census, for instance, registered 55 private slaves: 17 belonging to three clergymen and 38 to cobreros. Family Census of 1739, AGI-SD 385.

[6] In 1778, the proportion of people of color in El Cobre had been a bit higher: 98.7 percent, of whom 35.4 percent were free and 64.5 percent were enslaved. The racial breakdown of

to new settlers, the large number of free people of color suggests that many cobreros did return to El Cobre, some perhaps with children, spouses, lovers, and friends in tow. The promise of land; the reunification with remembered family, neighbors, and compatriots; and the reconstruction of native bonds may have drawn cobreros back, if not perhaps the condition of having to perform draft labor as free – or freed – cobreros.

Flagging the importance of instituting local self-governance, and not just material infrastructural improvements, the bishop noted in 1803 that the pueblo still needed council members and bailiffs (*regidores y alcaldes ordinarios*), that is, a duly constituted local government that would define them as a proper municipal body with self-rule.[7] By 1805, there was at least an alcalde, although the priest may have held undue (but not uncontested) power, as the incident of the internal *motín* mentioned in Chapter 8 suggests. In 1814, Justo Cruzata was one of two of the village's alcaldes, and he was again acting as apoderado for the village. An early 1814 regional census reported that El Cobre had an operating *ayuntamiento* (the new term for municipal council) of one alcalde, two regidores and one *síndico* (regent or solicitor), effectively half of a regular ayuntamiento, which called for two alcaldes and four councilmen.[8] A note in that census also suggested that El Cobre's (half) ayuntamiento did not have "established land, funds and taxes [*fondos y arbitrios*]" to manage its internal affairs, a sign of the vecinos' limited resources.[9] In this sense, although the cobreros' petitions referred to it as a villa, its ayuntamiento was not operating like the municipal councils of other established towns at the time. Without taking away the prestige or symbolic value of that standing, El Cobre was a villa in title only. It is well possible that its material poverty was due to the penury of the returnees who had lived as slaves for twenty years and to litigation debts. The flourishing pueblo imagined in the plaintiffs' memorials would have to wait.

The regional census of February 1814 revealed yet another caveat. A note in the census highlighted El Cobre's anomalous standing as a racialized pueblo. Because El Cobre was, the note stated, "a pueblo of

the population of color had been slightly different: 87.7 percent were pardos and 12.3 percent Blacks then. General Census of Cuba, 1778, AGI-Indiferente 1527.

[7] Report of Bishop Osés y Alzúa to Minister José Antonio Caballero, October 31, 1803, AGI-SD 2230.

[8] Regional census of Santiago de Cuba, Governor Pedro Suárez de Urbina, Santiago de Cuba, February 7, 1814, AGI-Ultramar 115. In this census, the population of El Cobre was down to 1,462 inhabitants from 1,529 in 1810.

[9] Ibid.

morenos and *pardos* [black and brown people]," its ayuntamiento was restricted "to their own governance" and "Santiago did not provide a salary for a secretary."[10] The census referred to El Cobre as a "pueblo," not a villa, and there seemed to be an irregular relation to Santiago due to its explicitly marked racial standing as a pueblo of African descendants. However, the note at least indicated that the village's ayuntamiento – or half ayuntamiento – provided some internal self-rule. Although we do not know what the real workings of that local "half" self-government and internal sovereignty entailed at this time, the natives and vecinos of El Cobre formally enjoyed some local political rights beyond individual civil rights, as Echenique's memorial had suggested in 1793 (see Chapter 3).[11] Paradoxically, however, internal self-rule in those years also implied a restriction of the cobreros' broader political rights.

Napoleon's invasion of Spain in 1808 and the deposition of the Spanish monarch Fernando VII led to a major crisis of empire. That crisis, however, created an opportunity to imagine and actualize, at least for a brief period, a future Spanish nation/empire under a mixed constitutional regime. Delegates from the American overseas territories participated in the constitutional convention of 1810 where highly controversial issues of the time such as the abolition of slavery and the slave trade and nativeness and citizenship in the Spanish nation were discussed. Yet, like other emerging liberal constitutional regimes at the time and thereafter (i.e., the United States and the soon-to-become independent nations of Spanish and Portuguese America), the Cádiz constitution of 1812 did not abolish slavery. Havana's delegates were the leading opponents to abolition in the constituent convention's deliberations.[12] And, although the new constitution extended native Spanish status and civil rights to every person born free or emancipated in the Spanish empire regardless of race (Title I, Chapter II), it did not grant citizenship political rights in the greater Spanish nation to African descendants, nor to women, minors, dependent

[10] Ibid.

[11] Although 1814 suggests the end of the constitutional regime with the return of Ferdinand VII to the throne, the king did not return to Spain until March and did not revoke the Cádiz constitution until May 4, 1814. Constitutional ayuntamientos were officially abolished by royal edict on July 30, 1814. Therefore, the census signed by the governor of Santiago on February 4, 1814 was reflective of the situation current during the short liberal regime. Expediente Jiguaní and El Caney, No. 31, f. 77v, AHN-Ultramar 1647.

[12] Sartorius, *Ever Faithful*, 23–35. Slavery would not be abolished in the Spanish peninsula until the liberal regime of 1837, but the law did not apply to the colonies, which would be ruled by separate colonial laws.

servants, the unemployed, or the disabled (Articles 22 and 25). Indians and Mestizos, however, became both natives and *ciudadanos* (citizens) of the transatlantic Spanish nation. Citizenship entailed the capacity to hold municipal office and elect those positions when specified by the law (Article 23). Although the constitution left a narrow door open for free people of African descent to acquire citizenship rights, the criteria to be fulfilled were stringent (Article 22).[13] The natives of El Cobre's standing in this context became ambiguous. Whereas they were ruled by colonial corporate Indian law, and held municipal offices in their village, they did not receive the expanded political rights of citizenship that native Indians did in the empire.

Recall that Echenique's memorial of 1793 had adumbrated that, regardless of their racial status, the cobreros enjoyed freedom and political rights by virtue of constituting a municipal body with self-rule. I argued in Chapter 3 that the memorial insinuated, and arguably advocated, that free subjects of color at large could also enjoy corporate life and municipal government as the cobreros once had. And if local political rights and internal sovereignty were enjoyed at the local level, could those rights not be eventually extended to the nation writ large in a possible future? And yet, as that opportunity came up with the Cádiz Constitution, the cobreros' citizenship was relegated to local self-rule. The Cádiz Constitution expanded ayuntamientos and saw them as an instrument to increase popular participation in the nation's government and democratize municipal rule.[14] Councilmen positions that had once been vendible and patrimonial were abolished. In 1812, following liberal mandates, an island wide census was made to determine the number of electors pertaining to each municipality. As a manifestation of popular sovereignty in opposition to previous local oligarchic control of cabildos, these

[13] The requirements were framed as "venues of virtue and merit." These included distinguished services to the Patria, or those who distingush themselves by their talent, dedication, and conduct. These vague requirements were qualified by having to be of legitimate birth from free born (not freed) parents; that is, they had to be third generation free. Candidates for citizenship also had to be married to a free born woman and reside in the domains of Spain. Additionally, they also had to exercise a useful profession or industry with their own capital. Cádiz Constitution, Article 22.

[14] De Castro, *Revolución Liberal*, 62. In support of municipal popular sovereignty, the Cádiz Constitution abolished perpetual and hereditary municipal positions, prohibited their sale, and made them elective by all municipal vecinos/citizens It restricted the formation of new ayundamientos to pueblos and towns with more than 1,000 inhabitants. For an extended discussion of the municipal reforms and the conflicts they spurred in the peninsula, see also 57–120.

electors would be voted on by all the (male) inhabitants in each municipality who had been endowed with citizenship status; and these electors, in turn, would vote for ayuntamiento officials, for delegates to the Spanish Cortes, and for other matters. Whereas the Indian pueblos of Jiguaní and El Caney were included in the electors' census of 1812 with seven electors each, El Cobre, as a pueblo of "pardos and morenos," was excluded from the census altogether since its Afro descendant members were not considered *ciudadanos* (citizens) and had no political rights beyond their own internal rule.[15] One wonders what kind of political disputes and reactions these new distinctions in the framework of political liberalism could have created among the discriminated cobreros. A new arena for political action could have well emerged in that new context.

Olga Portuondo offers an example of the kind of interactions that these new categories generated in the city of Santiago. The following incident was narrated in a local paper during this short period of freedom of the press. Intentionally employing the terms in use in the new regime, the author mentioned that having entered the house of a bailiff where some political event was taking place, he saw that "some *ciudadanos* and an *español* were present. The former [citizens] were given a seat, while the *español* [of color] remained standing until the event ended."[16] The author was critical of the unequal relations suggested by the incident. Although the doors of a political event were now open to all, racial hierarchy was reenacted not only in voting rights but also through social conventions like sitting and standing. Another writer criticized the treatment of people of color in the city from a liberal egalitarian position: "Conserving those classes [of color] in the contempt and withdrawal [*retiro*] in which they have been until now means non adherence to the liberal views of the supreme government."[17] The conflicts opened up during these few years of liberal rule suggest a re-surfacing of the local politics of race, nativeness, and citizenship in the context of a new liberal discursive regime.

Yet contestation also emerged between old regime–based identitarian political formulations and new liberal ones that attest to the continuing entanglements between municipal and national and imperial levels. Indian natives of El Caney and Jiguaní, for instance, received with

[15] Census of parishes of Santiago de Cuba for the appointment of deputies to Cortes, May 23, 1812, AHN- Ultramar 387.

[16] *Ramillete de Cuba*, in Portuondo Zúñiga, *Cuba*, 84. Adriana Chira narrates the same episode in *Patchwork Freedoms*, 114.

[17] *Ramillete de Cuba*, in Portuondo Zúñiga, *Cuba*, 85.

confusion and skepticism the offer of national Spanish *ciudadanía* that the constitutional regime of 1812 offered them.[18] Did citizenship as a native Spaniard, their petitions asked, mean the revocation of their status as native Indians and their protections as an Indian pueblo (mainly regarding corporate land)? Elsewhere in the empire similar questions came up.[19] Whereas El Caney seemed initially divided on the issue, Jiguaní opposed the revocation of Indian status, despite the fact that villagers were mostly Mestizos and had been labeled as Whites in eighteenth-century censuses (Table 1.1 and Chapter 4).[20] To them, acceptance of Spanish citizenship would have interfered with their corporate communal land regime, which liberals throughout the overseas empire sought to dissolve and transform into individual centered and market-oriented property regimes. The restoration of Fernando VII to the throne in 1814 temporarily suppressed the need to take a stand at the time, but the issue reemerged during subsequent liberal hiatuses in 1821 and 1837.[21]

In 1837, when the matter came up again for discussion, El Caney petitioned for the retention of Indian pueblo status; and in a local census of its own, classified all of its Mestizo population as native Indians to

[18] Sartorious, *Ever Faithful*, 35–38.

[19] On the Cádiz Constitution's requirements as applied in Indian republics in Oaxaca and Yucatan, see Caplan, "Indigenous Citizenship," 226–27. On how liberal projects of Indigenous erasure were navigated locally in postcolonial Mexico, see Caplan, *Indigenous Citizens*, 138–50, 170–80. For liberal and Republican projects to abolish Indigenous corporate landholdings in the Andean region, see Penry, *The People Are King*, 210–12. For Popayán, see Echeverri, *Indian and Slave Royalists*, 205–6, 224–26. In Spain, de Castro, *Revolución Liberal*, 86–88, and 214–18 on the issue of municipal land disentailments.

[20] Sartorious, *Ever Faithful*, 35–38.

[21] On February 28, 1817, El Caney petitioned the king to retain the "constitutional ayuntamiento" instead of reverting back to the old regime Indian pueblo standing. The petition disavowed Indian identity pointing that "there was no one left of the Indian race in the island." The petition also wanted the position of Protector of Indians abolished because it had been useless if not detrimental to the pueblo's improvement and only served to sustain legal disputes between vecinos and private landed interests. Most important was the issue of land, half of which was rented, and should be turned into private property for the development of agriculture. The petition's outcome is unknown. In Expediente Jiguaní and El Caney, No. 31, f. 79–85v, AHN-Ultramar 1647. The Protector de Indios was abolished during the liberal hiatus of 1820–23 but apparently reinstated with the return to absolutism in 1823 (Sartorious, *Ever Faithful*, 37– 38). The position of the Protector de Indios and the standing as Pueblo de Indios of Jiguaní also came under discussion in Madrid and Cuba in 1818, after the return to absolutism in 1814. A lieutenant governor was established in Jiguaní in 1819 and the villa placed under the jurisdiction of Santiago. Expediente Jiguaní and El Caney, No. 31, f. 16–20 and 30–33, AHN-Ultramar 1647.

defend their special corporate status (see Chapter 4).[22] In 1841, the Audiencia of Puerto Príncipe couched its position favoring the dissolution of Indian protected status in these two pueblos using the new Atlantic-wide discourse of modernity and progress: "The pueblos that have been subject to Protected status are the ones that now are most backward in the race toward civilization and progress and such an exotic institution could be extinguished by declaring them Spanish pueblos governed by the same judicial regime of the whole island."[23] During the Audiencia's investigation of the issue in 1841, a witness favoring the revocation of Jiguaní's communal status laid out clearly what was at stake: "I do not know what the ideas of these natives and their enthusiasm to be Indians may be, since up to now I have not seen the good that results from it . . . how much more would this population benefit if they became Spanish [*se españolizase*], their lands sold, [and if] foreigners [*forasteros*] came in to buy them, agriculture would develop better and commerce would increase and the Royal Treasury would see an increasing income."[24] Those were precisely some of the reasons why the natives of El Caney or Jiguaní may not have wanted to lose their protected corporate status entailing communal lands, even at the price of putting up with a Protector of Indians in Santiago to represent their causes. Other conceptions of rights, sovereignty, memory, and the common good may have also been at play.

The natives of El Cobre were not subject to the Spanish citizenship dilemma that the natives of El Caney and Jiguaní faced because per the Constitution of 1812 they were not eligible for citizenship status and rights in the first place. But because the Freedom Edict of 1800 constituted them as a corporate pueblo with attributes of Indian pueblos regarding communal land, they were also subject to efforts to block their corporate standing so that obstacles to the implementation of the land grant appeared at every turn. Cobrero politics since emancipation focused on the full enforcement of the Edict of 1800. In the mid-1810s, Justo Cruzata denounced the stalling of the land grant in several petitions. In one to the Council, he pointed out that the vecinos of El Cobre were

[22] Expediente Jiguaní and El Caney, No. 31, AHN-Ultramar 1647. The metropolitan context for the discussion was the liberal Constitution of 1837.

[23] Report of the Audiencia of Puerto Príncipe, December 24, 1841, No. 31, f. 40, AHN-Ultramar 1647.

[24] Ibid. Interview in Report of Jiguaní, December 24, 1841, No. 31, f. 45v–46. Natives had been renting village land to *colonos* (settlers) and *forasteros* (foreigners) for decades thereby funding their communal expenses. Litigation over village land went back to the eighteenth century. Now some wanted to open that land for alienation and sale.

beginning to "expatriate" themselves (*expatriarse*) from the pueblo due to lack of land to work.[25] Patria bonds, the use of the term suggested, were difficult to uphold without land (although perhaps, then as now, they were retained in heart and memory despite expatriation by migration). The Council, echoing Cruzata, acknowledged "the power [*poderío*] and relations that the interested families in that city have in that the land distribution should not take place."[26]

For decades, land in El Cobre's jurisdiction and from the community was granted to colonos, many of them French refugees. Ironically, the Haitian revolution may have also had another kind of indirect effect on the cobreros' community through the French refugees who sought land to settle in El Cobre's jurisdiction. The French entrepreneur Prudencio Casamayor bought large tracks of land in El Cobre's district, which he subdivided and resold to his exiled compatriots.[27] Because the cobreros were unable to demarcate El Cobre's boundaries, land grabbing, sale, and rentals went relatively unimpeded. Yet, even though El Caney's corporate land regime was on firmer ground, considerable settlement by aspiring French coffee producers also took place in that Indian pueblo's jurisdiction.[28] Despite the patriotic anti-French sentiment and protest that irrupted in Santiago and in Havana during the Napoleonic invasion of Spain that led to the deportation of these refugees, many of them returned after the defeat of Napoleon and resettled in eastern Cuba, including in

[25] Council's response and summary of dispute (hereafter Council's response), Madrid, June 6, 1815, AGI- SD 330.

[26] Ibid. Also, lack of capital in the village to finance the land survey and, more abstractly, political opposition to a corporate land-holding regime voiced by earlier liberal-oriented political sectors, such as that of El Caney's critic cited above, contributed to the stalemate over El Cobre's land survey. For instance, when Madrid asked the intendant to provide contiguous realenga land to El Cobre, the intendant refused, giving the pretext that the land had to be put up for sale due to urgencies of the treasury. The market for land trumped the Crown's commitment to the village's corporate land grant. Report on antecedents of land division of El Cobre, Madrid (hereafter Land Distribution Report), 1853, AHN- Ultramar 4638 (2)/24. In Cuba, there were at least two edicts since 1800, in 1815 and 1816, loosening land possession and land use restrictions and opening them to market exchange, see Knight, Slave Society in Cuba, 17–18. Another edict from 1817 allowed returning French refugees as foreigners to buy land in the island. For a broader account of the almost Kafkian trajectory of the 1800 edict's land grant provision from one governmental organism to another citing issues of jurisdictional competence and other pretexts (such as the intendant's above) to block the community land grant and for references to local litigation over boundaries, see the Land Distribution Report cited above.

[27] Ferrer, *Freedom's Mirror*, 180–81.

[28] Chira, *Patchwork Freedoms*, 84–85, 118.

the environs of El Cobre and El Caney.[29] A governor of Santiago summarizing the land situation of El Cobre to Madrid reported that "[a royal edict] in 1800 finally gave freedom to *all the Indians and inhabitants of color natives of El Cobre*. Subsequently, the emigrations from Santo Domingo and the [post-Independence] American continent brought to this province a multitude of illustrious persons who populated *great terrains of uncultivated land* [in El Cobre's district]" (my italics).[30] (Note that the governor echoed the Indian and Afro descendant local nativeness claim that the cobrero plaintiffs insinuated in the memorials and in which the Edict of 1800 partly relied; or perhaps he drew it from local living memory.) In any case, the 1800 edict's land provisions had not been actualized and other settlers had been taking possession of the community's land and land in the district.

Local litigation between cobreros and vecinos of Santiago over village land continued to take place at the individual and collective level in subsequent years.[31] In the late 1830s, the syndic of El Cobre's half-ayuntamiento, Don José María Díaz, collected a contribution of five pesos from each "of the natives of color for expenses regarding their [judicial] recourse without authorization of the government of Santiago."[32] The syndic was litigating the still-stalled land grant in the Audiencia of Puerto Príncipe on behalf of the cobreros: they seem to have been litigating collectively as natives of El Cobre since other vecinos were excluded from the collection for the litis. In 1841, the same syndic, Díaz, circulated a petition among the Whites and the free population of color in El Cobre in

[29] According to the governor of Cuba, the Royal Edicts of August 10, 1815, and October 21, 1817, allowed foreigners to sell, divide, and buy land in Cuba facilitating the return and settlement of French refugees on the island after their deportation in 1808–9 due to the Napoleonic invasion of Spain. The governor invoked these edicts in 1846 to justify the privatization of community land in El Cobre in 1842 saying that he amplified their reach to the colonos of El Cobre because "posterior orders [edicts of 1815 and 1817] nullify previous ones [the Edict of 1800]." The governor claimed these possessions had been granted for years and he was merely confirming possession and giving property title (with alienation rights) to them. Report of Governor Cayetano Urbina, Santiago, February 1846, AHN-Ultramar 4638 (2).

[30] Report of Governor Cayetano de Urbina, February 1846, No. 39, AHN-Ultramar 4638 (2)/24.

[31] Governor Pedro Suárez de Urbina, Santiago de Cuba, February 7, 1814, AGI-Ultramar 115; Council's response, Madrid, June 6, 1815, AGI-SD 330; Report on antecedents of land division of El Cobre, Madrid, August 28, 1842, No. 16, AHN-Ultramar 4638 (2)/24.

[32] Expediente contra el Capitán Don Felipe Pedroso (hereafter Expediente Peroso), ca. 1841, AHN-4513/8.

favor of the retention of the then lieutenant governor of the village, Captain Felipe Peroso, whom the governor wanted to remove from the post for political reasons.[33] In an interrogation of the vecinos who had dared to sign the petition, two cobreros referred to the land question (which was not part of that petition) in a noteworthy way. When asked why he signed the Díaz's petition backing Peroso, Raquemuado [*sic*] Campos, a fifty-year-old *labrador* (agricultural worker) identified as a "native and vecino of the Villa," who by age may have lived through the Freedom Edict of 1800's proclamation and the local politics of its aftermath, responded that he did not read the representation that Díaz presented to him but assumed that "it was related to the rights [*derechos*] of the pueblo [which was] what induced him to sign."[34] Taken aback perhaps by the phrase, the new lieutenant heading the investigation asked him to "manifest what are the rights of the pueblo that induced you to sign," to which Campos responded that "to his understanding those rights were about the litigation [*pleito*] that is pending in common [*en comunidad*] regarding the land [*los terrenos*] for which Don José María went as commissioner [*comisario*] to [the Audiencia of Puerto] Príncipe."[35] Campos saw the land question based on the Edict of 1800 as a communal claim and as a "pueblo's right" then under litigation at the Audiencia level with Díaz (the half-ayuntamiento's syndic) as their apoderado.

Similarly, the sixty-year-old Tomás Ortiz, another "native and vecino" of El Cobre who used the same excuse for signing the petition offered by Díaz, but who was not as bold as to suggest corporate "rights," mentioned the "pending litis about the community's land [*terrenos de la comunidad*]."[36] The old notion of community, communal land, and

[33] The lieutenant governor position representing colonial authority had been installed in 1838 in El Cobre to sit in, and directly oversee and control, the pueblo's half ayuntamiento, thereby reducing whatever little autonomy it may still retain even further. However, the colonial official won the backing of many vecinos and settlers (it is not clear to what extent the old cobreros backed him) as Captain Peroso defended some local interests against those of the foreign mining companies. In Jiguaní, a lieutenant governor had already been installed in 1819 when the villa was placed under the jurisdiction of Santiago de Cuba instead of nearby Bayamo. The lieutenant governor could mete out first instance justice, thereby reducing the former power of the local ayuntamiento. Expediente Jiguaní and El Caney, No. 31, f. 30–33, AHN-Ultramar 1647.

[34] Testimony of Campos, El Cobre, ca. 1841, Expediente Peroso, 1841, f. 27–27v, AHN-Ultramar 4613/8.

[35] Ibid. [36] Ibid. Testimony of Tomás Ortiz, ca. 1841, f. 26–26v.

municipal entity was after four decades still on the table for old-time cobreros.

Records at hand do not allow me to reconstruct further the many conflicts and litigation that took place, nor how the cobreros made claims based on their identity as natives of El Cobre and their local sovereignty rights against (White and racially mixed) *colonos*, *forasteros*, and *extranjeros* settling in the pueblo's jurisdiction (the distinctions between the terms and the rights associated with them at the local level at different points in the nineteenth century remain to be studied), but the comments about the communal land and the pueblo's rights are suggestive.

THE MINING REVIVAL AND TRANSFORMATIONS

Yet the greatest factor of change in El Cobre and the region emerged in the 1830s and it came from another corner of the Atlantic world. At this moment, a new historical period truly began: one that further eroded the limited political and land legal rights the cobreros had earned through the Edict of 1800. This time it was foreign British companies with an interest in exploiting the village's rich copper deposits who knocked at the door with some smaller Spanish companies following suit.[37] The Spanish imperial state's aspirations to find a new contractor to revive the mines of El Cobre, for which it had laid the ground in the Edict of 1800 by providing a labor pool with mita labor requirements in the village of El Cobre, never materialized. A lease to British companies with the capital and knowhow to exploit the mines constituted a new turn in Spanish imperial policy. Spain's coffers lay depleted by years of war and the loss of its American empire forced it to reconsider economic policy and accept foreign investment from its former enemy. But new trends of liberal economic thought and policy also were at work.[38] Ironically, despite Cuba's continuing colonial status under Spanish rule, British mining investment in El Cobre took place as British capital penetrated the mining sectors of postcolonial republics in Spanish and Portuguese America too.[39] Again, the well-connected French refugee entrepreneur Prudencio

[37] Gonzales Loscertales and de Montand, "La minería del cobre en Cuba."

[38] The Intendant José de Aguila, argued for the opening to foreign mining investment, for export of mineral to England for refinement and resale, and for an open door to foreign (White) immigration (without religious restrictions) as the basis for progress. Intendant's Mining Report, August 31, 1838, AHN-6(1).

[39] Randall, *Real del Monte*; Eakin, *British Enterprise in Brazil*. And for British copper mining investment in Spain, see Avery, *Not in Queen Victoria's Birthday*.

Casamayor, by then an extremely wealthy and powerful naturalized Spanish vassal and vecino of Santiago, initially served as liaison and Spanish front man for the British company.[40] These new actors also changed the internal politics of the pueblo and the region, which included now the powerful interests of the British mining companies, as well as of new vecinos and colonos, the church, the colonial government, and the cobreros politically aligning in new ways.

Steam engines and later a railroad, badges of industrial mining and modernity (and of coal-based greenhouse gas emissions) arrived in El Cobre with the new mining consortiums.[41] El Cobre became rapidly globalized. Skilled British miners from Cornwall (once a major copper mining center) were brought in too. Even though Britain was in the process of abolishing slavery in its Caribbean islands during the 1830s and was persecuting the international slave trade especially in Cuba and Brazil, hundreds of slaves arrived to work in the British-run mines of El Cobre from different Atlantic localities. By 1841, there were reportedly about 1,621 enslaved people in El Cobre's jurisdiction working in mining and agriculture.[42] The cobreros were not subject to mita labor for the British miners, although a handful (12 to 16) cobrera women were employed at a minimal wage in surface works separating the mineral.[43] As a major world producer of copper ore (exported to Swansea for

[40] Report of Governor Cayetano de Urbina, February 1846, No. 39, AHN-Ultramar 4638 (2)/24; Gonzales Loscertales and de Montaud, "La minería del cobre en Cuba." The partnership served to sidestep formal legal restrictions to foreign investment. For the logistics (and critique) of the partnership, see David Turnbull's account of his visit to the mines in 1838. Turnball was hosted by the British consul in Santiago, John Hardy, who was a co-proprietor of the Copper Mines and had a family residence in El Cobre. See Turnbull, *Cuba*, 5–15.

[41] On the magnitude of the British mining operations, see Turnbull's account of his visit, ibid. He also reported that there were almost 900 workers employed but that to his "great regret" he found that more than half were slaves, some property of the Mining Company and others hired out from their owners in Santiago. Yet, despite his abolitionist orientation, he did not press further the British connection regarding the origin of those slaves; he also reported Canarian workers and some 200 migrant Cornish miners, many of whom had recently died from a yellow fever epidemic.

[42] Intendant's Mining Report, Santiago, January 26, 1843, No. 14, AHN-Ultramar 6(2). An 1844 report by the governor of Santiago referred to 3,000 "souls" employed in the three main companies (two British and one Spanish) and in the mines. Report of Governor Cayetano Urbina, Santiago, February 1846, No. 39, AHN-Ultramar 4638 (2)/24.

[43] Intendant's Mining Report, Santiago, August 31, 1838, Interrogatory, AHN-Ultramar 6 (1).

refining),[44] El Cobre became fully inserted into global circuits and became a cosmopolitan place with a resident and working population from around the Atlantic world: cobreros; natives from other cities and villages in the island; Spaniards from the metropolis and former colonies; French, British, and enslaved workers from different localities in Africa. By the 1850s, even Chinese indentured workers were imported to toil in El Cobre's mining operations too.[45] This may not have been the sugar belt in the central-western part of the island, but it was not, by any stretch of the imagination, a hinterland. Nor was it the imagined agricultural villa from the past or the future once depicted in the cobreros' memorials. The physical landscape and the social profile of El Cobre had drastically changed.

By 1841, the village's population had tripled from 1,529 in 1810 to 4,636 in 1841.[46] The White population (881), many with British surnames related to the mines and others with French surnames to agriculture, constituted 19 percent of the villa's population. The number of slaves had increased to 1,614 or 35 percent of the total population, most of them working in the mines and related activities or in agriculture. Although the free of color population, among them the descendants of old time cobreros and new arrivals, had grown to 2,134 persons (1,736 or 81 percent of them racially mixed pardos), this group now constituted 46 percent of the village's population, down from 92 percent in 1810.[47] The villa of El Cobre had become a mix of mining enterprises digging copper ore, cattle ranches to supply the mining companies, coffee haciendas, and old-time small food producers.

Even the Marian sanctuary began to engage in litigation against the main British mining consortium over the penetration of the mining works into copper-rich sacred ground under the temple. Figure 9.1 shows the proximity of those works to the Marian sanctuary with the mouths of two old 1830s shafts (San José and San Juan) leading to copper deposits under the hill over which the sanctuary stood. Similarly, Figure 9.2 shows a boiler house (with its greenhouse gas emissions) and other mining

[44] Ibid. El Cobre took the third place, after Chile and China, as a world exporter of copper to Britain for refinement in the 1830s and '40s.

[45] González Loscertales and de Montand, "La minería del cobre en Cuba." A 1858 census, as reported in de la Pezuela's *Diccionario de la Isla de Cuba* (1863) under the entry of "El Cobre," registered 230 *colonos asiáticos* among a population of 12,676 souls.

[46] The population breakdown of 1841 was reported in the intendant's report of the mines, Santiago, January 26, 1843, No. 14, AHN-Ultramar 6(2).

[47] Ibid.

FIGURE 9.1 Mining works and old shafts next to the sanctuary, El Cobre, ca. 1904.
The photograph is from an anonymous mining album of the mining works in El Cobre probably commissioned by the North American mining company then reviving the mines. Note the names of the shafts that had been worked by a British consortium in the 1830s–1860s. Cuban Photograph Album Collection, Cuban Heritage Collection, University of Miami, Coral Gables, Florida

operations next to two other former British shafts, which by the turn of the twentieth century were owned by a US mining company.[48] Although both photographs were taken around 1904, during a later wave of "progress," they reflect the impact that mining works had on the landscape and environment of El Cobre back in the 1830s and '40s, when the old shafts were first made and worked.

In 1844, at the peak of the mining boom, the long-postponed land distribution finally took place in El Cobre. But it did not take place as prescribed in the Edict of 1800. Land was now privatized along patterns

[48] For the changes in ownership see Soto González, *Apuntes sobre la historia minerúa cubana*, 60–69.

FIGURE 9.2 Mining works and old shafts, El Cobre, ca. 1904.
The photograph from the anonymous mining album shows the industrial presence of steam engines in the boiler house and their impact on the landscape. Note the old shafts from the 1830s and 1840s. The Hardy shaft carried the name of the 1830s co-owner of the British mining consortium operating in El Cobre. Cuban Photograph Album Collection, Cuban Heritage Collection, University of Miami, Coral Gables, Florida

of usage and (legal and illegal) concessions made since the first decades of the nineteenth century. Although a number of cobrero small farmers retained land that they had inherited and worked for decades, considerable land was gobbled up and given out to foreign settlers, mainly to British foreigners and French "colonos" in the village and surrounding district for mining, pasturing, and agricultural purposes.[49] Colonos and cobreros were held as distinctly separate groups in the lists. One read: "Report of the *colonos* that have presented themselves and obtained a

[49] Land Distribution Report, 1842, AHN-Ultramar 4638/24, No. 43–46. The decision to confirm by usage may be read as a form of prescription now favoring established colonos and miners.

grant of the land that they *possessed of the community of El Cobre* [*del terreno que poseían de la comunidad del Cobre*]" (my italics), that is, community land that had been granted to these outsiders through the years and now formalized with titles.[50] Some 327 colonos (half of the recipients), most with French and English names and many with Monsieur, Madame, and Mister titles, received about 266 "urban" plots (*solares*) and 55 farm plots (*estancias*) from community land.[51] The other list included solely cobreros: "Report of the *cobreros* who have justified their origin [*procedencia*] and were included in the grant of land that they possessed of the community of El Cobre" (my italics).[52] Whereas about 329 cobreros received an urban plot (198) or an estancia (111), a few received both (33). It would be interesting to know how they justified their nativeness or origin as cobreros. Most of the surnames in the list were new, though not foreign sounding. In any case, the land distribution destroyed the communal aspect of the land grant of the Freedom Edict of 1800 and formally individualized, privatized, and made alienable all the community land through land titles. It is difficult to say how accurate these lists were or how much further conflict resulted from this land distribution scheme or what happened in its aftermath.

Moreover, as a result of local conflicts with the mining companies and in the midst of increased repression of slaves and free people of color elsewhere in the colony during the 1840s, the Spanish imperial government abolished El Cobre's half-ayuntamiento in 1844 and with it the villa's corporate municipal standing.[53] The governor of Santiago paved

[50] Ibid., No. 43. Of about 311 colono land recipients (some received more than one grant) about 131 (42 percent) had no titles preceding their names indicating non-Whiteness. Many of these non-White colonos had French names, however, so they were for the most part settlers from St. Domingue. But only 11 among them received a farm plot, while 25 colonos with titled names did so.

[51] Ibid., No. 44. Another 163, all with "Don" and "Doña" titles, White *hacendados* received land in the rural districts of the jurisdiction, not labeled "community land."

[52] Ibid., No. 45.

[53] The process had been more gradual. In 1838, a military lieutenant governor was named to sit and control the half-ayuntamiento of natives, who turned out to have some backing due to his opposition to the mining companies' power. When removed in 1841, another one was appointed to his position. At that time, El Cobre'sayuntamiento was restructured and the positions of councilmen were privatized, so to speak, or made *vendibles* (saleable) as allegedly was the case in other municipalities in the island. Thus, ironically, El Cobre had retained more democratic procedural protocols, while other municipalities had returned to pre- Cádiz constitutional elite proprietary municipal ayuntamiento regimes. In 1844, a further step was taken and the ayuntamiento was completely revoked and a military government installed until 1858. Report of Governor Cayetano Urbina, Santiago de Cuba, February 1846, AHN-Ultramar 4638 (2)/24. Urbina also made a passing reference to a slave

the way for this transformation when he alerted the captain general of the volatile situation that had developed in El Cobre during the last decade: "A pueblo where a considerable number of slaves are gathered and other persons of color for the work in the mines [and] where the natives [*naturales*] are also blacks and mulattoes and compose a half-ayuntamiento, and [a pueblo] that is surrounded by haciendas endowed with slaves to work the land" was a place in need of stronger colonial oversight and control.[54] That same governor, siding with the mining companies and voicing the need to support their interests against any contest from other groups in the pueblo such as those supporting Lieutenant Governor Peroso added: "The conflicts over jurisdiction of Captain Peroso with the Intendant Inspector of the Mines [are numerous] … because Peroso and his counselors [from Santiago] antagonize to death the Mining Enterprise [and] hinder an industry of so much utility to the country whose cash [*numerario*] is the only one that circulates in this garrison [*plaza*] … They have hindered it by obstructing the railroad project that the first [British mining] company was trying to build."[55] The governor's report alludes to the power of the mining company and the new political dynamics in El Cobre now involving global actors.

Soon after this report, El Cobre's half-ayuntamiento was completely dissolved and a full "energetic military government due to the numerous slaves that had to be watched over" was installed.[56] "Progress" called for further colonial militarization. With this change, any pretension of political rights for natives and vecinos of the villa that may have remained from the Edict of 1800 were rescinded. El Caney and Jiguaní also endured the revocation of their corporate status at this time, although they were not subject to El Cobre's militarization.[57] This final revocation of Indian

uprising in Hongolosongo, a rural district that was near of part of El Cobre's jurisdiction. For La Escalera rebellion and repression, see Paquette, *Sugar Is Made with Blood*; Reid-Vazquez, *The Year of the Lash*; Finch, *Rethinking Slave Rebellion.*

54 Governor Juan Tello, Santiago de Cuba, April 16, 1841, Expediente Peroso, 1841, AHN-Ultramar 4613/8, No. 8.

55 Ibid.

56 Report of Governor Cayetano de Urbina, Santiago de Cuba, February 1846, AHN-Ultramar 4638 (2)/24. According to de la Pezuela, a reorganized ayuntamiento was reestablished by royal order of July 27, 1858. *Diccionario*, "El Cobre" entry 12.

57 On the final liquidation of El Caney's and Jiguaní's Indian corporate standing in 1844, see Sartorius's short discussion in *Ever Faithful*, 38. See also "Expediente de tierras que la extinguida comunidad de Indios de El Caney poseía," 1850, No. 32, AHN-Ultramar 4632.

corporate status occurred in colonial Cuba even before it took full force in many postcolonial Spanish nations in the mainland. The land privatization and distribution policy and the abolition of corporate municipal status represented the final nail in the coffin to the Freedom Edict of 1800. To be sure, the cobreros' individual civil freedom was not revoked but what I have referred to as the local political freedom rights deriving from their limited municipal corporate standing slowly being dissolved as the global discourse of progress also burgeoned under Spanish colonial absolutism.

A shift to a more local perspective in the edict's afterlife story leads to an array of questions that cannot be answered at this point. How did the cobreros continue to use their identity as natives of El Cobre to make claims to land and to self-rule in the new historical contexts of a globalized space? What memory did cobreros retain of the edict and their rights after the revocation of corporate status and as new generations replaced older ones? These changes may well have set the stage for alignments in the first (failed) Independence War of 1868–78 (which also led to attacks on and closure of the mines). The dynamics of local, colonial, imperial notions of belonging in this globalized space generates new questions for future research that historians can compare with processes in postcolonial nations in Latin America too.

A photograph of "people of El Cobre" propels the story to the end of Spanish colonialism at the close of the century. The source allows the modern reader to "see" and not just "hear" the local people at the center of this book (Figure 9.3). Seemingly factual and authentic, the photo does not reveal much; it generates wonder instead. We see the barren landscape allegedly in the vicinity of El Cobre (although without specific markers it could be anywhere in the region). We wonder what brought this group of women and children of color to the semi-dilapidated wooden house on the right side of the picture and to its nonvisible residents. The larger historical context of the photo is 1898: a turning point that marked the end of Spanish colonialism with Cuba's last Independence war (1895–98) along with US intervention and a subsequent occupation leading to the photographer's visit to document (and publicize) the island and its people, including this seemingly spontaneous local gendered scene. The photographed subjects belonged to the generation who lived through the war and perhaps their gathering had to do with some claims related to its aftermath. Were they family of combatants? We can only wonder.

More importantly, in line with the queries of this book, and the history of local globalization sketched in this chapter, we may also wonder who

FIGURE 9.3 "People from El Cobre, Cuba," 1899.
First published in *Our Islands and Their People* by José de Olivares (redactor) and William Bryan Smith (editor). Vol. 1, 1899, 204. Ilbusca/Getty Images

these local women and children from El Cobre were. Were they, or some among them, direct descendants of the old emancipated cobreros? Or were they perhaps descendants of the colonos who settled in El Cobre and received land plots two generations before in the 1840s? Or were some of them the descendants of the enslaved people who had once toiled in the mines and coffee estates of El Cobre and had been emancipated with the abolition of slavery in 1886, only a dozen years before the picture was taken? Had they all become natives of El Cobre and developed bonds of local belonging with each other and the land? Or were the old cobreros a separate group linked through descent and the memory of the emancipation of 1800? Who, in short, were the natives and vecinos of El Cobre one hundred years after the edict of 1800? The photo makes us ponder these questions.

But the photograph becomes even more intriguing when paired with its original caption in *Our Islands and Their People as Seen in Camera and Pencil* (1899) where it first appeared. The caption was subsequently eliminated in the privatized digitized photo now part of the Getty Images commercial archive. The original publication labeled the photographed subjects "Group of El Cobre Indians." The longer caption originally accompanying the now uprooted photo is even more provocative:

> In the vicinity of El Cobre, near Santiago, there are still some remnants of the ancient aboriginal inhabitants of that island mixed more or less with Spaniards [*sic*] and negro blood. Some of those people are represented in the above group. *They trace their lineage* back to the people who occupied the island when Columbus made his discovery and are the remnants of that interesting and surely persecuted race (my italics).[58]

From where had this identification of racially mixed people as Indians of El Cobre come from? From the photographed subjects themselves, as the caption insinuates? From an intermediary or translator in situ guiding the photographer and his team? From the artist and editors' own spin on some local rumor or from consulted documents? Whose voice is represented in that caption? The question is important for it resembles the narratives of racial mixture and Indian ancestry constitutive of local nativeness that appeared in the memorials of the 1780s and '90s discussed in Chapter 4 or in passing official comments in reports such as that of Governor Urbina in 1846 mentioned above. The theme was here repurposed into a more general narrative of a persecuted Indigenous race under Spanish colonialism (perhaps to be liberated by the American occupation . . .). But one wonders to what extent vernacular narratives of Indian ancestry, racial mixture, and nativeness were circulating in the village in 1898 – and if so to whom did they apply now? To all the natives of the pueblo or selectively to some natives who claimed that ancestry? How was this identification invoked and used locally at this moment in history? We can only wonder at what future scholars may uncover about native identity–related mutations and their political and cultural deployments through time in this and other localities.

EL COBRE AND MEMORY SITES TODAY

Despite a stormy and fascinating history, El Cobre is in the present a quiet and seemingly ordinary village. Its small urban center today has a population of some 7,000 inhabitants, and some 17,000 people reside in

[58] José de Olivares (redactor) and William Bryan Smith (editor), *Our Islands and Their People*, vol. 1, 1899, 204. Getty Images changed the caption to "The people of El Cobre" and deleted the longer caption. No attribution of the image's source is provided in the new decontextualized market of (high-resolution) images. I was able to trace its source to the above-mentioned publication, which contained its own problems of attribution. The redactor who may have devised the title and the caption, José de Olivares, identified as a "noted author and war correspondent," was of Hispanic origin. In any case, the publication reflects the US imperial gaze at its new colonial acquisitions after the "Spanish American War" of 1898. For instance, El Caney lost all its allusions to an Indian past and was featured as a major scene of American operations during the war.

the municipality at large. The town's name echoes the legendary wealth of its mines and their importance at many points of its history going back to the early colonial period. Whereas in the first half of the nineteenth century (western) Cuba became the main world producer of sugar, by mid-century, as mentioned before, the mines of El Cobre in the eastern region became a major world producer of copper, an industry that globalized the town and nearby Santiago. Yet, despite the enormous mineral wealth once extracted from its mines, there is no charming colonial town left here: perhaps like other mining towns in the world, the town's architecture is bare and functional. Although British capital exploited El Cobre's copper mines until the late 1860s, when Cuba's first war of Independence interrupted production, US mining companies took over their exploitation in the early twentieth century at the dawn of the Cuban republic (Figures 9.1 and 9.2). The mines were nationalized after the Cuban Revolution of 1959. No longer productive or cost efficient, the nationalized mines closed again at the turn of the twenty-first century. An enormous pit lake of beautiful deep blue mineralized water two kilometers long, eighty meters wide and sixty meters in depth, now romantically called "El Lago Azul de El Cobre" (The Blue Lake of El Cobre), is a striking reminder of that mining past (Figure 9.4). However, the lake is a flooded pit full of toxic minerals that await treatment to avoid environmental and human harm.[59] Some hope it may one day become a touristic attraction.[60]

El Cobre has its share of fame in the island for other reasons too. The town is the seat of the sanctuary to the Virgin of Charity who became the patroness of the Cuban nation in the early twentieth century but whose local fame, as mentioned above, goes back to the seventeenth century.[61] After several decades of a low profile in the context of a socialist

[59] On the human and environmental hazardous aspects of the lake and research on how to remove contamination for water reuse, see the study of Rodríguez Gámez et al. "Assessment of Water Quality from the Blue Lagoon."

[60] The Blue Lagoon or Lake is also taking on touristic significance due to its striking visual contrasts, perhaps analogous to the tourism of Río Tinto (Red River) in Huelva, southwest Spain, where the red colored river (due to sulfide ore deposits also high in acidity) runs through the giant open cast abandoned copper mines. The walls of the pit have streaks of different hues due to the presence of other mineral ores that were also mined. The abandoned Río Tinto mines have been turned into a mining park that attracts considerable domestic tourism. The repurposing of the site is a way of extracting new value from the transformed landscape. See www.spain.info/en/leisure-parks/riotinto-mining-park/.

[61] Díaz, *The Virgin the King*; Díaz, "Rethinking Tradition and Identity." See also Portuondo Zúñiga, *La Virgen de la Caridad*; Ada Ferrer, *Cuba*, 34–39, 215.

FIGURE 9.4 Lake at copper mine of El Cobre, Santiago de Cuba Province, 2019. The lake is known locally as the "Blue Lake of El Cobre." The photograph shows the enormous open-pit mine that flooded after mining operations were discontinued in 1998. The water is acidic due to metal contamination and in need of remediation. Karol Kolowski Premium RM Collection/2019/Alamy

society unsympathetic to public religious worship, the sanctuary has become again in the last two or three decades a place of regional, national, and international pilgrimage for devotees of both the Christian faith and the Afro Cuban religion of Santería (Figure 9.5).

As the mines died and the sanctuary took on new life among devotees and tourists in the late twentieth century, El Cobre gained a new iconic status with the construction of a Monument to the Runaway Slave (Monumento al Cimarrón) in 1997 (Figure 9.6). Sponsored by UNESCO's program "Route of the Slave" and other local institutions such as Casa del Caribe in Santiago de Cuba, the monument maps another stream of Atlantic history and pushes back local memory to a period close to the story in this book. The giant sculpture by Santiago de Cuba's artist Alberto Debray represents a spirit flying out of a cauldron with a manifestly African allusion to the Palo Monte religion.[62] Freedom

[62] Monumento al Cimarrón, El Cobre, Cuba, 1997. Sponsored by Casa Caguayo, Casa del Caribe and UNESCO. Palo Monte or the Regla of Congo is an African diasporic religion that developed in Cuba during the nineteenth century (after the cobreros' late eighteenth-century acts of marronage). Perhaps the monument's allusion to this tradition constitutes a call for freedom of religion and for public recognition of this type of African presence in Cuba – or more ambiguously perhaps, as a diasporic African cultural ancestry claiming nativeness in the island too.

FIGURE 9.5 National Basilica of Our Lady of Charity, El Cobre.
The Basilica houses a seventeenth-century image of the Virgin of Charity said to be miraculous. Our Lady of Charity is the patron saint of Cuba. Rosita So Image/Getty Images

FIGURE 9.6 Monument to the Runaway Slave, El Cobre, 1997.
Monumento al Cimarrón. Iron and bronze sculpture by Alberto Lescay, El Cobre, Cuba. Cimarron Monument, Karol Kozlowski Premium RM Collection/Alamy Stock Photo, 2019

is an elusive notion and multiple ways of imagining it can be projected into the image of the iconic maroon.[63] While commemorating the struggles for freedom of this community in the past, the monument invites us to think about other battles and ways of imagining freedom and cultural identity in the present and future. However, enslaved villagers in the past did not only engage in flight to the mountains in pursuit of an elusive freedom. They also pioneered local, trans-local and transoceanic collective activism in the judicial arena to assert more explicit notions of freedom and enact political rights related to local native belonging. These stories of legal activism may lay hidden deep in the monument's cauldron of memories and merit to be remembered too. This book has dug out some of those stories and buried memories from the archive.

[63] For marronage as a trope of a continuous reimagining freedom, see Glissant, *Caribbean Discourse.*

Conclusion

The cobreros entered the Age of Revolutions on a bad footing but emerged from their trials and tribulations in 1800 in a stronger position with an edict recognizing their collective freedom and standing as a pueblo. Bourbon reforms aimed at the reconfiguration of empire led in eastern Cuba to the privatization of the mining jurisdiction of Santiago del Prado (aka El Cobre) in 1781 and to a massive enslavement of villagers deemed the king's slaves who had long lived alongside free people of color in an unconventional pueblo in the mining jurisdiction. This "modernizing" and development-oriented imperial assault on the precarious but long-established customary living and working arrangements of this community went hand in hand with other recent colonial policies such as the expansion of slavery and the slave trade, and in this case, with a stricter application of slave law and a tightening of coartación norms through higher assessment prices. The privatization and enslavement policy produced strong pushback from the cobreros through marronage actions and through a striking collective legal action for freedom that aimed to reconfigure their past and future.

Although the cobreros had made use of the judicial system before, they had only done so collectively as the king's slaves. In 1784, for the first time, the cobreros filed a wrongful enslavement legal action based on claims to collective freedom as natives of a pueblo and they did so directly in the Council of the Indies, the highest tribunal of empire. To be sure, the conception of freedom that emerged in their case was not one based on the universal rights of man that were part of the revolutionary ideas about freedom and equality circulating in some intellectual and political circles of the northern Atlantic at the time. Instead, the notions of collective freedom that emerged here represented jurists' and letrados' reflections on the cobreros' customary practices reworked in new ways through discursive, policy-oriented and legal instruments rooted in the Spanish Atlantic world. In line with the pro-slavery policies of the time and following a rigorous reading of slave law, the Council of the Indies initially rejected the cobreros' controversial claim to collective freedom and the criteria of freedom presented in the memorials on their behalf. By 1800, however, the cobreros emerged from their protracted battle for freedom with an official recognition of their civil freedom as well as a limited political freedom based on their standing as natives of a pueblo, a standing that imperial jurists eventually read mainly through the prism of colonial Indian law.

I embarked on this study wondering how the Freedom Edict of April 7, 1800, emancipating hundreds of enslaved cobreros could have come about in a period of frenzied slave expansion and deregulation of the international slave trade, though also a time of revolutions unfolding in the broader Atlantic world. Although a situational approach involving the dynamics between local, colonial, imperial, and global levels helped me explain the changing political context in the 1790s that produced the emancipation outcome in the cobreros' case, research on the heretofore neglected freedom suit also led me in other unanticipated directions. The freedom suit at the center of this book was a composite legal action that combined elements of traditional freedom suits with more novel claims advanced by and on behalf of racialized colonial subjects. Conjoined notions of civil and local political freedom linked to widespread notions of native local belonging throughout the empire were the most significant proposals that emerged from this remarkable case. However, whereas the emancipated natives of El Cobre retained the civil freedom recognized by the Edict of 1800, their limited municipal-based political freedom and rights were eroded in subsequent years and eventually dissolved by the 1840s as old and new Atlantic forces and interests together with ever harsher colonial policies converged in this increasingly globalized region of the island. The struggles of these Afro descendant subjects for land, civil freedom, and local political freedom through municipal level sovereignty may have had echoes elsewhere in the Spanish empire in the past and in some respects still have resonance in regions of Latin America more than 200 years later.

The most explicit and intriguing reflection on freedom presented to the court in this case was a discussion framed in Spanish political, philosophical, and juridical terms that distinguished between two kinds of freedom:

civil and political freedom. In this formulation, civil freedom was understood in opposition to slavery as personal freedom. It referred to an array of individual rights, however limited, that free subjects could enjoy as royal vassals even in the context of an absolute monarchy, if more restrictively in a colonial setting. These implicit rights of civil freedom included, for instance, possession of one's labor, right to property and to making contracts and wills, security of person from arbitrary violence, access to justice, protection by the law, the right to live as a family, and other negotiated and disputed rights, including proper treatment, that varied across time and place. These individual rights constituted the basic form of liberty rights that freedom suits disputed and that, if breached, free subjects, at least in principle, could claim in court (today they constitute a small part of a wider array of what are considered "human" rights, not just "freedom" and "citizenship" rights). Although the cobreros' legal briefs used traditional legal instruments to claim freedom in the Spanish empire (such as alleged manumission edicts and coartación), they also made use of a more rarified and controversial instrument that recognized practices associated with freedom performed uninterruptedly over a given number of years as prescriptive or emancipatory acts. This path to freedom was the most suggestive and controversial claim in this freedom case. What practices of freedom could carry such force? How were they disputed? And to what effect?

The other kind of freedom claimed and parsed in the cobreros' case was a locally based political freedom that rested on municipal belonging. This kind of freedom referred to a different order of rights, one associated with corporate belonging and limited local self-rule in political bodies or local republics such as pueblos, villas, and cities – a notion that went beyond the liberal notion of the bounded individual as full sovereign. Early modern Castilian municipal corporatist notions of local self-rule through cabildos, and later ayuntamientos, lived throughout the Spanish Atlantic, including in the overseas Spanish and Indian republics where the imperial and colonial state's grip was stronger. The boldest argument for freedom in the cobreros' case was based on the claim that, as members of a municipal entity, the cobreros had once enacted a collective political liberty that went beyond mere individual civil freedoms such as owning property or living in their own houses. In fact, the argument went, that having lived together as members (or natives) of a pueblo overrode any possible uncertainty regarding the individual status as free or slave of any member of the pueblo; and furthermore, that, by constituting a municipality (or a local republic), they also enjoyed rights to land. Arguably, here was in embryonic form a radical notion of natality rights suggesting that birth, co-residence and membership in a municipal body – in a local republic – upended bondage or effectively emancipated slaves. Although formulated in traditional local and corporativist terms, this was a bold assertion that writ large could also have important implications.

This kind of local corporate-based argument for collective freedom rights was especially significant because African descendants and other racially mixed subjects (castas) were not allowed by the laws of the Indies, at least not explicitly, to constitute themselves into pueblos or to hold municipal positions in those where they resided, and therefore they could not enjoy or enact locally-based political freedom. It was mainly in the interstices of the law that such situations emerged through informal arrangements and customary practices. In seeking official recognition of their pueblo through their legal action in Madrid, the cobreros were not only seeking civil freedom. They were also attempting to legitimize local political freedom through (limited) self-rule as a local republic – a political freedom that (male) cobreros had once enacted through their cabildo. Implicit in any legitimation of (local) political freedom were potential normative questions too: could the recognition of the cobreros' right to live as a racially mixed pueblo of pardos and morenos be extended to other free Afro descendants? Could Afro descendants throughout the empire who lived in informal communities become local republics and obtain political rights to self-govern and control local resources like Spanish and Indian republics? In this sense, the cobreros pressed on the imperial tribunal a novel proposal that called for reinterpreting, rethinking, and perhaps rewriting law.

Moreover, I suggested that there were also issues of participatory democracy at play in the cobreros' claims for local municipal and corporate based political freedom. Although the limited local participatory democracy implicit in early modern municipalities had for different reasons been significantly eroded by the eighteenth century in most localities of the empire, and especially in larger cities and towns, some impulses to open participation to commoners had emerged in Spain and more strongly from below in the Indigenous republics of the overseas empire. New research reveals that the concept of "*el común*" had gained traction in many Indigenous corporate communities where alleged immemorial practices that legitimized cacique and Indian noble local rule were being increasingly challenged by Indian commoners during the mid to late eighteenth century. Against this backdrop, racially mixed commoners of slave descent such as the cobreros represented an even greater potential for local participatory democracy by commoners: the royal slave and free men of color who once constituted the cabildo of El Cobre and the apoderados who now claimed official recognition of local self-rule as a villa effectively represented such a local democratic stance.

Although the cobreros obtained their civil freedom in 1800, the implications of collective political freedom based on municipal corporate self-rule that ensued was not fully actualized in subsequent years as only a half ayuntamiento was installed in El Cobre. More importantly, when the laws of the liberal Constitution of Cádiz briefly restructured and reformed municipal ayuntamientos throughout the empire, making them the basis of popular participatory democracy and of political freedom at the local and national level, paradoxically, those laws did not broaden political freedoms and participatory democracy to the cobreros' municipal community due to its racial standing. In fact, any political freedom implicitly recognized through the Freedom Edict of 1800 was eroded and eventually rescinded by the 1840s under a harsher colonial regime and the arrival of new globalizing actors to town.

Another related direction in which the study of the cobreros' legal action led me was into a close examination of the concept of local nativeness or *naturaleza* that these racially mixed subjects pressed on the court from below. Modern scholars have mostly examined the meaning and use of this notion at the supralocal scale of the (imagined) modern nation or of general Spanish or American (creole) identifications, or even of Indigeneity at large. Instead, in this book I explored the possible meanings of nativeness at the local municipal level and the category's potential for social, political, and legal mobilization by racialized colonial subjects such as the cobreros. I argued that because there were no legal precedents for African descendant or racially mixed pueblos in colonial law, the cobreros' case as natives of a municipal locality ambiguously straddled the plural legal regimes on which Spanish and Indian republics were based.

Based on a notion of natality and belonging in a local political community that went back to medieval and early modern times, the concept of local *naturaleza* or nativeness was a pillar of identity widespread throughout the Spanish Atlantic world. The strong bonds of solidarity and belonging that nativeness allegedly produced were naturalized as affective bonds of "love," solidarity, and obligation not unlike the alleged "natural" bonds of family and kinship. This naturalization of social bonds of belonging also entailed – and naturalized, so to speak – legal and political rights and duties that varied throughout the Spanish Atlantic. In *From*

Colonial Cuba to Madrid, I showed how the cobreros and their letrados mobilized this term (associated to municipal community) and linked it to specific rights such as collective freedom, litigation in common, self-representation, control over common resources such as land, and staying put in the place of birth. The mobilization of this identification by Afro descendant subjects was an assertion of their right to belong to the pueblo of their birth and residence with local citizenship rights and duties to each other as a community within the larger imperial state.

Although the situation and claims of the cobreros as natives of a pueblo of their own was sui generis, the centrality of the category of local nativeness in this case raises general questions about how other racialized subjects living in more racially diverse Spanish cities and municipalities may have invoked their standing as natives of, say, Santiago, Sancti Spíritus, or Bayamo to make claims too. Or, in the cobreros case, how the identity was deployed decades later against the arrival of *colonos* (settlers) and *extranjeros* (foreigners), especially regarding land. There is here an important social and political category of belonging at the local level of municipalities that calls for greater scholarly attention.

The case of El Cobre revealed yet other uses of the notion of nativeness in the Spanish empire, however. In the overseas empire, nativeness also had the connotation of Indianness or Indigeneity, a usage that was also insinuated in the cobreros' court briefs and memorials and that added another layer of ambiguity to the case. In this formulation, the natives of El Cobre were like colonial Indian native subjects, rather than slaves, Afro descendants, or racially mixed people in the plural legal regime of empire. In colonial law, Indians had individual civil freedom and could constitute semi-autonomous Indian republics; they also had rights to common land by virtue of belonging to these republics. The case for the cobreros' alleged partial Indian ancestry through blood, birth, or co-residence in what may have once been an Indian locality could have implicitly given them access to Indian legal standing, thereby expanding the reach of established Indian law. If in a pre-Hispanic past an Indian community had preceded the (colonial) site of El Cobre, the argument went, the arrival of other groups such as African slaves to work the mines made the descendants of all groups born, co-residing, and perhaps intermarrying in El Cobre natives of the pueblo and beholden to the same rights. In this formulation, racial mixture, genealogical confusion, birth, and co-residence were all used to claim Indian ancestry and its related rights (and to a lesser extent its burdens).

Although Indian standing indicated subordinate colonial status and burdens of labor and tribute, it also ensured corporate-held land, a legal protection that many communities regarded as a desirable right. Because the cobreros' standing as subordinate colonial subjects of color made their status closer to that of Indians than to Spaniards, the application of Indian law to their case seemed more feasible. The Freedom Edict of 1800 basically bridged colonial plural law to recognize the emancipated cobreros as a corporate community with common land and limited self-rule – but also with labor burdens – by applying colonial Indian law to them. But as scholars have recently shown, Indian laws were subject to further negotiation and disputation in many Indian republics throughout the empire at the time and throughout subsequent decades in the nineteenth century.

A general examination of the cases of the Indian pueblos of El Caney and Jiguaní took this investigation a step further in relation to the politics of native standing, racial classifications, and the play of plural legal regimes in this region of the Spanish empire. The natives of these two formally recognized Indian villages were also racially mixed subjects claiming Indian racial ancestry despite their fading Indian blood, a confusion that may have helped the ambiguous claims to Indian ancestry and rights made by the cobreros. My inquiry probed the racial confusions involved in determining Indian status in these communities. It also disclosed the pressure these communities came under to dismantle as Indian pueblos in the early nineteenth century, a trend that also had echoes in other localities of the former Spanish empire where postcolonial quasi liberal regimes sought to dissolve plural legal orders. The cobreros fought a similar battle for corporate land and community political rights but ultimately did so from a different racial position. The study of El Cobre and these other communities with Indian standing raises myriad potential questions regarding the possible social, legal, and political meanings that the local term of nativeness could take among racialized colonial subjects in the Spanish empire to make claims and shows that the term constitutes an important and dynamic category of historical analysis in need of closer local study in the Spanish Atlantic world.

Finally, another groundbreaking aspect of the collective legal action examined in this book was the trans local, trans regional and transoceanic character of these colonial subordinate subjects' mobilization through the courts and the political significance of this kind of mobilization in an absolutist regime with an extremely restricted civil society. Networks of communication and action in this case spanned from El Cobre to Madrid, including Santiago, Havana, and other towns in colonial Cuba. Cobrero litigants took their case directly to the highest court of empire, where colonial subjects of color were not supposed to venture on their own. At both ends of the web, cobreros acted as apoderados or legal representatives of the community thereby showing a remarkable capacity for autonomous and collective action through the judicial system. Solidarity was enacted through shared political and financial resources.

Because of their previous informal organization as a pueblo, the plaintiffs of El Cobre were able to act more powerfully in a communal way, a possibility not open to most African descendants in the Spanish empire. In this sense, their collective judicial mobilization was closer to that of Indian subjects living in corporate communities than to that of other Afro descendant free or enslaved subjects in the empire. However, acting communally in court was a controversial enactment of the cobreros' claimed native and corporate standing. In any case, the role that Gregorio Cosme played in Madrid as apoderado of his community seems unprecedented even in the cases of the few Indigenous and Mestizo litigants that we know about. In some ways, Cosme redefined the role of a subordinate colonial apoderado by direct representation of his native community in the imperial court.

In El Cobre's case, triangulation of the conflict through litigation at the colonial and imperial levels enabled a more complex political dynamic beyond the usual binary of colonizers and colonized or masters and slaves. Although imperial court rulings regarding the privatization of the mines and the attendant enslavement of former royal slave cobreros converged with colonial private slaveholders' interests and colonial officials' implementation of imperial mandates during the 1780s, by the 1790s new global geopolitical factors that included international warfare and the absence of a mining revival in El Cobre motivated a shift in imperial policy in favor of the cobreros' emancipation. However, despite the security issues at hand, royal officials in the colony resisted imperial orders and tried to protect slaveholders' alleged rights to the enslaved cobreros. The triangulation of the conflict opened a space for the cobreros' mobilization and eventually worked to their advantage in the 1790s.

The cobreros mobilized for freedom not only through the judicial system. They also did so, especially after the mid 1790s, through extrajudicial actions such as marronage. I argued that both forms of political mobilization, judicial and extrajudicial, became strongly intertwined in this case. My situational approach suggests that neither legal action nor marronage would have made the Freedom Edict of 1800 possible on their own and that the force of these mobilizations was also contingent on political factors such as the Crown's mining policy imperatives and the security concerns in the context of global conflict with republican France, Saint Domingue and later Britain during the 1790s. Similarly, the afterlife of the Edict of 1800 was also contingent on Atlantic, imperial and colonial forces and economic interests at play in Cuba's eastern region during the first half of the nineteenth century. Local, colonial, imperial, and global forces interacted in unforeseen ways. I have approached their interaction from the prism of the local that El Cobre's case makes possible.

In short, as the title of this book suggests, this study has mainly focused on the meanings of freedom presented in this remarkable collective legal action at the end of the eighteenth century, a time when the notion of freedom was expanding and garnering increasing discursive force in the Age of Transformations and Revolutions. The cobreros litigated a proposal of collective freedom linked to the notion of local native belonging at the municipal level, a pervasive, yet still insufficiently understood category and form of belonging throughout the Spanish Atlantic until the nineteenth century and beyond as I have pointed out in this study. Although the category could take on different meaning at various levels, this study has emphasized the importance of probing its usages at the municipal level, particularly in the case of colonial racial subjects excluded from wider notions of Spanishness and Indianness. Yet, even as other levels and meanings of nativeness (as the greater nation) became dominant and displaced municipal level iterations, the latter retained their force in many localities of the former Spanish empire in subsequent decades.

I want to end this book by making reference to recent manifestations of municipal belonging and collective rights, including communal landholding rights, that have emerged in various Latin American nations at the end of the twentieth century. Since the 1980s and '90s, the general turn in these countries from authoritarian rule to democratic regimes has seen the emergence of social and political movements advocating multicultural and pluri-national legal regimes of citizenship and using global human rights discourse to ground these claims. Some movements have called for decentralization of national level governments and more participatory forms of democracy grounded at the local municipal level, effectively along corporate traditions from early modern and colonial times.

Although collective rights based on notions of Indigeneity as cultural difference or customary norms have been generally recognized by the state and the public for Indigenous people, Afro descendant citizens (as was the case with El Cobre) have met with more difficulties in generating normative justifications for collective rights. The recently minted constitutions of Columbia (1991) and Ecuador (1998) are among the charters offering more constitutional protections and collective rights to Afro descendant citizens.[1] In Colombia, however, and probably elsewhere, Afro descendant citizens are divided between, on the one hand, those favoring increased participation in traditional national politics even as they call for greater access to resources and, on the other, those supporting more "ethno-cultural" goals linked to identity, local territory, and autonomy from the national state. Citizens in the first group oppose the codification of special rights for Afro descendants because they consider that the measure treats Blacks "as Indians" and they prefer to integrate into the nation-state as "Colombians" (or as natives of the greater nation of Columbia).

Afro Colombians in the second group are largely located in the Pacific Coast. Although they do not deny Columbian national citizenship, they stress local nativeness and seek incorporation as autonomous municipal bodies with formal title of communal land (as natives of El Cobre in the late eighteenth and early nineteenth centuries did).[2] Some of these Afro descendant local communities, like Indigenous ones, have redefined themselves in modern times as environmentalists and portray themselves as stewards of communal natural resources in their local territory. As advocates of sustainable development, they also oppose large extractive industries such as mining and they fight encroachment on their territory by large landowners from the private sector. Stressing local autonomy rights and the right to consultation, these communities also oppose state-backed public utility projects such as the construction of the Pan American highway through their territory. Although they mobilize through their own cultural and political organizations in civil society, they also make active use of the courts to make claims and protect rights. Moreover, women now take on prominent roles as local activists and leaders in these communities.

[1] Van Cott, *The Friendly Liquidation of the Past*, 258. See also Hooker, "Indigenous Inclusion/Black Exclusion, and *Race*."

[2] Van Cott, *The Friendly Liquidation of the Past*, 95–98.

The current vice-president of Colombia, Francia Márquez, local activist and winner of the Goldman Environmental Prize in 2018 for stopping illegal gold mining in her community and protecting water resources, headed one such group called "Soy Porque Somos" (I Am Because We Are). The movement's name speaks to the "natural" community bonds that prop up the individual self in this collective formulation of local nativeness that also coexists with notions of belonging to the greater nation. Although according to Márquez, the notion proceeds from an African communal philosophy termed "Ubuntu," it is not far from the notion of local nativeness and the bonds of love among local natives from the place of birth and residence found in the *Siete Partidas* and examined in this book. When journalist Carolina Sarín asked Márquez to explain what place meant to her ("you feel more from there than I from here [Bogotá], and I would like to understand that"), Márquez referred to the local practice in her community of burying the umbilical cord of a newly born infant in the land thereby creating a bond to the place where one was born and to which one belongs. She parsed further the local meaning of her movement putting an environmental spin on the land connection: "We are not if mother earth is not, I am not if you are not, and we construct ourselves collectively and this is very important ... We think as an extensive family, because everyone in the Pacific region feels like that, ... [we are like] cousins, and the elders [like] uncles and aunts, even if there are no blood ties ... [it is] being from a place and being with others."[3] She then projected this affective and social ideology of local nativeness to the greater nation of Colombia still so turned apart by violence.

Elsewhere, Márquez referred to the "Ley 70," which is enabling her community to consolidate itself legally but "we have not been able to exercise self-government yet as we want to, but that is part of the process."[4] Looking into the past, she remarked that in the Afro descendant settlements: "We are raised defending our territory. There have always been territorial conflicts in this territory with the slave run haciendas, the slave run mines [in the past] ... we are nothing without territory, territory is our reason for being as a pueblo and as a community. That is why when

[3] Interview of Francia Márquez Mina by Carolina Sanín in "Mesa Capital," "Dominio Público" program, ca. April 27, 2021. The interview begins at 16:20 and the discussion on place and community in 21:20–29:00, https://m.facebook.com/CanalCapitalOficial/videos/930509294383153/?locale2=ur_PK.

[4] Interview of Francia Márquez, "Perspectivas" Universidad del Cauca. https://www.youtube.com/watch?v=5e_lOxXnHwc.

they displace them, they destroy their culture, they destroy them as a pueblo."[5] Turning to the present she counterposes the (capitalist) developmentalist rationale based on extraction and accumulation from these territories to a human-based one grounded on the well-being of the people who belong to the territory and own it. The cobreros faced that conflict between the Bourbon Crown's extractive project of exploiting the mines, the private sector property rights over land and persons, and the cobreros' human-based bonds and rights to live in El Cobre as natives of a pueblo.

The projects and conflicts of the past are not completely past. They reemerge in new guises in other times and places. Notions of local nativeness and local forms of political autonomy are still important for many. There is no teleology of modernity that eradicates them. People still mobilize in terms of these identifications and make claims through them. Local notions of nativeness also coexist and mix with notions of belonging to the greater nation in many places in Latin America and elsewhere. And looking toward the future, they can also coexist, overlap, and alternate with even more encompassing and ecologically based ("terrestrial") notions of belonging to our native planet.[6]

[5] Ibid. [6] Latour, *Down to Earth*.

References

Ablavsky, Gregory. "Making Indians 'White': The Judicial Abolition of Native Slavery in Revolutionary Virginia and Its Racial Legacy." *University of Pennsylvania Law Review* 159 (2011): 1457–1531.

Aguirre, Carlos. *Agentes de su propia libertad: Los esclavos de Lima y la desintegración de la esclavitud: 1821–1854*. Lima: Pontificia Universidad Católica, 1993.

Amores, Juan B. *Cuba en la época de Ezpeleta, 1785–1790*. Pamplona: Ediciones Universidad de Navarra, 2000.

Anderson, Benedict. *Imagined Communities: Reflections on the Origin and Spread of Nationalism*. London: Verso, 1983.

Andrew, N., and N. Cleven. "Ministerial Order of José de Gálvez Establishing a Uniform Duty on the Importation of Negro Slaves into the Indies; and Convention between Spain and the United Provinces Regulating the Return of Deserters and Fugitives in Their American Colonies." *Hispanic American Historical Review* 4, no. 2 (May 1, 1921): 266–76.

Andrews, George Reid. *Afro-Latin America, 1800–2000*. New York: Oxford University Press, 2004.

Aptheker, Herbert. *Nat Turner's Slave Rebellion: Including the 1831 "Confessions."* Mineola, NY: Dover, 2006.

Araujo, Ana Lucía. *Reparations for Slavery and the Slave Trade: A Transnational and Comparative History*. New York: Bloomsbury Academic, 2017.

Arrelucea Barrantes, Maribel. "Slavery, Writing, and Female Resistance: Black Women Litigants in Lima's Late Colonial Tribunals of the 1780s." In *Afro-Latino Voices: Narratives from the Early Modern Ibero-Atlantic World, 1550–1812*, edited by Kathryn J. McKnight and Leo J. Garofalo, 285–301. Indianapolis, IN: Hackett, 2009.

Arrom, Silvia. *The Women of Mexico City, 1790–1857*. Stanford, CA: Stanford University Press, 1985.

Avery, David. *Not on Queen Victoria's Birthday: The Story of the Rio Tinto Mines*. London: Collins, 1974.

Bacardí Moreau, Emilio. *Crónicas de Santiago de Cuba.* Tomo 1. Barcelona: Tipografía de Carbonell y Esteva, 1908.

Barbier, Jacques. "The Culmination of Bourbon Reforms, 1787–1792." *Hispanic American Historical Review* 57, no. 1 (February 1977): 51–68.

Barcia, Manuel. *The Great African Slave Revolt of 1825: Cuba and the Fight for Freedom in Matanzas.* Baton Rouge: Louisiana State University Press, 2012.

Barrett, Elinore M. *The Mexican Colonial Copper Industry.* Albuquerque: University of New Mexico Press, 1987.

Beckles, Hilary. *Britain's Black Debt: Reparations for Caribbean Slavery and Native Genocide.* Kingston, Jamaica: University of West Indies Press, 2013.

Belmonte, José Luis. *Ser esclavo en Santiago de Cuba: Espacios de poder y negociación en un contexto de expansión y crisis, 1780–1803.* Madrid: Ediciones Doce Calles, 2011.

Bennett, Herman L. *Africans in Colonial Mexico: Absolutism, Christianity, and Afro-Creole Consciousness, 1570–1640.* Bloomington: Indiana University Press, 2003.

Borah, Woodrow. *Justice by Insurance: The General Indian Court of Colonial Mexico and the Legal Aids of the Half-Real.* Berkeley: University of California Press, 1983.

Borrego Plá, María del Carmen. *Palenques de negros en Cartagena de Indias a fines del siglo XVII.* Seville: Publicaciones de la Escuela de Estudios Hispano-Americanos de Sevilla, 1973.

Borucki, Alex. *From Shipmates to Soldiers: Emerging Black Identities in the Río de la Plata.* Albuquerque: University of New Mexico Press, 2015.

Brading, David. A. *Miners and Merchants in Bourbon Mexico 1763–1810.* New York: Cambridge University Press, 1971.

The First America: The Spanish Monarchy, Creole Patriots, and the Liberal State 1492–1867. New York: Cambridge University Press, 1991.

Brooks, Roy L. *Atonement and Forgiveness: A New Model for Black Reparations.* Berkeley: University of California Press, 2004.

Bryant, Sherwin K. "Enslaved Rebels, Fugitives, and Litigants: The Resistance Continuum in Colonial Quito." *Colonial Latin American Review* 13, no. 1 (October 21, 2010): 7–46.

Burkholder, Mark A. "The Council of the Indies in the Late Eighteenth Century: A New Perspective." *Hispanic American Historical Review* 56 (August 1976): 404–23.

Burns, Kathryn. *Into the Archive: Writing and Power in Colonial Peru.* Durham, NC: Duke University Press, 2010.

Cáceres Gómez, Rina. "La Puebla de los Pardos en el siglo XVII." *Revista de Historia* 34 (July 1996): 83–113.

Campos, Clarissa, and Miguel A. Martínez. "Squatting Activism in Brazil and Spain: Articulations between the Right to Housing and the Right to the City." In *Comparative Approaches to Informal Housing Around the Globe,* edited by Udo Grashoff, 110–29. London: UCL Press, 2020.

Cañizares-Esguerra, Jorge. *How to Write the History of the New World: Histories, Epistemologies, and Identities in the Eighteenth-Century Atlantic World.* Stanford, CA: Stanford University Press, 2001.

Caplan, Karen D. *Indigenous Citizens: Local Liberalism in Early National Oaxaca and Yucatan*. Stanford, CA: Stanford University Press, 2009.

"Indigenous Citizenship: Liberalism, Political Participation, and Ethnic Identity in Post-Independence Oaxaca and Yucatan." In *Imperial Subjects: Race and Identity in Colonial Latin America*, edited by Mathew O'Hara and Andrew Fisher, 225–47. Durham, NC: Duke University Press, 2009.

Carabalí Angola, Alexis. "Los afronortearaucanos: de la autonomía a la miseria. Un caso de doble reparación?" In *Afro-reparaciones: Memorias de la Esclavitud y Justicia Reparativa para negros, afrocolombianos y raizales*, edited by Claudia Mosquera Rosero-Labbé and Luiz Claudio Barcelos, 389–403. Bogotá: Panamericana Formas e Impresos S.A., 2007.

Carroll, Patrick J. "Mandinga: The Evolution of a Mexican Runaway Slave Community, 1735–1827." *Comparative Studies in Society and History* 19, no. 4 (October 1977): 488–505.

Castañeda Fuertes, Digna. "Demandas judiciales de las esclavas en el siglo XIX cubano." *Mujeres iberoamericanas: historia y cultura, siglos XIX y XXI* (1997): 221–30.

Castro, Concepción de. *La revolución liberal y los municipios españoles (1812–1868)*. Madrid: Alianza Editorial, 1979.

Chang, David A. *The Color of the Land: Race, Nation and the Politics of Landownership in Oklahoma, 1832–1929*. Chapel Hill: University of North Carolina Press, 2010.

Chaves, María Eugenia. *Honor y libertad: Discursos y recursos en la estrategia de libertad de una mujer esclava (Guayaquil a fines del período colonial)*. Gothenburg, Sweden: Departamento de Historia e Instituto Iberoamericano de la Universidad de Gotemburgo, 2001.

María Chiquinquirá Díaz: Una esclava del siglo XVIII: Acerca de las identidades de amo y esclavo en el puerto colonial de Guayaquil. Guayaquil, Ecuador: Archivo Histórico del Guayas, 1998.

"Slave Women's Strategies for Freedom and the Late Spanish Colonial State." In *Hidden Histories of Gender and the State in Latin America*, edited by Elizabeth Dore and Maxine Molyneux, 108–26. Durham, NC: Duke University Press, 2000.

Childs, Matt D. *The 1812 Aponte Rebellion in Cuba and the Struggle against Atlantic Slavery*. Chapel Hill: University of North Carolina Press, 2006.

Chira, Adriana. "Affective Debts: Manumission by Grace and the Making of Gradual Emancipation Laws in Cuba, 1817–68." *Law and History Review* 36, no. 1 (February 2018): 1–33.

Patchwork Freedoms: Law, Slavery, and Race beyond Cuba's Plantations. New York: Cambridge University Press, 2022.

Clarkson, Thomas. *An Essay on the Slavery and Commerce of the Human Species, Particularly the African*. Whitefish, MT: Kessinger, 1786.

Clifford, James. *Returns: On Becoming Indigenous in the Twenty First Century*. Cambridge, MA: Harvard University Press, 2013.

Coates, Ta-Nehisi. "The Case for Reparations." *The Atlantic*, June 2014. www.theatlantic.com/magazine/archive/2014/06/the-case-for-reparations/361631/.

"Ta-Nehisi Coates Revisits the Case for Reparations." *New Yorker*, June 10, 2019. www.newyorker.com/news/the-new-yorker-interview/ta-nehisi-coates-revisits-the-case-for-reparations.

Cooper, Frederick. *Colonialism in Question: Theory, Knowledge, History*. Berkeley: University of California Press, 2005.

Costner, Charlotte. *The Golden Leaf: How Tobacco Shaped Cuba and the Atlantic World*. Nashville: Vanderbilt University Press, 2015.

Couso, Javier A., Alexandra Huneeus, and Rachel Sieder, eds. *Cultures of Legality: Judicialization and Political Activism in Latin America*. Cambridge: Cambridge University Press, 2010.

Cowen, David and Lorna Fox O'Mahoney. "Unlawful Occupation of Land: Squatting and Adverse Possession." In *Great Debates in Land Law*. 2nd ed., edited by Dave Cowen et al., 113–33. New York: Palgrave, 2016.

Curtin, Philip D. *The Atlantic Slave Trade: A Census*. Madison: University of Wisconsin Press, 1969.

Cutter, Charles. *The Legal Culture of Northern New Spain, 1700–1810*. Albuquerque: University of New Mexico Press, 1995.

The Protector de Indios in Colonial New Mexico, 1659–1821. Albuquerque: University of New Mexico Press, 1986.

de la Cadena, Marisol. *Indigenous Mestizos: The Politics of Race and Culture in Cuzco, Peru, 1919–1991*. Durham, NC: Duke University Press, 2000.

de la Fuente, Alejandro, and Ariela J. Gross. *Becoming Free, Becoming Black: Race, Freedom, and Law in Cuba, Virginia, and Louisiana*. Cambridge: Cambridge University Press, 2020.

"Slave Law and Claims-Making in Cuba: The Tannenbaum Debate Revisited." *Law and History Review* 22, no. 2 (Summer 2004): 339–69.

"Slaves and the Creation of Legal Rights in Cuba: Coartación and Papel." *Hispanic American Historical Review* 87, no. 4 (November 1, 2007): 659–92.

de la Pezuela, Jacobo. *Diccionario Geográfico, Estadístico Histórico de la Isla de Cuba*. Vol. 2. Madrid: Imprenta del Establecimiento de Mellado, 1863.

de la Puente Luna, José Carlos. *Andean Cosmopolitans: Seeking Justice and Reward at the Spanish Royal Court*. Austin: University of Texas Press, 2018.

de Olivares, José, and William Smith Bryan. *Our Islands and Their People as Seen with Camara and Pencil*. Vol. 1. St. Louis: N. D. Thompson, 1899.

de Solano, Francisco, and Agustín Guimerá, eds. *Esclavitud y derechos humanos: La lucha por la libertad del negro en el siglo XIX*. Madrid: Consejo Superior de Investigaciones Científicas, Grafipren, S.A, 1986.

Deschamps-Chapeaux, Pedro. *El negro en la economía habanera del siglo XIX*. Havana: Unión de Escritores y Artistas de Cuba, 1971.

Los batallones de pardos y morenos libres. Havana: Editorial Arte y Literatura, Instituto Cubano del Libro, 1976.

Díaz de Espada y Landa, Juan José. "Informe sobre diezmos." In *Esclavitud y sociedad: Notas y documentos para la historia de la esclavitud negra en Cuba*, edited by Eduardo Torres-Cuevas and Eusebio Reyes, 103–18. Havana: Editorial de Ciencias Sociales, 1986.

Díaz, María Elena. "Beyond Tannenbaum." *Law and History Review* 22, no. 2 (Summer 2004): 371–76.

"Mining Women, Royal Slaves: Copper Mining in Colonial Cuba, 1670–1780." In *Mining Women: Gender in the Development of a Global Industry, 1670 to 2005*, edited by Laurie Mercier and Jaclyn J. Gier, 21–39. New York: Palgrave Macmillan, 2006.

"Of Life and Freedom in the (Tropical) Hearth: El Cobre, Cuba: 1709–73." In *Beyond Bondage: Free Women of Color in the Americas*, edited by David Barry Gaspar and Darlene Clark Hine, 19–36. Urbana: University of Illinois Press, 2004.

"Rethinking Tradition and Identity: The Virgin of Charity of El Cobre." In *Cuba, the Elusive Nation: Interpretations of National Identity*, edited by Damián J. Fernández and Madeline Cámara Betancourt, 43–59. Gainesville: University Press of Florida, 2000.

The Virgin, the King, and the Royal Slaves of El Cobre: Negotiating Freedom in Colonial Cuba, 1670–1780. Stanford, CA: Stanford University Press, 2000.

"To Live as a *Pueblo*: A Contentious Endeavor, El Cobre, Cuba, 1670s–1790s." In *Afro-Latino Voices: Narratives from the Early Modern Ibero-Atlantic World, 1550–1812*, edited by Kathryn J. McKnight and Leo J. Garofalo, 126–41. Indianapolis, IN: Hackett, 2009.

Domínguez Ortiz, Antonio. *Sociedad y Estado en el siglo XVIII español*. Barcelona: Ariel, 1976.

Dubois, Laurent. *A Colony of Citizens: Revolution and Slave Emancipation in the French Caribbean, 1787–1804*. Chapel Hill: University of North Carolina, 2004.

Avengers of the New World: The Story of the Haitian Revolution. Cambridge, MA: Harvard University Press, 2004.

Dueñas, Alcira. *Indians and Mestizos in the "Lettered City": Reshaping Justice, Social Hierarchy, and Political Culture in Colonial Peru*. Boulder: University Press of Colorado, 2010.

Eakin, Marshall C. *British Enterprise in Brazil: The St. John d'el Rey Mining Company and the Morro Velho Gold Mine, 1830–1960*. Durham, NC: Duke University Press, 1989.

Echeverri, Marcela. *Indian and Slave Royalists in the Age of Revolution: Reform, Revolution, and Royalism in the Northern Andes, 1780–1825*. New York: Cambridge University Press, 2016.

Edwards, Laura F. *The People and Their Peace: Legal Culture and the Transformation of Inequality in the Post- Revolutionary South*. Chapel Hill: University of North Carolina Press, 2009.

Erakat, Noura. *Justice for Some: Law and the Question of Palestine*. Stanford, CA: Stanford University Press, 2019.

Ferrer, Ada. *Cuba: An American History*. New York: Scribner, 2021.

Freedom's Mirror: Cuba and Haiti in the Age of Revolution. New York: Cambridge University Press, 2014.

Finch, Aisha K. *Rethinking Slave Rebellion in Cuba: La Escalera and the Insurgents of 1841–1844*. Chapel Hill: University of North Carolina Press, 2015.

Fisher, John R. *Silver Mines and Silver Miners in Colonial Peru, 1776–1824*. Liverpool: Centre for Latin-American Studies, University of Liverpool, 1977.

Flin, Briana. "Growing Up Undocumented When Your Siblings Are Citizens." *The Atlantic*, August 22, 2018. www.theatlantic.com/politics/archive/2018/08/undocumented-children-mixed-status-families/567610/.

Franco, José. Luciano,. *Las minas de Santiago del Prado y la rebelión de los cobreros, 1530–1800*. Havana: Editorial Ciencias Sociales, 1975.

García Rodríguez, Gloria. *Voices of the Enslaved in Nineteenth Century Cuba*. Chapel Hill: University of North Carolina Press, 2011.

"Impact of the French and Haitian Revolution." In *The Impact of the Haitian Revolution in the Atlantic World*, edited by David P. Geggus, 3–9. Columbia: University of South Carolina Press, 2001.

"Slavery, War, and Revolution in the Greater Caribbean, 1780–1815." In *A Turbulent Time: The French Revolution and the Greater Caribbean*, edited by David B. Gaspar and David P. Geggus, 1–150. Bloomington: Indiana University Press, 1997.

"Slave Resistance in the Spanish Caribbean." In *A Turbulent Time: The French Revolution and the Greater Caribbean*, edited by David B. Gaspar and David P. Geggus, 131–55. Bloomington: Indiana University Press, 1997.

Genovese, Eugene D. *From Rebellion to Revolution: Afro-American Slave Revolts in the Making of the Modern World*. Baton Rouge: Louisiana State University Press, 1979.

Glissant, Edouard. *Caribbean Discourse*. Charlottesville: University Press of Virginia, 1989.

Gómez de la Serna, Ramón. *Historia de la Puerta del Sol*. Madrid: Almarabu, 1996.

Goodman, David C. *Power and Penury: Government, Technology and Sciencein Philip II's Spain*. Cambridge: Cambridge University Press, 1988.

González Díaz, Antonio Manuel. *La esclavitud en Ayamonte durante el Antiguo Régimen*. Huelva, Spain: Diputación Provincial de Huelva, 1997.

González Enciso, Ignacio, and Rafael Torres Sánchez, eds. *Tabaco y economía en el siglo XVIII*. Pamplona: Ediciones de la Universidad de Navarra, 1999.

González Loscertales, Vicente, and Inés Roldán de Montaud. "La minería del cobre en Cuba. Su organización, problemas administrativos y repercusiones sociales (1828–1849)." *Revista de Indias* 40 (January 1, 1980): 255–99.

Gordon, Jane Anna. "The Limitations and Possibilities of Freedom as Flight: Engaging Neil Roberts's Freedom as Marronage." *Theory & Event* 20, no. 1 (2017): 182–87.

Graubart, Karen. "Pesa más la libertad: Slavery, Legal Claims, and the History of Afro-Latin American Ideas." *The William and Mary Quarterly* 78, no. 3 (July 2021): 427–58.

Republics of Difference: Religious and Racial Self-Governance in the Spanish Atlantic World. New York: Oxford University Press, 2022.

"'So color de una cofradía': Catholic Confraternities and the Development of Afro- Peruvian Ethnicities in Early Colonial Peru." *Slavery and Abolition* 33, no. 1 (2012): 43–64.

Grinberg, Keila. *A Black Jurist in a Slave Society: Antonio Pereira Reboucas and the Trials of Brazilian Citizenship*. Chapel Hill: University of North Carolina Press, 2019.

"Freedom Suits and Civil Law in Brazil and the United States." *Slavery & Abolition* 22, no. 3 (2001): 66–82.

Liberata, a lei da ambigüidade: As ações de liberdade da corte de apelação do Rio de Janeiro no século XIX. Rio de Janeiro: Relume Dumará, 1994.

"Slavery, Manumission and the Law in Nineteenth-Century Brazil: Reflections on the Law of 1831 and the 'Principle of Liberty' on the Southern Frontier of the Brazilian Empire." *European Review of History* 16, no. 3 (June 2009): 401–11.

Gross, Ariela. "Beyond Black and White: Cultural Approaches to Race and Slavery." *Columbia Law Review* 101, no. 3 (April 2001): 640–90.

What Blood Won't Tell: A History of Race on Trial in America. Cambridge, MA: Harvard University Press, 2008.

Helg, Aline. *Slave No More: Self-Liberation before Abolitionism in the Americas*. Chapel Hill: University of North Carolina Press, 2019.

Hernández Cuevas, Marco Polo. "The Mexican Colonial Term 'Chino' Is a Referent of Afrodescendant." *Journal of Pan African Studies* 5, no. 5 (June 2012): 124–43.

Herzog, Tamar. *Defining Nations: Immigrants and Citizens in Early Modern Spain and Spanish America*. New Haven, CT: Yale University Press, 2003.

"The Appropriation of Native Status: Forming and Reforming Insiders and Outsiders in the Spanish Colonial World." *Rechtsgeschichte Legal History* 22 (2014): 140–49.

"The Colonial Expansion and the Making of Nations: The Spanish Case." In *History of Nationhood and Nationalism*. Vol 1., edited by Cathie Carmichael, Mathew D'Auria and Ariel Roshwald, 145–62. Cambridge: Cambridge University Press, 2022.

Upholding Justice: Society, State and the Penal System in Quito (1650–1750). Ann Arbor: University of Michigan Press, 2004.

Hooker, Juliet. "Indigenous Inclusion/Black Exclusion: Race, Ethnicity and Multicultural Citizenship in Latin America." *Journal of Latin American Studies* 37, no. 2 (May 2005): 285–310.

Race and the Politics of Solidarity. New York: Oxford University Press, 2009.

Howard, Philip A. *Changing History: Afro-Cuban Cabildos and Societies of Color in the Nineteenth Century*. Baton Rouge: Louisiana State University Press, 1998.

Hunefeldt, Christine. *Paying the Price of Freedom: Family and Labor among Lima's Slaves, 1800–1854*. Berkeley: University of California Press, 1994.

Irisarri Aguirre, Ana. "El informe del obispo Joaquín de Osés y Alzúa: Un intento ilustrado de promocionar el oriente cubano." *Temas Americanistas*, no. 16 (2003): 81–95.

Jennings, Evelyn P. "Paths to Freedom: Imperial Defense and Manumission in Havana, 1762–1800." In *Paths to Freedom: Manumission in the Atlantic World*, edited by Rosemary Brana-Shute and Randy J. Sparks, 121–42. Columbia: University of South Carolina Press, 2009.

Jensen, Larry R. *Children of Colonial Despotism: Press, Politics, and Culture in Cuba, 1790–1840*. Tampa: University of South Florida Press, 1988.

Johnson, Lyman. "Manumission in Colonial Buenos Aires, 1776–1810." *Hispanic American Historical Review* 59, no. 2 (1979): 258–79.

Johnson, Sherry. *The Social Transformation of Eighteenth Century Cuba*. Gainesville: University Press of Florida, 2001.

Johnson, Walter. *Soul by Soul: Life Inside the Antebellum Slave Market*. Cambridge, MA: Harvard University Press, 1999.

Jones, Martha S. *Birthright Citizens: A History of Race and Rights in Antebellum America*. New York: Cambridge University Press, 2018.

Kagan, Richard L. *Lawsuits and Litigants in Castile, 1500–1700*. Chapel Hill: University of North Carolina Press, 1981.

Katzew, Ilona. *Casta Painting: Images of Race in Eighteenth-Century Mexico*. New Haven, CT: Yale University Press, 2004.

Kellog, Susan, and Ethelia Ruiz Medrano, eds. *Negotiation within Domination: New Spain's Indian Pueblos Confront the Spanish State*. Boulder: University Press of Colorado, 2010.

Knight, Franklin W. *Slave Society in Cuba during the Nineteenth Century*. Madison: University of Wisconsin Press, 1970.

Kuethe, Allan J. *Cuba, 1753–1815: Crown, Military, and Society*. Knoxville: University of Tennessee Press, 1986.

"Mining and the Bourbon Reforms: The Entrepeneurs and the State in Eighteenth Century Peru." HAHR 61, No. 2 (1981): 217–38.

La Rosa Corzo, Gabino. *Runaway Slave Settlements in Cuba: Resistance and Repression*. Chapel Hill: University of North Carolina Press, 2003.

Landers, Jane. *Black Society in Spanish Florida*. Champaign: University of Illinois Press, 1999.

"Gracia Real de Santa Teresa de Mose: A Free Black Town in Spanish Colonial Florida." *The American Historical Review* 95, no. 1 (February 1990): 9–30.

Larson, Brooke. *Trials of Nation Making: Liberalism, Race, and Ethnicity in the Andes, 1810–1910*. New York: Cambridge University Press, 2004.

Latour, Bruno. *Down to Earth: Politics in the New Climate Regime*. Cambridge: Polity Press, 2018.

Lavallé, Bernard. *Las promesas ambiguas: Ensayos sobre el criollismo colonial en los Andes*. Lima: Pontificia Universidad Católica del Perú, Instituto Riva-Agüero, 1993.

Littlefield, Daniel F., Jr. *The Cherokee Freedmen: From Emancipation to American Citizenship*. Westport, CT: Greenwood Press, 1978.

Lockhart, James, and Enrique Otte, eds. *Letters and People of the Spanish Indies: Sixteenth Century*. Cambridge: Cambridge University Press, 1976.

López García, José Miguel. *La esclavitud a finales del Antiguo Régimen: Madrid, 1701–1837*. Madrid: Alianza Editorial, 2020.

López García, José Tomás. *Dos defensores de los esclavos negros en el siglo XVII: Francisco José de Jaca y Epifanio de Moirans*. Caracas: Universidad Católica Andrés Bello, 1982.

Lucena Salmoral, Manuel. "El segundo Código negro español, la religión, la humanidad y la tranquilidad y quietud públicas: La crítica realizada en 1788 al Código carolino." *Estudios de Historia Social y Económica de América*, no. 12 (1995): 117–32.

Marina Barba, Jesús. "La reforma municipal de Carlos III en Ciudad Real (1766–1780)." *Chronica Nova* 14 (1984–85): 249–91.

Marrero, Levi. *Cuba: Economía y sociedad*. Vol. 11. San Juan, Puerto Rico: Editorial San Juan, 1972.

Martínez López, Miguel, ed. *The Urban Politics of Squatters' Movements*. New York: Palgrave MacMillan, 2018.

McDaniel, W. Caleb. *Sweet Taste of Liberty: A True Story of Slavery and Restitution in America*. New York: Oxford University Press, 2019.

McKinley, Michelle A. *Fractional Freedoms: Slavery, Intimacy, and Legal Mobilization in Colonial Lima, 1600–1700*. New York: Cambridge University Press, 2016.

McKnight, Kathryn J., and Leo J. Garofalo. "Introduction." In *Afro-Latino Voices: Narratives from the Early Modern Ibero-Atlantic World, 1550–1812*, edited by Kathryn J. McKnight and Leo J. Garofalo, ix–xxii. Indianapolis, IN: Hackett, 2009.

Miles, Tiya. *The House on Diamond Hill: A Cherokee Plantation Story*. Chapel Hill: University of North Carolina Press, 2010.

Ties that Bind: The Story of an Afro-Cherokee Family in Slavery and Freedom. Berkeley: University of California Press, 2006.

More, Anna. *Baroque Sovereignty: Carlos de Sigüenza y Góngora and the Creole Archive of Colonial Mexico*. Philadelphia: University of Pennsylvania Press, 2013.

Moreno Fraginals, Manuel R. *El ingenio: El complejo económico cubano del azúcar*. Cuba: Comisión Nacional Cubana de la UNESCO, 1964.

Morgado García, Arturo. "Zinda (1804), de María Rosa Gálvez de Cabrera y las reflexiones sobre la esclavitud en la España finidieciochesca." In *Mujeres esclavas y abolicionistas en la España de los siglos XVI al XIX*, edited by Aurelia Martín Casares and Rocío Periáñez Gómez, 187–219. Madrid: Iberoamericana Editorial Vervuert, 2014.

Mosquera Rosero-Labbé, Claudia, and Luiz Claudio Barcelos, eds. *Afro-reparaciones: Memorias de la Esclavitud y Justicia Reparativa para negros, afrocolombianos y raizales*. Bogotá: Panamericana Formas e Impresos S.A., 2007.

Murray, David R. *Odious Commerce: Britain, Spain and the Abolition of the Cuban Slave Trade*. Cambridge: Cambridge University Press, 1980.

Nader, Helen. *Liberty in Absolutist Spain: the Habsburg Sale of Towns, 1516–1700*. Baltimore, MD: Johns Hopkins University Press, 1990.

O'Hara, Matthew D. *A Flock Divided: Race, Religion, and Politics in Mexico, 1749–1857*. Durham, NC: Duke University Press, 2009.

O'Malley, Gregory E. *Final Passages: The Intercolonial Slave Trade of British America, 1619–1807*. Williamsburg, VA: Omohundro Institute of Early American History and Culture; Chapel Hill: University of North Carolina Press, 2016.

Ortiz, Fernando. *Contrapunteo cubano del tabaco y el azúcar*. Las Villas: Universidad Central de las Villas, [1947] 1995.

Osorio, F. Eduardo, ed. *Clamor de los indios americanos*. Mérida, Venezuela: Consejo de Publicaciones de la Universidad de los Andes, 1993.

O'Toole, Rachel Sarah. *Bound Lives: Africans, Indians, and the Making of Race in Colonial Peru*. Pittsburgh: University of Pittsburgh Press, 2012.

Owensby, Brian P. *Empire of Law and Indian Justice in Colonial Mexico*. Stanford, CA: Stanford University Press, 2011.

"How Juan and Leonor Won Their Freedom: Litigation and Liberty in Seventeenth Century Mexico." *Hispanic American Historical Review* 85, no. 1 (February 1, 2005): 39–79.

"Legal Personality and the Processes of Slave Liberty in Early-Modern New Spain." *European Review of History: Revue europeenne d'histoire* 16, no. 3 (June 2, 2009): 365–82.

Palacio Atard, Vicente. *Carlos III, el rey de los ilustrados*. Barcelona: Ariel, 2006.

Paquette, Gabriel B. *Enlightenment, Governance, and Reform in Spain and Its Empire, 1759–1808*. London: Palgrave Macmillan, 2008.

Paquette, Robert L. *Sugar Is Made with Blood: The Conspiracy of La Escalera and the Conflict between Empires over Slavery in Cuba*. Middletown, CT: Wesleyan University Press, 1988.

Peabody, Sue, and Keila Grinberg, eds. *Free Soil in the Atlantic World*. New York: Routledge, 2015.

Slavery, Freedom, and the Law in the Atlantic World: A Brief History with Documents. Boston: Bedford/St. Martin's, 2007.

Penry, S. Elizabeth. *The People Are King: The Making of an Indigenous Andean Politics*. New York: Oxford University Press, 2019.

Phelan, John Leddy. *The People and the King: The Comunero Revolution in Colombia, 1781*. Madison: University of Wisconsin Press, 1978.

Pierson, William W. "Francisco de Arango y Parreño." *Hispanic American Historical Review* 16, no. 4 (November 1, 1936): 451–78.

Portuondo Zúñiga, Olga. *Cuba: Constitución y liberalismo (1808–1841)*. Santiago de Cuba: Editorial Oriente, 2008.

La Virgen de la Caridad del Cobre: símbolo de cubanía. Santiago de Cuba: Editorial Oriente, 1995.

Premo, Bianca. *The Enlightenment on Trial: Ordinary Litigants and Colonialism in the Spanish Empire*. New York: Oxford University Press, 2017.

Price, Jacob M. "Summation: The American Panorama of Atlantic Port Cities." In *Atlantic Port Cities: Economy, Culture, and Society in the Atlantic World, 1650–1850*, edited by Franklin W. Knight and Peggy K. Liss, 262–76. Knoxville: University of Tennessee Press, 1991.

Price, Richard, ed. *Maroon Societies: Rebel Slave Communities in the Americas*. Norwell, MA: Anchor Press, 1973.

Randall, Robert W. *Real del Monte: A British Mining Venture in Mexico*. Austin: University of Texas Press, 1972.

Reid-Vazquez, Michele. *The Year of the Lash: Free People of Color in Cuba and the Nineteenth-Century Atlantic World*. Athens: University of Georgia Press, 2011.

Restall, Matthew. *The Black Middle: Africans, Mayas, and Spaniards in Colonial Yucatan*. Stanford, CA: Stanford University Press, 2009.

Roberts, Neil. *Freedom as Marronage*. Chicago: University of Chicago Press, 2015.

Rodríguez Gámez, Odalys, Isabelle Laffont-Shwob, Pascale Prudent, et al. "Assessment of Water Quality from the Blue Lagoon of El Cobre Mine in Santiago de Cuba: A Preliminary Study for Water Reuse." *Environmental Science and Pollution Research* 26, no. 5 (June 2019). doi.org/10.1007/s11356-019-05030-3.

Sachs, Honor. "'Freedom by a Judgement': The Legal History of an Afro-Indian." *Law and History Review* 30, no. 1 (2012): 173–203.

Los códigos negros de la América Española. Alcalá de Henares: Universidad de Alcalá de Henares, 1996.

Saunt, Claudio. *Black, White, and Indian: Race and the Unmaking of an American Family*. New York: Oxford University Press, 2005.

Sartorius, David. *Ever Faithful: Race, Loyalty, and the Ends of Empire in Spanish Cuba*. Durham, NC: Duke University Press, 2013.

Schafer, Judith Kelleher. *Becoming Free, Remaining Free: Manumission and Enslavement in New Orleans, 1846–1862*. Baton Rouge: Louisiana State University Press, 2003.

Schmidt-Nowara, Christopher. *Empire and Antislavery: Spain, Cuba and Puerto Rico, 1833–1874*. Pittsburgh: University of Pittsburgh Press, 1999.

"Still Continents (And an Island) with Two Histories?" *Law and History Review* 22, no. 2 (Summer 2004): 377–82.

Schneider, Elena A. "African Slavery and Spanish Empire: Imperial Imaginings and Bourbon Reform in Eighteenth-Century Cuba and Beyond." *Journal of Early American History* 5, no. 1 (April 6, 2015): 3–29.

The Occupation of Havana: War, Trade, and Slavery in the Atlantic World. Williamsburg, VA: Omohundro Institute of Early American History and Culture; Chapel Hill: University of North Carolina Press, 2018.

Schweninger, Loren. *Appealing for Liberty: Freedom Suits in the South*. New York: Oxford University Press, 2018.

Scott, Julius S. *The Common Wind: Afro-American Currents in the Age of the Haitian Revolution*. London: Verso, 2018.

Scott, Rebecca J., and Carlos Venegas Fornias. "María Coleta and the Capuchin Friar: Slavery, Salvation, and the Adjudication of Status." *The William and Mary Quarterly* 76, no. 4 (October 2019): 727–62.

Scott, Rebecca J., and Jean M. Hébrard. *Freedom Papers: An Atlantic Odyssey in the Age of Emancipation*. Cambridge, MA: Harvard University Press, 2012.

Scott, Rebecca J. "Slavery and the Law in Atlantic Perspective: Jurisdiction, Jurisprudence, and Justice." *Law and History Review* 29, no. 4 (November 2011): 915–24.

"Social Facts, Legal Fictions, and the Attribution of Slave Status: The Puzzle of Prescription." *Law and History Review* 35, no. 1 (February 2017): 9–30.

Slave Emancipation in Cuba: The Transition to Free Labor, 1860–1899. Pittsburgh: University of Pittsburgh Press, 1985.

Seed, Patricia. *To Love, Honor, and Obey in Colonial Mexico: Conflicts over Marriage Choice, 1574–1821*. Stanford, CA: Stanford University Press, 1988.

Sherman, Charles P. "Acquisitive Prescription – Its Existing World-Wide Uniformity." *The Yale Law Journal* 21, no. 2 (December 1911): 147–56.

Sieder, Rachel. "Legal Cultures and the (Un)Rule of Law: Indigenous Rights and Juridification in Guatemala." In *Cultures of Legality: Judicialization and Political Activism in Latin America*, edited by Javier Couso, Alexandra Huneeus, and Rachel Sieder, 161–81. Cambridge: Cambridge University Press, 2010.

Sinha, Manisha. *The Slave's Cause: A History of Abolition*. New Haven, CT: Yale University Press, 2016.

Soto González, Luis. *Apuntes sobre la historia de la minería cubana*. Santiago de Cuba: Editorial Oriente, 1981.

Stern, Steve J. *Peru's Indian Peoples and the Challenge of Spanish Conquest: Huamanga to 1640*. Madison: University of Wisconsin Press, 1982.

Taylor, William B. "Between Global Processes and Local Knowledge: An Inquiry into Early Latin American Social History, 1500–1900." In *Reliving the Past: The Worlds of Social History*, edited by Olivier Zunz, chapter 3. Chapel Hill: University of North Carolina Press, 1985.

"The Foundation of Nuestra Señora de Guadalupe de los Morenos de Amapa." *The Americas* 26, no. 4 (April 1970): 439–46.

Thomas III, William G. *A Question of Freedom: The Families Who Challenged Slavery from the Nation's Founding to the Civil War*. New Haven, CT: Yale University Press, 2020.

Tieney, Brian. *The Idea of Natural Rights: Studies on Natural Rights Natural Law, and Church Law, 1150–1625*. Atlanta: Scholars Press for Emory University, 1997.

Tomba, Massimiliano. *Insurgent Universality: An Alternative Legacy of Modernity*. New York: Oxford University, 2019.

Tomich, Dale. *Through the Prism of Slavery: Labor, Capital, and World Economy*. Lanham, MD: Rowman & Littlefield: 2004.

"The Wealth of Empire: Francisco Arango y Parreño, Political Economy, and the Second Slavery in Cuba." *Comparative Studies in Society and History* 45, no. 1 (January 2003): 4–28.

Tomlins, Christopher. *In the Matter of Nat Turner: A Speculative History*. Princeton, NJ: Princeton University Press, 2020.

Torres-Saillant, Silvio. "The Tribulations of Blackness: Stages in Dominican Racial Identity." *Latin American Perspectives* 25, no. 3 (May 1998): 126–46.

Townsend, Camilla. "Half My Body Free, the Other Half Enslaved: The Politics of the Slaves of Guayaquil at the End of the Colonial Era." *Colonial Latin American Review* 7, no. 1 (1998): 105–28.

Turnball, David. *Cuba: With Notices of Porto Rico, and the Slave Trade*. London: Orme, Brown, Green, and Longmans, 1840. Facsimile by Adamant Media Corporation: Elibron Classics, 2005.

United Nations General Assembly. *Universal Declaration of Human Rights*. Paris: United Nations, 1948.

Vallejo, Jesus. "Paradojas del sujeto." In *Historia y constitución: Trayectos del constitucionalismo hispano*, edited by Carlos Garriga, 173–89. Mexico: Centro de Investigación y Docencia Económica, 2010.

Van Cott, Donna Lee. *The Friendly Liquidation of the Past: The Politics of Diversity in Latin America*. Pittsburgh: University of Pittsburgh Press, 2000.

Van Deusen, Nancy E. *Global Indios: The Indigenous Struggle for Justice in Sixteenth-Century Spain*. Durham, NC: Duke University Press, 2015.

VanderVelde, Lea. *Redemption Songs: Suing for Freedom Before Dredd Scott*. New York: Oxford University Press, 2014.

Varella, Claudia, and Manuel Barcia. *Wage-Earning Slaves: Coartación in Nineteenth-Century Cuba*. Gainesville: University of Florida Press, 2020.

Vinson, Ben III. *Bearing Arms for His Majesty: The Free-Colored Militia in Colonial Mexico*. Stanford, CA: Stanford University Press, 2002.

von Germeten, Nicole. *Black Blood Brothers: Confraternities and Social Mobility for Afro- Mexicans*. Gainesville: University Press of Florida, 2006.

Walker, Charles F. *The Tupac Amaru Rebellion*. Cambridge, MA: Harvard University Press, 2016.

Wallenstein, Peter. "Indian Foremothers: Race, Sex, Slavery, and Freedom in Early Virginia." In *The Devil's Lane: Sex and Race in the Early South*, edited by Catherine Clinton and Michele Gillespie, 57–73. New York: Oxford University Press, 1997.

Welch, Kimberly M. *Black Litigants in the Antebellum American South*. Chapel Hill: University of North Carolina Press, 2018.

Wilder, Gary. "The Promise of Freedom and the Predicament of Marronage: On Neil Roberts's Freedom as Marronage." *sx salon* 24 (February 2017). smallaxe.net/sxsalon/reviews/promise-freedom-and-predicament-marronage-neil-robertss-freedom-marronage.

Yannakakis, Yanna. *The Art of Being In-Between: Native Intermediaries, Indian Identity, and Local Rule in Colonial Oaxaca*. Durham, NC: Duke University Press, 2008.

Since Time Immemorial: Native Custom & Law in Colonial Mexico. Durham, NC and London: Duke University Press, 2023.

Yingling, Charlton W. "The Maroons of Santo Domingo in the Age of Revolutions: Adaptations and Evasions, 1783–1800." *History Workshop Journal* 79, no. 1 (Spring 2015): 25–51.

Index

www.ingramcontent.com/pod-product-compliance
Lightning Source LLC
LaVergne TN
LVHW091524200926
848483LV00002B/299

* 9 7 8 1 0 0 9 4 9 4 1 9 9 *